D0163349

Farmers and Village Life in Twentieth-century Japan

This is a book about rural Japan from the early 1900s, when the majority of Japanese were farmers, to the end of the twentieth century, when farmers formed only a very small proportion of the Japanese labor force and the future of domestic agriculture itself was uncertain. Although attention is paid to the changing economics of agriculture over time and to the policies of the Japanese state, the emphasis throughout is on farmers themselves and the ways in which they have sought, individually and collectively, to sustain and improve their lives. This 'rice roots' approach seeks to bring the rural Japan of the past and present to life, and to suggest that many of the characterizations of farmers that appear in the general literature about modern Japan – in particular, those which stress their innate conservatism, their exceptional enthusiasm for militarism and aggression in the 1930s, and their cosseted existence in a regime of agricultural subsidies after 1945 – distort a much more diverse and complicated reality.

The contributors include six Japanese scholars, some of whose research appears in English for the first time, and five western scholars with established reputations in the history, sociology and anthropology of twentieth-century rural Japan. Their analyses should prove of considerable interest not only to scholars specializing in other spheres of modern Japanese studies, but also to those working on the past and present of agriculture, farmers and rural communities elsewhere in the developed and developing world.

Ann Waswo is Lecturer in Modern Japanese History at the University of Oxford, a member of the Nissan Institute of Japanese Studies, and a fellow of St Antony's College, Oxford.

Nishida Yoshiaki is Emeritus Professor, University of Tokyo, and Professor in the Faculty of Economics, Kanazawa University, Japan.

Farmers and Village Life in Twentieth-century Japan

Edited by Ann Waswo and
Nishida Yoshiaki

LONDON AND NEW YORK

First published 2003
by RoutledgeCurzon
11 New Fetter Lane, London EC4P 4EE

Simultaneously published in the USA and Canada
by RoutledgeCurzon
29 West 35th Street, New York, NY 10001

RoutledgeCurzon is an imprint of the Taylor & Francis Group

Typeset in Times by
Florence Production Ltd, Stoodleigh, Devon
Printed and bound in Great Britain by
Biddles Ltd, Guildford and King's Lynn

British Library Cataloguing in Publication Data
A catalogue record for this book is available from the British Library

Library of Congress Cataloging in Publication Data
Farmers and village life in twentieth-century Japan/edited by
Ann Waswo and Nishida Yoshiaki.
p. cm.
Includes bibliographical references and index.
1. Farm life – Japan – History – 20th century. 2. Villages –
Japan – History – 20th century. 3. Farmers – Japan – History –
20th century. I. Waswo, Ann. II. Yoshiaki, Nishida, 1940–
HT421.F348 2003
307.76′2′0952 – dc21 2002073979

ISBN 0–7007–1748–X

Contents

Illustrations

Tables

Figures

Plates

Notes on contributors

Iwamoto Noriaki (Professor of Agricultural and Resource Economics in the Graduate School of Agricultural and Life Sciences, University of Tokyo) is now doing comparative studies of rural communities in Japan and Indonesia.

Raymond A. Jussaume Jr (Associate Professor in the Department of Rural Sociology, Washington State University) continues research on the political sociology of agri-food systems, east and west.

Kase Kazutoshi (Professor, Institute of Social Science, University of Tokyo) is working on the modern history of employment in Japan and on the history of the Japanese civil engineering and construction industry.

John Knight (Lecturer, School of Anthropological Studies, Queen's University, Belfast) will soon publish *Waiting for Wolves in Japan: An Anthropological Study of People–Wildlife Relations*.

Mori Takemaro (Professor, Department of Economic Research, Hitotsubashi University Graduate School) is working on the social history of rural Japan in the past century and on villages and regional cities in the postwar era.

Nishida Yoshiaki (formerly of the Institute of Social Science, University of Tokyo; now Professor, Faculty of Economics, Kanazawa University) is studying night elementary schools in Tokyo as part of a larger project on forms of school attendance in modern Japan.

Ōkado Masakatsu (Professor, Faculty of Economics, Yokohama National University) is continuing research on women in Japanese farm families and on primary education in rural and urban Japan.

Kerry Smith (Associate Professor, Department of History, Brown University) is now studying the social and cultural histories of the Great Kanto Earthquake of 1923.

Tsutsui Masao (Professor, Department of Economics, Shiga University) is continuing research on the development of Japanese agriculture and is also studying the history of local cities and the Japanese folk craft movement.

Ann Waswo (University Lecturer in Modern Japanese History, Oxford University) has recently published *Housing in Postwar Japan: A Social History*.

Sandra Wilson (Associate Professor, School of Asian Studies, Murdoch University) is now working on a study of Japanese nationalism in the nineteenth and twentieth centuries.

Acknowledgments

This volume is the product of two workshops, the first held in Tokyo in March 2000 and the second held in Oxford in December of that same year, and a lot of traffic in cyberspace thereafter. The editors would like to express their gratitude to the University of Tokyo, its Institute of Social Science and St Antony's College, Oxford, for funding this project. We would also like to thank the discussants at each workshop for their very helpful comments on draft papers and the enterprise as a whole. At the Tokyo workshop the discussants were: Iwamoto Noriaki (who subsequently became a contributor to the volume), Nagae Masakasu, Nakamura Masanori, Noda Kimio, Ōkawa Hiroshi, Ōmameuda Minoru, Shimizu Yōji, Tama Shinnosuke, Teruoka Shūzō, Usami Shigeru, Ushiyama Keiji, Yamaguchi Yoshito and Yasaka Masamitsu. At the Oxford workshop the discussants were Penelope Francks and Nakashima Yasuhiro. Thanks are also due to Inge Egebo, Neil Evans, Daniel Gallimore and Mizutani Satoshi for their hard work in preparing draft translations of four of the papers by Japanese contributors.

Finally we wish to acknowledge the following for permission to reproduce copyright material:

Cover photograph (Communal dredging of a drainage ditch in Niigata): from Nishikanbara tochi kairyōku, ed., *Nishikanbara tochi kairyōshi, shasshin hen* (Niigata: Nishikanbara tochi kairyōku, 1981), p. 201, reproduced by permission of Majima Tatsuichi, Chairman, Nishikanbara tochi kairyōku.

Plate 2.1: reproduced by permission of Nishida Yoshiaki and Tokyo University Press.

Plates 3.1, 3.2, 9.1, 9.2 and 9.3: from 'Shashin ga kataru Shōwa nōgyōshi' kankōkai, ed., *Shashin ga kataru Shōwa nōgyōshi* (Tokyo: Fumin kyōkai,

1987), reproduced by permission of Kido Minato, Chairman, Fumin kyōkai.

Plate 8.1: reproduced by permission of Togashi Eiji.

Chapter 5: 'In search of equity: Japanese tenant unions in the 1920s,' originally published in T. Najita and J.V. Koschmann, eds, *Conflict in Modern Japanese History: The Neglected Tradition* (Princeton: Princeton University Press, 1982), reproduced by permission of Princeton University Press.

1 Introduction

Ann Waswo

The 1990s and early 2000s have been difficult years for many farmers in many parts of the developed world. Their incomes have fallen sharply, and may well fall further as the subsidies designed to boost food production in the aftermath of the Second World War are progressively withdrawn and agriculture is increasingly exposed to unfettered market forces in the national, regional and global arena. Their intensive, industrialized production methods, celebrated in the recent past, are now the targets of criticism on both environmental and food-safety grounds. Theirs is a steadily aging population, as their children vote with their feet and move to urban areas to take up 'jobs with a future.' Young men who do opt for farming find it increasingly difficult to find young women willing to marry them, even in some parts of the United States (*New York Times*, May 6, 1999; see also *Country Living*, August 1999 for a response to the bride shortage in rural England). There has been severe population decline in some rural areas, and an influx of former city dwellers in search of the rural idyll in others, who then object to the noises and odors of the farming that still takes place nearby. Protesting farmers have become a familiar sight on the nightly television news. Less visible, but certainly no less significant, is the rising suicide rate among farmers in at least some countries. A debate about the future of farming and of food – in some instances, about the rural landscape itself – appears to have begun among politicians and policymakers, farmers and farmers' organizations, and consumers and consumer lobbying groups in virtually every OECD country. What the outcome of those debates will be remains to be seen, but it is likely that another great era of change for farmers and farming, comparable to the sea changes of the early postwar era, is in the offing.

In all probability, the future of farmers and farming in Japan will strike most of the intended readers of this volume as an eminently clear-cut case, lacking any of the ambiguities and anxieties that bedevil consideration of the fate of farmers and farming elsewhere. After all, to most observers of agriculture and agricultural policies in the contemporary, overwhelmingly western portion of the OECD, farming in Japan is inefficiency incarnate, sustained only by a very slowly crumbling wall of protectionism, and hence a prime candidate for extinction in favor of more cheaply produced food imported from abroad. That urban residents in Japan might benefit from better housing if given access to building sites on former farmland is seen as an additional benefit, and not only by Australia and other members of the so-called Cairns group of agricultural free traders. There is also a small but increasingly vocal constituency within Japan for the elimination of most if not all of Japanese agriculture, consisting primarily of macro-economists at present but possibly poised to enjoy somewhat broader support among business interests and at least some members of the Japanese public.

Moreover, to most western scholars of modern Japan – other than to a relative handful among them who study its rural society and economy – the countryside and its purported ethos are seen as overwhelmingly negative factors in Japan's development past and present. Granted, the agricultural sector fed the nation for a crucial interval in the aftermath of the Meiji Restoration of 1868 and made other contributions to the consolidation of the new Meiji regime and the launching of efforts to promote industrialization, by providing the major share of tax revenues, significant foreign exchange earnings from the export of raw silk and tea, and ample factory labor. But farmers themselves are widely characterized as a major source of problems for the modernizing 'rest' of the country, especially after the turn of the twentieth century. Their traditional ethos of communal solidarity has been portrayed as the linchpin of emperor-centered nationalism in the early 1900s, impeding the spread of individualism and other values deemed essential to a liberal political order. Overwhelming rural support is said to have enabled Japan's 'fascist' or 'militarist' transformation in the 1930s and the reckless attempt to establish Japanese hegemony in Asia during the Second World War. Farmers' interests as petty property owners in the aftermath of the Occupation-led land reform, combined with their 'innate conservatism' and the over-representation of rural districts in elections, are frequently cited as an obstacle to the development of a vigorous and healthy democracy in postwar Japan. Given these perceived problems, releasing Japan from the dead weight of its rural heritage might very easily be construed as offering socio-political, as well as economic, benefits.

A common feature of most western assessments of farming and farmers in Japan is sweeping generalization. *The* agricultural sector, *the* rural village, *the* Japanese farmer feature in the discourse, such as it is. At the very least, the contributors to this volume hope to muddy these suspiciously simple conceptual waters by providing evidence of the considerable diversity within rural Japan at any given time, as well as evidence of fairly constant processes of adaptation and change at the local level, and not only in response to directives from government officials or other elites. Our focus is not on the economics of Japanese agriculture past or present, although prevailing economic realities will figure in most of the papers. Nor will state policy receive more than passing attention. Rather, we seek to emphasize the actions and attitudes of farmers themselves as they have confronted and coped with new opportunities and new challenges during the twentieth century. In contrast to the modernist paradigm, which posits a sharp dichotomy between the 'old'/rural/agrarian and the 'new'/urban/industrial and which generally portrays the old as a drag on development, we seek to demonstrate that Japanese farmers played an active and largely positive role in Japan's modern trajectory. Far from being 'innately' conservative, they have proven themselves consistently innovative, and their support for the conservative Liberal–Democratic Party (LDP) in the postwar era was by no means a foregone conclusion. The Japan Socialist Party (JSP) had been very active in the countryside in the first few years after Japan's surrender in 1945, after all, and might well have made further headway among rural voters had its significant left-wing not decided after poor results in the election of 1949 that it should concentrate on being the party of the industrial proletariat, rather than a more broadly based party of the lower and lower middle classes as a whole. Conservative politicians then proved willing and able to fill the void the JSP's retreat from the countryside created.

We focus in this volume on the twentieth century in part because a reasonably accurate portrayal of rural Japan in the late nineteenth century has found its way into textbooks of Japanese history and other western scholarship dealing at least in part with agriculture's role in Japan's development at that time. A further, and more salient, reason is that it was from the turn of the twentieth century that Japan's industrial transformation began in earnest, posing for Japan as for other countries at other times the challenge of defining a place for farming and farmers within a dramatically changing economic order. It is in this respect that Japan's experience may prove most relevant in comparative perspective, thus contributing to a better understanding of an important phase in the long history of agriculture itself.

In Chapter 2 Nishida Yoshiaki presents an overview of the century, based primarily on the diary of Nishiyama Kōichi, a farmer in Niigata prefecture. In Chapter 3 Ōkado Masakatsu introduces the neglected topic of rural women during the same period. In Chapters 4 and 5 Tsutsui Masao and myself discuss developments in rural Japan in the early 1900s and 1920s, respectively, each in its own way a time of increasing empowerment for 'ordinary' farmers, whether owner-cultivators or tenant farmers, within a stratified rural social order. Three chapters on the profoundly disruptive consequences of the Great Depression of the 1930s follow. In the first of these Kerry Smith explores the response of the overwhelming majority of Japanese farmers to the depression: working together for rural revitalization in Japan. Sandra Wilson and Mori Takemaro then examine efforts to promote rural emigration to Manchuria, a Japanese puppet state after the Manchurian Incident of 1931, and the decidedly lukewarm responses of Japanese farmers to those efforts. The next four chapters deal with the postwar era. In Chapter 9 Raymond Jussaume Jr discusses the evolution of part-time farming, or the pluriactivity of farmers, from its prewar origins to the mid-1990s. Iwamoto Noriaki examines farmers' changing attitudes toward land and land use in the context of rapid economic growth and urban land price escalation in Chapter 10, and Kase Kazutoshi examines the impact of the same external developments on farmers' enthusiasm for farmland and agricultural improvements in Chapter 11. In Chapter 12 John Knight considers the phenomenon of rural resettlement in a depopulated rural region and the implications of such resettlement for an agrarian future in Japan. In a concluding chapter the editors discuss some of the main themes that emerge from the preceding chapters and assess the prospects for farmers and farming in Japan at the outset of the twenty-first century.

Although rural Japan is the setting in the pages that follow, many of the issues dealt with will come as no surprise to observers of farming and farmers in the twentieth-century West. That said, however, there are certain distinctive features of the Japanese case that need to be borne in mind. Chief among these are, first, the relatively high proportion of farm households within the total population and total labor force of Japan, at least until fairly recently. Between 1868 and 1940, the number of farm households remained relatively stable at some 5.5 million, each with an average of about five household members, within a population that grew from some 35 million to 72 million persons. By and large, the non-agricultural economy in this period only provided new employment opportunities for the surplus (non-inheriting) younger sons and daughters of farm households, and no net decrease in the number of households engaged in farming occurred. That would not begin to take place until the early 1960s and the onset of Japan's so-called 'economic miracle' of sustained high rates of growth and structural change, and it would gather speed both as the non-agricultural economy soared in the years ahead and as the early postwar generation of farmers/heads of farming households progressively aged. There had been some 5.7 million farm households in 1965. By 1985 the number had fallen to 4.4 million, and it would fall to 3.4 million in 1995. During those same years the Japanese population had grown from 98 to 125 million, and the total labor force had increased from 48 to 64 million. Roughly 70 percent of the total labor force at the turn of the century, and still 45 percent in 1950, farmers would constitute only about 10 percent in 1980 and about 5 percent in 1995.

Second, we must note the persistence of family farming on relatively small holdings throughout the century. The average holding of farm households before the Second World War was about one *chō* (.992 hectares or 2.45 acres) in size, and it remained one *chō* after the postwar land reform, which virtually eliminated farm tenancy but did not – indeed could not – address the problem of land scarcity in a mountainous and densely populated country. There were, of course, significant regional and local variations in the scale of holdings which average figures obscure, but, more importantly, both before and after the war there was significant potential for productivity increases even on such small holdings and, as we shall see, much of that potential was realized. What might well appear to be market gardening by the standards of extensive western agriculture could prove to be reasonably profitable in Japan, and certainly adequate to supporting a respectable standard of living, provided the cultivator either owned the land concerned or paid only modest rents.

The third feature concerns the centrality of one crop, rice, in agricultural production. In Japan, as elsewhere in Asia, rice has long been grown in flooded paddies, and located as Japan is on the fringes of the monsoon zone, rainfall alone could not be counted on to provide the necessary water as and when needed. A considerable infrastructure of irrigation and drainage facilities was required to service the paddies in a given locality. As a result, no one farmer could own or control all of the essential means of production himself, and needed the community in order to survive as a rice producer. Herein lay the basis for communal solidarity and cooperation in the rural settlements of Japan. Other crops were grown, to be sure, on drained rice paddies in the winter, where climate allowed (generally in the southwestern half of the archipelago), and on upland or dry fields (*hatake*) beyond the reach of existing technology for paddy rice or – more recently – on former rice paddies that have been converted to the raising of 'upland' or dry field crops. Throughout the twentieth century, however, the area devoted to rice production generally has exceeded the area planted to all other crops combined. Moreover, the varieties of rice grown were of a specific type, shorter-grain *japonica* rice, that would germinate at the lower temperatures prevailing in Japan than was the case with the longer-grain *indica* type of rice grown in monsoon Asia, and that differed in luster, texture and taste from *indica* rice (Francks 1983: 28; Ohnuki-Tierney 1993: 13). So long as domestic demand for that rice continued to increase, Japanese rice farmers prospered. When demand started to fall in the mid-1960s, a 'rice mountain' of surplus production began to accumulate, which no other major rice-consuming country wanted in any meaningful quantity, even if that rice had been sold at a discount well below the price the Japanese government was then paying its domestic rice producers.

Given the near equivalence between *chō* and hectares, the two measurements of area will be used interchangeably in the chapters that follow. As *hatake* fields are no longer confined to upland areas, they will be described as dry fields. The names of all Japanese persons cited in the text or as authors will be given in the standard Japanese order: surname followed by personal name.

References

Country Living. 1999. 'Lonely Hearts Campaign: The Farmer Wants a Wife,' August, pp. 54–6.

Francks, Penelope. 1983. *Technology and Agricultural Development in Pre-war Japan*. New Haven, Connecticut: Yale University Press.

New York Times. 1999. 'Scrambling to Find Cupid in a Haystack,' May 6.

Ohnuki-Tierney, Emiko. 1993. *Rice as Self: Japanese Identities through Time*. Princeton: Princeton University Press.

2 Dimensions of change in twentieth-century rural Japan

Nishida Yoshiaki

Introduction

In this chapter I will discuss the many changes that occurred in Japanese villages and in the lives and livelihoods of Japanese farmers during the twentieth century, basing my assessment primarily on a diary kept by a farmer in the Nishi-Kanbara district of Niigata Prefecture. The diary's writer, Nishiyama Kōichi, was born in August 1908 and died in December 1995 at the age of 87. His entries start in October 1925 when he was 17 and continue on an almost daily basis until the early 1990s, a span of some 65 years. At the beginning of this period, his family were pure tenant farmers, cultivating slightly more than two *chō* (one *chō* = 2.45 acres) of rented land in the hamlet of Koshin in the village of Sakaiwa. The hamlet was located between the Shinano and Nishikawa rivers, only about two miles from Niigata City on the Japan Sea, and the five tracts of marshland within its borders were held as common land to which all farmers residing in the hamlet had rights of access.

During Kōichi's tenure as head of the family, the Nishiyamas made considerable economic strides forward, first acquiring title to the land they cultivated not long before the end of the Second World War and then thriving as owner-cultivating farmers for over two decades, even becoming 'cultivating landlords' for a brief period in the early 1970s. Stock market speculation by Kōichi's son and heir thereafter, using the dramatically enhanced value of their land as collateral, proved the family's undoing, however, and by the late 1980s they owned no land but that on which their family home stood and were no longer involved in farming.

Entries in the diary record the main daily activities of Kōichi and other members of his family and all their income and expenditure, giving us a clear record year by year of the labor they devoted to farming and to by-employments and hence of changes in their household economy. Kōichi was also concerned with the life of his village and hamlet, recording the major events and campaigns that took place in his lifetime. These entries make it possible to trace developments within the local community and to see how solidarity and mutual cooperation among residents were from time to time affected by tension and conflict. Although it is very definitely micro-data, this diary provides us with rare insight into the realities of rural life and is a valuable source for the study of farmers and villages during the twentieth century. Entries up until 1975 have been published in Nishida and Kubo 1991 and 1998.

Since the diary begins in 1925, however, it cannot tell us anything of the first quarter of the twentieth century. For that period, I will draw on the *Zenji Nisshi* (*Diary of Zenji*), kept by an owner-tenant farmer in Yamagata Prefecture between 1893 and 1934 (reprinted, with helpful commentaries, by Toyohara Kenkyūkai 1977), and also on the novel *Tsuchi* (*The Soil*) by Nagatsuka Takashi (English translation by Waswo 1989), which provides a very realistic portrait of rural life in the early 1900s.

The worlds of Zenji and *Tsuchi* (1900–25)

Zenji was born in 1878 in the village of Toyohara in the district of Akumi in northeastern Yamagata Prefecture, the second son of an owner-tenant farmer cultivating some 14 to 15 *tan* (one *tan* = .245 acre) of land. He started his diary in 1893 when he was 15 and continued it until 1934. Until 1896 he worked on his natal family's holding and did occasional labor for a nearby large landowner. In 1898 he was taken on as a hired employee by the Gotō family, who cultivated eight *tan* of land that they owned and another nine *tan* that they rented, and who had no sons to help with the work. In 1904 he married the Gotō's second daughter (the eldest having died) and so was adopted as their family heir.

What then was the household economy and the daily life of the Gotō family and Zenji like during the early 1900s? It goes without saying that their core business was as farmers cultivating rice, but they also carried out a wide variety of subsidiary activities, such as rice brokerage (i.e. purchasing rice wholesale for later sale at a profit, known locally as *kedashi*), seasonal work transporting rice to dealers in the coastal city of Sakata (known as *dachinmai*, 'rice carriage'), polishing rice, selling sake and brokering the ropes that local farmers made, and it is evident that it was the profits from these subsidiary activities that made it possible for them to acquire more land. By around 1910, the Gotō had risen considerably in their world, even though they remained owner-tenant farmers, because they had managed to expand the acreage they owned to 12 *tan*, bringing their total holding – including the nine *tan* still rented – to 21 *tan* (2.1 *chō*). Such an advance into the upper ranks of Japanese farmers was highly unusual at the time, especially in the Tohoku region, where a widening disparity between the economic status of landlords on the one hand and of tenant farmers on the other had been the norm. Yet it was an advance made at the cost of 'ceaseless labor' by people working for the Gotō, none more so than Zenji (Usami 1977a: 16). The Gotō were known as particularly 'strict' employers, such that it was said that 'if you had survived working for the Gotō you could survive working anywhere' (Usami 1977b: 142). Their draconian exploitation of all available labor as a means of expanding their operations also made them rather unusual.

Even so, the strongest impression one gets from Zenji's diary entries at this time is not how much work he had to do, but how relentlessly repetitious that work was year after year. Of course, it could be argued that such relentless repetition of tasks is an enduring feature of paddy rice farming in Japan, rather than a distinctive characteristic of the early 1900s. Indeed, the author of another of the commentaries on the diary has calculated that there was essentially no difference in the time Zenji devoted to various tasks when he was in his twenties, at the turn of the century, and when he was in his fifties, in the 1930s (Kawaguchi 1977: 36). But I think the diary does illustrate the general stasis that prevailed in rural Japan at this time, which would not be disrupted until after the First World War. There was an established pattern in place, in which farming and its demands took precedence over everything else. Although the Gotō were one of only two families in Toyohara to engage in rice brokering, an activity that along with rice carriage took Zenji to Sakata far more frequently than was usual for local farmers, there is no evidence that commercial involvement of that sort changed their – or his – outlook or approach to securing the household's future in any significant way. On the contrary, the brokering was also routinized, continuing to pretty much the same extent and in the same manner in the early 1900s as had been the case a generation or so earlier, and slotted in at the very end of the established agricultural calendar: deep-digging the paddy fields with a horse-drawn plow → transplanting the rice seedlings → weeding → harvesting → winnowing → manufacture of bags and rope from rice straw. It was not something that was going to disrupt village life in any way. Moreover, it appears from the diary that from the time of Zenji's adoption as Gotō heir in 1904 until the end of the Meiji era in 1912 there were no incidents of tension, much less conflict, among village residents. Indeed, the only unusual entries Zenji made in his diary concerned essentially private matters, such as a surprisingly long 16-day stay at a hot springs spa in 1910 and the running away of his wife with a young male employee for a month that same year. Rural life in Toyohara during the early years of the twentieth century was decisively centered on the seasonal agricultural cycle, and although the village was not far from Sakata, with which its commercial relations were gradually deepening, the diary gives no real indication of the village having experienced economic, political or social development of any sort during that time.

Nagatsuka Takashi's novel *Tsuchi* (*The Soil*) is set in a village on the west bank of the Kinu river in Ibaraki Prefecture and revolves around the life of a desperately poor tenant farmer. The novel has been praised as 'a seminal work in the rural literature of our country' (Usui 1956: 326), and since it was first published as a book in 1912 more than 200 separate studies of it have appeared in print (Murakami 1997: 11). There can thus be no doubting its high reputation as a work of literature, but it is also essential to note that the author was committed to realism and intimately familiar with the community about which he wrote, thus providing readers with vivid details about the lives of those at the lower reaches of rural society in the early twentieth century and their relations with other residents. While still a graduate student, Ann Waswo was told by the late Professor Furushima Toshio that if she wanted to know what rural life was actually like in the Meiji era she should read *Tsuchi*, and she eventually decided to translate the whole of it into English because, as she put it, '[A]lthough *Tsuchi* was undeniably a novel it was simultaneously an informal ethnography of a rural community and its inhabitants in the early 1900s and, as such, a valuable historical document' (Waswo 1989: vi). Indeed, as she also observed, '[A]s a place where labor-intensive, small-scale family farming prevailed, the community depicted in the novel was fairly typical of rural Japan in the early 1900s' (Waswo 1989: xi).

I am inclined to agree with those observations for the following four reasons. First, the novel depicts the impoverished lives of tenant farmers and their dependence on the benevolence of their landlords. After Kanji's wife Oshina died, he found himself down to a single sack of rice with which to feed his children, and so:

> he went and appealed to his landlord to let him borrow back half of the rice he owed until the following fall. The landlord, the former head of EastNeighbor's house, consented.
>
> (Waswo 1989: 29; Nagatsuka 1956: 50)

This was a time when tenant farmers could not survive hard times of one sort or another unless their landlords benevolently reduced or deferred rent payments, a fact that is supported by the records kept by the Nishiyama family in Niigata Prefecture, which report that in almost every year between 1902 and 1914 one or another of their landlords benevolently consented to reduce rents. Second, the novel sheds light on the circumstances that constrained poor tenant farmers to make themselves available for paid work:

> During the growing season itself they had to abandon their own fields to do day labor for others to earn money for that day's food. . . . Even when their own crops most needed attention they might not be able to provide it for days at a time. Nor could they do much about fertilizer.
>
> (Waswo 1989: 47; Nagatsuka 1956: 74–5)

In other words, they were caught up in a vicious circle: because they were poor they had no choice but to do day labor; because they did day labor they were unable to tend their own crops as and when necessary; and as a result, their crops would produce poor yields, leaving them at least as dependent on day labor for income as before. More affluent farmers were not caught up in this vicious circle, and not surprisingly their yields were thus more abundant. My third point is related to the first and second: that many of the opportunities for day labor were provided by landlords themselves, for example in projects to reclaim land for farming within the woodlands that they owned (Waswo 1989: 94; Nagatsuka 1956: 142). Finally, there is the sense that one is left with after reading the novel that poor farmers faced very bleak prospects indeed at this time of ever improving their farming operations or their livelihoods. Granted, there were opportunities for day labor in the village and off-season work at more distant construction projects. Like Kanji, they just might manage finally to have a little cash to hand and to feel that after years of struggle life was getting better at last. But as if to sweep this more optimistic interpretation aside, the novel ends with a disastrous fire that spreads from Kanji's house to his landlord's nearby and leaves everything in ashes in its wake. What *Tsuchi* conveys is an image of a poor farmer entrapped in his poverty, no matter how hard he has worked, and in that sense it captures the situation confronting all poor farmers in the period before the First World War.

In the rural villages of Japan early in the twentieth century, cases like that of Zenji, whose position as a farmer improved to a notable degree, were exceptional. The majority of tenant farmers and owner-tenant farmers remained dependent (as in *Tsuchi*) on the benevolence of their landlords and were forced to make up their threadbare existence by day labor and off-season employment elsewhere. Moreover, as Zenji's diary entries make clear, the lives of farmers were tied to the agricultural cycle, unaffected by significant economic, social or political change. Stasis prevailed, as indeed appeared to be the case in the village portrayed in *Tsuchi*, especially among its poorest residents. As Tsutsui argues later in this volume, changes were under way in this period owing to the steadily growing commercialization of the countryside, but not until after the First World War would those changes become manifest.

Zenji and farming during the First World War

The First World War gave rise to unprecedented economic growth in Japan. In a single stroke she turned from being a net importer to a net exporter and from a debtor nation to a creditor nation, giving rise to considerable economic change throughout the nation, including the countryside.

Toyohara and the lives of its inhabitants (of whom Zenji was in this sense no exception) experienced significant changes. The first of these, completed just before the war began, was a large-scale project of land adjustment (*kōchi seiri*), which transformed some 7,500 *chō* of fields in the Akumi district into uniformly sized parcels of one *tan* each and enabled local landowners to exchange parcels with others so that they ended up with less scattered holdings than in the past. That in itself made farming operations considerably easier and more efficient than previously and seems to have encouraged other improvements as well, most notably in the application of fertilizer. It was from this time that such commercial fertilizers as soybean cakes began to be used in earnest, leading to dramatic increases in the productivity of land. That entries such as those Zenji recorded in his diary in April 1916 to the effect that he had 'bought ten soybean cakes and one bag of bone meal' and 'bought twenty soybean cakes' became more frequent thereafter is suggestive of this trend. It should be noted, too, that this land adjustment project, like most others carried out in Japan at the time, also eliminated the 'extra land' (*nobi*) that tenant farmers had been able to cultivate in the past, when the area of irregularly shaped fields had been estimated rather than accurately determined as now was possible, but no corresponding reduction in the rents they were charged was effected. This would prove to be a cause of tenancy disputes in the Akumi district, and elsewhere in Japan, in the future (Isobe 1977: 208–12).

Second, Zenji's involvement in rice brokerage expanded rapidly during the war years. In 1913 he had bought only 235 *hyō* of rice (one *hyō* = 60 kg), whereas in 1916 he bought 603 *hyō* and in 1917, 501 *hyō* (Takeda 1977: 170–1). His profit amounted to ¥130 in 1916 and ¥165 in 1917, or almost enough in total to purchase a *tan* of arable land, then costing

350 to 400 yen (Takeda 1977: 184–5). In fact, there does appear to have been a close connection between the expansion in the rice brokering business and the acquisition of additional land. In 1915 the Gotō purchased 12 *tsubo* (.04 *tan*, or 39.7 sq. m.) of dry field, in 1916 they purchased 4.7 *chō* of woodland, and in 1917 they purchased 149 *tsubo* (almost half a *tan*, or 493.2 sq. m.) of rice paddy and 29 *tsubo* (.097 *tan*, or 96 sq. m.) of housing land (Isobe 1977: 198–9).

Third, and very significantly, Zenji's rice brokering business declined markedly in 1918 and 1919, even though rice prices soared in those years, and both that business and his rice carriage business came to an end in 1920. This was because the Uetsu railway line along the Japan Sea coast had been extended to the north of Sakata in 1919 and a branch of the Sankyo rice warehouse built at Motodate station, not far from Toyohara. Local farmers no longer had any need for the services he had been providing, as they could now take their rice to the nearby warehouse and sell it themselves (Takeda 1977: 187). Zenji's most profitable business activities had been rendered useless by the expansion of the railway network, but thanks in large measure to those activities the Gotō family had acquired more land and could now make a fairly comfortable living as full-time farmers.

As shown in Table 2.1, rice yields per *tan* increased considerably during the years of the First World War, mostly because of the greater use of commercial fertilizers. With the expansion of the railway network during the same period and on into the early 1920s, the commodification of rice also increased dramatically. The average annual volume of rice traded nationwide between 1911 and 1914, for example, had amounted to 89.53 million *koku* (one *koku* = 150 kg), or only about 1.78 times the average annual output of 50.25 million *koku*. In contrast, between 1915 and 1924 the average annual volume traded rose to 309.65 million *koku*,

Table 2.1 Changes in rice yields, 1910–21

Years	*Planted area (in million chō)*	*Total yield (in million koku)*	*Yield per tan (in koku)*
1910–12	2.97	49.5	1.67
1913–15	3.03	54.3	1.79
1916–18	3.08	55.8	1.82
1919–21	3.12	59.7	1.91

Source: Kayō Nobufumi, *Kaitei Nihon nōgyō kiso tōkei* (1977), pp. 194–5.

Notes:
Yields shown are averages for each 3-year period.
1 *tan* = 0.1 *chō*; 1 *koku* = 150 kg.

or 5.38 times the average annual output of 57.59 million *koku* (Niigata-ken keizai nōgyō kumiai rengōkai 1957: 342). It was as a consequence of these and other developments during the war years that the lives and livelihoods of Japanese farmers began to change in important ways.

The era of tenancy disputes and challenges to landlord ascendancy

The growth in agricultural productivity during the First World War served to transform Japanese farmers, including many tenant farmers, into small-scale commodity producers. As shown in Table 2.2, even the family of Nishiyama Kōichi, who rented all of the land they cultivated, sold a steadily increasing volume of rice during the 1920s, the (estimated) amount rising from 11.6 *koku* (29 *hyō*) in 1921 to 32.7 *koku* (82 *hyō*) in 1929. Like other tenant farmers, they also had to pay rents in kind to their landlords, and the more involved they became in commodity production, the more keenly aware they became of the real value of the rice they were handing over. The stage was set for tenant demands for rent reduction.

The tenant farmers of Koshin hamlet joined the Northern Japan Farmers' Union in 1922, and in 1923, even though yields were down only slightly on those of the previous year, they demanded a 32 percent rent reduction and persuaded all local landlords to agree to it. Then in December of 1925 Miyake Shōichi and Inamura Ryūichi, well-known leaders of the farmers' movement in Niigata Prefecture, were invited to address a gathering of tenant farmers at the Man'eiji Temple in Koshin. As Nishiyama Kōichi wrote in the diary he had begun just a few months earlier: 'The meeting went off very well with a large attendance from all parts of the hamlet and an ostentatious presence by the Uchino police.' It was decided to establish the Koshin branch of the Japan Farmers' Union and to press for 30 percent rent reductions between 1925 and 1927. These efforts, too, met with considerable success. Once organized, and benefiting from the support of a nationwide farmers' union, the tenant farmers of Koshin were able to wrest considerably more favorable terms from their landlords.

They were not alone in organizing and seeking lower rents. As shown in Table 2.3, both the number of tenant unions and the number of tenancy disputes escalated during the 1920s, with most disputes in that decade involving demands for rent reductions. Most such disputes resulted in at least a degree of success for tenant farmers. For example, the data published annually by the government in *Kosaku Nenpō* (*The Annual Report on Tenancy*) indicate that in 1926 tenants pressed for rent

Table 2.2 Rice farming operations by the Nishiyama family, 1911 and 1921–44

Year	*Planted area (in tan)*	*Total yield (in koku) a*	*Yield per tan*	*Tenant rents paid (in koku) b*	*Rice sold (in koku) c*	*Rice retained a – (b+c)*	*% rent reduction secured*
1911	15.7	22.66	1.443				40.2
1921	17.5	33.00	1.886	10.6 (32.1)	(11.6)		0
1922	17.5	34.50	1.971	10.6 (30.7)	(13.1)		0
1923	17.6	33.80	1.920	7.2 (21.3)	(15.8)		32.0
1924	14.4	33.75	2.344	10.6 (31.4)	(12.4)		0
1925	17.0	37.74	2.220	7.4 (19.6)	(19.5)		30.0
1926	17.0	33.68	1.981	5.3 (15.7)	(17.6)		50.0
1927	17.3	39.21	2.266	7.4 (18.9)	(21.0)		30.0
1928	21.6	48.50	2.245	9.7 (20.0)	(28.0)		41.0
1929	21.6	53.15	2.461	9.7 (18.3)	(32.7)		41.0
1930	22.4	68.80	3.071	12.3 (17.9)	(45.7)		12.5
1931							20.0
1932	17.1	47.80	2.795				10.0
1933		61.65		9.8 (15.9)	28.4	(23.5)	7.0
1934	22.5	49.52	2.201		41.6		29.0
1935	22.5				35.2		0
1936	22.5	65.80	2.924	13.4 (20.4)	35.2	(17.2)	0
1937	22.5	63.98	2.843	10.7 (16.7)	36.8	(16.5)	0
1938	24.1	67.65	2.807	11.7 (17.3)	38.8	(17.2)	0
1939	24.1	72.55	3.010	12.0 (16.5)	46.0	(14.6)	0
1940	24.3	63.20	2.061	11.3 (17.9)	34.8	(17.1)	0
1941	23.7	66.80	2,819		46.4		40.0
1942	20.6	50.02	2.428		31.6		0
1943	24.5	62.50	2.551				0
1944	22.3	61.50	2.758				0

Source: Calculated from tables 48, 49 and 75 of the explanatory chapter in Nishida Yoshiaki and Kubo Yasuo, *Nishiyama Kōichi nikki* (Tokyo: Tōkyō daigaku shuppankai, 1991).

Notes

1 Rice sales from 1921 to 1930, in parentheses, are estimated, using the known figure of 27 bales (10.8 *koku*) of rice consumed by the family in 1930. Total yield less rent paid and rice consumed = estimated rice sold.

2 The figures in parentheses after ‘tenant rents paid’ indicate the percentage of the total yield paid as rent.

3 The figures in parentheses for ‘rice retained’ indicate the rice remaining from the harvest after rent payments and recorded rice sales.

朋友会記念写真（昭和２年８月15日）

より高田義夫(19歳)，西山光一(18歳)，西山久作(16歳)，高田春三(17歳)，山下善三(16

林徳治(17歳)，西山由衛(19歳)

Plate 2.1 Nishiyama Kōichi (second from the left), aged 18. Reproduced from Nishida Yoshiaki and Kubo Yasuo, eds, *Nishiyama Kōichi Nikki, 1925–50 nen* (Tokyo: Tōkyō daigaku shuppankai, 1991).

reductions averaging 34.9 percent and secured reductions averaging 23.6 percent; in 1928, they pressed for reductions averaging 34 percent and secured reductions averaging 21.7 percent. That disputes were concentrated at this time in western Japan was a reflection of the earlier increases in agricultural output there and, hence, the earlier involvement of local tenant farmers in small-scale commodity production. It is worth noting, however, that, wherever such commodity production occurred, interest in rent reduction was likely to occur, too. As Waswo argues later in this volume, tenant farmers had relied on the benevolence of their landlords in the past, going to them individually to request rent reductions whenever yields were poor, but now they joined together and presented most if not all local landlords with a uniform set of demands. There is evidence of this shift in attitude in Zenji's diary, which records in December 1924 that 'Yozō has gone to [one of his landlords] to request a rent reduction' and in March 1925 that 'I went to a meeting to see about getting rents reduced.'

Table 2.3 Tenant unions and tenancy disputes, 1920–37

Year	*Number of tenant unions*	*Number of tenancy disputes*	*Principal tenant demands*		*Number of participants*	
			Related to rents	*Related to tenancy rights*	*Landlords*	*Tenants*
1920		408	350 (85.7)	–	5,236 (12.8)	34,605 (84.8)
1921	681	1,680	1,409 (83.8)	–	33,985 (20.2)	145,898 (86.8)
1922	1,114	1,578	1,527 (96.7)	–	29,077 (18.4)	125,750 (79.7)
1923	1,530	1,917	1,872 (97.6)	15 (0.7)	31,712 (16.5)	134,503 (70.2)
1924	2,337	1,532	1,433 (93.5)	24 (1.5)	27,223 (17.8)	110,920 (72.4)
1925	3,496	2,206	1,957 (88.7)	162 (7.3)	33,001 (15.0)	134,646 (61.0)
1926	3,926	2,751	2,324 (84.4)	313 (11.3)	39,705 (14.4)	151,061 (54.9)
1927	4,582	2,052	1,508 (73.5)	417 (20.3)	24,136 (11.8)	91,336 (44.5)
1928	4,353	1,866	1,238 (66.3)	464 (24.8)	19,474 (10.4)	75,136 (40.3)
1929	4,156	2,434	1,595 (65.5)	703 (28.8)	23,505 (9.7)	81,998 (33.7)
1930	4,208	2,478	1,357 (54.7)	996 (40.1)	14,159 (5.7)	58,565 (23.6)
1931	4,414	3,419	1,918 (56.0)	1,315 (38.4)	23,768 (7.0)	81,135 (23.7)
1932	4,650	3,414	1,464 (42.8)	1,468 (42.9)	16,706 (4.9)	61,499 (18.0)
1933	4,810	4,000	1,285 (32.1)	2,305 (57.6)	14,312 (3.6)	48,073 (12.0)
1934	4,390	5,828	2,479 (42.5)	2,668 (45.7)	34,035 (5.8)	121,031 (20.8)
1935	4,011	6,824	2,877 (42.1)	3,055 (44.7)	28,574 (4.2)	113,164 (16.6)
1936	3,915	6,804	2,117 (31.1)	3,674 (53.9)	23,293 (3.4)	77,187 (11.3)
1937	3,879	6,170	1,795 (29.0)	3,509 (56.8)	20,236 (3.3)	63,246 (10.3)

Sources: Calculated from annual editions of *Kosaku chōtei nenpō* and *Kosaku nenpō*.

Notes

1 The figures in parentheses for tenant demands show the percentage of all disputes in a given year involving that demand. (Less frequently made demands are omitted here.)

2 The figures in parentheses for participants show the average number involved in each dispute.

Nor was taking a united stance toward rent reductions the only change in the behavior of tenant farmers at this time. They also began challenging the ascendancy of landlords in village politics and agricultural affairs. In the elections for town and village assemblies held in 1925 under de facto universal manhood suffrage, fully 9,061 (or 21.2 percent) of the 42,738 successful candidates were tenant farmers, almost 2.5 times as many as had been elected under a restricted franchise in the last elections held in 1921. In 761 town and village assemblies, tenant farmers now constituted more than one-third of members, and in 340 assemblies they now constituted the majority, a fivefold increase over the last elections (Nōchi seido shiryō shūsei hensan iinkai 1969: 64). In addition, there was a notable increase in the number of tenant farmers joining village agricultural associations, agricultural cooperatives and fire brigades. Not surprisingly, the attention of tenant and owner-tenant farmers also turned to gaining a voice in hamlet decision-making, which had until then been controlled by the wealthiest residents. In Koshin hamlet, my focus here, what eventuated in 1929 were demands for fairly radical reform: As Kōichi noted in his diary in February of that year, 'From now on, the headman of each ward [within the hamlet] should receive 11 *koku* of rice per year in compensation for services rendered,' and 'The council of prominent residents should be replaced with a representative assembly, with 5 members elected from the lower ward and 3 each elected by middle and upper wards.' The first of these demands meant that the post of headman would no longer be confined to men of means, who could afford the time and expenditure the post demanded, and the second meant that all households, not just the most affluent among them, would have a voice in deciding hamlet affairs. The stipulation that the lower ward, which contained the most households and in which many tenant farmers lived, would elect five representatives to the hamlet assembly was intended to insure that the interests of tenant farmers would get a fair hearing. Both demands were accepted, and Kōichi's father Komakichi was soon elected for the first time as one of the *nōji gakari* (agricultural officials) who were responsible for all farming matters in the hamlet.

As is well known, the Peace Preservation Law was passed at the same time as the Universal Manhood Suffrage Law of 1925, and it became no easy matter for those leading the farmers' movement and other social reform movements to pursue their objectives. That said, however, it should be noted that, as a result of tenancy disputes and other initiatives, a degree of rural democratization was achieved during the 1920s, some of it even penetrating to the hamlet level. The actual cultivators of the land gained a greater voice in local affairs and, as we shall see, in Koshin that voice would survive the harsh years ahead.

Rural life during the Showa depression

Rice prices had been declining since 1926, but they dropped dramatically in October 1930, plunging rural Japan into a deep depression. In order to weather the crisis and generate a little cash, the Nishiyamas began first to manufacture, sell and repair rice-hulling devices, then to sell threshing apparatus, next to produce mechanically made rope for sale, and finally to make and sell powdered soap, as well as selling green tea. Yet capital was needed to start each of these businesses, and as the depression left them without cash to hand they ended up borrowing all the money required. Kōichi had gone 'to the Hachisuke house to borrow funds for the threshing apparatus' that he had designed himself and then had 'mortgaged some industrial bonds to borrow 30 yen' (both entries, December 1930). But none of these ventures made a go of it in the harsh economic climate of the time, and their debts swiftly mounted. In January 1932, seeing no other escape from their predicament, Kōichi wrote in his diary: 'Having discussed matters with my father until midnight, we eventually decided to sell everything we own to pay off our debts.' After consultation with their relatives, however, Kōichi was relieved to record in February that: 'We had been prepared to settle our debts now, but it seems we have another year before having to do so.'

The loans taken out by the Nishiyama family certainly were considerable. As of 1932, the sum they owed amounted to ¥5,752, which was more than 11 times the average ¥514 of debt per tenant farmer household reported in the Economic Survey of Farm Households for that year (Nōrinshō 1974: 20–5). Their determined efforts to generate income from first one new activity and then another, using borrowed capital, had without exception failed. An extreme case they obviously were, but it should be stressed that all farmers suffered from mounting debt during the depression years. The average ¥514 indebtedness of tenant farmers cited above was, after all, considerably greater than their average income of ¥385 that same year. It was the rapid spread of debt among farmers throughout the country in the initial years of the depression that prompted the government to pass the Farm Village Debt Arrangement Union Law in March 1933, although most scholars would agree the law did little to resolve the problems that Japanese farmers faced.

One noteworthy trend observable in rural Japan during the depression era was a decline in tenant militancy. In Koshin, instead of demanding substantial rent reductions every year as in the mid- to late 1920s, union members now stood by while others decided what sort of reduction might be given in view of current crop conditions. As Kōichi recorded in September 1930, 'We got our landlords to come and see how our rice was ripening,' and in October, 'The men from the prefecture came, and all the tenants spent the day showing them their fields.' As Table 2.2 shows, the rent reductions Kōichi and other tenant farmers in Koshin obtained by these means were considerably lower than in the recent past, even though they were reeling from the effects of the depression: 12.5 percent in 1930, 20 percent in 1931 and 10 percent in 1932. Clearly, Koshin's tenant farmers had lost the initiative in dealing with their landlords and seeking, by means of united action, to improve their lives.

Why was this the case? One reason was that many tenant farmers had borrowed money from their landlords in the past, and their inability to repay what they owed during the depression years made it difficult for them to adopt a strong stance toward rent reductions. To cite the case of the Nishiyamas again, Kōichi recorded in February 1932 that 'my inability to repay the interest due on the loan from Mr Kazama of Aoyama hamlet [his main landlord] is inexcusable.' Another reason was that, while some tenant farmers opted, as had the Nishiyamas, to attempt to ride out the depression by increasing their cash income from non-agricultural sources, others remained focused on securing rent reductions on the plots of land they cultivated. Such differing survival strategies, not to mention the success of some at new cash-generating activities and the failure – and increasing indebtedness – of others, made it difficult for tenant farmers in any one community to agree on what steps to take. As shown in Table 2.3, the number of tenancy disputes nationwide concerning demands for rent reductions stagnated between 1930 and 1933, and the number of disputes concerning tenancy rights – that is, disputes triggered by landlord attempts to evict tenants, typically so that the landlords could farm the land themselves – rapidly increased. During the Showa Depression, the tenant farmers' movement was thrown on the defensive.

Another trend observable in Koshin during the depression years was the division of residents into two rival political camps, one (the Sonseikai) associated with the Seiyūkai political party and the other (the Shinbokukai), with the Minseitō. This first became apparent in 1931, when the residents of the upper ward within the hamlet were unable to agree on a single headman and so elected two, one from each camp. That in itself would complicate the running of the hamlet until 1937, when the standoff ended, and it would lead to similar polarization among all hamlet residents while it lasted. What was noteworthy about that polarization was that most Koshin tenant farmers came to support the camp associated with the Seiyūkai, generally regarded as a bastion of landlord interests throughout Japan and opposed to any legislation that might bolster tenancy rights, while most landlords and owner-cultivators came to support the Minseitō camp. Granted, there were no proletarian political parties for

Koshin's tenant farmers to support at this time, the Rōnōtō (Labor–Farmer Party) having already been banned by the authorities and no successor groups formed in Niigata, but the outcome is still startling to say the least. It probably can be explained by the fact that the Seiyūkai favored efforts to induce recovery in rice prices, something that appealed to tenant farmers in a major rice-producing region, while landlord support for the Minseitō might be explained by that party's advocacy of economic austerity, which coincided with their reluctance to bear the costs of irrigation improvements and other agricultural public works (Nishida and Kubo 1991: 1056–9). Whatever the explanation, it appears that a political divide now opened between landlords and tenants in Koshin. Disputes of the sort that had prevailed in the 1920s were no longer possible, but their confrontation continued, and deepened, in new form.

Toward equality in rural Japan during the war years

The so-called Fifteen Years War may have begun with the Manchurian Incident of 1931, but it was not until after the outbreak of hostilities with China in 1937 that national mobilization was proclaimed in Japan, and not until after Japan's attack on Pearl Harbor in December 1941 that the war effort began affecting virtually every aspect of the lives of the Japanese people. Kōichi's diary recorded the first funeral for a soldier from the village of Sakaiwa in December 1937. The number of local men killed in action steadily increased thereafter, and from 1941 on the village held joint rather than individual funerals for them, including for the first time in December of that year a soldier born and raised in Koshin hamlet. The number of war dead escalated in the final two years of the war, with 25 of the total of 37 deaths in combat of young men from Koshin occurring in 1944 and 1945. Almost one in four of the 139 households in the hamlet had experienced the death of a family member (Nishida and Kubo 1991: 1071). Nor was that the only burden they had to endure. As the war situation worsened after 1942, they were called upon to surrender all metal objects in their possession to the authorities, including 'the handing over of Buddhist altar fittings' (Kōichi's diary, August 1943), and to dig up their allotted share of 'pine roots to make turpentine' for military use (December 1944).

But far and away the greatest pressure placed on rural Japan during the war was for increased food production. The rural economy had begun to recover from the depression in about 1935, and from 1937 on, with a boost from the inflation induced by increased military spending, farming had become profitable again. By dint of increased rice sales and once-again flourishing by-employments, the Nishiyamas were able to begin paying off their massive debts, and by 1942 they had completed the task, owing nothing. As their example illustrates, during the early years of the war tenant farmers had re-emerged as small-scale commodity producers. Buttressing their position even further was a series of measures implemented by the state to assure adequate food supplies in wartime, which had the effect of rewarding tenants as the actual cultivators of the land and curtailing the rights of their landlords: the 1938 Farmland Adjustment Law, which aimed at encouraging the establishment of owner-cultivators and the reinforcement of cultivating rights (reviving and expanding on earlier efforts in that sphere that had lapsed during the depression); the 1939 Farm Rent Control Ordinance; the 1941 Emergency Measures for the Management of Farmland and Special Control Ordinance on Farmland Prices; and the 1942 Staple Food Control Law, which established a two-tier pricing structure for the now mandatory delivery of all rice except that needed for subsistence to government warehouses, with a considerably higher price paid to tenant-producers than to landlords delivering rent rice.

There would be two notable developments in Koshin during the latter part of this period. The first was in 1941, when residents of the most densely populated lower ward of the hamlet demanded that their ward be divided into two, with each given the same quotas for deliveries of rice and receipt of rationed goods as the other wards. Protests from some of the wealthier residents elsewhere in the hamlet that this would 'divide the community' caused delay, but the reform was implemented in 1942, leading to a better deal for the many tenant farmer households in the original lower ward and more equitable burden-sharing among all households in the hamlet.

The second development was the launching of a campaign among Koshin's tenant farmers, Nishiyama Kōichi included, for the right to purchase the land they cultivated under the terms of the state program to establish owner-cultivators, as revised in 1943. Rents on paddy fields in Koshin had always been comparatively low, a legacy of the periodic land redistribution system (*warichi seido*) of past centuries in this and other districts that were subject to harsh weather and frequent crop failures. Simply put, tenants rented a standard 'household's worth' (*ikken mae*) of land that consisted of 1.8 *chō* of paddy, 2.9 *tan* of dry fields and 1.6 *tan* of housing and other land, a total of 2.25 *chō*, and paid a flat rate of 11.12 *koku* of rice in rent on the lot. That might be recalculated as a rent of 6.17 *to* (.617 *koku*) per *tan* on the rice paddy in their allotment and, given that the Nishiyama's yield per *tan* of paddy in 1943 amounted to 2.55 *koku*, that worked to a rent of slightly less than 25 percent of output. With the increase in rice prices payable to cultivators on the one hand, the value of tenancy rights (what might be earned by selling what one produced above subsistence and rent payment needs) also rose, and with state controls on rents and land prices on the other hand, the value of paddy and other land to landlords declined. When the state issued new guidelines to encourage the creation of owner-cultivators in 1943, which included changes in how the purchase price of land would be calculated to reflect recently imposed controls on both rents and land prices, the increasing value of tenancy rights per *tan* in Koshin came to coincide with the declining official price of land per *tan* at some 300 yen. For the first time, the land they cultivated was available for purchase at a price that made economic sense to local tenant farmers, and they seized the opportunity to attempt to become landowners. Not all local landlords proved willing to accept the offers they made at those low official prices, however, and not until May of 1945, after what Kōichi noted in his diary as 'a request that they cooperate in resolving the crisis facing the nation by permitting the creation of owner-cultivators', did the last of them concede.More than 90 percent of the tenanted land in Koshin was then purchased by its cultivators, at 24 times its rental value in the case of paddy (the multiple would rise to 40 times during the postwar land reform), and 33 times its rental value in the case of dry fields (to rise to 48 times during the land reform) plus the payment of fairly modest 'gratuities' (*tsutsumi gane*) to former landowners in both cases. Calling for cooperation in the war effort, as Koshin's tenant farmers did, was in marked contrast to the anti-war stance taken in the late 1930s by leaders of the National Farmers' Union, testifying to the powerful effects of national mobilization thereafter, but their determination to gain ownership of the land they cultivated also testifies to the potential that existed for solution of the land tenure problems of rural Japan even before the postwar land reform. Nor were Koshin's tenant farmers alone in seizing the chance that the 1943 revision of the program to establish owner-cultivators provided. More than 50 percent of all the households to take advantage of the program since its inception in 1926 did so during or after 1943, and more than 50 percent of all the land transferred under its auspices was transferred during or after that same year.

Japan's wartime regime had exacted a heavy toll on Koshin's residents, not only in the lives of its young men lost in battle, but also in the increasingly difficult struggle they themselves faced in meeting the hamlet's quotas for rice deliveries to the state and supplying other requisitioned goods. And yet that very wartime regime had also contributed to irreversible movement toward equality within the community. Even before Koshin's tenant farmers had campaigned successfully to rise into the ranks of owner-cultivators – itself made possible by the government's intense concern about the impact of urban food shortages on the war effort – they had lobbied successfully for fairer burden-sharing among the wards and, as fellow rice-producers, joined together with existing owner-cultivators in frequent ward and hamlet meetings to agree how production targets might be met. Their status within the hamlet rose, as did the status of tenant farmers elsewhere in Japan, as their contributions to the community became increasingly clear.

Farmers' responses to the postwar Occupation and its reforms

For farmers like Nishiyama Kōichi who had done everything they could to sustain the war effort on the home front, the announcement on August 15, 1945 by Emperor Hirohito that the war had ended was like a bolt of lightning in a clear blue sky. Kōichi recorded on that day, 'it seems that the whole household has fallen into the depths of despair,' and on the next that 'I'm in no mood for work, when I think of our being ruled by the Americans, British, Russians and Chinese.' On August 25, the order having come down to disband the local Military Reservists' Association and destroy its records, he wrote that 'fighting back the tears, I helped . . . set fire to everything.' Then in December 1946 he attended a feast in honor of the hamlet chief, who had been forced to resign in the purge of public officials, and 'about 30 of us in posts in all the wards made merry.' It is clear that Kōichi was not looking forward to the Occupation and remained caught up in the psychology of the wartime era.

And yet that Occupation was to bring an unprecedented measure of democratization to the Japanese countryside, as well as to the rest of Japan, and men like Kōichi and communities like Koshin were soon to be actively involved in many of the reform initiatives emanating from Occupation headquarters in Tokyo. As is well known, a new constitution was promulgated in 1947, giving the right to vote to women as well as men and making such posts as prefectural governor and city, town and village mayor subject to election for the first time. Members of the city, town and village agricultural land committees that played such a crucial role in the postwar land reform were also elected, according to the formula of two owner-cultivators, three landlords and five tenant farmers per committee as a means of limiting the influence of landlords. So, too, were elections held for members of the food regulation committees that insured the smooth delivery of food supplies at a time of great scarcity, and for directors of the newly created agricultural cooperatives.

Kōichi was elected as one of the two owner-cultivators on the agricultural land committee in his area and quickly became deeply involved in the land reform. While the role of Occupation headquarters and officials in the Ministry of Agriculture and Forestry in that reform should not be ignored, neither should the contributions of those land committees and the many individuals mobilized at the hamlet level be overlooked. Enjoying the trust of other rural residents and intimately familiar with local farming and land tenure, they carried out all the basic work at the 'front lines' of the reform, insuring both the rapidity and thoroughness with which it was effected.

Similarly, the food delivery system depended on continued cooperation within rural hamlets. Hamlets had been made responsible for meeting delivery targets during the war, and because of the severe food shortages that still afflicted Japan's cities until late in 1947, the same system was maintained in the early years of the Occupation. That it provided most of the food supplies needed was an important element in restoring social stability and sustaining popular support for Occupation policies, but doing so was no easy matter for farmers, especially not when crops were poor. In Koshin in the autumn of 1946, for example, it was clear that the rice harvest was disappointing and that some two dozen households had experienced a disastrous year. After a long series of ward meetings in which farmers debated what to do, it was finally decided at a hamlet-wide meeting that (1) the volume of rice the community was expected to hand over that year was the absolute maximum it could manage without endangering local subsistence; and (2) while every household would contribute its fare share of the total requisition, any households left without sufficient food to tide them over until the next year's harvest would be given rice by other members of the community (Kōichi's diary, May 11, 1947). This was a notable example of 'rice roots' democracy in action, reflecting the willingness of hamlet residents to do their part in feeding the nation, but at the same time demonstrating their determination to protect the most disadvantaged within their midst.

Farmers' commitment to raising output during the 1950s

With virtually all Japanese farmers now owner-cultivators in the aftermath of the land reform, rural interest in measures to increase agricultural output rose dramatically. In Koshin, a portion of local paddy fields was transformed into uniform parcels of one *tan* each in a program of land adjustment carried out between the autumn of 1948 and spring of 1949, and a survey of agricultural land committees in August 1950 to assess the impact of the land reform confirmed that similar land improvements were now being considered throughout the country (Nishida 1998: 201–14).

Unlike food deliveries, however, land adjustment was not something that farmers in a given hamlet could manage strictly on their own. The cooperation of neighboring hamlets in the determination of new field boundaries, the transfer of some ownership rights and the location of new irrigation and drainage channels were needed, as were united efforts throughout the improvement district in securing subsidies from the prefecture and the state. According to his diary, Kōichi, then a hamlet official, made numerous visits to the adjacent hamlet of Kitaba in 1953 'as a representative of Koshin' to negotiate land transfers, finally succeeding a few months later. Then at the end of 1954 he travelled to Tokyo with officials of the local land improvement district to seek state assistance in the construction of drainage culverts and the laying out of drainage channels:

> We divided the assignments up among ourselves, with some going to the Ministry of Agriculture and Forestry and others going elsewhere. I went on my own to visit the home of Section Chief Ogawa, who was in charge of the drainage work at Tsudanuma in Chiba Prefecture.

Table 2.4 Hamlet meetings (*yoriai*) in Koshin, 1942–60

Year	*Hamlet meetings*	*Ward meetings*	*Officials committee*
1942	13	7	14
1943	12	9	20
1944	10	11	9
1945	8	5	1
1946	8	12	19
1947	8	25	17
1948	15	14	13
1949	11	18	30
1950	5	16	41
1951	7	18	35
1952	6	9	32
1953	3	4	16
1954	5	3	42
1955	3	1	–
1956	5	3	–
1957	5	3	–
1958	3	2	–
1959	4	6	25
1960	3	7	29

Source: Calculated from *Nishiyama Kōichi nikki*, 1925–50 and 1951–75.

The more deeply rural hamlets became involved in land improvements to increase and stabilize agricultural output, the more power inevitably accrued to the hamlet officials who were directly involved in the necessary negotiations, and the committee of hamlet officials steadily developed into the key organ in determining and executing hamlet policy. As shown in Table 2.4, the number of ward and hamlet-wide meetings in Koshin decreased during the 1950s, while the number of meetings held by hamlet officials increased markedly. At the same time, the attention of farmers was inevitably drawn to those politicians and bureaucrats whose influence at the prefectural and national level might prove useful in securing funding for the land improvements they wanted. No doubt that was a factor in the higher than average turnouts at elections for the lower house of the Diet in Niigata, a predominantly agricultural prefecture, during the 1950s, and the higher than average support for candidates from the Socialist and Communist parties during the same decade (Tables 2.5 and 2.6).

At any rate, it can be said that during the 1950s farmers dedicated themselves to any and all efforts to increase agricultural output. In Koshin, young farmers organized a rice cultivation research group in 1951, and in July of that same year they held a conference, to which they invited engineers from the prefecture, to consider reclaiming new arable land from the marshes the hamlet owned. In July of 1956 local farmers established an association to reclaim about 20 *chō* of marshland, each farmer agreeing to contribute toward the cost, and efforts to secure additional government funding for the project began. That same year, the Nishiyamas joined with some of their neighbors to purchase a mechanical cultivator

Table 2.5 Voter turnout in Lower House elections, 1946–60

	Niigata Prefecture			*National average*		
Year	*Men*	*Women*	*Total*	*Men*	*Women*	*Total*
1946	80.2	63.2	70.3	78.6	67.0	72.1
1947	72.8	55.2	63.5	74.9	61.6	67.9
1949	81.8	64.4	72.5	80.7	67.9	74.0
1952	87.3	77.2	81.9	80.5	72.8	76.4
1953	86.0	76.3	80.7	78.4	70.4	74.2
1955	88.0	80.6	84.1	80.0	72.1	75.8
1958	86.7	78.4	82.3	79.8	74.4	77.0
1960	84.4	79.1	81.6	76.0	71.2	73.5

Sources: For 1946 and 1947, *Mainichi nenkan*, 1948 and 1949; for 1949, 1952, 1953 and 1955, *Nihon tōkei nenkan*, 1950, 1952–54; for 1958, *Dai 28 kai shūgiin giin sōsenkyo ichiran*; for 1960, *Dai 29 kai shūgiin giin sōsenkyo ichiran*.

Table 2.6 Voting rates for progressive and conservative parties, 1947–60

	Niigata Prefecture		*National average*	
Year	*Progressive parties (%)*	*Conservative parties (%)*	*Progressive parties (%)*	*Conservative parties (%)*
1947	32.9	60.7	30.0	59.6
1949	33.3	64.0	23.3	63.0
1952	29.3	69.6	23.8	66.9
1953	35.7	59.5	28.5	65.4
1955	36.5	57.8	31.2	63.2
1958	38.1	49.9	35.5	57.8
1960	39.4	55.1	30.5	57.6

Source: *Shūgiin giin sōsenkyo ichiran* for each year.

Notes:

1 Progressive parties: Japan Socialist Party and Japan Communist Party.

2 Conservative parties:

1947: Japan Liberal Party, Japan Democratic Party and National Cooperative Party
1949: Democratic Liberal Party, Japan Democratic Party and National Cooperative Party
1952: Liberal Party, Japan Progressive Party, Cooperative Party
1953: Liberal Party, Japan Progressive Party
1955: Japan Democratic Party, Liberal Party
1958 on: Liberal Democratic Party

for shared use. Many similar examples of the initiative taken at this time by farmers elsewhere in the country to increase output could be cited. To mention only one, farmers in 32 of the 48 hamlets in Azuma village in Ibaraki Prefecture decided to establish agricultural research groups during the 1950s for such purposes as developing better seed strains and improving the local soil (Nishida and Kase 2000: 13–14).

A final point to be made about the 1950s is that most agricultural legislation of the early postwar era – for example, a land improvement law passed in 1949, a law to provide exceptional aid to farming in regions subject to harsh winter weather in 1951, a law to stabilize the prices of agricultural commodities in 1953 and a law to provide financial aid to agricultural improvement projects in 1955 – sought to establish a solid basis for farming operations in Japan and therefore provided welcome support for the efforts of farmers themselves.

The era of rapid economic growth and its impact on farmers

Japan's so-called 'economic miracle' – the sustained high rates of economic growth that began in the late 1950s and continued until the early

1970s – brought about profound structural changes in Japanese agriculture. As a result of the rapidly expanding industrial and tertiary sectors, the primary sector's share in national income fell from 14.6 percent in 1960 to 6.7 percent in 1975, and the proportion of the labor force engaged in agriculture fell from 30 percent to 12.6 percent in the same period. As Jussaume discusses later in this volume, there was also a rapid increase in part-time farming during these years, and the share of income that farm households earned from their agricultural operations fell from a national average of 52.2 percent in 1960 to 32.2 percent in 1975. Nevertheless, both the income of farm households and the value of their assets rose dramatically, together increasing by 8.4 times between 1960 and 1975, well in excess of the threefold increase in consumer prices during that period (calculated from data in Nōsei chōsa iinkai 1977). In other words, despite the decline of the agricultural sector as a source of national income and employment, the growth of the farm household economy kept pace with the growth achieved in the rest of the economy because of ever greater income from non-agricultural employment and the rising value of the land and other assets that farm households owned. Nowhere was the seeming paradox of declining family farming, on the one hand, and the improving economic status of farm households, on the other, more noticeable than in rural communities that were located close to cities.

As mentioned previously, farmers in Koshin had decided in 1956 to drain some of the hamlet's communally owned marshland to create additional paddy fields, but their repeated efforts to secure additional funding for the project from the prefecture and the Ministry of Agriculture and Forestry had not met with any success. Objections to the project surfaced in the hamlet in the early 1960s, as Niigata City began to expand into nearby rural areas and local land prices rose, and a series of meetings was held to consider whether to proceed with land reclamation for farming or opt for urban development instead. Kōichi himself leaned toward the view of Niigata construction companies and politicians that urban development was preferable, but others remained unconvinced. As he noted in his diary on December 25, 1963, 'Serious debate over the pros and cons of the reclamation project went on until half past midnight.' Finally, a vote was taken on February 3, 1964 at a gathering of all those who had agreed to take part in the reclamation project, and Kōichi reported the results as follows: 'Of 91 votes cast, 35 were in favor [of reclamation], 54 were opposed, and 2 votes were invalid. So reclamation [of arable land] has been postponed indefinitely.' It is fair to say that at this point the majority of Koshin's residents were no longer interested in expanding acreage for farming, but rather had their eye on the conversion of farm land to non-agricultural use. In fact, in 1966, after further steep rises in agricultural land prices, paddy fields were converted to housing land in Shimohara, that part of Koshin closest to Niigata City , and the No. 1 and No. 2 Koshin housing developments were soon under construction.

The growing interest of Koshin's farmers in the non-agricultural development of their land in the early 1960s was matched by their growing involvement in politics at all levels. Indeed, development and politics would become increasingly intertwined in the years ahead. Elections were held in April 1963 for the prefectural assembly, mayor of Niigata City (in which Koshin was now included as part of its rural districts) and the city assembly. Kōichi recorded in his diary on March 9 that:

> A joint briefing was held at the Man'eiji by Ōsawa on city politics and Diet Member Takahashi and Assemblyman Yoshida Yoshihei on the prefectural assembly. The place was bursting at the seams with people.

The incumbent mayor of Niigata City, Watanabe Kōtarō, had not attended, but it was generally thought that Koshin would support his re-election. On election day itself Kōichi wrote that he 'was up all night getting reports by telephone of the votes cast for mayor and city assemblyman,' and as he appears to have hoped, Watanabe and Ōsawa, as well as Yoshida, emerged victorious. Then at the general election in November of that same year, Kōichi paid 'a courtesy visit' to the office of incumbent Diet Member Takahashi Seiichirō (of the conservative Liberal Democratic Party), and went the day after the election with the head of Koshin hamlet to congratulate Takahashi on his victory and drink some 'celebration *sake*.'

In 1967, as the creation of further building sites on marshland in Koshin commenced and as both regional and national elections were scheduled to take place in April and June respectively, hamlet officials found themselves devoting just about equal time to issues of 'development' and 'elections' at virtually every meeting they held. As Kōichi recorded on February 18 of that year:

> At the meeting of officials we discussed Mayor Watanabe's supporters' association and the future of rice paddies near the marshes. We now know what the costs of developing those paddies will be, and so we decided to get all those concerned together to decide what to do. We also discussed the election for the city assembly and how we should handle it.

Or again on March 2: 'Discussion of the marshes and the city assembly.' Such entries were repeated in subsequent weeks, and so it is pretty obvious that hamlet officials were aiming at the election of a mayor and a city assemblyman who would support the sort of 'development' they and other residents had in mind.

A concrete example of the links between 'elections' and 'development' and between politicians and hamlet residents was the purchase of one of the hamlet's marshes by Diet Member Takahashi in 1968. It is clear from Kōichi's entry of July 21 of that year that the person who had raised the possibility of purchase was Takahashi himself:

> When we heard that Diet Member Takahashi was interested in buying the marsh, hamlet officials and Assemblyman Kaneda went to see him, and we also talked about the need for new roads to ease farm work. I had a drink and got home at 5.30.

Yet there is no doubt that most local farmers were enthusiastic about the sale. On August 2, Kōichi wrote:

> After discussions at the ward level about whether the sale of the marsh to Diet Member Takahashi should be made, we held a hamlet meeting to decide the matter. Although a few people from wards 1 and 2 expressed opposition, we agreed in the end that the sale should go ahead on terms decided by the hamlet officials, *because the sooner the marsh was developed, the sooner the value of nearby paddy fields would rise*.
>
> (emphasis added)

The overwhelming majority of hamlet residents favored the sale on the grounds that it would lead to higher prices for other land in the community. Attention now turned to the selling price, in which everyone developed a keen interest. On August 21, Kōichi wrote:

> We seesawed back and forth between ¥400,000 and ¥600,000 before agreeing that the midway figure of ¥500,000 might stand a greater chance of success. I alone had pressed for asking for ¥600,000 as the starting price for negotiations, but to no avail. Then Takahashi's secretary Hirashima was summoned, and Ōsawa managed to control his nerves and tell him calmly that we wanted ¥500,000. That was accepted without any quibbles whatsoever, and the contract was signed and sealed when Takahashi-sensei returned home a few days later.

It is no wonder that hamlet representatives had 'seesawed back and forth' in deciding the price for the marsh, and no wonder that they had been nervous about putting their agreed price forward. After all, they were attempting to maximize the return from what had long been regarded as a pretty useless bit of hamlet property, and it probably surprised them that the fairly high price they announced was accepted 'without quibble.' It is no doubt also the case, however, that Diet Member Takahashi profited from the transaction, given the continued increases in local land prices thereafter. Deals such as this one and the other assistance conservative politicians provided to increase the income of farm households and the value of farm household assets played an important role in generating ever greater electoral support for the Liberal Democratic Party in rural Japan during the high growth era.

Farming and farmers since 1970: whither rural Japan?

While rice production remained at high levels during the 1960s, rice consumption steadily declined. Faced with a structural surplus that was also costing a great deal in subsidies to producers, the government launched measures in 1970 to reduce the acreage (*gentan*) planted to rice. The theory among policymakers was that rice farmers would diversify to other crops but, as we shall see, these *gentan* policies tended to promote their 'diversification' out of farming itself and, ironically, to make many of them focus ever more exclusively on rice in their remaining farming operations.

In Koshin, where rice continued to be the major crop, a general meeting had been held in January 1970 to discuss whether or not to undertake drainage improvements in some paddy fields near a marsh that were still subject to excessive dampness. Opinion was generally against the plan:

> Various views were expressed, but what with all the talk about cutting back on rice output we just don't think we can undertake such a project unless substantial funding comes from elsewhere.

In April, a conclusion was reached:

> A general meeting of all farmers. There was discussion as to whether or not to carry forward the drainage project . . . but it was decided that in this era of reduced rice output it made no sense and so the project was abandoned.

The number of farmers in the hamlet who were dedicated to efforts to improve agriculture had already decreased, and, as mentioned in the preceding section, most farmers had been drawn to getting as high a price as possible from the sale of reclaimed marshland for urban development, expecting that the value of their own land would increase as a result. Indeed, the two topics that were discussed most enthusiastically in the hamlet in 1970 were whether Koshin would be named a district for urban development under the terms of the new city planning law of 1969 and how much the hamlet would earn from selling reclaimed marshland as sites for the new vocational high school and police academy that the prefecture had decided to build. In Koshin, located as it was so close to Niigata City, a retreat from farming was well under way.

What about farming communities that were located at a considerable distance from cities? To answer that question I would like to refer once again to the case of Azuma village in Ibaraki Prefecture (for details, see Nishida and Kase 2000: chapter 2). Although non-agricultural employment had risen somewhat during the 1960s, especially among the school-leaving children of local farmers, most households in the village remained engaged 'solely' or 'mainly' in agriculture. After 1970, however, when measures to reduce rice acreage went into force, non-agricultural employment increased markedly, and by the mid-1970s most local farm households derived more of their income from non-agricultural than from agricultural activity. Yet at the very same time, and despite official efforts to discourage rice production, the number of farm households growing nothing but rice had also increased markedly. For example, the proportion of farm households in the Toyoshima section of Azuma who concentrated exclusively on rice production rose from 67.4 percent in 1965 to 93.9 percent in 1975. The explanation for this unexpected outcome is twofold: that hardly any other crop could yield more profit than rice, and that all other crops required considerably more time to cultivate successfully than farmers who were simultaneously engaged in non-agricultural employment could possibly manage to provide. That Japan had then and continues to have the lowest rate of food self-sufficiency among the developed nations of the world (just 42 percent on a calorie basis in 1999) and produces more than is needed for domestic consumption only in rice is largely owing to the above considerations.

Let us return now to the experiences of the Nishiyama household and Koshin hamlet after 1970. Dealing with the Nishiyamas first, they purchased nine *tan* of paddy fields in Iwamuro village in 1973, paying for the purchase with a bit over half of the ¥13 million they had received from the sale of only one *tan* of their original holding in Koshin for construction of an access road to the Hokuriku expressway. They now owned a total of 3.6 *chō*, which would prove to be the most land they ever owned and would mark the height of their prosperity. As the fields they had just purchased were some six miles from Koshin, instead of cultivating them themselves they leased them out (which recently relaxed regulations dating from the land reform era allowed) for an annual rent of ¥370,000. In one sense, the tenant farmers who had become owner-cultivators back in the mid-1940s had now risen to the status of 'cultivating landlords.' In another sense, however, they had become speculators in land, and speculation of that and other sorts would prove to be their undoing.

What one should bear in mind is that the purchase of those nine *tan* in Iwamuro had been made possible not by the Nishiyama's profits from farming, but by their profits from development – more specifically, from the dramatic increases in land values that property in the path of development, such as theirs in the case of the Hokuriku expressway, had produced. Nor does the purchase seem to have been based as much on expectations of a favorable return from renting the land out for farming as on expectations of substantial increases in the value of that land in future. Kōichi had by now retired as head of the household, and his eldest son was in charge of their affairs. Like others in the community, the latter saw little point in striving to increase yields on their paddy fields now that *gentan* policies were in operation and turned his attention to other means of increasing the family's wealth, mainly by playing the stock market. By 1976 his investment losses had mounted to ¥18 million, and they had no option but to sell three *tan* of dry fields to cover the debt. Further losses by 1981 led to an impasse between father and son – as Kōichi noted in his diary: 'We talked about what to do with all those debts but could come to no agreement' – but in 1983 they had to sell 2.6 *tan* of rice paddy. And even then his son did not stop investing, and making losses, in shares. With debts of almost ¥300 million in 1987, they were obliged to surrender 'title to all the farm land' still in their possession, leaving them 'with only the house and the land on which it stood.' In short, the prosperous cultivating landlords of 1973 had nothing to do with farming 14 years later. The dramatic rise in land prices during the era of rapid economic growth had transformed the family's attitude toward its land holdings from a site of agricultural production to a capital asset. Without the inflated values of that land as collateral, it would have been impossible for Kōichi's son to become so deeply – and disastrously – involved in the stock market.

Life in Koshin, too, became increasingly troubled after 1970, with 'disharmony in the hamlet' (*buraku no fuwa*) surfacing early on and proving well-nigh impossible to resolve. Here, too, the main source of the problem was development. In 1970 itself, 15 local farmers who had withdrawn from the reclamation association back in 1956 because they objected to the costs they were expected to bear now insisted that as reclamation had ceased and property development begun they were entitled to their share of the proceeds from the sale of a communal asset, a position with which those who had stuck with the association as its purpose changed from reclamation to development did not agree. Differences also emerged among the members of the association as to whether the proceeds from sales of marshland should be shared out among them or deposited in the community's account. Toward the end of 1970, Kōichi noted with a degree of exasperation: 'We've looked at why things are not going well in the hamlet from every angle, but there's still no solution in sight.' These first two issues eventually were resolved in 1972, when it was decided to share out most of the proceeds and, thanks to the mediation of high-ranking officials of the land improvement district, to give each of the 15 farmers who had left the association ¥770,000, or ¥100,000 less than the others, but squabbles over money continued to erupt within the community. In 1973, for example, there was disagreement over whether the owners of the rice seedling beds that were being taken for the access road to the Hokuriku expressway should receive more money than the owners of ordinary paddy fields, and residents polarized into 'a seedling bed faction and a paddy field faction,' as well as arguing among themselves about what to do with the payment that would be made into the hamlet's account. Numerous meetings were held from 1974 onward to 'restore communal harmony,' but relations among residents remained strained and, as a result, hamlet officials had to spend more of their time in managing conflict than in carrying out their normal duties.

Granted, the situation in Koshin was exacerbated by its location in the immediate environs of an expanding city, but no part of rural Japan proved totally immune to the sort of changes described above. Even in Azuma, located in a fairly remote part of Ibaraki Prefecture, there was a retreat from farming as *gentan* policies took effect, with the acreage planted to rice declining by 21 percent between 1970 and 1990 and the total acreage, including dry fields, devoted to farming declining by 9 percent in the same period (Nishida and Kase 2000: 12–13). As local households became more and more involved in non-agricultural employment, it is highly likely that there, too, it became increasingly difficult to organize residents for the performance of essential communal tasks and to maintain any sort of viable consensus in local affairs.

An even more recent trend throughout the country has been a marked increase in the rate at which rural communities themselves have been disappearing. According to the *World Census of Agriculture and Forestry*, the number of farming hamlets in Japan declined from 142,377 in 1980 (of which 13,869 contained nine or fewer households) to 140,144 in 1990 (of which 21,721 contained nine or fewer households), which by a simple calculation means that hamlets were disappearing at the rate of more than 220 a year. By the year 2000, only 135,179 hamlets remained (of which 29,955 had nine or fewer households in residence), meaning that the pace of disappearance had quickened to almost 500 a year. Given the rising number of hamlets containing nine or fewer residents, it is not unreasonable to expect that even more hamlets will disappear even more quickly in future. Rapid economic growth since 1960 had led to increases in the income of farmers and the value of their assets, bringing unprecedented prosperity to rural Japan, but in that very process farming became increasingly marginalized within many rural communities, and those communities themselves, on which local farmers had depended so heavily in the past, faced mounting problems and, in a growing number of cases, ceased to exist. I believe it is no exaggeration to say that Japanese agriculture is now faced with a crisis that will decide its whole future.

References

Isobe Toshihiko. 1977. 'Kōchi seiri o kakki to suru tochi hensei no tenkai.' In '*Zenji nisshi*' *kaidai* 8, ed. Toyohara kenkyūkai. Tokyo: Tōkyō daigaku shuppankai.

Kawaguchi Akira. 1977. '"Nisshi" ni miru nichijō seikatsu no keisei to shutai.' In '*Zenji nisshi*' *kaidai* 2, ed. Toyohara kenkyūkai. Tokyo: Tōkyō daigaku shuppankai.

Murakami Rinzō. 1997. *Tsuchi no bungaku: Nagatsuka Takashi, Akutagawa Ryūnosuke*. Tokyo: Kanrin shobō.

Nagatsuka Takashi. 1956. *Tsuchi*. 1956 edition. Tokyo: Kadokawa bunko.

Niigata-ken keizai nōgyō kumiai rengōkai. 1957. *Kome ni kansuru shiryō*.

Nishida Yoshiaki. 1998. 'Nōchi kaikaku to nōson minshushugi.' In *Demokurashii no hōkai to saisei*, ed. Minami Ryōshin, Nakamura Masanori and Nishizawa Tamotsu. Tokyo: Nihon keizai hyōronsha.

—— and Kase Kazutoshi. 2000. *Kōdo keizai seichōki no nōgyō mondai*. Tokyo: Nihon keizai hyōronsha.

—— and Kubo Yasuo. 1991. *Nishiyama Kōichi nikki, 1925–1950*. Tokyo: Tōkyō daigaku shuppankai.

—— 1998. *Nishiyama Kōichi nikki, 1951–1975*. Tokyo: Tōkyō daigaku shuppankai.

Nōchi seido shiryō shūsei hensan iinkai. 1969. *Nōchi seido shiryō shūsei*. Tokyo: Ochanomizu shobō.

Nōrinshō. 1974. *Nōgyō keizai ruinen tōkei*, vol. 1, ed. Nōrinshō tōkei jōhōbu and Nōrin tōkei kenkyūkai.

Nōsei chōsa iinkai. 1977. *Kaitei Nihon nōgyō kiso tōkei*. Tokyo: Nōrin tōkei kyōkai.

Takeda Tsutomu. 1977. 'Kome "kedashi" gyō no eigyō keitai to seikaku.' In '*Zenji nisshi*' *kaidai* 7, ed. Toyohara kenkyūkai. Tokyo: Tōkyō daigaku shuppankai.

Toyohara kenkyūkai. 1977. *Zenji nisshi – Yamagata ken Shōnai heiya ni okeru ichi nōmin no nisshi, Meiji 26–Shōwa 9 nen*. Tokyo: Tōkyō daigaku shuppankai.

Usami Shigeru. 1977a. '"Zenji nisshi" – Zenji to Tanzo ke no hitobito.' In '*Zenji nisshi*' *kaidai* 1, ed. Toyohara kenkyūkai. Tokyo: Tōkyō daigaku shuppankai.

—— 1977b. 'Wakase renchū no sekai.' In '*Zenji nisshi*' *kaidai* 6, ed. Toyohara kenkyūkai. Tokyo: Tōkyō daigaku shuppankai.

Usui Yoshimi. 1956. 'Kaisetsu.' In Nagatsuka Takashi, *Tsuchi*. Tokyo: Kadokawa bunko.

Waswo, Ann (trans.) 1989. *The Soil by Nagatsuka Takashi: A Portrait of Rural Life in Meiji Japan*. London and New York: Routledge.

3 The women of rural Japan

An overview of the twentieth century

Ōkado Masakatsu

Introduction

Writing in 1995, a Japanese economist reported that '60 per cent of all agricultural labor is now performed by women' (Imamura 1995: 3). He was correct, but his apparent surprise at this finding was misplaced. As shown in Table 3.1, the proportion of women among those primarily employed in farming has remained at approximately 60 percent since the 1960s. It is clear, therefore, that rural women have played an important role in family farming for many years, but it seems equally clear that most scholars – and, it might be added, agricultural policy makers – have tended to overlook this fact.

Taking Imamura's 'finding' as her starting point, Kumagai Sonoko has noted in a recent literature survey that, although there was some research on rural women carried out during the prewar period, most notably by Maruoka Hideko (1937; reprinted 1980), it tended to focus on the problems those women faced as wives and mothers, and their labor in farming was largely ignored (Kumagai 1995: 8–9). Nor was much attention paid to the role of women in the extensive research into the history of family farming and changes in the farm household economy during the nineteenth and early twentieth centuries that was carried out by agricultural economists and rural sociologists during the first four decades of the postwar era. The labor contributions of women to farming remained largely invisible.

Since the early 1990s, however, more and more research on the history of rural women during the early modern and modern eras has been published, in part reflecting contemporary concerns with the aging (and 'feminization') of the agricultural labor force, and in part reflecting the development of women's studies in general and greater sensitivity to gender issues. Broadly speaking, that research can be divided into three strands. First, research on the daily lives of rural women, as exemplified

Table 3.1 Percentage of women among those primarily employed in farming

Year	*Persons primarily employed in farming*	*Of whom, % women*
1946	16,320,822	54.6
1960	14,541,624	58.8
1970	10,451,956	61.2
1980	6,973,085	61.7
1990	5,653,321	60.2

Source: Nōrinsuisanshō tōkei jōhōbu, *Nōgyō sensasu ruinen tōkeisho*, 1992.

Note
'Persons primarily employed in farming' includes those whose only work was in farming and those who did more days of farm work than any other sort of work during the year in question.

by Itagaki Kuniko's study based on an analysis of articles in *Ie no hikari* (*Light of the Home*), a magazine that began publication in 1925 and was widely read in the countryside (Itagaki 1992). Second, research shedding new light on the functioning of farm families as economic units: for example, Nishida Yoshiaki on the differences between farm households and the households of industrial workers (Nishida 1997: 41–51); Tanimoto Masayuki on the economic strategies adopted by farm households and their responsiveness to market stimuli (Tanimoto 1998); and Saitō Osamu on the choices made by families (*kazoku no sentaku*) and the effect of those choices on the farm household economy over the long term (Saitō 1998). Third, research dealing specifically with the role of women within farm households (Saitō 1991; Ōkado and Yanagizawa 1996).

In this chapter I will focus on the latter topic, tracing the continuities and changes in the role of women in the operation of farm households over the course of the twentieth century. No doubt there are some interesting historical comparisons to be made with rural women elsewhere in the developing/developed world, but I will have to defer consideration of that topic to another time. Only a few contemporary comparisons will be brought out in the concluding section.

Women in farm households during the early 1900s

Perhaps not surprisingly, given the 'invisibility' of rural women, there is very little documentation available on the working hours of farm families that distinguishes between the tasks performed by men and by women

Table 3.2 Hours of work performed by male and female members of farm households, 1933 (national averages)

Age range	*Farm work*		*By-employments*	*House-work*	*Other*	*Total*
	(days)	*(hours)*	*(hours)*	*(hours)*	*(hours)*	*(hours)*
Males						
Under 15	75	515	15	167	43	739
16–20	186	1,563	406	222	158	2,350
21–30	238	1,900	752	301	280	3,232
31–50	241	2,156	492	405	341	3,394
51–60	251	2,180	273	486	276	3,216
61–70	188	1,538	291	459	126	2,414
Over 70	200	1,167	53	574	67	1,860
Females						
Under 15	50	314	57	407	36	814
16–20	140	1,090	151	924	59	2,224
21–30	197	1,530	103	1,340	91	3,064
31–50	210	1,666	124	1,554	95	3,440
51–60	163	1,106	101	1,710	95	3,012
61–70	130	748	29	1,680	53	2,510
Over 70	40	179	6	1,208	10	1,403

Source: Teikoku nōkai, *Nōgyō no rōdō jōtai ni kansuru chōsa*, 1938.

in the early decades of the twentieth century. One particularly valuable set of data that is available is that for 1933, which was published by the Imperial Agricultural Association (Teikoku nōkai) on the basis of its rural household economic surveys (see Table 3.2). From this we will now examine how the tasks of farming, housework and by-employments were distributed within farm families.

If we look at the age group from 31 to 50 years, people in the prime of their working lives, it is apparent that the annual number of working hours was almost the same for men and women at about 3,400 hours, with both men and women spending a massive number of hours at work. The distribution of labor tasks differed considerably between men and women, however, with men being engaged in farm work for 2,100 hours, in by-employments for 500 hours, in housework for 400 hours and in other tasks for 300 hours. In contrast, women spent 1,600 hours in farm work, 1,500 hours in housework, and 100 hours each in by-employments and additional tasks. Unfortunately, we do not know how the distinction was drawn between farm work and housework in this particular survey. Moreover, the data reflect the average hours worked by farm families, with no regard to regional or class differences. But in spite of these shortcomings, the data in the table do allow us to get a rough understanding of how labor tasks were allocated between men and women in prewar farm households. Male members of farm families worked principally at farming and were then to some extent engaged in tasks relating to by-employments and housework. In contrast, women spent more or less the same amount of time on farm work and housework. It is quite likely that the type of housework carried out by men and women differed, with women shouldering among other things the tasks of providing food and clothing, childcare and care for the sick and elderly, while men tended to such tasks as repairing the house and maintaining the household's tools and equipment. These differences notwithstanding, it is clear that women in Japanese farm households were deeply involved in farm work as well as in housework, and that the role they played, although different from the role played by men, was indispensable to the household.

Let us now examine that role more closely. Table 3.3 shows the allocation of labor tasks in four farm households in Niigata Prefecture in 1915. According to these data, with the exception of Household B where the wife of the head of the family was the only adult woman present, two or three women were needed to carry out the housework in the household, and accordingly two or three women remained in residence. The wife of the head of household (or inheriting son) was almost constantly engaged in childbirth or childrearing during her younger years and, because of the high rate of infant mortality at the time, giving birth and bringing up the children placed a very great burden on her (Kobayashi 1974: 75–84; Ōkado 1995: 67–69). It was therefore necessary for her to have the support of one or two other women in the housework, who spent any additional time available to them doing farm work.

As these examples show, the household economy was sustained both by women's work (in the form of housework and farming) and the farm work of the head of household and eldest son. If additional farm labor was needed, younger sons might remain in the household; if not, they were sent away to work (e.g. the third son of Household B, the second son of Household C).

Table 3.4 presents data on the work performed by women in three farm households in Ibaraki Prefecture in 1913, and in its breakdown of housework reveals the importance of tasks related to clothing: the weaving of cloth and the sewing and repair of garments. That was a considerable undertaking for women, given the large size of most farm households at the time, and was typically carried out during the winter months. It usually required the labor of two or three women during that season, and those women would then perform other housework and agricultural

Table 3.3 Allocation of tasks in four farm households in Niigata Prefecture, 1915

Household	*Family members*	*Age*	*Farming (days)*	*House-work (days)*	*Other (days)*
A					
Cultivating landlord	head of household	45	**132**	34	**135**
(owned 3.8 *chō*,	wife of head	43	**162**	**182**	24
farmed 1.3 *chō*)	eldest son	22	**209**	32	**62**
	eldest son's wife	18	**111**	**106**	6
	eldest daughter	18	**126**	**193**	12
	part-time employee		21	79	53
B					
Owner-tenant	head of household	46	**277**	12	17
(owned 0.9 *chō*,	wife of head	42	**96**	**148**	20
farmed 2.1 *chō*)	second son	18	**307**	21	14
	third son[1]	16	2	3	
	third daughter[2]	12	8	11	
	fourth daughter[2]	9			
	fifth daughter	7			
C					
Owner farmer	head of household	59	**220**	10	5
(owned 2.8 *chō*,	wife of head	56	**143**	**167**	21
farmed 2.6 *chō*)	mother of head[3]	69			
	eldest son	34	**260**	10	21
	eldest son's wife	30	**192**	**127**	2
	second son[4]	28	38	1	
	third son	25	**301**	5	10
	eldest daughter	18	**189**	**145**	6
	3 young grandchildren				
	part-time employees		73	1	
D					
Owner farmer	head of household	45	**277**	3	9
(owned 2.7 *chō*,	wife of head	41	**122**	**152**	15
farmed 2.2 *chō*)	eldest son	16	**267**	3	1
	eldest daughter	19	**203**	**157**	1
	second daughter[2]	13			
	third daughter	6			
	second son	3			

Source: Niigata ken nōkai, *Niigata ken nōka keizai chōsa*, 1915.

Notes

1 started work in a shop in April.

2 elementary school student.

3 age as given in source, but must have been some 8 to 10 years older; did some housework from time to time.

4 helped with silkworm rearing only.

Table 3.4 Work performed by women in three farm households in Ibaraki Prefecture, 1913 (in days or portions of days)

Status	*Age*	*Agriculture*		*Housework*		
		Farm work	*Seri-culture*	*Routine chores*	*Clothes making*	*Sewing lessons*
A						
wife of head	49	**96**	**69**	**119**	17	
wife of adopted son	29	**147**	21	**49**	**86**	
second daughter	17	**163**	24	25	**56**	33
mother of head	75					
B						
wife of head	42	**95**		**107**	**85**	
wife of eldest son	22	**113**		**61**	**66**	
mother of head	67					
C						
wife of head	42	**128**		**51**	**75**	
eldest daughter	22	**153**		20	**99**	
second daughter	17	**134**		24	**119**	

Source: Ibaraki ken nōkai, *Nōka keizai chōsa*, 1913.

Note

All four households were owner farmers, owning from 2.7 to 3 *chō* of land. Household A had 9 members, of whom 3 were children; Household B, 10 members, of whom 3 were children; Household C, 8 members, of whom 4 were children. Most of the farm work done by women related to rice cultivation.

tasks during the rest of the year (such as the silkworm breeding of the wife and other women in Household A). Not surprisingly, daughters who were expected to remain in the family were made to learn needlework (Household A's second daughter), and the others were sent out to work just like surplus sons, in the case of daughters as household servants or factory workers.

As these examples show, women were deeply involved in both reproductive and productive work within their families. Some housework tasks, such as childcare and cooking, were performed daily, while others, such as making and repairing clothing, were performed in the agricultural off-season. The work load was distributed as 'rationally' as possible among the two or three adult women present in most farm households, all of whom devoted their spare time – that is, the time not needed for housework – to farming.

The examples cited above are for the 1910s. Unfortunately, no similar material exists for the 1920s and 1930s, and so two examples from the

Table 3.5 Labor performed by family members, 1950 (○ = main tasks △ = subsidiary tasks)

Member	*Age*	*Agriculture*		*Housework*					
		Farm work	*Seri-culture*	*Cooking*	*Clothing*	*Cleaning*	*Shopping*	*Child care*	*Bath fires*
A									
head	47	○	○						
his wife	44	○		○	○	○	○	○	○
his mother	64			○	△	○	○	○	○
his brother	38	△	△			△			
eldest son	21	○	△			△			
second son	18								
third son	14								
fourth son	9								
second daughter	11					○			
third daughter	5								
B									
head	54	○					○		
his wife	51	○	○	○	○	○			
eldest son	27				△	△	○		
second son	21								
third son	18	△		△			○		
fourth daughter	13	△		○	△	○			○
fourth son	9	△							

Source: Rōdōshō fujin shōnen kyoku, *Nōson fujin no seikatsu*, 1952.

Note

The second son of Household A was employed as an agricultural laborer. The eldest son in Household B was a company employee and the second son was apprenticed to a shopkeeper.

early 1950s will be introduced to show how, if at all, the role of women in farm households changed over time. Table 3.5 shows the labor performed by family members in two farm households, one in northeastern Japan (Household A in Yamagata Prefecture) and one in southwestern Japan (Household B in Aichi Prefecture). In both cases, the similarities with the 1910s are clear, in that two women in each household were needed to do the housework, devoting any spare time they had to farming. In Household A, housework was done by the wife and her mother-in-law, while in Household B, which did not include a mother-in-law, housework was performed by the wife and her 13-year-old fourth daughter (a middle school student). In Household B both the eldest and second son were employed elsewhere, and for this reason the wife shared farming and livestock rearing tasks with her husband, with help during the busy season from the children who remained at home and were still in school, the third and fourth son (in high school and elementary school, respectively) and the fourth daughter (as noted above, in middle school). In contrast, in Household A, where farm labor was provided by the head of the household, his wife, his younger brother and their eldest son, it seems that the primary and middle school children of the family helped only a little in the farm work and housework. This point may be considered a new characteristic of the postwar period: now that attendance at middle school had become compulsory (that is, now that nine years of schooling were required, instead of six), it became increasingly difficult for farm households to use children between the ages of 12 and 16 as an auxiliary labor force in either farming or housework.

The era of the Showa Depression

If one examines the various bibliographies that are available on the subject of rural women, it is immediately obvious that almost no sources dating from before the First World War are listed. Only in the 1920s did articles on rural women begin to appear in newspapers and magazines, reflecting a growing awareness of the contrasts between countryside and city in Japan at that time. The volume of such articles and other materials increased markedly in the aftermath of the Showa Depression, mostly in connection with the on-going rural economic revitalization campaign. Two themes stand out in the sources dating from the depression era as far as rural women are concerned: (1) the problems facing young women from the countryside who were at work in factories; and (2) the campaign for the improvement of daily life (*seikatsu kaizen*) in the countryside itself. Only Maruoka Hideko, mentioned earlier, dealt with a third theme, the heavy workload of women in farm households. Apparently, such heavy workloads were taken as perfectly normal by other observers, not meriting any special attention.

What did attract the attention of these observers was the role women were to play in rural economic revitalization. The campaign of that name may have been based on the mobilization of 'middling farmers' – that is, the adult men who as owner-cultivators or owner-tenants managed their family's farming operations – but it also sought to mobilize the women and children in those families in the cause of self-help efforts to rescue both their families and their communities from the devastating effects of the depression (Ōkado, 1994: 306–8, 310–18).

To illustrate the role rural women were expected to play in the campaign, I will use Yamagata Prefecture as an example. Two things were expected from rural women in that prefecture, i.e. 'the reform of daily life in the home' and 'the promotion of education within the home.' The first of these, 'reform of daily life in the home' consisted of the following three objectives: (1) the improvement of food, clothing, and shelter (better nutrition, suitable work clothes and children's clothing, improved cooking facilities), better management of hygiene and health (establishment of a hygiene day, protection of expectant and nursing mothers, greater attention to the care of infants and children), and reduced expenditure on weddings and funerals; (2) the rationalization and reduction of household expenditure by means of the keeping of detailed household accounts and making as many purchases as possible through the local industrial cooperative; and (3) the improved performance of communal tasks by better time management and the establishment of day nurseries (Yamagata ken rengō jokyōin kyōgikai 1935: 48–68). As can be seen, the home (*katei*) was here identified as a key institution in daily life, consumption and the community, and women (*fujin*) were portrayed as responsible for its proper management. Moreover, they were also portrayed as responsible for 'the promotion of education within the home,' that is, for the traditional maternal task of teaching their children proper behavior and, in addition, teaching them basic farming skills (Ōkado 1994: 317–19).

The magazine *Nōson fujin* (Rural Women) which was published between 1932 and 1936, provides further insight into the roles envisaged for rural women at the time of the rural economic revitalization campaign. In the inaugural issue of March 1932 the editors stated:

> The desire for modern luxuries has finally spread to the countryside, and we note with extreme regret that some women have even fled their rural homes [in the hope of bettering their lives]. . . . But if all rural women awaken to their economic, occupational and familial

> roles in agriculture, we can expect prosperity to return to the rural villages of our country.

What was needed, the editors continued, were efforts to create 'a pious rural culture, in contrast to the decadent culture of the city.' Women were thus expected to contribute to rural recovery in three spheres: the 'economic,' the 'occupational' and the 'familial.'

About the articles that appeared in this and subsequent issues of the magazine, the following five observations can be made. First, rural women were identified as the persons in charge of the reform of daily life, as family managers and as educators of children. As a reflection of this there were many articles relating to meal planning, kitchen improvements, more 'rational' expenditure on family weddings and funerals, child-rearing and education. Second, there were numerous articles on the activities of groups such as industrial cooperatives, young women's associations and housewives' associations, all emphasizing the importance of collective action in solving rural problems. Third, there were relatively few articles on farming itself and quite a few articles on vegetable gardening and such by-employments as poultry raising, horticulture, rope making and other uses of leftover straw, with rural women encouraged to take the lead in such activities. Fourth, there were regular articles introducing readers to rural women in other countries, for example in Denmark, Korea, the United States and Russia. Fifth, each issue of the magazine invariably contained articles explaining the goals of the rural economic revitalization campaign and exhorting readers to strive for their achievement.

On the basis of the above observations about the content of articles in *Nōson fujin*, it can be said that the magazine located rural women outside of farming itself, stressing their role in the operation of by-employments and portraying them as the managers of the home and improvements to daily life. And those latter improvements were generally confined to simple techniques and technologies, with essentially no mention made of such problems as patriarchy, primogeniture or overwork. That said, it did mark a new departure that the 'home' (*katei*) was identified as a distinct domain within family farming operations and women were given a responsible position within that domain. Where previously farm households had tended to subordinate how they lived to the needs of their farming activities, now for the first time the importance of the domestic domain was acknowledged. Despite that acknowledgment, however, it is important to remember that the rural economic revitalization campaign stressed collective action by such organizations as youth groups, women's associations and industrial cooperatives to bring about improvements in that domain. In that sense, the campaign drew rural women out of their dwellings and gave them a role in their communities, but it did not intervene in any way to help them as individuals or to encourage changes in the situation of women within family farming.

Women in wartime Japan

It was only during the wartime period that the role of women in farm operations began to attract attention, especially from those involved in the design and execution of wartime economic controls. Now that rural men were being drawn away for military service and factory work, it was clear that the agricultural labor force was becoming increasingly feminized (Ōkado and Yanagizawa 1996: 34–6).

Table 3.6, which is derived from census and other data, shows changes in the employed population by industry and by gender during the years 1936 to 1940 (the time of the Sino-Japanese War) and 1940 to 1944 (the time of the Asian-Pacific War). The last three columns show the increase or decrease of those so employed in each period, providing an indication of the major sources of military manpower and labor in heavy industry at the time. At the time of the Sino-Japanese War, those major sources were males from agriculture and forestry and from commerce and males and females from the textile industry. From the outbreak of the Asian-Pacific War, the major sources were males and females from commerce, males from agriculture and forestry and males and females from the textile industry. What should be noted here is that the number of females in agriculture and forestry increased in both periods. It is clear that labor shortages in that sector were being compensated for, at least to a considerable extent, by females throughout the Sino-Japanese and the Asian-Pacific Wars.

In that connection, it would be relevant to compare the reliance on foreign and prisoner-of-war labor in both wartime Germany and Japan. On the one hand, in 1944 the proportion of foreign workers and prisoners of war in the total German labor force reached 20 percent. On the other hand, in that same year the proportion of Korean and Chinese workers in the total Japanese labor force has been estimated at only 4 percent (Yamazaki 1993: 196–7). Koreans and Chinese were certainly subjected to a severe forced labor regime in wartime Japan (as were a comparatively small number of western prisoners of war), but viewed in terms of the degree of dependence on that form of labor, there was clearly a striking difference between Germany and Japan. I believe that a major reason for this difference rests with the nature of family farming in Japan and the role of women within farm households. That is, wartime mobilization in Japan drew heavily on the manpower from the many farm

Table 3.6 Changes in the employed population by industry and gender, 1936–47

	October 1, 1936	*October 1, 1940**	*October 1, 1940***	*February 22, 1944*	*October 1, 1947*	*Variation*		
						1936–40	*1940–44*	*1944–47*
Male employees								
agricultural and forestry	7,814	6,618	6,626	5,787	8,431	**–1,196**	**–839**	2,644
machine industry	789	1,897	1,870	3,524	971	1,108	1,654	–2,553
textile industry	869	689	583	239	409	–180	–344	170
commerce	3,072	2,652	2,464	879	1,497	**–420**	**–1,585**	618
restaurants, etc.	530	395	552	279	349	–135	–273	70
Female employees								
agriculture and forestry	6,714	7,223	7,223	7,784	8,671	**509**	**561**	887
machine industry	33	227	225	787	148	194	562	–639
textile industry	1,263	1,122	1,044	570	641	–141	–474	71
commerce	857	1,193	1,119	684	693	**336**	–435	9
restaurants, etc.	951	742	811	573	389	–209	–238	–184
All employees								
agriculture and forestry	14,528	13,842	13,850	13,571	17,102	–686	–279	3,531
machine industry	822	2,123	2,095	4,312	1,120	1,301	2,217	–3,192
textile industry	2,132	1,811	1,626	809	1,050	–321	–817	241
commerce	3,929	3,845	3,583	1,555	2,190	–84	–2,028	635
restaurants, etc.	1,480	1,137	1,363	852	738	–342	–511	–114

Source: Umemura Mataji *et al.*, *Chōki keizai tōkei 2: rōdōryoku* (Tokyo: Tōyō keizai shinpōsha, 1988), pp. 208–15, 260–1.

Notes: *1940 census data
**1940 census data as re-calculated on the bases used in the extraordinary censuses of 1944 and 1947

households throughout the country, and 'womanpower' in those same households to a great extent filled the gap that their departure for the front or factory left.

In fact, the feminization of the agricultural workforce progressed conspicuously during the wartime period. While the number of males aged 20 to 39 in that workforce decreased from 2.91 million in 1930 to 2.13 million in 1940 and to only 1.5 million in 1944, the number of females in that same age group increased from 2.81 million in 1930 to 3.02 million in 1940, and again to 3.36 million between 1940 and 1944. As a result, the percentage of women in the agricultural workforce rose from 49.1 percent in 1930 to 58.7 percent in 1940 and to 69.1 percent in 1944. On the eve of Japan's defeat and surrender, roughly 70 percent of all labor in agriculture was provided by women (Ōhara shakai mondai kenkyūjo 1964: 181).

Thus, wartime mobilization depended heavily on farm households, and the fact that women were already involved in farming and capable of even deeper involvement was a fundamental factor in making possible the mobilization of men from those households. Herein lies the reason why rural women were given increased attention during the war years.

A lot was expected from rural women during those years, both in farming and in fecundity. Because they were supposed to take over much of the agricultural work in place of the young men who had been mobilized for the war and war-related work, they were taught farming techniques – for example, how to dig fields with an ox-drawn plow and how to cope with shortages of fertilizer and other essentials (Niigata ken nōkai 1942). The training given to such women at this time no doubt had something to do with the emergence of 'housewife farming' (*shufu nōgyō*) in the postwar period, as many wives had the necessary skills to tend the crops while their husbands went off to perform non-agricultural work. At the same time, rural women were expected to give birth to as many babies as possible during the war years, to replenish and augment the nation's population, and this led to a variety of health problems, especially related to childbirth and infant care, as well as problems related to housing.

These two expectations placed a great strain on many women. According to one source, for example, infant mortality rates in Tohoku in the early 1940s were the highest not among the poorest farm families, but among those of middling economic status, and the major cause of mortality was not malnutrition but maternal exhaustion from overwork and the poor condition of even 'middle-class' rural dwellings (Itaya 1942: 151–2, 295). Nor did women gain any higher status within their families for taking the place of absent males and becoming responsible for farming as well as housework. They may have sustained the family's farming operations, but as before males remained the principle successors to family property. Women were not recognized as the mainstays of family farming, but regarded as mere caretakers while the 'proper' head of the family or male heir to the family's landholding was away.

None of these problems was addressed during the war years. Granted, there were surveys carried out by the Institute for the Science of Labor, which carried forward the previously mentioned research of Maruoka Hideko to portray the role of rural women in all of its dimensions, including agricultural labor as well as housework and by-employments, and which highlighted the problems caused by overwork and the state's pro-natal policies during wartime (Rōdō kagaku kenkyūjo 1933–42). In a different way, *Ie no hikari* continued to highlight the need for the improvement of daily life in the countryside and the aspiration of rural women to achieve progress in that. It may well be that the editors of that magazine were aware of the Institute's findings and hoped for policy initiatives on a much wider front, but the financial and other demands of waging war rendered that impossible.

From the Occupation through the 1950s

The 'liberation of women' was put forward as an essential part of the democratization sought by the Occupation in early postwar Japan. In September 1947 the Women's and Minors' Bureau (*Fujin shōnen kyoku*) was created in the Ministry of Labor, and women and minors' offices (*fujin shōnen shitsu*) were established in every prefecture. In addition, in November 1948 the Home-Life Improvement Section was established in the Ministry of Agriculture and Forestry, and agents were dispatched to the countryside to promote improvement projects, many of which had a bearing on 'women's liberation.' Thereafter, in the wake of the democratization effected by the new constitution and revision of the civil code, and as a result of continued American influence and concern about the gap in living standards between rural and urban Japan, many surveys on the labor and lives of rural woman were carried out. Indeed, the overwork experienced by rural women was a major theme in the literature published at this time, along with the more familiar themes of the need for improvements in housework and daily life. One notable example of this was *The Lives of Rural Women* (*Nōson fujin no seikatsu*), published by the Women's and Minors' Bureau in the Ministry of Labor in 1952. This marked the first time an official government agency had published material on the heavy workload of rural women, and, moreover, in attributing the causes of that heavy workload to the privileged positions

Plate 3.1 A bountiful rice harvest in Niigata, 1954. Reproduced from 'Shashin ga kataru Shōwa nōgyōshi' kankōkai, ed., *Shashin ga kataru Shōwa nōgyōshi* (Tokyo: Fumin kyōkai, 1987), p. 75.

of the male patriarchs of farm families and their wives (the mothers-in-law of the brides of eldest sons), it clearly reflected early postwar concerns with the democratization of Japanese society.

But in reality efforts to tackle the problems facing rural women even in the postwar period ended up being confined to the improvement of daily life. On the assumption that men were responsible for the management of farming and family property, including issues of succession and inheritance, women were placed in charge of the family home (Ichida 1995). Under the strong influence of contemporary American thinking about rural policies, that meant that women were responsible for such things as the rationalization of housework, beginning with improvements to kitchens, and other efforts to make the home safer and more comfortable for family members. As already mentioned, the campaign for the improvement of daily life can be traced back to the prewar period, but it is probably correct to say that it did not get started in earnest until after the Second World War.

For rural women, who had to perform heavy labor in both farming and housework, such issues as simplifying food preparation tasks by means of kitchen reform were of pressing concern, but it also seems that many rural women aspired to the status that at least some of their urban counterparts had already achieved as 'professional housewives.' Consequently, the campaign to improve daily life in the rural areas of early postwar Japan was implemented not simply because the Ministry of Agriculture and Forestry had made it policy, but also because rural women themselves enthusiastically embraced and carried forward its objectives. During these years, the zeal for admittedly much-needed improvements to the daily life and living standards of farm families deflected attention from the other problems facing rural women.

Rural women since the 1960s

In the concluding section of what is, of necessity, a brief overview, I will begin with a summary of the discussion so far and then make some observations about rural women in Japan since the 1960s.

As has been made clear, rural women were largely ignored until after the First World War, and it was not until the launch of the rural economic revitalization campaign in the aftermath of the Showa Depression that much attention was paid to them. The emphasis then, however, was on their newly defined role as managers of the home and of improvements to daily life. So great was the gap between that externally defined role, however, and the lives that most rural women actually led, that very little was accomplished in the way of tangible improvements to daily life at the time. What was achieved, largely on account of the activities of local industrial cooperatives, youth groups and women's associations, was the placing of the issue of such improvements on the agenda of most rural communities, and that in turn helped lay the basis for renewed attempts at a similar range of improvements in the postwar era.

During the war years, women became more heavily involved than ever before in farming, as they stepped in to replace the labor of the men who had been called up for military service or recruited for essential factory work. Only the Institute for the Science of Labor took note of the overwork from which many of them suffered, however. As before, magazines such as *Nōson fujin* and *Ie no hikari* continued to stress the role of rural women as managers of the home and agents of improvement to daily life.

It finally seemed that action would be taken to improve the lot of rural women in the early postwar years, when for the first time government

Plate 3.2 Woman at work with a pitchfork, Ibaraki, 1961. Reproduced from *Shashin ga kataru Shōwa nōgyōshi*, p. 113.

officials acknowledged the heavy burden of work women shouldered and attributed that burden to the way in which farm households themselves were structured. As the report published by the Women's and Minors' Bureau made clear, only by the democratization of those households would that burden be eased. Despite some progress on that front, however, most farm families maintained the long-standing practice of succession by the first-born son, and so far as government officials were concerned, the main role played by rural women was as manager of the family home. This situation did not change in any fundamental way even after the start of the High Growth Era in the late 1950s, when male labor was siphoned away from the countryside to non-agricultural employment, leaving rural women with even more farm work to do. As was pointed out in the introduction, it was only in the 1990s that scholars and officials noticed how much farm work rural women were actually performing. Their important role in family farming as well as in farm families, although a continuing feature of their lives throughout the twentieth century, had finally become visible.

A recent international survey of the attitudes and situation of rural women in four countries including Japan highlights the problems that Japan's rural women face at present, suggesting some of the policy initiatives and the research topics that might well be pursued in future.

The survey was conducted by the Ie no Hikari Association in 1998 among rural women in the United States, France, Thailand and Japan (Ie no hikari kyōkai 1999a and 1999b). One of the most significant features of this survey is that it includes not only such fairly concrete issues as property and management rights, but also such otherwise elusive issues as the extent to which women are 'entrusted' with certain tasks, how rural women themselves assess farming, and how they think about their lives (*ikigai*). Both the nature of the questions asked and the diverging results from country to country bring the current situation of rural women in Japan into clear relief.

Figure 3.1 shows the responses by country to statements about the merit of taking part in farming. So to speak, this becomes the self-appraisal of rural women engaged in agriculture. What is clear from just one glance is that among the four countries Japanese women had the lowest percentage of respondents saying that there is merit in being engaged in farming. The questionnaire items included many different aspects, but the self-appraisal by the Japanese rural women is low in almost all items. If we look at the four countries together, respondents in Thailand had the highest level of self-appraisal and the most pride in being part of agriculture, followed by the United States, then by France, and finally by Japan.

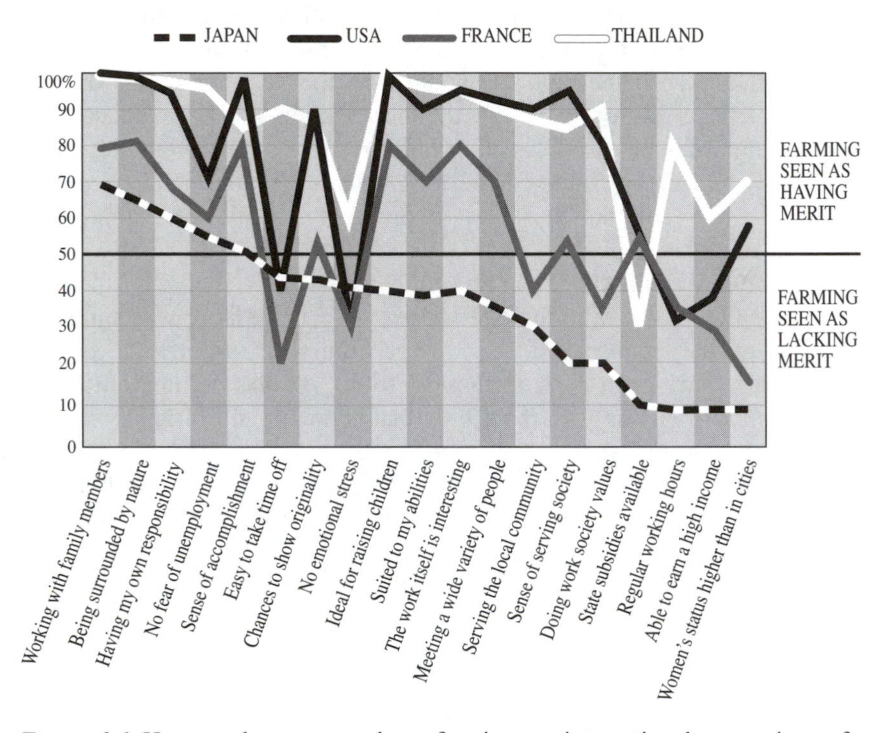

Figure 3.1 How rural women evaluate farming: an international comparison of Japan, France, the United States and Thailand.

Note

In the original survey rural women were asked to select one of the following responses to each of the 19 statements: (1) completely agree; (2) agree to an extent; (3) disagree to an extent; and (4) completely disagree. The above figure presents the percentages of those agreeing with each statement (responses 1 and 2). The statements themselves are arranged in descending order of agreement by rural women in Japan.

Source: Ie no hikari kyōkai, *Nōson josei no ishiki to jittai ni kansuru kokusai hikaku chōsa hōkokusho*, 1999.

If we look at Japan in more detail, to only five of the 19 statements in Figure 3.1 did the level of assessment of merit reach more than 50 percent, and to many statements the assessment level remained between 10 and 30 percent. Japan in particular differs from the other countries by having low assessment levels on statements related to the pride in and appeal of farming, e.g. 'work that society values,' 'suited to one's own abilities,' and 'the work itself is interesting.' In contrast, statements where there is no major difference between Japan and the other countries included 'no fear about unemployment' and 'no emotional stress.' With the progressive aging of Japan's agricultural labor force, some commentators and policymakers have suggested that even more rural women might now be expected to take up farming. However, the fairly positive image of rural women in agriculture on which this suggestion is based and the image of rural women that emerges from this questionnaire survey are rather different. From the survey we learn that many rural women do not have much interest in farming itself or take much pride in the farm work they do.

And why do Japanese rural women not feel positively attracted to farming? Figure 3.2 shows the responses related to the ownership of different kinds of assets, and reveals that a fairly high percentage of rural women in other countries have gained title to the family home and land, which is in contrast to Japan, where only a low percentage of respondents hold title

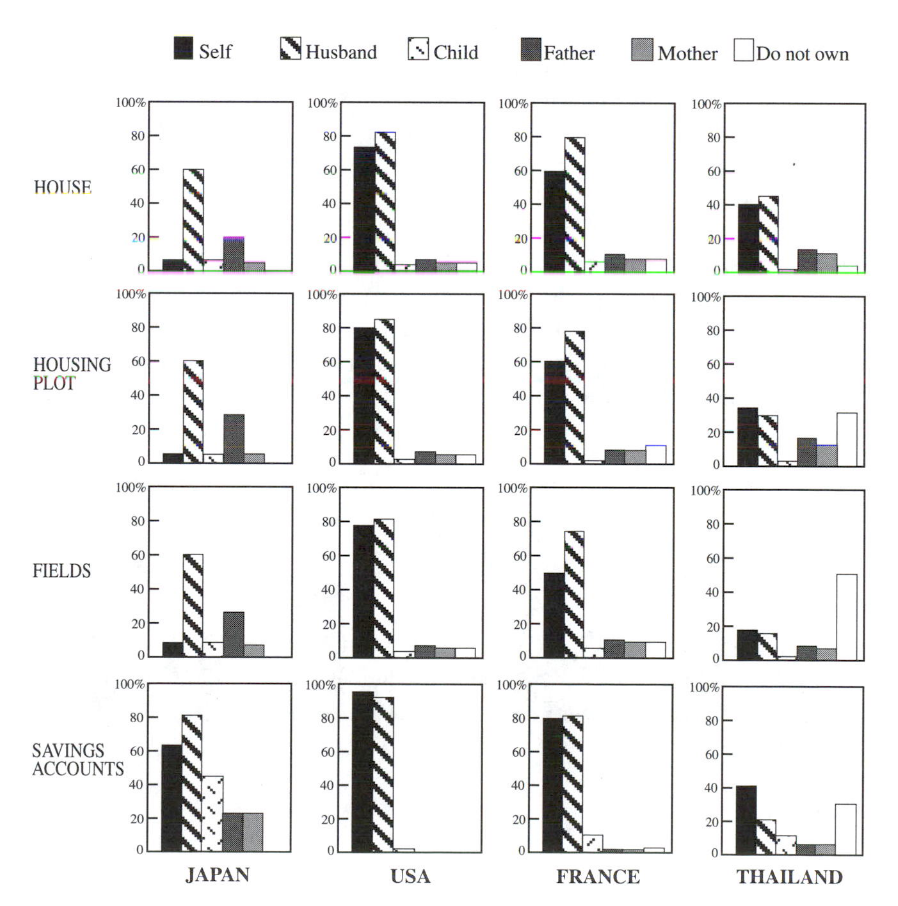

Figure 3.2 Ownership of assets within the family.

Source: as in Figure 3.1.

to such property. In the case of Japanese farm families, not only is it often the husband who owns the farmhouse and land, but cases where title to both remains in the name of the father even after a successor son's marriage are also still numerous. The only property that is in the name of Japan's rural women is savings accounts. It is perhaps only natural that rural women are not attracted to or have no pride in agriculture, when they are excluded from the ownership of farmhouses and land.

In addition, another interesting finding of the survey concerns the degree to which rural women are entrusted with tasks relating to farming and the daily life of the household (Figure 3.3). With regard to farming management and agricultural techniques men play the leading role not only in Japan but also in the United States and France, and rural women feel that they are only entrusted with a low degree of responsibility. But Japan differs considerably from the other countries on the issues of domestic life and the upbringing of children. In contrast to the high proportion of rural women in the United States, France and Thailand who feel that they are 'entrusted with responsibility' for the domestic household and upbringing of the children, only a low percentage of Japanese women report this feeling. In short, many rural women in Japan feel that they are neither entrusted with responsibility for farm work nor entrusted with responsibility in the home.

The latter finding is particularly interesting, given the emphasis since the 1920s on rural women in Japan as managers of the home. They may have done most of the housework, but further research will be needed to uncover precisely how the work has been delegated, and by whom, within

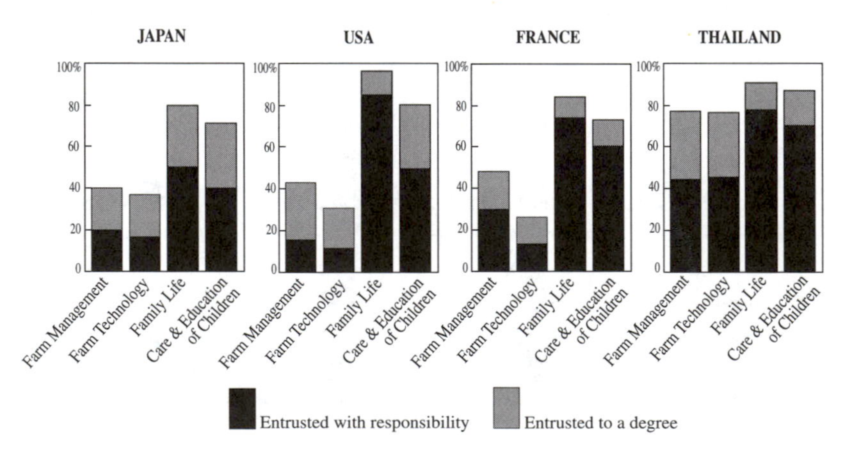

Figure 3.3 Degree of responsibility in farming and home for rural women.
Source: as in Figure 3.1.

farm households. Moreover, the exclusion of rural women from the ownership of family assets – that is, from inheritance of the family's land – will have to be addressed if in future women are to play a greater role in Japanese agriculture.

References

Ichida Tomoko. 1995. 'Seikatsu kaizen fukyū jigyō no rinen to tenkai.' *Nōgyō sōgō kenkyū* 49(2).

Ie no hikari kyōkai. 1999a. *Nōson josei no ishiki to jittai ni kansuru kokusai hikaku chōsa hōkokusho*. Tokyo: Ie no hikari kyōkai.

—— 1999b. *Nōson josei ni miru okunigara no chigai.*

Imamura Naraomi. 1995. 'Nōgyō no shinjin kakumei jidai.' *Nōgyō to keizai*, January.

Itagaki Kuniko. 1992. *Shōwa senzen, senchūki no nōson seikatsu*. Tokyo: Sanrei shobō.

Itaya Eisei. 1942. *Tōhoku nōson ki*. Tokyo: Tōkyō daidō shokan.

Kobayashi Hatsue. 1974. *Onna sandai*. Tokyo: Asahi shinbunsha.

Kumagai Sonoko. 1995. 'Kazoku nōgyō keiei ni okeru jōsei rōdō no yakuwari hyōka to sono igi.' In *Kazoku nōgyō keiei ni okeru josei no jiritsu*, ed. Nihon sonraku kenkyū gakkai. Tokyo: Nōsangyoson bunka kyōkai.

Maruoka Hideko. 1937; reprinted 1980. *Nihon nōson fujin mondai*. Tokyo: Kōyō shoin; Domesu shuppan.

Niigata ken nōkai. 1942. *Joshi nōsakugyō kenkyūkai yōkō.*

Nishida Yoshiaki. 1997. *Kindai Nihon nōmin undōshi kenkyū*. Tokyo: Tōkyō daigaku shuppankai.

Ōhara shakai mondai kenkyūjo. 1964. *Taiheiyō sensōka no rōdōsha jōtai*. Tokyo: Tōyō keizai shinpōsha.

Ōkado Masakatsu. 1994. *Kindai Nihon to nōson shakai*. Tokyo: Nihon keizai hyōronsha.

—— 1995. 'Nōmin no seikatsu no henka.' In *Kōza sekaishi*, 4. Tokyo: Tōkyō daigaku shuppankai.

—— and Yanagizawa Asobu. 1996. 'Senji rōdōryoku no kyūgen to dōin: nōmin kazoku to toshi shōkōgyōsha o taishō ni.' *Tochi seido shigaku*, 151.

Rōdō kagaku kenkyūjo. 1933–42. *Nōgyō rōdō chōsasho hōkoku*, 1–59.

Saitō Osamu. 1991. 'Nōgyō hatten to josei rōdō.' *Hitotsubashi dakigaku keizai kenkyūjo keizai kenkyū*, 42(1).

—— 1998. *Chingin to rōdō to seikatsu suijun*. Tokyo: Iwanami shoten.

Tanimoto Masayuki. 1998. *Nihon ni okeru zairaiteki keizai hatten to orimonogyō*. Nagoya: Nagoya daigaku shuppankai.

Yamagata ken rengō jokyōin kyōgikai. 1935. *Joshi kyōin no shakaiteki katsudō.*

Yamazaki Hiroaki. 1993. 'Nihon no sensō keizai.' In *Rekishi to Identity*, ed. Yamaguchi Yasushi and Ronald Ruprecht. Tokyo: Shibunkaku.

4 The impact of the local improvement movement on farmers and rural communities

Tsutsui Masao

Introduction

Victorious in the Russo-Japanese War of 1904–5, Japan expanded its colonial empire and reveled in its newly achieved status as one of the five great powers of the world. The industrial revolution that had begun in the early Meiji era appeared to be nearing success. But the Japanese people remained burdened with the increased taxes that had been levied during the war so that the foreign loans made to help finance the conflict could be repaid and the expenditure on industrial, transport and social infrastructure that had been suspended during the conflict could be resumed. Meeting that tax burden caused hardship in the Japanese countryside and led to financial and administrative paralysis in many rural communities, as well as to greater tensions between landlords and tenant farmers. It was at this time that the Japanese government announced the local improvement movement (*chihō kairyō undō*) to effect widespread change in provincial (especially rural) Japan and create a local population willing and able to support the needs of the emerging Japanese Empire.

The movement was launched during the second Katsura government (July 14, 1908–August 30, 1911) and directed by the Home Ministry, with support from both the Ministry of Agriculture and Commerce and the Ministry of Education. Its main areas of concern were: (1) strengthening the financial and administrative base of towns and villages by such measures as the transfer of hamlet property to the larger administrative villages of which they were a part, establishing local councils (*jichikai*) to assist in administration and, with the 1911 local government reform, the granting of greater powers to town and village mayors; (2) expanding the economic base of villages by means of greater reliance on agricultural associations and industrial cooperatives; (3) promoting the values of diligence, frugality and united action among people of all social classes as set forth in the Boshin Rescript of 1908 and further promoting unity under the emperor by merging local shrines into a nationwide hierarchy of State Shinto shrines; (4) encouraging patriotism and loyalty to the emperor in the classrooms of elementary schools and in the activities of youth groups and military reservists' associations; and (5) by such means as the selection of 'model villages' and training courses, creating enthusiasm for local improvement and nurturing local leaders in towns and villages who would carry the movement forward. It was thus a multi-faceted undertaking, involving local government, the economy, society, education and ideology.

Not a little scholarly controversy surrounds the interpretation of the local improvement movement. To Ishida Takeshi (1956), Ōshima Mitsuko (1970) and others of the school of political history inspired by Maruyama Masao, for example, the movement was an attempt to shore up the underpinnings of an imperial state unsettled by the Russo-Japanese War by revamping and revivifying the traditional – and inherently anti-modern – hamlet solidarities of rural Japan. In contrast, Miyaji Masato (1973) has argued that those traditional hamlets were to be subordinated to the larger administrative units of which they nominally were part, and the latter would be strengthened as the 'financial and manpower base' of imperial Japan. Given the political focus of these scholars, very little attention is paid in their work to the bearing of the local improvement movement on rural society itself, or its effects on the commercialization of agriculture and landlord–tenant relations. Nor do they pay much attention even to local politics and the on-going activities of political parties to gain support in the regions and rural areas of Japan (Ariizumi 1976: 247–55). On the contrary, the political literature tends to revolve around a rather simplistic either/or proposition – either the hamlet solidarity was strengthened or the administrative village was strengthened – and to be concerned primarily with the character of the imperial Japanese state.

There has been similar controversy among economic historians over whether the agricultural economy was in crisis after the Russo-Japanese War (Takahashi 1926) or whether the commercialization of agriculture was proceeding apace, albeit it not entirely without problems (Kurihara 1949) and, in the decades after the Second World War, on the relevance of economic developments in the agricultural sector after the Russo-Japanese War on class relations in the countryside – especially landlord–tenant relations – and tenancy disputes in the 1920s (Teruoka 1970: chapter 3). With the benefit of hindsight, the latter certainly was an important issue, but at the time – that is, in the early 1900s – the central problems facing Japanese villages were those very much on the agenda of the local improvement movement: elementary education, hamlet common lands, the burden of taxation and other public charges, and discontent with local financial administration (Aoki 1967: 159; Senoue 1985). Tenancy disputes were still very rare. Moreover, the very commercialization of agriculture that has attracted so much attention was not unaffected by the high taxation that constituted rural residents' main complaint about local financial policy. Thus it can be said that economic historians, too, have tended to ignore some of the key features of the local improvement movement.

In this chapter I will attempt to present a suitably comprehensive account of the local improvement movement in all of its aspects in one rural district of Japan. Moreover, I will also discuss the hitherto rather neglected topics of the penetration of emperor-centered nationalism into the Japanese countryside and the realization of a substantially new local power structure in the Japanese countryside.

The district on which I will focus is the northern portion of Sunto county (*gun*) in Shizuoka Prefecture, usually abbreviated as Hokusun and now part of the city of Gotenba and the nearby town of Oyama. Hamlets in the district each owned tracts of forested land, either at the foot of Mt Fuji or in the vicinity of Mt Hakone. There were a few large landlords with holdings of about 30 hectares each and numerous cultivating landlords and substantial owner-cultivators with holdings of five to ten hectares each. A stretch of the Tokaido Railway Line (now the Gotenba Line) had opened to traffic in the district in 1889, the Fuji Spinning Company had opened a large, modern cotton mill in Oyama in the mid-1890s, and local farming had become steadily more commercialized thereafter. All in all, the district is well suited as a case study of the nature and impact of the local improvement movement.

The reform of elementary education

In the aftermath of the Russo-Japanese War the Japanese government took steps to expand the elementary education system that had been initiated in the 1870s and to insure that appropriate values were taught to all children. Tuition fees at the elementary level had been abolished (in principle, at least) in 1900, and in 1907 the number of years of schooling required was increased from four years to five and then six. During the local improvement movement, all towns and villages were encouraged to reach the six-year target and to take steps to insure enrollment and regular attendance by all local children, including girls. As a result, the overall enrollment and attendance rates reached 95 percent or more in the 1910s.

The issuance of the Boshin Rescript in 1908 gave impetus to the incorporation of imperial ideology into the elementary school curriculum, as well as into local society itself. For example, in Shizuoka Prefecture the Imperial Rescript on Education of 1890 was thereafter taught to pupils in years 1 to 4, and the Boshin Rescript was taught to those in added years 5 and 6. Moreover, it became compulsory to give both rescripts a respectful formal reading at the local elementary school on such public occasions as Army Day, Navy Day, the anniversaries of Japan's victories in the Sino-Japanese and Russo-Japanese Wars, the anniversary of Emperor Jimmu's accession and the annual celebration of entrance to elementary school itself. Readings were also encouraged at major ceremonies at local Shinto shrines and during the late summer Buddhist *bon* festival for the dead.

However useful to the state in inculcating such virtues as frugality, diligence and social harmony in young minds, or indeed in promoting basic literacy and numeracy among the young, the expansion of elementary education posed great problems for the towns and villages of Japan. In the first place, it was municipalities such as these (as well as cities) that were expected to pay for the additional classrooms, teachers and playgrounds needed to achieve first five-, then six-year elementary education provision. That constituted a considerable financial burden and necessitated increases in local household tax levies. Faced with that additional expenditure, the landlord who headed Harazato village raised the household tax levy paid by those with the lowest incomes in the village, on the one hand, and joined with other local landlords in raising the rents they charged their tenants, on the other, thereby shifting the increased burden away from themselves (Tsutsui 1984: 20–2).

Second, the need to provide additional classroom space led to proposals in many villages to consolidate the smaller schools that had been built earlier in various hamlets into one, centrally located school as a means of saving money in the longer term, and those proposals immediately led to controversy about precisely where in the village the new school should be located and intense rivalry among the constituent hamlets of the villages concerned that would continue for years (Tsutsui 1999a: 236–43). A contributing factor in that inter-hamlet rivalry was the effect of railway and industrial development in the district since the late 1890s, which had already benefited some hamlets more than others.

Hamlet common lands

The transfer of hamlet-owned forests and fields to administrative villages was also one of the policies vigorously pursued during the local improvement movement, partly as a means of bolstering village finances (and weakening hamlet autonomy), but primarily in order to protect the timber and other natural resources on such common lands from over-exploitation.

During the earlier Tokugawa period, the common lands which played such a vital role in subsistence agriculture had been infused with religious significance by local farmers, and hamlet rules had governed both access to and use of the precious resources they contained. Other substantial tracts of forested land were managed by the Tokugawa shogunate and domain rulers (the daimyo), and access even more severely restricted. This changed with the Meiji Restoration of 1868, however, as Japan's incipient industrial revolution generated greatly increased demand for railway sleepers, timber for the construction of factories and other new buildings, wood and charcoal for fuel and scrap wood for matches. Moreover, the land tax reform implemented during the 1870s, which made newly recognized land owners responsible for paying taxes in cash not kind, spurred the commercialization of agriculture and the development of by-employments to earn cash incomes throughout rural Japan. As a result, farmers began cutting ever more grasses for green manure for their fields and taking ever more twigs and other raw materials needed for handicraft production from local common lands. Hamlet regulations about the use of those common lands were increasingly relaxed or simply ignored as farmers competed for the resources they provided (Tsutsui 1984: 23–4, 1993: 243, 1999b: 341–5). Traditional nature worship ceased to structure the daily lives of farmers to the same degree as in the past, and gradually a new deity – the emperor – began to figure more prominently in their thoughts (Miyamoto 1960: 3). Nowhere was this more apparent than in the leading by-employment among farmers in the Meiji era, the rearing of silkworms. As they were told by the speakers who toured the countryside promoting sericulture, the silk thread produced from the cocoons farmers supplied earned the foreign exchange Japan needed to pay for imports of weapons of war and industrial technology, and therefore all those who reared silkworms were performing service to the emperor and the empire (Tsutsui 1984: 27).

Shortly after the Russo-Japanese War, officials in Tokyo were warning of the impending deforestation of much of Japan. Severe flooding had been reported throughout the country since the late 1880s, as denuded mountains and hillsides could no longer absorb spill-off from heavy rains, and local residents were becoming increasingly alarmed about the threat of water-borne diseases (Tsutsui 1993: 243, 1998: 99–107).

Because official efforts since the late 1880s to regulate the exploitation of forests and promote conservation had failed to produce notable results, the government opted for the transfer of hamlet forests to administrative villages as part of the local improvement movement. Precisely because those villages were, unlike hamlets, part of the legally established local government system and hence subject to supervision by prefectural officials and the Home Ministry in Tokyo, it was anticipated that better management of forests could finally be achieved.

In Hokusun, as elsewhere, the transfers did not go as smoothly as the government had hoped, and in many cases were not effected until the 1920s (Tsutsui 1999c: 450–8). Strong opposition from hamlets was the key factor in delay, because hamlet residents still needed the firewood and thatch that the common lands provided and, despite the increased use of commercial fertilizer, most farmers still needed grass cuttings as green manure. Negotiations between village officials and representatives of hamlets often ended in deadlock as a result and had to be suspended. Only when the government took note of this opposition and amended the transfer policy in 1919 to allow hamlets to lease parcels of common land were agreements on transfers finally reached at the local level. A contributing factor at this time was the further commercialization of agriculture during and after the First World War, and the greater use of commercial fertilizer, which made farmers less dependent on common lands than had been the case in the years immediately following the Russo-Japanese War.

And so ownership of common lands was finally transferred from hamlets to administrative villages. Income from access fees, etc. never amounted to much, however. Far more revenue was earned for the village coffers from timber operations or the occasional sale of a parcel of land as an industrial site, and it was now possible for the village office to reach decisions about such revenue-generating measures without undue concern about hamlet opinion and interests (Tsutsui 1999c: 456–8).

Shrine mergers

An attempt was also made during the local improvement movement to replace the separate shrines that existed in hamlets, each one dedicated to the community's own guardian deity and closely associated with traditional folk beliefs, with a single village shrine that would be part of a State Shinto hierarchy of shrines. The emperor would be the living god at the apex of the system, the guardian deity of the Japanese nation as a whole.

The first steps in the creation of State Shinto had been taken immediately after the Meiji Restoration, and in Hokusun as elsewhere some Shinto rites and festivals reflecting State Shinto teachings had taken place in the early Meiji era. But until the Sino-Japanese War most rural residents still associated local shrines with their own communities and with traditional natural spirits and deities. In one Hokusun village, Kitagō, for example, a later village history observed:

> Back in those days [the early Meiji era], when there was no sanitation and no one knew how to prevent disease, many families fixed Shinto or Buddhist charms to the doors of their houses to ward off sickness, or they hung up a *hiru* root to keep evil spirits from entering. . . . Priests went [into the houses of the sick] and said prayers to drive the sickness-producing god away.
>
> (*Kitagō sonshi* n.d.: 136–9)

Nor were local shrines resorted to only to ward off disease in the days before modern hygiene and medicine reached the countryside. They were also used to resist state efforts to conscript young men into military service in the early Meiji era. As the same village history noted:

> Although the village chief read the imperial instructions to consider military service an important duty in a formal assembly and lectures were held in every hamlet to persuade residents of this great obligation, there were those who sought to evade the rigors of that service. When they were summoned for the physical examination, they and their relatives visited all the shrines and temples in the area, praying that they would fail, and the neighbors would gather to carry out a ritual purification of the young men and pray to the local guardian deity to secure exemptions for them.
>
> (*Kitagō sonshi* n.d.: 144)

The situation changed radically after the Sino-Japanese and Russo-Japanese Wars, however. According to the village history:

> The youth of the village were awestruck when they saw soldiers who had returned home after the 1894/5 war striding about, their tunics sporting brilliant medals. Some decided they must enlist, and some even applied, although in most cases their fathers and elder brothers withheld consent, not only because they feared putting a younger son's life at risk, but also because his absence for three years in uniform would disrupt the household's work. After the 1904/5 war, enthusiasm for everything military grew even stronger, and now young men prayed at shrines and temples not to fail the physical examination, but to have the strong, healthy bodies needed to pass, so they could accomplish brave deeds. Some night school classes were organized so they could improve their skills before heading off

> to the barracks. Now those young men who fail the physical examination feel ashamed, and those who pass but are not actually called up resent their exclusion from the great work of the nation.
>
> (*Kitagō sonshi* n.d.: 144–5)

And so, Japan's victories in these two wars can be seen to have raised popular awareness of the Empire of Japan to an ever greater extent and, in the process, to have transformed local shrines from places with the power to protect young men from conscription to places that would enable them to 'accomplish brave deeds.' Shrines were in the process of changing from sites of resistance to the modernizing policies of the state to sites mobilizing a spirit of service to that state.

The state also pursued specific shrine policies to encourage further change. In 1900, a Home Ministry communiqué was transmitted to villages, stating that they should consider merging all shrines that were not fully self-supporting financially. In 1906 an imperial edict announced that towns and villages should provide funding for religious observances at shrines of exceptional significance – that is, those with connections to the imperial house or nation, those venerating members of the warrior class or daimyo, and those whose enshrined deity had performed meritorious deeds in the area. Those purely local shrines dedicated to the worship of nature were excluded. In response, the head of Sunto county announced in 1909 that all small shrines lacking any particular historical significance should now be merged, that is, enshrined together in one location.

How did this work out in practice? The government had envisioned shrine mergers to create just one shrine in each administrative village, but this proved unfeasible, especially in villages with many local shrines, and in the end efforts were concentrated on producing just one shrine in each hamlet or section of administrative villages. According to my survey in what is now the town of Oyama, but where six administrative villages existed in the early 1900s, between 1903 and 1918 some 34 shrines were merged into just 17. Roughly two-thirds of these mergers took place between 1907 and 1910.

It was mostly small shrines dedicated to such natural deities as mountains, forests and trees, to the harvest god Inari or to the ancestors of residents that were selected for merger, and most of the merged shrines were either local branches of shrines found throughout Japan – for example, Hachiman shrines or Sengen shrines – or they bore the name of the administrative village or village ward in which they were located.

Shrine mergers did not proceed at all as quickly as government officials seem to have expected, and even today there are shrines in provincial

Japan, including in the Oyama area, that exist in their original form and location. That said, however, many mergers did occur eventually, and the demise of the local shrines that sustained the nature worship of local residents contributed to the waning of nature worship itself, no doubt facilitating the indiscriminate taking of natural resources from nearby mountains and meadows by local residents at just about this time.

Moreover, merged shrines receiving financial support from administrative villages increasingly became sites for ceremonies relating to the emperor and the state. One of the first such occasions in Hokusun was in July 1912, when news of the Meiji emperor's grave illness reached the district. In Kitagō, all village officials, elementary schoolteachers and schoolchildren gathered at the main shrine in the community to pray for the emperor's recovery, and village residents, too, 'paid visits to the shrine in great numbers to watch as priests performed rites on behalf of the stricken emperor. Popular sentiment focused on the shrine during His Majesty's illness' (quoted in Tsutsui 1999a: 253). The enhanced role played by village shrines such as this one no doubt facilitated further shrine mergers later on.

The promotion of agricultural improvements

Here, it will be useful to review changes in Japanese agriculture during the earlier decades of the Meiji era before examining efforts to improve agriculture during the local improvement movement.

By about 1900 such commercial crops as cotton, rape and indigo that had flourished during the Tokugawa period had been displaced by cheaper imported cotton, kerosene and chemical dyes, and the planting of such subsistence crops as millet and buckwheat had also decreased. In addition, farm households throughout the country were increasingly buying the cotton cloth, bean paste (*miso*) and rice wine (*sake*) they had once produced themselves.

What farmers were raising instead were cocoons for the rapidly expanding raw silk industry, mulberry trees for the leaves to feed those cocoons and rice, maize and vegetables to feed the expanding urban population. During the winter slack season, they made charcoal, straw sandals and other craft items of straw or bamboo. Both in their farming and in their by-employments, they were seeking cash income with which to pay taxes and to purchase chemical fertilizers as well as clothing and other items they had once produced at home (Wagatsuma 1937: 491–9).

If farmers were going to be able to pay the heavy taxes that remained in effect after the Russo-Japanese War, it was imperative that they commercialize their operations even further. Village leaders who were responsible for collecting the greatly increased household tax and other village imposts were keenly aware of this need. For example, as the mayor of Harazato (now in Gotenba City) announced at the inaugural meeting of the village council set up during the local improvement movement:

> The main purpose of creating this council in our village is to insure that our tax obligations are fully met. It is obvious that the ability to pay taxes stems from economic enterprise. Therefore, to improve agriculture we will establish plots for testing alternative strains of rice and encourage seed selection by the salt water method. To promote by-employment, we will have training courses on how to improve mulberry yields. I urge you to support progress by this means.
> (quoted in Tsutsui 1984: 30–1)

The mayor in this case was the landlord owning ten hectares mentioned earlier. His family's tax burden had more than trebled between 1895 and 1911, and especially because of increases in the household tax he was now actually paying more in village taxes than in national taxes. That is the main reason why he saw to it that the household tax levied on the poorest group in the village was increased and secured roughly a 10 percent increase in the rents his tenants paid. Other landlords in the Hokusun district also sought to increase their incomes by raising rents or, in some cases, by changing the form in which rents were paid. On upland (dry) fields, for example, rents had traditionally been payable in soy beans, leaving tenants to profit from the sales of the vegetables and other commercial crops they had begun to grow. Now landlords demanded rents in cash on those fields, the amount based on average prices for those commercial crops. Faced with increased taxes and rents, not to mention expenditure on fertilizer and other necessities, ordinary and poor farmers had no choice but to assent to the agricultural improvement projects advocated by the state and by landlords. Only by means of the further development of commercial agriculture could they increase their cash incomes (Tsutsui 1987: 164, 1999b: 329).

There had, of course, been earlier attempts at promoting agricultural improvement in Japan. In the Hokusun district, for example, from the 1880s a group of cultivating landlords and substantial owner-cultivators known as 'industrious farmers' (*seinō*) had worked enthusiastically to promote scientific farming of the sort then advocated by the state. An agricultural school had been established in Gotenba in the late 1890s, and its graduates, mostly the sons of local farm households of fairly modest means, had become instructors and officials of village agricultural associations, working to promote proper seed selection, the use of horses in plowing and the planting of superior strains of rice. But such efforts had had limited effects in the area by the turn of the century, in part because they had concentrated almost exclusively on the cultivation of rice and wheat. It was not until after the Russo-Japanese War that more effective measures to promote agricultural productivity were implemented. These were of three main sorts.

The first was the encouragement of improvements tailored to the particular farming conditions in the various villages of the district, less by the imposition of changes from above than by motivating local farmers to increase output. In low-lying villages well suited to paddy rice cultivation, experimental plots were established to try out new rice strains, and the farmers who produced the best rice, winter wheat or compost were rewarded with prizes at local agricultural fairs. In upland districts, on the other hand, experimental plots of mulberry trees were established, and prizes given for the best mulberry or maize produced. Moreover, village agricultural associations allocated some funding to their constituent hamlets to encourage improvements at an even more local level (Tsutsui 1984).

Second, some town and village agricultural associations launched into the cooperative purchase of such fertilizers as ammonia, superphosphate lime and soybean cakes on behalf of local farmers, and some industrial cooperatives functioning primarily as credit associations were established. The latter replaced or supplemented the hamlet-based *kō* and *mujin* mutual savings and credit associations on which farmers had long depended, many of which were in serious trouble in the years following the Russo-Japanese War (Tsutsui 1986: 84–6, 142–3). Although it would not be until the 1920s and beyond that these new activities by village agricultural associations and industrial cooperatives developed in earnest, they began to appear at this time as a means of shoring up the economic status of small farmers and stabilizing landlord – tenant relations.

Third, full-time agricultural instructors, all of them graduates of agricultural schools, were attached to town and village agricultural associations. Most such inspectors now were the sons of local cultivating landlords and substantial owner-cultivators, and they made regular visits throughout the year to all the hamlets in the village, providing detailed guidance to farmers, not only on the planting, cultivation and harvesting of rice, wheat and vegetables, but also on sericulture and the proper management of mulberry fields. Their very 'hands-on' approach and their field trials aimed at finding the varieties and cultivating techniques best suited to the area helped to implant the ideas of scientific farming that had begun to spread in the Meiji era and the new imperative of greater commercialization among local farmers.

As a result, there was a considerable increase in the production of such commercial crops as rice, vegetables and silkworm cocoons in the Hokusun district following the Russo-Japanese War. Not only did this bring greater economic security to small farmers in the area, it also boosted the local average of actual tenant rents paid to landlords from a postwar low of 70 percent of the stipulated amount due to over 90 percent in the early Taisho era (1912–26).

It is also noteworthy that agricultural inspectors played an active role in directing repairs of local roads and bridges, giving talks in elementary schools, leading youth groups and encouraging attendance at village council meetings and the payment of taxes. Rather than being a completely separate undertaking, agricultural improvement developed as an integral part of the multifaceted efforts to achieve 'local improvement' in the years following the Russo-Japanese War.

A final feature of the agricultural improvements carried out at this time was their role in spreading the ideology of the imperial Japanese state among farmers. The Boshin Rescript was solemnly read at the start of agricultural training sessions, and the importance of sericulture as an industry producing the foreign exchange that sustained the empire was constantly reiterated. In Harazato a particularly ingenious effort to link agricultural improvement with both the village shrine and respect for imperial ideology took place in 1914 under the auspices of a newly organized First Fruits Association. At the agricultural fair held on the day of the Harvest Festival (*Niinamesai*), the winning exhibits were offered to the shrine as 'first fruits,' the names of the winning farmers were displayed in the shrine compound, and a donation to shrine expenses in the amount of the market value of the winning exhibits was made by the association. According to its founding charter: 'By impressing children with divine virtues, making offerings to the Emperor and uniting our hearts in worship, [we seek] to foster the improvement of agriculture, public morals and devotion to the public good' (Tsutsui 1984: 26–9).

The organization of youth

Revamping the traditional young men's groups (*wakamono-gumi*, *wakashū-yado*) that had existed in virtually all rural hamlets since the Tokugawa period into a new federation of young men's associations was another measure implemented during the local improvement movement.

Those traditional youth groups had functioned as highly autonomous clubs, which undertook preparations for local festivals, cleaned shrines and paths and carried out night patrols in their communities, as well as holding regular meetings. In the early Meiji era, their penchant for drunken carousing at festivals was viewed with disdain by the authorities in Tokyo as one of the 'base customs of the past' that impeded Japan's progress toward proper civilization and enlightenment, and local officials were urged to reform their 'barbarism.' Meanwhile, in the countryside itself, many young men had been inspired by the on-going freedom and people's rights movement (*jiyū minken undō*) and had created associations to study and debate the political issues of the day. In Hokusun, too, a variety of such associations were created by the sons of leading local families who belonged either to the Gakunan Liberal Party or to the Shizuoka Progressive Party. In addition to speech meetings and political campaigning on behalf of people's rights, these associations also organized night school classes for their members (Matsumoto 1999: 100–3; Nagahara 1999: 128–31, 146–8).

By the 1890s, however, a nationwide system of compulsory elementary education and optional middle-school and higher education had been established, a constitution had been promulgated, and from the National Diet in Tokyo to the towns and villages of Japan a governmental system had been established, with various political parties having branches in local districts. In these circumstances, the activities carried out by the educational and political associations that young men had organized during the heyday of the quest for 'civilization and enlightenment' were subsumed into the state educational system, on the one hand, and political party organizations, on the other. At about the same time, in response to Japan's on-going industrial revolution and its recent victory in the Sino-Japanese War, the long-existing young men's groups in Japan's rural communities began to look for new activities that seemed suited to the new circumstances in which they found themselves and their country to add to the activities in which they had always engaged.

In Rokugō village in Hokusun in the mid-1890s both a Progress Society (*Shinpōkai*) and a night school were organized in order to 'provide the technical education needed to plan the reform and progress of the nation,' to promote 'enlightenment and the advance of wealth and power,' and 'to curb loose habits among youth . . . promote education . . . and foster morality' (quoted in *Oyama chō shi* 1992: 779). During the Sino-Japanese War the youth in the village presented 1,213 pairs of straw sandals to the army's soldiers' relief department, collected donations to make a commemorative object in the shape of a phoenix and prayed that the army and navy would secure a great victory (Tsutsui 1999a: 200). The critical stance toward the state that had characterized some youth activities in Hokusun during the freedom and people's rights era was gone, and local youth groups now were seeking of their own volition to acquire the practical skills and proper morality for the role their members would perform in an increasingly industrialized and powerful Japan.

Steps were taken in the aftermath of the Russo-Japanese war to capitalize on these changes among local youth and on the even greater patriotic sentiment which that war had engendered. The existing hamlet-based youth groups were reorganized into branches of a young men's association in the villages of which they were part, and activities such as late-night carousing were prohibited as totally inappropriate in a civilized nation.

We can gain insight into the activities of these newly reorganized youth groups from the diary kept by the 15-year-old Serizawa Kunio, member of the Harazato Young Men's Association, between 1913 and 1915 (Tsutsui 1984: 28–9). While such traditional activities as preparations for festivals, cleaning of shrines and fire patrols at night continued, a range of new activities was added. As young Kunio's entries reveal, the first of these related to farming and to the training of young men as new agents of agricultural improvement:

> Attended the prize show for rice and wheat of the Kawashimata branch of the agricultural association, as well as the branch meeting of the youth association (January 14, 1913).
>
> Attended a training course on sericulture at the elementary school (March 1, 1913).
>
> Did work at the youth group's trial plot on . . . fertilizer application and cultivating techniques (March 8, 1913).
>
> Attended a branch meeting of the agricultural association at the agricultural instructor's house, combined with a meeting of the youth association branch (January 20, 1915).
>
> Must really learn all I can next year about rice seedlings and try out my own ideas, too, so that I can produce seedlings that no one will find fault with (October 30, 1915).

Second, greater contact with village officials and the local military reservists' association was encouraged as a means of promoting patriotic sentiment among rural youth. As Kunio noted in his diary, at the night school classes on farming that he and other young men attended, they were 'prompted to hold a ceremony [at which the Imperial Rescript on Education and Boshin Rescript would feature] to honor the work of the village mayor and the enterprise of Mr Katsumata' (October 27, 1913). He also recorded on the same day: 'had a welcome home party for the returning soldiers' and 'held foot races and lantern races with the reservists.' On November 10, 1915, the anniversary of the Taisho emperor's enthronement, Kunio made it clear that he saw himself as a subject of the emperor:

> If on this day . . . we truly give thanks for the blessings bestowed by the Emperors who have reigned in our country since the beginning of time and pledge to maintain the same spirit of veneration the Japanese people have demonstrated in the past, then people in other countries, too, even though not part of the Great Empire of Japan, will come to celebrate this day with us.

Third, young men's associations set up small lending libraries and published newsletters, as well as once again launching the debating and speech societies that had flourished during the freedom and people's rights era (Ōkado 1993: 257–66). Naturally, state and village officials sought to use activities in this sphere to promote their own vision of Japanese youth, but it is important to note that these same activities also made the young men who took part in them steadily more conscious of their own autonomy and distinctiveness. They gained new knowledge of the outside world from the books they read, published their own assessments of village life and other subjects in their newsletters, and regularly exchanged views among themselves. During the 1910s most of the opinions they expressed in speeches or in newsletters were broadly in accord with official policy, but the potential for a more critical stance toward the government of the day and toward village politics was being created and, with it, one of the bases for the up-welling of 'rice roots' democracy in rural Japan in the 1920s.

The strengthening of village finances and the restructuring of local politics

As previously noted, the special emergency taxes levied during the Russo-Japanese War remained in place thereafter, and the household taxes on which towns and villages depended for most of their revenue more than doubled between 1904 and 1909 as those municipalities were called upon to expand local elementary school provision and to embark on diverse public works projects that had been neglected during wartime. Non-payment of village taxes became common, jeopardizing the ability of villages to carry out their appointed tasks.

Moreover, the very projects of expanded schooling, shrine mergers and assertion of control over hamlet common lands that villages were urged to carry out during the local improvement movement created tensions between villages and their constituent hamlets, as well as creating tensions among hamlets in the same village. Those tensions, in turn, led to a loss of confidence in village officials among local residents and even greater resistance to paying taxes. Not a few villages found themselves on the verge of financial collapse, and the government also was alarmed, especially when the non-payment of village taxes spread to prefectural and national taxes. As a result, both the state and village officials perceived the urgent necessity of measures to shore up village finances, on the one hand, and to restore peace and harmony within the community, on the other. The measures implemented to achieve these twin goals can be divided into four categories.

The first was the strengthening of financial mechanisms and procedures within administrative villages. County (*gun*) officials, who bore responsibility for supervising the towns and villages in their jurisdictions, began making regular tours to inspect local financial operations and to recommend such changes as they deemed warranted. They also attempted to mediate any disputes they encountered. Then in 1911, the local government system itself was reformed, not only to give village mayors greater powers, but also to provide salaries to their deputies, previously honorary posts in most cases, as a means of insuring the professional expertise in accounting and other financial matters that villages seemed to need.

Second, various steps were taken to promote enthusiasm for the goals of the local improvement movement among town and village employees and to get the residents of those municipalities to unite in seeking their realization. The Home Ministry organized lectures on the local improvement movement in every part of the country and publicized the achievements of so-called 'model villages' as a means of spreading the local improvement ethos. A variety of town- and village-wide organizations were established to combat hamlet parochialism and inter-hamlet rivalry and to unite all residents in commitment to promoting school attendance, diligence and frugality and the prompt payment of taxes. Those who contributed to effective village administration received public commendation (Tsutsui 1984: 29–30, 1999a: 250–2). Moreover, branches of the village-wide assembly, agricultural association, youth associations, etc. were established in every hamlet or ward. By the early Taisho era the problem of non-payment of village taxes had begun to ease.

Third, towns and villages themselves began petitioning higher authorities at the county, prefectural and national level for financial assistance in meeting some of their funding responsibilities for local schools, roads and bridges or for the transfer of funding responsibility itself to the prefecture for county schools (for which towns and villages paid) or for local and county roads. In these efforts, towns and villages were aided by members of county and prefectural assemblies and by the Diet Members for their districts, who since the mid-1890s had functioned as the upper stratum of men of high repute and influence (*meibōka*) and become involved in defending and promoting local interests as part of their role as politicians. In the hard economic times following the Russo-Japanese War, they became even more willing to use their good offices to provide help to their constituencies (Tsutsui 1984: 14–15; 1999a: 217–19).

Fourth, not just county officials but also many of the politicians mentioned above were enlisted in resolving the disputes engendered by such projects as school expansion, shrine mergers and the transfer of hamlet common lands to administrative villages. In most cases, they sought to bring rival factions together and negotiate a 'give-and-take' solution. In Hokusun, for example, what that meant in villages that were divided over where the expanded elementary school would be located was getting the losing side to agree to the location of the school in the rival area in exchange for the promise that desirable road improvements would be carried out in its part of the community (Tsutsui 1999a: 239–43).

Thus did the activities of the upper stratum of political elites in the countryside to promote local interests and mediate local disputes merge with the on-going efforts of the local improvement movement to organize the rural population into a variety of functionally specific groups that were centered on the administrative villages in which they lived to form a local power structure that was qualitatively different from the power structure of the past. 'Local notables' no longer operated simply as the heads of the wealthiest local families, but as members of political parties, and the interests they sought to promote transcended the particular hamlet in which they might live to incorporate the administrative village, county and prefecture as a whole. Moreover, as a result of the local improvement movement, a much greater number of formal organizations existed in every village, with branches in every hamlet, each with posts that needed to be filled. Now smaller, cultivating landlords and substantial owner-cultivators were appointed to such posts and incorporated into the lower reaches of the power structure (Tsutsui 1993: 246).

Conclusion

Nor was that all. As a result of the local improvement movement and the commercialization of agriculture it promoted, even ordinary and poor farmers became caught up in local conflicts of interest and increasingly politicized. On the one hand, such farmers usually depended to a greater extent than did their more affluent neighbors on the benefits that hamlet membership had traditionally conferred, especially on access to common lands, and as a result they became involved in efforts to protect hamlet interests, even at times challenging powerful local landlords in the process. On the other hand, and perhaps more significantly in the longer term, the very pressure such ordinary and poor farmers experienced to commercialize their operations so that they could bear the burden of local taxes and pay their rents in full focused the attention of others on their role as the direct agents of agricultural improvement and made them increasingly aware of that role as well. In this sense, the local improvement movement also contributed to the eventual undermining of the new local power structure that crystallized at this time, by creating some of the dynamics that would result in challenges to the ascendancy of local notables, especially the large landlords among their ranks, in the 1920s and beyond. That said, it should be remembered that, while becoming aware of themselves as agents of agricultural improvement, ordinary and poor farmers were also becoming increasingly aware of themselves as loyal subjects of the emperor, and the two new consciousnesses would reinforce each other without any sense of contradiction in the years ahead.

References

Aoki Kōji. 1967. *Meiji nōmin sōjō no nenjiteki kenkyū*. Tokyo: Shinseisha.

Araiizumi Sadao. 1976. 'Meiji kokka to minshū tōgō.' In *Iwanami kōza Nihon rekishi*, kindai 4.

Ishida Takeshi. 1956. *Kindai Nihon seiji kōzō no kenkyū*. Tokyo: Miraisha.

Kitagō Sonshi. n.d. Deposited in Oyama chōritsu toshokan.

Kurihara Hyakujū. 1949. 'Nōgyō kiki no seiritsu to hatten.' Reprinted in *Kurihara Hyakujū chosaku zenshū*. Tokyo: Kōkura shobō.

Matsumoto Hiroshi. 1999. 'Oyama no Meiji ishin.' In *Oyama chō shi*, ed. Oyama chō shi hensan senmon iinkai. Oyama: Oyama chō.

Miyaji Masato. 1973. *Nichi-Ro sengo seijishi no kenkyū*. Tokyo: Tōkyō daigaku shuppankai.

Miyamoto Tsuneichi. 1960. *Wasurareta Nihonjin*. Tokyo: Iwanami bunko.

Nagahara Kazuko. 1999. 'Bunmei kaika to dentō no kurashi.' In *Oyama chō shi*, ed. Oyama chō shi hensan senmon iinkai. Oyama: Oyama chō.

Ōkado Masakatsu. 1993. 'Nihon no kindaika to nōson seinen no sekai.' *Shinano* 45(4).

Ōshima Mitsuko. 1970. 'Chihō zaisei to chihō kairyō undo.' In *Kyōdoshi kenkyū kōza* 7, ed. Furushima Toshio, Wakamori Tarō and Kimura Ishizue. Tokyo: Asakura shoten.

Oyama chō shi. 1992. *Oyama chō shi* 4 (*kin-gendai shiryō hen*), ed. Oyama chō shi hensan senmon iinkai. Oyama: Oyama chō.

Senoue Yuki. 1985. '1910 nendai no nōson shakai jōkyō: Shizuoka ken Suntō gun Izumi mura burakuyū rinya tōitsu hantai undō o jirei to shite.' *Shizuoka ken kindaishi kenkyū*, 11.

Takahashi Kamekichi. 1926. *Meiji Taishō nōson keizai no hensen*. Tokyo: Tōyō keizai shinpōsha.

Teruoka Shūzō. 1970. *Nihon nōgyō mondai no tenkai*, vol. 1. Tokyo: Tōkyō daigaku shuppankai.

Tsutsui Masao. 1984. 'Nihon teikokushugi seiritsuki ni okeru nōson shihai taisei – Shizuoka ken Harazato mura no jirei o chūshin ni.' *Tochi seido shigaku*, No. 105.

—— 1986. 'Buraku kyōyū kinkoku no un'yō to meiboka shihai,' 1 and 2. *Hikone ronsō,* Nos. 236 and 237.

—— 1987. 'Seitō seiji kakuritsu ki ni okeru chiiki shihai kōzō 1 – Shizuoka ken Gotenba chiiki no jirei ni sokushite.' *Hikone ronsō*, No. 244.

—— 1993. 'Nōson no hensen.' In *Shiriizu Nihon kin-gendaishi*, ed. Sakano Junji *et al.* Tokyo: Iwanami shoten.

—— 1998. 'Kōjō no shutsugen to chiiki shakai – sangyō kakumei ni okeru Fuji bōseki kaisha to Shizuoka ken Oyama chiiki,' 2. *Shiga daigaku keizai gakubu kenkyū nenpō*, 5.

—— 1999a. 'Chōsonsei kara Nisshin, Nichi-Ro sensō e.' In *Oyama chō shi*, 8, ed. Oyama chō shi hensan senmon iinkai. Oyama: Oyama chō.

—— 1999b. 'Oyama no sangyō kakumei.' In *Oyama chō shi*, 8, ed. Oyama chō shi hensan senmon iinkai. Oyama: Oyama chō.

—— 1999c. 'Taishō kara Shōwa e.' In *Oyama chō shi*, 8, ed. Oyama chō shi hensan senmon iinkai. Oyama: Oyama chō.

Wagatsuma Tōsaku. 1937. *Nōson sangyō kikōshi*. Tokyo: Tōkyō Sōbunkaku.

5 In search of equity

Japanese tenant unions in the 1920s

*Ann Waswo**

That the Japanese bureaucracy sought to extend its control to the very lowest reaches of rural society and to prevent the emergence among the rural population of organizations based on social class is beyond doubt. That these goals were easily achieved is another matter entirely.

From its inception in 1900, the government's local improvement movement, a series of initiatives designed to integrate rural communities and pre-existing rural interest groups more fully into the central administrative structures of the state, met with both active and passive resistance. The effort to merge the Shinto shrines of individual hamlets into one central shrine for each administrative village in the country aroused considerable opposition among hamlet residents, as did the effort to transfer control of hamlet common lands and forests to the villages. In both cases the bureaucracy found it necessary to scale down its original objectives. Similarly, many administrative villages responded without enthusiasm – or failed to respond at all – to the bureaucracy's request for local development plans.[1]

Nor did efforts to 'declass' social and economic interests in the countryside proceed without setback. By early Taishō the bureaucracy had indeed acquired a high degree of control over a number of grass-roots organizations in the countryside – for example, the youth groups that had long existed at the hamlet level and the associations of ex-servicemen that had appeared in increasing numbers after the Russo-Japanese War. Yet at the same time the bureaucracy was confronted with the emergence of the very sort of class-based organizations its social policy had been designed to prevent. These were of two kinds: organizations of landlords,

* This paper was originally published in *Conflict in Modern Japan History: The Neglected Tradition*, ed. T. Najita and J. V. Koschmann (Princeton: Princeton University Press, 1982). It is reprinted in this volume with the permission of Princeton University Press. It was not possible to recast the references into the form used elsewhere in the volume, and a rather long list of endnotes has been provided instead.

which the bureaucracy did not find especially troubling,[2] and organizations of tenant farmers, which it did. My concern in this paper is with the latter – with the internal organization, activities, and goals of tenant unions.

My focus will be on the 1920s. After a general description of tenant unions, I will present a detailed analysis of tenant unions and the tenant movement in the Izumo region of Shimane Prefecture. Finally I will discuss the ways in which the bureaucracy dealt with tenant unions. Before I turn to these topics, however, I should comment briefly on the dimensions of the phenomenon I am considering.

Roughly 50 tenant unions had been established in Japan by 1908, the first – in Gifu Prefecture – as early as 1875. Thereafter unions began to multiply at a faster rate. By 1917 some 173 unions were known to exist; by 1921, 681, and by 1923, 1,530. In 1923, the first year for which membership figures are available, 163,931 tenant farmers, or 4.3 percent of all tenant farmers in the nation, belonged to unions. Four years later, in 1927, the figure had risen to a peak of 365,331, or 9.6 percent of all tenant farmers.[3]

In common with popular movements in other times and places, the tenant movement in Japan was unevenly dispersed throughout the country. Some prefectures, primarily those in northeastern Japan and Kyushu, had few unions, whereas others, primarily those in central Honshu and the Inland Sea region, had large numbers. In many of the latter a considerably higher than average percentage of the tenant population was unionized. In 1927, for example, over 41 percent of the 4,582 unions in existence were located in only seven of the nation's 47 prefectures. The percentages of tenant farmers in those prefectures who belonged to unions were as follows: Yamanashi, 41.6 percent; Niigata, 32.0 percent; Kagawa, 29.9 percent; Tokushima, 22.0 percent; Gumma, 20.1 percent; Gifu, 18.5 percent; and Okayama, 17.1 percent.[4]

However an outside observer might evaluate these statistics, it is clear that contemporary Japanese perceived them as significant.[5] Bureaucrats in particular regarded the increase in tenant unions and union membership in late Taishō with considerable misgivings. They monitored the phenomenon carefully, keeping close track of numbers and gauging their responses accordingly. In short, the degree of unionization achieved was sufficient, in a society that was sensitive to manifestations of class consciousness, to merit definition as a social problem.

Tenant unions: an overview

Collective action on the part of the lower strata in rural society was by no means a new phenomenon in Japan. As Stephen Vlastos has shown, many participants in the 'world renewal' (*yonaoshi*) uprisings of the Bakumatsu era were small-scale landholders, tenant farmers, or day laborers.[6] In the immediate aftermath of the Meiji land settlement, too, tenant farmers in various regions of the country acted in concert to protest rent increases or the loss of permanent tenancy rights. Indeed, in subsequent years whenever harvests were poor and the rent reductions landlords were expected to give were not deemed adequate, tenants were likely to band together to express their grievances.[7] What was unprecedented about the situation in the countryside in the 1920s, then, was not that tenant farmers were resorting to collective action as such. Rather, it was the form that their collective action took, and its thrust.

With some exceptions, to be sure, earlier protest movements in the countryside had been ad hoc in structure and relatively short-lived; the product of a particular perceived crisis, the collectivity dissolved when that crisis had passed. In contrast, the tenant unions that came into being in the Taishō era were formal organizations, with detailed rules of procedure set forth in written bylaws (*kiyaku*). Although established in many cases at a moment of crisis – for example, when heavy rains had damaged the rice crop – tenant unions were designed to function in perpetuity, or at the very least for an extended period of time.[8]

Like earlier rural protest movements, tenant unions were concerned with improving the economic and social status of their members, and they employed a number of familiar means – the drafting of petitions, for example – to achieve that end.[9] In their conception of the measures that constituted improvement and of the agency by which improvement was to be brought about, however, tenant unions differed markedly from earlier movements. To state the contrast baldly, the 'world renewal' protesters of the Bakumatsu era sought to eliminate economic and social inequality in the countryside, first by destroying the homes and property of wealthy peasants, and second by obtaining the intervention of feudal authorities on their behalf. The former, in fact, was conceived of not only as a desirable end in itself but also as a means to the latter. Faced with unambiguous evidence of discontent among the peasantry, rulers would be obliged to demonstrate their benevolence (*jinsei*) by removing the causes of that discontent and restoring rural society to its natural, harmonious state.[10]

Tenant unions, on the other hand, sought to lessen economic and social inequality in the countryside by *upgrading* the status of tenant farmers. This was to be accomplished primarily by the efforts of tenant farmers themselves, by means of various forms of self-help, and by the united front they presented to others. The latter was conceived of as a crucial instrument of power. By employing it, unions attempted to manipulate their environment in constructive ways. They negotiated with landlords rather than destroying their property, and they pressured the government to provide them not with benevolent treatment but with the equity to which they felt they were entitled. Implicit in the activities of unions, and at times explicit in their public statements, was a recognition that the social order was both man-made and malleable. Justice lay in the future, not the past; it was to be achieved, not restored.

Both the form and the thrust of tenant unions attracted the attention of bureaucrats in the Ministry of Agriculture and received fairly extensive coverage in the reports of the tenant union movement they issued from time to time throughout the 1920s.[11] Their reports, which were based primarily on analysis of union bylaws, constitute a useful source for examining the structure and aims of tenant unions in greater detail.

In 1925, roughly 35 percent of the tenant farmers who belonged to unions were members of what the bureaucracy termed associated unions (*keitōteki kumiai*), that is, unions that were themselves members of some larger federation or alliance of tenant unions; 65 percent of the tenant farmers who belonged to unions were members of autonomous unions (*tandoku kumiai*), that is, unions that maintained no formal ties with other tenant organizations.[12] Whether associated or autonomous, however, all unions appear to have been markedly similar in structure.

Each union was organized as a voluntary association of individuals within a specified geographical area. Membership generally was open to anyone cultivating leased land within that area, that is, to pure tenant farmers who leased all the land they cultivated and to part-tenants who leased a portion of the land they cultivated and owned the rest.[13] The majority of unions encompassed a single village district (*ōaza*), equivalent in many, though not all, cases to one of the traditional hamlets of which the village was constituted. The next most common basis was the village. In 1925, for example, 63.6 percent of all unions were organized at the *ōaza* level; 93.8 percent of all unions were organized at the village level or below.[14]

The entire union membership was convened once or twice a year into a general assembly to hear reports on union activities and financial outlays, to decide on future undertakings, and, if necessary, to elect officers. In most cases, decisions were reached by simple majority vote, although in special cases, such as a change in the union's bylaws, a two-thirds or three-quarters majority might be required. Extraordinary assemblies could be convened whenever deemed necessary by the union president or demanded by a specific percentage, usually one-fifth to one-third, of union members.[15]

Union officers included a president (usually designated *kumiaichō*, sometimes *sōdai*) whose duty it was to represent the union in dealings with others, direct the union's internal affairs, and preside at union meetings; one or two vice presidents to assist the president and substitute for him whenever he was unable to perform his duties; one or more secretaries (*kanji*, *riji*) to carry on the union's day-to-day operations; and a number of councilors (*hyōgiin*) to advise the president and to decide on matters delegated to them by the general membership. The union president and vice president(s) were elected by and from the membership as a whole, for terms varying in length from one to three years. Other officers were either elected by the membership or appointed by the union president. Officers generally served without salary, although in many cases their out-of-pocket expenses were reimbursed from union funds.

In most cases no qualifications for holding office were specified in union bylaws. All members were therefore eligible for election in theory. In practice, however, most union officers, the president in particular, were men of some influence (*kuchi kiku no mono*) among local tenant farmers and in their communities as a whole.[16] What constituted that influence seems to have varied from place to place. Sometimes it was a higher than average level of education, sometimes a distinguished military record. Probably the most common requirement was a degree of affluence, based on a larger than average landholding and/or a source of non-agricultural income, which provided individuals with the economic independence and the social status to carry out official union duties.[17]

All unions collected membership dues, although the way in which they assessed them and the amounts they charged varied considerably. Some unions required an equal sum from every member, whereas others levied dues according to the area of land individual members tenanted or the amount of rent they paid to landlords. Dues might be payable in rice (as were tenant rents in most cases) or in cash. If in cash, they might be as low as one *sen* per month or range upward to as much as 30 *sen* per month.[18]

In addition to articles defining organizational structures, the bylaws of all tenant unions contained articles setting forth objectives and enumerating the means that would be employed to achieve them. Although some unions cited only a single objective, most listed two or more. Bureaucrats grouped the objectives that appeared in union bylaws under six headings, which they then divided into two separate categories. In the first category were objectives they termed non-confrontational (*hitaikōteki*). These were: the promotion of harmonious relations between landlords and tenants; the promotion of friendship and mutual aid among tenants; the improvement of agriculture; and the prevention of competition for land among tenants. In the second category were a pair of confrontational (*taikōteki*) objectives: the maintenance and improvement of the terms of tenancy; and the social advancement of the tenant class.[19] Early in the Taishō period the majority of unions had concerned themselves with what bureaucrats considered non-confrontational objectives. Beginning in 1918, however, there had been a dramatic increase not only in the total number of unions, but also in the number of unions with confrontational objectives. In 1922, 88 percent of all unions cited at least one such objective in their bylaws, typically in combination with other non-confrontational objectives. In 1926, 92 percent of all unions cited at least one confrontational objective.[20]

For each of the six objectives they identified, bureaucrats further identified a corresponding set of union activities. Their findings, although based on measures stipulated in the bylaws of individual unions, were presented in summary form with little or no attention to how frequently those measures were cited. No one union necessarily engaged in all the activities in any one set, nor did many unions engage in more than two or three sets of activities. What follows, then, is not a description of typical union activity, but rather a description of the entire range of union activities.[21]

- *The promotion of harmonious relations between landlords and tenants*. Bureaucrats were able to find only a few activities relating specifically to this objective. The most common were inviting landlords to social gatherings, and offering to mediate disputes over tenanted land.
- *The promotion of friendship and mutual aid among tenants*. Other than the holding of social gatherings for tenants and their families, all the activities bureaucrats listed related more directly to mutual aid. They were: the establishment of a fund for emergency relief to members in the event of natural disaster; the creation of flood and fire brigades; the provision of needed labor to families who had fallen behind in their work owing to the sickness or conscription of a family member; assistance to members wanting to lease additional land; the cooperative purchase of such everyday necessities as bean paste and soy sauce; and the loan of union-owned funeral goods to members.
- *The improvement of agriculture*. Bureaucrats divided the activities relating to this objective into two categories, improvements to agricultural technology and improvements to farm management. The former included: the exchange of seeds; the standardization of seed strains; cooperation in insect control; the encouragement of deep plowing; the furnishing of materials to construct racks for drying rice; the encouragement of improved composting techniques; the construction

of drainage ditches; the improvement of field paths; the joint use of farm tools; cooperative rice planting; research on possible secondary crops and by-employments; employment of a trained agricultural expert; and training courses in farming methods. The latter included: the cooperative purchase of livestock, fertilizers, and other necessities for farming; the cooperative sale of farm produce; the provision of loans for farm operations; and the encouragement of efforts to enable tenant farmers to purchase land.

- *The prevention of competition for land among tenants*. More in the nature of agreed-upon rules of procedure than activities, the stipulations related to this objective were: that no union member would try to secure tenancy rights to additional land by offering to pay higher rents than were paid by the current tenant of that land; that decisions on whether or not to agree to higher rents demanded by landlords would be made by the union's general assembly, not by individuals; that whenever a member relinquished his cultivating rights to a plot of land he would notify the union immediately so that another member would have a chance to assume them; that no union member would agree to cultivate land currently cultivated by another member without the latter's consent; and that if a union member acquired title to land that another union member tenanted he would not demand that the latter surrender the land to him until after a specified period of time had elapsed.[22]
- *The maintenance and improvement of the terms of tenancy*. Activities related to this objective were divided by bureaucrats into three groups. First were those designed to standardize the terms of tenancy in a given locality, which included efforts to secure uniformly worded tenancy agreements and to eliminate variations in the due date for rent payments. Second were activities designed to maintain existing terms of tenancy, which usually involved resistance to landlords' demands for rent increases or the surrender of tenanted land. Third were activities designed to improve existing terms of tenancy. The latter included efforts to secure recognition of cultivating rights, temporary or permanent rent reductions, abolition of 'added rice' payments and the double-baling of rent rice, and reform of the system of inspection imposed on rents.[23]

Bureaucrats observed that efforts to maintain or improve terms of tenancy often led to conflict with landlords, in which case tenant unions were likely to take one or more of the following steps: survey and prepare reports on local rent levels and crop yields; study the laws pertaining to the points at issue in the dispute; agree on a united front among union members in dealing with landlords during the dispute, with sanctions to be imposed against anyone who violated it; refuse to do farm labor or any other type of work for landlords while the dispute was in progress; provide land or monetary aid to anyone who was evicted from the land he cultivated during the course of the dispute; threaten to abandon all of the land involved in the dispute unless the union's demands were met; and make partial rent payments only.[24]

- *The social advancement of the tenant class*. Bureaucrats noted that this was an objective found in the bylaws of recently organized unions, constituting evidence that the tenancy problem was moving into 'a stage of class conflict.' Most commonly tenants sought to achieve recognition of the right to engage in collective bargaining and, in the early 1920s, urged speedy passage of a universal manhood suffrage law. Other activities aimed at promoting the awareness (*jikaku*) and knowledge of tenant farmers included publishing union newsletters and organizing lecture meetings or training courses for union members.[25]

In their reports, bureaucrats placed far greater emphasis on describing tenant unions than on explaining why unions had been organized. When they did deal fleetingly with issues of causation, they attributed both the increase in number of unions after 1918 and the concurrent shift from non-confrontational to confrontational union objectives to exogenous forces. Chief among those cited were the Russian Revolution and the First World War, events external to Japan. Also important were the rice riots of 1918, the industrial labor union movement, and the various democratic and socialist movements of the Taishō era, all essentially urban phenomena within Japan.[26] Other than making passing reference to the dislocating effects on tenants of the First World War economic boom and subsequent bust, bureaucrats did not discuss precisely (or even generally) how these events and developments impinged on tenants, wrought changes in their attitudes and aspirations, and resulted in tenant unions.

I will consider the policy initiatives that stemmed from this assessment of tenant unions as an 'alien growth' upon the countryside in the concluding section of this paper. Here I want to examine two aspects of the descriptive material bureaucrats presented in their reports that seem to suggest another, more basic explanation: that unions were responses to endogenous changes within rural society itself and to exogenous forces that stemmed not from outside Japan or from Japanese dissidents but from the policies and procedures of the Japanese state.

As bureaucrats noted (without comment), the majority of unions were organized at the *ōaza* (or hamlet) level. In my view, that is a very intriguing fact. If the forces creating tenant unions came from outside rural society, how did they penetrate directly and immediately to the very core of that society, the 'natural community,' where traditional values and attitudes inimical to self-assertiveness and class consciousness supposedly remained very strong?

'Without the hamlet one cannot even get to paradise.'[27] So went a rural proverb that summed up the hamlet's power over the individual and over individual households. One needed the community to obtain a proper funeral, just as one needed it in life to obtain water, firewood, recreation, or aid and comfort when disaster struck. Social cohesion and acceptance of status distinctions were necessary to survival. In theory, the poorer members of the community were most affected, and most constrained, by these imperatives. Far from identifying with others in the same situation, they competed with them for the favor of the local elite and the small but crucial benefits that favor bestowed on them.[28] Yet it was in these very communities that the poorer members abandoned competition for cooperation and organized unions.

Not every hamlet, of course, had a tenant union. What, then, might distinguish those that did from those that did not? Since, to my knowledge, bureaucrats never compiled a directory of unionized communities, one must rely on information gleaned from various case studies of tenant unions and tenancy disputes. On that admittedly imperfect basis, it appears that unionized communities differed from non-unionized communities in one or more of the following three ways.

First, unionized communities were located where agriculture had become relatively highly commercialized. Communities with unions where thus more likely to be found in the Kinki or Chubu regions of central Honshu than in the Tohoku or other economically backward regions of the country. Within the latter regions, however, communities with unions did exist in major rice-producing districts and/or in districts where sericulture was an important by-employment among local farmers. Tenant farmers in these communities were all involved in commercial farming in one way or another. Some, typically those with substantial holdings of paddy, participated directly and actively in the marketplace, selling what at times amounted to considerable quantities of rice. Those with smaller holdings often relied on wage labor, a product of commercial farming, to make ends meet. If they sold any rice at all they were likely to do so immediately after the harvest, when prices were lowest, because of their pressing need for cash. Later they might have to buy rice, at higher, early summer prices, to tide them over until their next crop was in. Whatever the size of their holdings, tenants in these communities were affected by rice (or silk) prices and were interested in maximizing the amount of their harvest they could retain, that is, in reducing rent levels.[29]

Second, unionized communities tended to contain considerable amounts of reclaimed land. This meant, on the one hand, that local tenants farmed holdings that were larger and/or less fragmented than did tenants in neighboring communities, and, on the other, that they possessed, or believed they possessed, permanent tenancy rights (*eikosaku ken*) by virtue of their labor, or an ancestor's labor, in reclaiming the land they tilled.[30]

Third, unionized communities tended to be what one observer has termed 'headless.' That is, few if any landlords were in residence. The community consisted primarily of owner-cultivators and tenants or, in some cases, of tenants alone. Landlords might live in another hamlet of the same village, in a neighboring village, or far away in a town or city. Their absence from the community itself created both the need for self-help among remaining residents since there was no local elite to bestow favors, and the opportunity for self-help since there was no local elite to demand subordination and deference.[31]

This brings me to the second aspect of the descriptive material in official reports that bears examination: the activities of tenant unions. In my view, even the activities bureaucrats identified as non-confrontational can be construed as challenges to established norms. Mutual aid that the community was supposed to provide was provided by the union. The union also engaged in agricultural efforts that duplicated those assigned to the hamlet branch of the village agricultural association (*nōkai*).[32] Indeed, instead of the sharp (and conveniently timed) break circa 1918 between non-confrontational and confrontational activities, one can perceive a gradual and steady evolution. That is, tenants found it necessary or desirable to provide certain services for themselves. One of those services was not competing among themselves for land, since competition drove rent levels up; having found that they could, by cooperation, keep rent levels from rising, they began to experiment with joint action to get rents reduced; finding that lower rents did not solve all their problems, they became interested in other objectives, among them their 'social advancement.'[33]

That exogenous forces influenced this process is evident. Among those that bureaucrats characterized as 'alien' and later Japanese scholars have viewed as 'progressive' were labor union activists who returned to their native villages, typically after having been fired from their jobs for participating in strikes; university professors, writers, and intellectuals who toured the countryside giving speeches on the tenancy system, monopoly capitalism, and the proletarian movement in Japan and abroad;

and books, journals, and newspapers that dealt with these and other 'radical' themes.[34]

An even more powerful stimulus to new attitudes and behavior among tenants, however, was the Japanese state. It trained agricultural experts and sent them out into the countryside where, among other things, they taught tenants how to keep detailed records of their incomes and expenditures. It conscripted young tenant farmers and taught them discipline and organizational skills.[35] By means of conscription and compulsory elementary education, the state imbued tenant farmers with nationalism and with a new vocabulary of nationalistic symbols that could be and, as will be discussed later, were used to legitimate tenant grievances.

More fundamentally, the state established a system of laws and administrative procedures to organize all of Japanese society, including the countryside. Under that system tenants continued – as they had before the Meiji Restoration – to occupy an inferior status. The civil code of 1898 recognized property rights as superior to leasing rights. Until 1925 only property owners were granted a voice in local and supralocal politics. But what had once been defined by custom was now, in principle, justiciable. As in the past, tenants could appeal to a higher authority for redress of their grievances, but now that authority was impartial law, not benevolent rulers. It was not coincidental that one of the measures tenant unions resorted to in conflict with landlords was 'study of the laws pertaining to the points at issue in the dispute.' Law had replaced bamboo spears as one of tenant farmers' major weapons, just as formal organizations, similar to those of bureaucratically controlled youth, reservists, and agricultural groups, had replaced ad hoc and transitory collectivities.

Thus far I, like the bureaucrats whose reports I have summarized above, have not discussed at all precisely how the diverse events and developments I have mentioned impinged on tenants, wrought changes in their attitudes and aspirations, and resulted in tenant unions. To do that it is necessary to move from the general to the specific and examine tenant unions in one particular region of the country.[36]

Tenant unions and the tenant movement in Izumo

Shimane Prefecture lies along the Japan Sea coast of western Honshu, bordering to the east on Tottori, the south on Hiroshima, and the southwest on Yamaguchi Prefecture. There were some 91 tenant unions in Shimane in 1925, with an overall membership of 5,545 (roughly 7 percent of the tenant population). These unions were not evenly distributed throughout the prefecture as a whole. Rather, they were concentrated in its eastern portion, in the region known as Izumo, one of the three *kuni*, or provinces, from which the prefecture had been constituted in the early Meiji era.

Identified in Japanese myths as the earthly place to which Susano-o was banished for such transgressions as letting piebald colts loose in the heavenly rice paddies of his sister the Sun Goddess, Izumo may have seemed to government officials in the mid-1920s to be living up to the unruly reputation of its first divine inhabitant. There were 62 tenant unions in the region in 1925, 60 of them in Nōgi and Yatsuka *gun*, its two largest administrative districts. The unions in these two *gun* had a total of 3,195 members, 57.6 percent of all the unionized tenants in the prefecture. Roughly 26 percent of all tenant farmers in Nōgi and 23 percent of all tenant farmers in Yatsuka belonged to unions, and the unions they belonged to were almost all of the sort bureaucrats recognized as confrontational, that is, unions that sought to maintain and improve the terms of tenancy and/or to bring about the social advancement of the tenant class.[37]

The confrontational stance of unions in Izumo was a fairly recent development. As late as 1920 most unions in the region were informal, clandestine organizations at the hamlet or *ōaza* level, whose leaders met under cover of darkness to discuss the state of the upcoming harvest and to decide the amount of rent reduction each tenant should request from his landlord.[38] Those unions that were formally and openly organized generally avoided use of the words 'tenant farmer' or 'union' in their bylaws, styling themselves 'friendship societies,' 'cultivators' associations,' or 'agricultural clubs' instead.[39]

In dealing with landlords these unions generally based their appeals on expectations of benevolent treatment: once aware of their tenants' problems, landlords would, it was assumed, grant relief. Those landlords who failed to do so were subjected to various forms of ostracism, or *murahachibu*. Tenants would refuse to take part in funerals, weddings, and other occasions involving the offending landlords. Their ultimate and most explicitly economic weapon was the joint return of the land they leased; no tenant in the community would cultivate the land of any landlord who behaved improperly toward tenants.[40]

By 1925 the situation was radically different. The majority of tenant unions were formally organized as voluntary associations and openly employed the words 'tenant farmer' and 'union' in their bylaws. They held public meetings in the hamlet hall, local schoolhouse, or Buddhist temple. Instead of requesting benevolence, tenants now demanded equity, and did so collectively, not individually.[41] Moreover, a considerable proportion of unions in Izumo, although still organized at the hamlet or *ōaza* level, now belonged to a regional body, the Tenant Federation of Nōgi and Yatsuka Districts. In place of isolated tenant unions there was now a tenant union movement.

Toward confrontation

This development of tenant unions in Izumo can be attributed to two closely related causes: the accumulation of new or newly perceived grievances among tenant farmers during late Meiji and early Taishō, and the emergence of an able group of local tenant union leaders. A contributing cause was the founding in 1922 of the Japan Farmers' Union (Nihon nōmin kumiai, or Nichinō), the country's first national tenant union federation, by Sugiyama Motojirō and Kagawa Toyohiko.

Since relatively few ordinary tenant farmers could or did commit their thoughts to paper, one must infer their grievances from their actions. For that purpose, reports on early tenancy disputes in Shimane Prefecture constitute the best available source. In those reports one finds a number of new complaints in company with such old and familiar ones as poor harvests and the threatened loss of cultivating rights owing to the sale of tenanted land or the owner's desire to farm the land himself. The two new complaints that figured most prominently were the added burdens imposed on tenants by rice inspection, and the hardships imposed by land adjustment.

Shimane did not institute a mandatory program for inspecting all rice grown in the prefecture until the late 1920s. Beginning in late Meiji, however, various steps were taken to improve the quality and marketability of local rice. In 1906 regulations were issued to standardize the size of rice bales throughout the prefecture. At roughly the same time, a program was established for inspecting rice destined for sale outside the prefecture, and landowners were encouraged to establish procedures at the local level for improving rice quality. In response, many landlords organized fairs and awarded prizes to tenants who produced superior rice. Others established local inspection facilities and began to require rent payments in rice that met minimum standards of quality. One of the most ambitious undertakings of this sort was organized by landlords in Nōgi *gun*, a major rice-producing district in the prefecture.[42]

From the very start tenants found much to complain about in these efforts, correctly perceiving that they bore the added expenses involved while landlords reaped the profits. Among other things, tenants had, in most cases, to manufacture smaller and more durable rice bales than had been necessary in the past and spend more time in threshing and drying their rice before baling it. They objected, too, to continued demands from landlords for 'added rice' payments, the extra quantity per bale traditionally required to compensate for leakage and spoilage, perceiving that stronger packaging and longer drying made such additional rice payments unnecessary. Protesting that soil and drainage conditions on the land they cultivated limited the quantity of high-grade rice they could produce, they opposed the imposition of quality standards on rent payments, or, if they accepted the idea of such standards, demanded that they be set as low as possible to reflect accurately local growing conditions.[43]

The land adjustment projects carried out in many parts of the prefecture in the early 1900s were designed to improve the irrigation and drainage of paddy fields, thereby solving one of the problems tenants faced in meeting quality standards for rent, and to straighten boundaries between fields, thereby making cultivation easier and more efficient. In the short run, however, land adjustment elicited far more opposition than enthusiasm among tenant farmers. They complained about the difficulties of growing crops while adjustment projects were under way, about slight but disturbing declines in the fertility of the soil in some newly adjusted fields,[44] and, most of all, about rent increases in the aftermath of adjustment. The latter, for example, was the cause of a dispute in three villages of Nōgi *gun*, where a large-scale adjustment project had been carried out in 1907. Before work commenced, landlords had agreed to hold rents at their current level for a year or two after the project was completed. Then rents might be raised in accordance with increased productivity. During 1907, however, prices for both materials and labor rose dramatically, bringing the actual cost of adjustment to almost 16 yen per *tan*, more than twice what landlords had estimated. Most landlords thereupon decided to raise rents immediately. Protesting the unfairness of such a step, tenants in the three villages banded together and refused to pay any rents at all until landlords agreed to abide by their initial promise not to raise rents for a few years.[45]

In addition to grievances such as the above, prefectural officials also cited the behavior of landlords as a source of discontent among tenants. Some landlords acted arbitrarily and arrogantly in their dealings with tenants, like the *jitō*, or estate managers, of Japan's feudal past. Where, at the same time, landlords showed no interest in their tenants' well-being or in improving local agriculture – where, in other words, landlords were functionally if not physically absent from their communities – a particularly volatile situation existed. This was clearly the case in Araijima, a village in Nōgi *gun*, where a dispute involving 10 of the village's 12 hamlets erupted in 1921. The most militant stance in the dispute was taken by tenants in Kami-Araijima hamlet where, officials noted, landlords had not supported the hamlet agricultural association or permitted the establishment of a hamlet cooperative for the purchase of tools, fertilizers, or other supplies. Instead they had established a bank and sought to make it the sole source of loans and credit in the community. Finding this state of affairs unsatisfactory, tenants organized their own association, the Kami-Araijima Tenant Farmers' Friendly Society, and began to provide for themselves many of the services – including the cooperative purchase of essential supplies – their landlords had denied them.[46]

Without these and other grievances to fuel it, the tenant movement in Izumo would have been impossible. But the existence of grievances alone was not enough. Most tenants, however upset they might be at one time or another over specific issues, lacked the verbal and conceptual skills to link those issues into a generalized indictment of the status quo. Still dependent on landlords for access to land and on their communities for access to water, fuel, and other necessities, they were wary of openly defying authority and established norms of behavior. They might organize a self-help society in their own hamlet, but they remained unaware that tenants in other hamlets or villages faced problems similar to theirs.[47] The movement, therefore, had to be engineered. Someone had to articulate the grievances of tenant farmers, formulate a systematic statement of the problems they faced, create a program for solving those problems, and build a viable organization for achieving desired change. In Izumo this was accomplished by a small group of young, educated, and determined union leaders, chief among them Yamasaki Toyosada.

Yamasaki was born in 1898 in Mori, a village in Nōgi *gun*. Although there were several large landlords resident in the village, none lived in Ido hamlet where his home was located. Of the 15 families in the hamlet, 14 owned no land at all, not even the plots on which their houses stood. Yamasaki's was the only family of means in the hamlet, owning one *chō* of paddy fields, one *tan* of upland fields, and two *chō* of forest land. In addition, they leased four or five *tan* from a village landlord and rented out one *tan* to another cultivator.[48]

Yamasaki graduated from the village elementary school in 1913 and enrolled in a nearby agricultural school. He soon quit attending courses, however. Thereafter he subscribed to a few correspondence courses offered by Nihon and Meiji universities, and in the process became interested in the philosophy of Henri Bergson, but for all practical purposes his formal education ended when he was 15 years old.

One reason he quit school was his growing involvement in local politics and the tenant movement. Yamasaki's father had long served as head (*kuchō*) of Ido hamlet, and from an early age Yamasaki had assisted him in performing his duties, first running errands and later taking a more active part in hamlet business. Yamasaki appears to have enjoyed dealing with people – as he recalled years later, if there was something his father found difficult to say to someone, he would volunteer for the task – and there seems to have been a lot of dealing for him to do. Ido was, by Yamasaki's account, a tempestuous community. Adultery was not uncommon. In addition, local residents enjoyed gambling, which tended to bring them into conflict with one another over the repayment of debts, and they produced considerable quantities of 'moonshine' sake, which brought them into conflict with the authorities. In late Meiji, money-lending *kō* (mutual financing clubs) were introduced into the hamlet. Many residents had difficulty repaying the loans they received, and for several years Ido was 'a nest of process servers.'[49]

Yamasaki seems to have regarded the trouble his neighbors got into as a product of poverty, not of moral failings on their part. He also regarded their poverty as a problem to be solved. A poor hamlet, in his view, was destined to become even poorer unless its inhabitants took measures to defend themselves. All the administrative reforms in the village during the early 1900s – the merger of shrines, consolidation of common lands, definition of water rights – had been carried out to Ido's disadvantage. Just as wealthy hamlets asserted themselves at Ido's expense, wealthy landlords took advantage of Ido's tenants, charging high rents and taking back their land – 'an everyday occurrence' – if tenants fell at all behind in rent payments.

Yamasaki attributed his initial commitment to the tenant movement to an essay he read at the age of 12 in the journal *Nihon oyobi Nihonjin*. It concerned the death of the last aboriginal Tasmanian in a Melbourne hospital and the dispatch of his bones to the British Museum. Moved to tears by the obliteration of an entire people, Yamasaki began to reflect on what had already happened in his own community. His family had once been residents of Nakatsubo hamlet, adjacent to Ido and home to 30 households. One by one the families had died out or moved away, until only his was left. No one remained to look after the graves, and finally the hamlet had been erased; the Yamasakis, as the sole survivors, were absorbed into Ido. A sinister progression of events occurred to him: the death of an individual, a family, a hamlet, and, ultimately, a people. Resolved to do something to prevent Ido from following the same sad course as Nakatsubo, Yamasaki started working to improve local conditions.

That resolve manifested itself in two ways, both of which later figured importantly in Yamasaki's career as a tenant union leader. First, he began to study law, buying for himself an inexpensive edition of the revised penal code and a copy of the civil code. He carried one or another with him wherever he went and studied the contents at every opportunity.

By the age of 17 he was known in the hamlet and in the village as something of a legal expert.[50]

Second, Yamasaki began experimenting with agricultural improvements. With several other youngsters from the local boys' association (*shōnendan*) he reclaimed some wasteland on the outskirts of his hamlet and began growing vetch.[51] As it turned out, the land in question was in the public domain and within the boundaries of another hamlet. In 1918, 20 years after the promulgation of the civil code, the government began a survey of public lands throughout the country to determine whether individual plots should revert to state ownership or be granted to their cultivators. Yamasaki and the others received a formal notice from the head of Nōgi *gun*, acting on behalf of the prefectural governor and the home minister in Tokyo, informing them that the land they cultivated was deemed state property and should be returned forthwith. On Yamasaki's advice, the group sent back a postcard stating that as far as they were concerned the land was theirs by virtue of occupancy and reclamation. Under no circumstances would they surrender it. Whenever *gun* officials appeared on the scene to confront them, the boys managed to disappear.

On August 30, the day before the deadline for resolving ownership rights, the entire group received a summons to appear at the *gun* office. This time they agreed to go, and for several hours they were subjected to severe scolding for their recalcitrant behavior. Toward evening they were handed forms in which they renounced their claims to the land and were ordered to sign. Yamasaki nodded, and everyone signed. Then he announced that, of course, their signatures were invalid. As minors they could make no binding legal agreement without the approval of an attorney. Unfortunately it was too late in the day to arrange for that. Abruptly the boys left for home. The deadline came and went, and their right to cultivate the land was confirmed. The episode became something of a cause célèbre in the area, and as Yamasaki later recalled gave him confidence in his legal knowledge.[52]

In 1921, the Mori Agricultural Friendly Society, the first village-wide tenant union in Shimane, was created, and Yamasaki, then aged 23, became a member. The following year he read a newspaper announcement about the planned organization of a nationwide tenant union by Sugiyama Motojirō and Kagawa Toyohiko. Interested parties were invited to attend a meeting at Kagawa's church that April. Intrigued, Yamasaki went to the meeting, finding himself one of a handful of 'real farmers' among the 50 or 60 people present. Both the idea and the platform of the Japan Farmers' Union (Nichinō), the organization established at that meeting, appealed to him. In particular, he was impressed by Sugiyama's call for efforts to raise the awareness (*jikaku*) of tenant farmers and for 'moderate, steady, rational and legal' efforts to reform the tenancy system.[53] Yamasaki returned home determined to organize a Nichinō branch in his own village and to join with tenant leaders in neighboring Tottori Prefecture to form a Nichinō federation in the San'in region. In the end, he did neither, although he did become leader of a regional federation in Izumo that incorporated Nichinō's original goals.

In the first place, his proposal to affiliate with Nichinō did not appeal to the leaders of the Mori Friendly Society. 'They were all old men in their fifties,' Yamasaki wrote later. The head was a member of the village assembly and did only what the mayor told him to do. Several landlords served as advisors to the organization. Yamasaki therefore decided to bypass the society and form his own Nōgi-wide organization. Using Ido hamlet as his base, and with the aid of several young tenant farmers from Ido and a hamlet in a nearby village, he set to work. The young men toured Nōgi by bicycle, stopping at every hamlet with a tenant union and sounding out its leaders about their willingness to join a regional federation.[54]

At the time, Yamasaki was still interested in taking part in the planned Nichinō San'in rengōkai, a federation of unions in Shimane and Tottori. By July of 1923, however, he had abandoned the idea. As early as its second national congress that year Nichinō had begun a 'turn to the left' of which Yamasaki thoroughly disapproved. Proposals were made (unsuccessfully for the time being) to create an alliance between farmers and industrial workers and to replace the organization's original emphasis on economic reforms with an emphasis on politics. In addition, steps were taken to centralize the decision-making structure of the federation, reducing the autonomy of affiliated unions.[55] As Yamasaki recalled later:

> Nichinō [leaders] began to proclaim that tenancy disputes were merely rehearsals for the revolution. That frightened farmers. I believed that it was possible for farmers to create a rational tenancy system and achieve fair rent levels all by themselves. Ultimately, they could abolish tenancy altogether, but it was necessary to proceed step by step.[56]

Another factor was his dislike of what he termed the formulaic (*kōshikishugi*) stance of Yuihara Genzō, one of the key leaders of the tenant movement in Tottori. The man was 'not a farmer' and did not pay adequate attention to actual conditions in the countryside.[57] Yamasaki therefore dissociated himself from the San'in Rengōkai and later withdrew from

Nichinō itself. When Nichinō experienced its first split in 1925, Yamasaki participated in the splinter organization established by Hirano Rikizō, the All Japan Farmers' Union League (Zen Nihon nōmin kumiai dōmei). Once again, however, he rapidly became disillusioned and withdrew: 'I found that I'd been misled. [The league] was merely an effort to use the farmers' movements as a base for getting ahead in politics . . . It was wrong to use unions as political tools.'[58]

Instead, Yamasaki pursued an independent course, following his own ideas and instincts and building what he later described as 'an organization of real farmers with their feet firmly planted on the soil.'[59] In December of 1923 13 unions throughout Nōgi joined together to form the Nōgi Tenant Federation (Nōgi gun kosaku rengōkai), with Yamasaki as its head. In 1924 a similar federation was established in neighboring Yatsuka. The two united in 1925 as the Tenant Federation of Nōgi and Yatsuka Districts (Nōgi Yatsuka gun kosaku rengōkai). In July of 1926 the Shimane Prefecture Tenant Federation (Shimane ken kosaku rengōkai) was formed, with over a hundred branches in the five *gun* of eastern Shimane. Yamasaki served as head of the federation, which controlled the tenant movement throughout Izumo.[60]

Building an organization

At its inception in 1923, the Nōgi Tenant Federation was composed of pre-existing tenant unions in the district, whose leaders had responded favorably to proposals for a *gun*-wide body. Once the federation had been created, Yamasaki and his associates began to expand its scale, encouraging the formation of affiliated unions in communities where no tenant unions had existed before. The strategy they followed then and in later years consisted of four stages: the selection of appropriate communities; the identification of a local leadership cadre; the enrollment of members within the community; and the education of those members in the principles of unionism and the means of achieving rural reform.

Yamasaki was less interested in creating an extensive movement than in creating a strong one. Rather than simply moving from one community to the next, he preferred to concentrate on those communities – in most cases, hamlets – that he thought could sustain an effective local union. To him that meant communities where farming was the principal occupation of inhabitants and rice their major crop, and where few, if any, landlords resided. Landlords might live elsewhere in the village, but the farther away they lived and the larger their holdings in the community concerned, the better. Hamlets in which there were many small landlords and/or many small, part-time farmers were to be avoided.[61]

In Yamasaki's view the best choices for leaders of a new union were: adopted sons who had been born and raised in other communities; newly returned soldiers or activists in the local reservists' association (*zaigō gunjinkai*); anyone who had left the community for a time and then returned; former landlords who had 'sunk to the status of tenant farmers'; sons of owner-cultivators who were 'on the verge of ruin'; men with experience as sawyers, stonemasons, or in other skilled occupations; and Buddhist priests or faith healers (*kitōshi*).[62] As indicated by this list, Yamasaki had a decided preference for 'outsiders,' defined either literally (individuals who came from elsewhere and had no deep roots in the community) or figuratively (individuals who had had experiences in the community or elsewhere that made them dissatisfied with the status quo). How successful he was in identifying such people in hamlets throughout Izumo is unknown. What is clear is that 'outsiders' constituted the majority of the movement's top leadership. Another characteristic they had in common was youth, as the following examples suggest.

Terada Noriaki, son of a tenant farmer, was a childhood friend of Yamasaki's from Ido. He had served two years in the army and on the basis of his past education and military record returned home in the early 1920s with a non-commissioned officer's certificate. Thereafter he helped Yamasaki organize the Nōgi federation and, as will be discussed later, took charge of the movement's publicity and publishing efforts. His union activities came to the attention of the military police who, according to Terada, prevented his promotion to corporal in the local reservists' association.

Ishiwara Toshio had been a member of the Buddhist Socialist party in Izumo before becoming interested in the federation. Although subjected to various pressures to abandon his union activities – he had to resign the headship of the fire brigade in his village, his brother was turned down for admission to military cadets' school on the grounds that a close relative was 'a suspicious character,' and at one point his in-laws threatened to make his wife leave him – he remained involved, specializing, like Terada, in publicity work.

Adachi Iwao became involved in federation activities at the age of 17, later serving as head of the youth bureau in the Shimane federation. Born in neighboring Yatsuka *gun*, he developed an interest in socialism at an early age. That proved awkward because the government had designated the community in which he lived a 'model village' that embodied the best of purely Japanese virtues. Made to feel unwelcome at home, Adachi moved to Nōgi and volunteered to work with Yamasaki. The two subsequently toured Yatsuka by bicycle, organizing the *gun*-wide federation there.[63]

Enrolling members in a new union was a relatively easy task if the first two stages of organizational strategy had been carried out properly, that is, if an appropriate community had been selected and appropriate leaders identified. As full-time farmers, local tenants had no sources of non-agricultural income to distract their attention from the tenancy system. Producing rice as their major crop, they were aware of the burdens imposed by high rents in kind and recently instituted standards for baling and rice quality. Subject to relatively few face-to-face contacts with landlords, they were not as constrained by traditional expectations of deferential behavior as were tenants who saw their landlords regularly. That men from their own communities were leading them (however alienated or marginal those men might be) muted the defiance of norms of community solidarity that membership in a union necessarily involved.

Also helpful in attracting members were Yamasaki's growing reputation as a champion of tenant farmers in Izumo and the success of unions already affiliated with the federation in winning meaningful gains (principally, but not exclusively, rent reductions) for their members. The proclamations of Yamasaki's regional federations, which were designed to persuade ordinary farmers of the legitimacy of their grievances, were another factor. Avoiding unfamiliar and therefore threatening terminology, these proclamations portrayed class action – objectively a radical departure from established norms – as a higher form of patriotism. Both to mollify fears among tenants and to forestall reprisals by officials, they invoked imperial symbols on behalf of the tenant movement. The proclamation of the Tenant Federation of Nōgi and Yatsuka Districts (1925) provides a good example:

> The majority of Japanese are farmers, and the majority of farmers are tenants. By their efforts the nation is protected, its land cultivated, and its people fed. But for many years now the evils brought about by the unimpeded power of wealthy landlords have hung like a dark cloud over the countryside, obstructing the infinite benevolence of His Imperial Majesty. Moreover, rural living standards have not kept pace with progress in the rest of the country. As a result tenant farmers have truly suffered. At this time, we tenant farmers, inspired by the fundamental principles of the Empire and by the spirit of love for humanity, stand in the forefront of rural reform. We reject all violent means, for we are convinced that championing righteousness and morality gives us greater strength.
>
> Until the light shines brightly on the countryside – we shall persevere steadily until both the fields that we love and we ourselves are favored with boundless Imperial grace. In striving to reach our goals

> we must resist all blandishments and be prepared to face untold persecution. Whatever voices are raised against us, we must remember that our cause is just.[64]

Yamasaki was sharply criticized by contemporary leftists for 'misguiding' tenant farmers with such notions as imperial benevolence and love of humanity. Later Japanese scholars of the tenant movement have also criticized him for his acceptance of 'the emperor system,' his use of army reservists as union leaders, and, above all, his 'defection' from Nichinō. To most of these scholars, Yamasaki ranks with the leaders of the two other independent regional federations, Sugai Kaiten of Niigata and Yokota Hideo of Gifu, as a reactionary within the tenant movement and 'traitor' to its revolutionary cause.[65] Although I tend to feel that major social and political restructuring – perhaps even a revolution – was needed in Taishō Japan, I cannot accept this negative evaluation of Yamasaki. It ignores, among other things, the success he had – greater, I think, than the more explicit and ideologically 'advanced' efforts of Nichinō or its affiliates – in mobilizing tenant farmers and nurturing in them a new and implicitly revolutionary consciousness. Far from being a reactionary, he used what later came to be regarded as reactionary symbols and reactionary rhetoric with consummate skill to accomplish the crucial task of getting farmers into unions and into his federation. Once that was achieved, Yamasaki and his associates began educating those tenants, instilling in them new knowledge and new ideas that enabled them both to perceive the need for change and to act to bring it about.

One of the most important facets of the fourth, educational stage of the movement's organizational strategy was publication of a newspaper, *Kosakunin* (*The Tenant Farmer*). Realizing that there were limits to what could be accomplished by personal contacts alone (*kuchi dake de wa ikenai*), Terada Noriaki suggested in 1923 that some sort of newsletter be produced to publicize the federation's activities and goals. He and a few other young men from Ido collected 30 yen, bought a mimeograph machine, and began experimenting with it.[66]

From this modest beginning evolved an increasingly polished and effective publication. In 1926 six-page issues of *Kosakunin* appeared on a regular monthly basis and were distributed to over 3,000 subscribers.[67] Professionally printed instead of mimeographed, the paper appears to have become more relevant and accessible to its intended audience than it had been initially. 'You were once just a paper for literary youth,' a reader wrote in 1926, presumably referring to a plethora of abstract and theoretical essays in earlier issues, 'but now you have developed into something completely different.'[68] That 'something completely different' consisted of useful advice and inspirational messages written in straightforward Japanese that most tenant farmers could comprehend. *Furigana* were printed beside each Chinese character, giving its phonetic reading. Plain verb forms and a conversational style were employed.[69] Except in articles about politics, which I will discuss at a later point, the vocabulary usually was simple and concrete. On the rare occasions when a technical term or abstraction appeared, it was carefully defined.

Most of the writing for *Kosakunin* was done by Yamasaki, Terada, and other federation officers, but subscribers too were invited to submit news items, essays, poems, and reflections. The following letters from two Izumo tenant farmers give some idea of the kind of response the paper generated:

> I just received your paper. I too am a propertyless tenant farmer. I am a miserable creature who lives at the very bottom rung of capitalist society. The key to our liberation is a class newspaper like yours. By reading this kind of newspaper we get the weapons to break our chains. In that connection, please add my name to your list and lead me to the goal of liberation. I enclose stamps for a two-year subscription.
>
> When the factory where I worked was destroyed in the recent [Kanto?] earthquake, I came back to the countryside. What shocked me most about my village was the credit union. Everyone including tenant farmers contributes money, and then the landlords and wealthy people borrow that money at low interest rates and use it as capital for their investments. Poor people like us, who don't have anything to put up as collateral, can't get a loan at all. So that credit union is just a money-making tool for landlords. I'll let you know if I uncover anything else about this credit union. Your paper has a lot to do in the future. Keep up the struggle. I got you thirty subscribers here. Goodbye.[70]

In addition to items on such practical topics as how to set up a cooperative to purchase farm tools,[71] *Kosakunin* devoted considerable space to legal questions of concern to tenant farmers. In the March 1926 issue, for example, an extended discussion of ordinary and permanent tenancy rights was printed. It began with the observation that one of the reasons landlords threatened lawsuits over rent arrears and other issues was to intimidate tenants; ignorant of the law and 'terrified of going to court,' tenants would, landlords hoped, give in to demands without a struggle. Only by knowing their rights and conquering their fear of the law could tenants protect themselves. Moreover, they could use that knowledge to improve tenancy conditions. Getting rents reduced, the article observed, was a particularly easy task: *Kosakuryō o makesasu koto mo asameshi mae no koto da*.[72] In the May issue the more specific question of how a tenant should go about protecting his rights of occupancy in the face of an eviction attempt by his landlord was discussed. Like most other articles containing useful information, this one also contained an exhortation to rely upon the union; its officers and legal advisers would do the necessary paperwork free of charge and help the tenant if he went to court.[73]

Other articles were devoted entirely to exhortation. Each issue of the paper began with an introductory essay (*kantōgen*) about some aspect of the tenancy system or the tenant movement, often taking the season as its starting point:

> It is March. The plum trees are in blossom, the nightingales sing. But tenant farmers are too exhausted from . . . hard work and their miserable diet of pickled radishes to take any pleasure in the fragrance of the blossoms or the silvery voices of the birds.
>
> All they can think about is getting some rice to eat. The crop they raised last year . . . is now completely gone. . . . [They tell themselves] the seeds they planted weren't good enough. They didn't tend their fields carefully enough. . . . This year they will use better seeds and work harder so the rice will not desert them in their time of need.
>
> What fools tenants are to think this way! 'Poverty can be overcome by diligence.' That is what they've learned at school. But it's not so. No matter how hard they try, they can't solve their problems by diligence alone.[74]

Another introductory essay, this one written by Yamasaki for the June issue, invoked the experiences of farmers in early summer to attract attention:

> It's that busy time of year when everyone could use some extra help in harvesting the vetch or the wheat and getting ready for planting rice. With the silkworms coming out of molt again we get hardly any sleep at night. Our joints ache from weariness . . . when we get up in the morning.
>
> Why must we work so hard? . . . What rewards do we tenants get for our labor? Do we even get enough food to fill our bellies, or clothing to keep us warm, or decent houses to protect us from the rain?
>
> We're not machines . . . or draft animals. We're human beings. . . . That our labor goes to make idle landlords richer . . . is enough to make me weep. Were we growing crops for the benefit of society

> as a whole, it wouldn't matter how hard we had to toil. If more rice or more cocoons were needed so that many people could live, we'd work for nothing if need be. . . . But we aren't going to be the means by which a few human beings can live in . . . luxury.[75]

The theme of the injustice of the status quo was dealt with in numerous other articles, among them one rather provocatively titled 'Why are Tenant Unions Trying to Destroy Landlords?' Like the June introductory essay quoted above, it too made the point that tenants were not seeking change for purely selfish reasons, this time citing their dedication to the villages in which they lived:

> [People ask] why have tenant farmers organized unions and set out to destroy the landlords they used to honor and obey? . . . Consider the condition of villages today. On the one hand there are tenant farmers who find it hard to make ends meet no matter how hard they work. On the other hand are landlords, who don't work at all. . . . These landlords are few in number, but the number of hard-pressed tenants has increased steadily. More and more of them have had to abandon their native villages and head for the cities. The fields of the idle landlords are no longer carefully tended and may eventually become wasteland. . . .
>
> We feel no hatred toward landlords as individual human beings. But when we consider them as members of a community who ought to . . . be concerned about that community's future, we can only regard them as enemies. They are traitors who are destroying the villages in which they live by their own lust for riches. . . . If they would abandon their petty concerns and strive to serve the community as a whole, they would benefit too. It is to get them to recognize this fact and stop charging excessive rents that we have organized tenant unions. . . . We do this out of duty and love toward our ancestors who settled those villages originally and brought the land under cultivation. We will go on . . . until [landlords] change their mistaken ways and vow to strive for the benefit and happiness of the entire community. We're not out to destroy landlords. We're trying to educate them.[76]

Yamasaki wrote frequently for *Kosakunin*, returning again and again to the theme that tenant farmers could improve their lives by solidarity and solidarity alone. Although aware of developments in the tenant movement in other parts of the country, he rarely referred to them. Indeed, he seems to have held both his wider knowledge of the world and his youth in check, adopting instead the homespun approach of a wise old man. Building on what local tenant farmers knew, he sought to lead them to new perceptions. 'One can't tell the value of a house when the weather is fine,' he wrote on one occasion.

> But in a heavy storm one knows right away if the roof is strong enough or not. . . . The same thing is true of villages. A village that has a tenant union and one that doesn't or a village with a solid union and a village with a weak union – they're all the same when things are going smoothly. . . . But in this world we don't get bumper crops every year. Landlords change too, as sons take over from their fathers. It happens sometimes that a greedy fellow becomes head of the house. . . . It's at times like that that the value of a union becomes clear. . . .
>
> The weakest tenants are those who've formed a union under their landlord's direction. They think they're well off, but they end up paying higher rents than anybody else. Next . . . are tenants in villages with no unions at all. They get summoned one by one [to the landlord's house]. Terrified, they prostrate themselves and . . . pay whatever the landlord asks. Then come villages with unions that don't belong to a federation. At first, just the very existence of a union in the village will scare the landlords. . . . But landlords are no fools. After a few years at most they'll start studying the law and talking with lawyers. Then the union starts having trouble. . . . Nobody is there to help. . . . The landlords sense that the union is weak and move in for the kill. . . . That's when the advantages of belonging to a federation will be clear.[77]

In an unusually long essay titled 'The Power of Unions to Transform Dogs and Cats into Human Beings,' Yamasaki cast his thoughts about unions in yet another way, this time clearly revealing his commitment to achieving dignity, as well as equity, for tenant farmers:

> 'Beg for three days and the taste will last three years.' By relying on the benevolence of their landlords as if they were dogs or cats, tenant farmers have led a beggar's existence for a long time. . . . They and their families barely scrape by on the basis of the favors they receive – the relief, the sympathy presents, the patronage, the pity. . . . Whether they live or die, eat or starve, depends on their landlords' generosity. If tenants don't do exactly as their landlords say . . . landlords will turn them away just as they'd turn away stray dogs. . . .
>
> There is absolutely no reason for landlords to treat tenants like beggars, and yet they persist in doing so. . . . Recently, too, some

tenant farmers have allowed themselves to be organized into landlord–tenant conciliation unions. They pride themselves on belonging to the committees that dispense bonus rice, sympathy rice when crops are poor, relief rice, and money for fertilizer or farm tools. Despite the high-sounding name and fancy organization [these conciliation associations] are nothing more than the latest means landlords have seized upon to keep tenants in their place, the latest means to keep them living like beggars. The tenants who serve on the committees think they're doing grand work, but in reality they are nothing but the landlords' cats-paws. . . .

Landlords know that they take an unfair share of the crop from tenants, and they're afraid tenants will realize it. They try to divert the tenants' attention by doling out relief rice, sympathy rice, and bonus rice. Portraying themselves as benevolent *oyakata*, they give tenants as charity what they ought to give them as their due. As a result, tenants get cheated not only out of their property, but out of their self-respect as well. . . .

The only way to change this – to free tenants from the opiate of benevolence and paternalism that oppresses them in everything they do and reduces them to groveling for favors like dogs and cats, the only way to elevate them from the demeaning status of beggars to the dignity of human beings – is by means of tenant farmer unions. Only when landlords . . . have been subjected to the pressure of a union created by tenant farmers themselves will tenant farmers become aware of their own power. Then they will begin to develop pride and self-respect. They will come to see that by relying on their own united strength they can do without favors. . . . That will be the day that dogs and cats become human beings, the day that tenants forever free themselves from humiliating dependence on landlords.[78]

The organization in action

One can divide the activities of the successive federations of tenant unions in Izumo into three general categories: those concerned with landlord–tenant relations and the tenancy system; those concerned with farm management and community life; and those concerned with politics at the local and supralocal level. Not surprisingly, given the strong views and considerable influence of Yamasaki himself, the movement continued to emphasize activities in the first category throughout its existence. Activities in the second category played in retrospect a pivotal role. On the one hand, they constituted a logical extension, which Yamasaki actively encouraged, of efforts to improve the lives and livelihoods of tenant farmers. On the other hand, they led – equally logically, it would seem – to concern with village politics and, ultimately, to concern with the policies of Shimane Prefecture and the central government. Political activities, in turn, involved the movement in the rivalries of the national tenant movement, which contributed to growing dissension among leaders of the Shimane tenant federations and resulted, in late 1927, in the expulsion by Yamasaki of several federation members. The tenant movement in Izumo never recovered from this rupture.

Among federation activities concerned with landlord–tenant relations and the tenancy system, two figured most prominently. The first was what Yamasaki termed, not without a touch of wit, rent adjustment (*todai seiri*), *todai* being a local term for rent payments. If land itself could be adjusted (*kōchi seiri*) so too could tenant rents. The latter should be just as rational and efficient as the former. Instead of being determined by custom or by what Yamasaki termed 'exploitation' (charging whatever the market would bear), rents should be based on the productivity of the land concerned and on an equitable sharing of risks and costs between landlord and tenant.[79]

Based partly on Yamasaki's own assessment of what was wrong with the tenancy system and partly on his reading of 'A Treatise on Fair Rents' by Nasu Hiroshi, professor of agricultural economics at Tokyo University,[80] the movement's program of *todai seiri* evolved through several stages. Initially, local tenant unions sought reform of the traditional system of granting rent reductions when harvests were poor. Since the Meiji era, if not earlier, it had been customary for local landlords to reduce rents in bad years so that tenants were left with a minimum of four *to* of rice per *tan*. By whatever means they could devise – sometimes a petition would suffice, in other cases prolonged negotiations were required – tenants sought to raise that minimum, to six *to* at least, and up to eight, ten or twelve *to* if their bargaining position was exceptionally strong.[81]

Next, local unions began carrying out detailed surveys to determine the productivity level of each plot of land within their communities and compiling equally detailed accounts of costs of production and income earned per *tan*. It is significant and by no means coincidental that both tasks were assigned to tenant farmers themselves. In Yamasaki's view, tenant farmers knew the land better than landlords or so-called agricultural 'experts' from elsewhere and therefore could do a better job of surveying it.[82] That they might gain satisfaction from accomplishing the task and useful insights from keeping records of their incomes and expenditures had also, one can safely conclude, occurred to Yamasaki.

The penultimate stage of *seiri* was the calculation of fair rent levels. Yamasaki advocated, and the federation appears to have adopted, what he termed the 8:3/4:6 system as a guiding principle. Of the first eleven *to* of rice produced per *tan*, eight *to* would go to the tenant to cover his costs of production and three *to* would go to the landlord to cover his tax liabilities. Any remaining produce above the eleven *to* thus accounted for, which constituted only 42 percent of average yields per *tan* in Shimane for the period 1916–20, would be divided on a 4:6 basis between landlord and tenant, respectively, compensating the former for his investment and the latter for his labor.[83]

The final stage was the presentation of proposed new rent levels to the landlords concerned. According to Yamasaki, by 1927 roughly two-thirds of all landlords in Izumo had agreed to rent adjustment, more or less along the lines described above. In some cases, the prospect of a virtually automatic determination of rents even in years of poor harvest had been enough to gain their consent. In other cases, landlords had agreed to adjustment only after tenants had showed their solidarity and determination during months or even years of disputes.[84]

The second federation activity concerned with landlord–tenant relations and tenancy conditions was conflict itself, that is, the theory and practice of tenancy disputes. As promised in the pages of *Kosakunin*, the federation came to the aid of tenants or tenant unions involved in disputes, providing advice on strategy and tactics and, when necessary, free legal aid. Equally important as far as Yamasaki was concerned, the federation organized training courses and workshops throughout Izumo to inform tenant farmers about laws relating to tenancy, and in particular the tenancy conciliation law of 1924.[85]

Although Nichinō took a formal stand against the conciliation law, Yamasaki concluded after careful study of its provisions and of the proceedings of the parliamentary committee that had considered it that it had potential; if well-coached in its intricacies, tenants could use what was basically 'bourgeois' legislation to their own advantage. Among other things, both sides of a dispute subject to conciliation could be made to appear personally in court. Used to delegating such tasks to their lawyers, landlords would be on unfamiliar ground.[86] While conciliation was in progress, moreover, landlords could not file suit against tenants to recover unpaid rents or to secure return of their land. Tenants therefore could use the law to gain time, negotiating privately with some of the landlords who were party to the dispute in the hope of reaching a favorable and precedent-setting settlement of outstanding differences.[87] Given the primacy accorded to private property rights in Japan, tenants could not expect a favorable decision in all cases of conciliation. But if they presented a legitimate reason for the position they took in the dispute, provided evidence to back up their claim, and observed the correct forms and terminology in all their communications with the judge, they stood a reasonable chance of success. In cases involving eviction, the only legitimate claim tenants had was possession of permanent tenancy rights. In cases involving rent arrears, their only legitimate claim was a poor harvest.[88] In addition to discussing these points at workshops, the federation made general guidelines and sample petitions available to all affiliated unions.[89]

Like tenants elsewhere in the country, tenants in Izumo were not interested solely in lower rents and more secure cultivating rights, important as those issues were. They also wanted improvements in farm management and community life. At the annual meeting of the Nōgi federation in 1924, for example, nine of the 25 proposals for action submitted to the membership by participants concerned the latter two issues. Among the specific problems identified in these proposals were the high cost of everyday necessities and farm tools, excessive demands made by the community for donated labor and monetary contributions, and lack of uniformity in the scheduling of holidays.[90]

The federation's basic response to these and other concerns was to provide information and encourage self-help by member unions. Workshops on new farming techniques and demonstrations of new tools were scheduled at annual meetings or local union gatherings, and simply written pamphlets on a variety of topics were made available below cost.[91] In December 1926, an entire page of *Kosakunin* was devoted to information about why and how local unions should establish consumer cooperatives for the purchase of salt, sugar, and other staples.[92] Earlier the same year *Kosakunin* reported in glowing terms an experiment in cooperative farming under way in Ido and Yokoyama hamlets of Mori village. Tenants in the two hamlets had pooled the land they cultivated and formed teams to carry out all farming tasks. By early June the team had planted rice in seed beds and harvested the vetch crop. In early July they transplanted the rice seedlings into the paddy fields. Afterwards a commemorative photograph was taken, and the tenants marched triumphantly though the village.[93]

There were limits, however, to the improvements in farm management or community life that tenants could effect on their own. Even if, as in Ido, they constituted the entire hamlet population and therefore could decide hamlet affairs as they saw fit, they had to deal with other hamlets, and other interests, in the village if they were to realize desired changes in the allocation of water for irrigation, the scheduling of repairs on roads and bridges, or other matters that fell within the purview of the village assembly. Similarly, numerous policies of the prefectural government – concerning taxes and surtaxes, for example, or the location of agricultural experiment stations – impinged on the economic interests of tenants, just as prefectural police regulations (to be discussed later) impinged on the very existence of tenant unions and the conduct of tenancy disputes. In short, tenants were impelled toward involvement in politics.

Until 1925 that involvement was limited by property qualifications on the franchise at both the local and supralocal levels. Tenants might lobby successfully for voting rights in their own hamlets, which were not affected by government regulations on that score.[94] But only tenants who owned a fair amount of their own land could vote or run for office in village elections, and only a tiny minority of tenants owned enough land to qualify to vote in prefectural or national elections. In general, then, tenant unions relied on indirect (though not necessarily ineffectual) means to change village policies, and from time to time they petitioned *gun* or prefectural officials on issues of concern to them.

The passage of the universal manhood suffrage law in 1925 enabled tenants throughout Japan to vote and run for office at all levels, a right they exercised with some success that very year when village elections were held. Out of 9,331 villages in which elections occurred, tenants were elected to assembly seats in 3,142, acquiring a total of 9,061 seats. In 761 of those villages, tenants acquired one-third or more of the total number of seats, possessing an absolute majority of seats in 340 villages and occupying all seats in 38.[95]

As a result of village elections in Shimane, the number of tenant farmers holding assembly seats rose from 51 to 172 (out of a total of 878). Of these tenants 147 (86 percent) had 'no connection' with tenant unions, a situation that prevailed throughout Japan. Eleven successful candidates were members of Nichinō-affiliated unions, located predominantly in the Iwami region of western Shimane. Fourteen were members of 'other unions,' including an unspecified number who belonged to unions in the Nōgi Yatsuka federation in Izumo.[96] Federation leaders may have encouraged individual tenant farmers to seek office at the village level, but no formal policy was established in that connection.

Nor was more than a modest effort made to mobilize Izumo tenants for the prefectural assembly election of 1926. Several articles about politics appeared in the February issue of *Kosakunin*. One presented a program for 'the rationalization of prefectural government,' which called primarily for reform of local taxes and improvement of the educational system. Another article pointed out the need for attention to prefectural politics, urged tenants to support candidates who would work on their behalf, and, significantly, called for candidates to come forward: 'Anyone with common sense will do. . . . Not having money or education makes no difference at all.'[97] At the time, the election was less than three weeks away. No tenant candidates had yet been selected, and none would be.[98]

After February 1926 there was relatively little mention of politics in the pages of *Kosakunin*. When the subject did appear, it was treated in a manner that contrasted sharply with the newspaper's general style. Both the language and the concepts employed were complex, not simple; the erudition, not the experience, of readers was being addressed. Rather than being presented as a concern of all tenant farmers, politics was dealt with as the special concern, indeed, the mission, of rural youth.

'We know well,' one article began, 'that all of nature is divided into predators and prey. Every living thing, be it plant or animal, must fight for its survival.' The article then pointed out that youth had a vital role to play in the ongoing struggle for survival with society:

> The exploiters and the exploited are now in conflict . . . and it is our duty as members of the exploited class to join the fray. . . .
>
> History shows that all change has been carried out by youth. Is there no lesson there for us? . . . Youth must attack all systems of thought based on customs of the past. We cannot leave this task to the older generation. They've lost hope. They've lost the will to prevail. We must lead the way in building a new society.[99]

Another article in the same issue called upon young tenant farmers to use their new political rights to reform local government:

> Just as a jewel, if left uncut, has no value, a human being who has never battled adversity cannot develop his full potential. . . . Lincoln, who freed hundreds of thousands of Negro slaves at the time of the American Civil War, endured great hardship [as a boy], as did Napoleon, who spent his childhood in wretched poverty. Haven't young men of the tenant class, who have fought against adversity [all their lives], developed more character than young landlords? I fervently hope these propertyless young men will soon be brandishing the sword of reform in village politics.
>
> In every country of the world the energy of youth has played a crucial role in history. Our own Meiji Restoration, carried out by a mere handful of young men from Satsuma and Chōshū, is but one example. Like a great ball of flame their energy brought about the end of Tokugawa tyranny and the establishment of a national government. Youth easily defeated age and took command of political reform. Reflecting on their victory, it seems fit and proper that the youth of today . . . stand up against the tyranny of landlords. . . .

> Fabius, a hero of ancient Rome, retreated before the overwhelming force of Hannibal's invading army rather than face him in battle. Then when Hannibal's soldiers had grown lax and dropped their guard, Fabius mobilized all his troops and launched a massive counterattack. The invading army was smashed to pieces.
>
> Today the old guard [in the villages] has grown lax. They have no idea of the passions that stir our young blood. This is the time to act, to sound the cry for political reform spearheaded by youthful vigor. The corrupt old system will be buried, and a new village politics embodying [our] glorious aspirations will be born.[100]

While some enthusiastic young federation members wrote articles like the above, others tried to get the federation to adopt an active political program and, in particular, to cooperate with other organizations in the prefecture and the country in electoral campaigns. Initially their efforts met with a degree of success. The federation took part in a conference of proletarian groups (*musansha dantai hyōgikai*) in the San'in region in October 1925. In April 1926 Yamasaki attended the inaugural meeting of Hrano Rikizō's All Japan Farmers' Union League in Tokyo and agreed to become one of its directors. As mentioned earlier, however, he withdrew after a brief period, disillusioned that Hirano and others were using tenant unions to further their own political careers. Already critical of Nichinō for advocating 'revolution,' Yamasaki decided against formal cooperation with other tenant or proletarian organizations. The program of the Shimane Prefecture Tenant Federation, which was established in July 1926, did not foreclose the possibility of political action – as one of its goals, the organization called for passage of a law 'that firmly established tenancy rights' – but it included no specific plans for getting such a law enacted. Moreover, it reiterated the movement's longstanding commitment to 'moderate, rational, and legal methods' and, in what constituted a rejection of the ideological tone of recent political essays in *Kosakunin*, stated the organization's resolve to 'put an end to class conflict' (*kaikyū tōsō zetsumetsu o kisu*).[101]

Rebuffed in their efforts and increasingly isolated within the movement in Izumo, a number of young federation members began to look with increasing favor on the tenant movement in western Shimane, or Iwami. Affiliated with the regional Nichinō federation in Tottori Prefecture, the Iwami movement had emphasized leftist politics from its inception. One of its principal leaders, Ogawa Shigetomo, was a graduate of Kansai University. Returning home to Iwami in 1924, he had first worked as an elementary schoolteacher and then had resigned to devote all his energies to organizing tenant farmers. The other leader,

Toyowara Goro, had been a labor union activist in Tokyo and had been arrested for his role in a textile workers' strike in 1926. Returning to his native village in Iwami to recover from the severe case of pleurisy he had developed in prison, he became involved in the local tenant movement. In March of 1927 Ogawa and Toyowara organized their own regional federation in Iwami, the Nichinō Shimane ken kosaku rengōkai, with 13 branches and 572 members. Two months later they staged a May Day celebration in Iwami that resulted in numerous arrests and, in Toyowara's opinion, heightened the political consciousness of all the tenants who had taken part.[102] Another focus of interest for would-be political activists in Izumo was the Seiji kenkyūkai (Political Study Group) in Matsue. Organized in 1923 by Fukuda Yoshisaburō, a Marxist with experience in the Tokyo labor movement, the kenkyūkai became active after 1925 in efforts to create a Labor–Farmer party organization in Shimane.[103]

Early in 1927 Nichinō experienced its second split, like the first, over the issue of whether or not to support the Labor Farmer party. Sugiyama Motojirō, president of Nichinō since its creation, resigned and in March organized the Zen Nihon nōmin kumiai (All Japan Farmers' Union, or Zennichinō). Now opposed to the Labor–Farmer party and in favor of more moderate political efforts, Sugiyama appealed to and received the support of Yamasaki. With two 'defecting' unions from the Nichinō federation in Tottori, Yamasaki organized the Zen Nihon nōmin kumiai San'in rengōkai (All Japan Farmers' Union Federation of the San'in Region) in April 1927. That step precipitated a clash with pro-Nichinō and pro-Labor–Farmer party members of the Izumo movement.

In July 1927, after several weeks of jockeying for position, Kimura Kamezō, a young federation member from Yatsuka *gun* who was also involved in the Seiji kenkyūkai, issued a proclamation calling for a united front between the competing Nichinō and Zennichinō federations in Shimane 'in response to historical necessity and the will of the masses.' Opposed to any dealings with Nichinō and, one suspects, offended at this direct challenge to his leadership, Yamasaki expelled Kimura from the federation. Kimura then rallied his supporters in Yatsuka and succeeded in getting the *gun* tenant organization to withdraw from Zennichinō and affiliate with Nichinō. Several months later Yamasaki experienced another and more painful blow. Adachi Iwao, who had worked with him since 1923 and who was then in charge of youth affairs within the federation, issued a proclamation calling, as had Kimura, for a united front. Yamasaki responded by firing Adachi forthwith. Taking a number of supporters with him, Adachi moved to Matsue. In mid-October he, Kimura and other Nichinō supporters in Shimane joined with the Nichinō-affiliated unions in Tottori to form the San'in chihō nōmin dantai kyōgikai (Conference of Farmers' Organizations in the San'in Region).[104]

Finally, in the spring of 1928, the breach between Nichinō and Zennichinō at the national level was healed, the result being the creation of the Zenkoku nōmin kumiai (National Farmers' Union, or Zennō). That June the two competing organizations in Shimane united as well, although each wing maintained its own leadership structure 'so as not to upset its members.'[105] Yamasaki took part in the new Zennō federation in Shimane, but without enthusiasm. In his view, the movement was at a stalemate, caught between 'landlords and bureaucrats on the one hand, and communists on the other.'[106] Local organization in Izumo was 'paralyzed,' its older leaders 'tired' from an endless stream of late-night meetings, and many of its younger leaders tending to regard the movement as a 'game.' Members had fallen into debt because they had spent more than they had gained in rent reductions. Lacking confidence in local union leaders, they did not pay their dues.[107] In Shimane as a whole, membership in the Zennō federation had declined to 520. The most active part of the federation was its youth branch, which engaged in literary study, conducted experiments in proletarian theater, and advocated reduction of the voting age to 18, conscription reform, support of public libraries, and the abolition of bourgeois sports.[108]

Bureaucratic responses

In early August of 1926, five tenant union leaders from throughout Japan were invited to present their views to a special committee of the Kosaku chōsakai, a committee headed by the minister of agriculture and charged with considering proposals for new legislation concerning tenancy relations and tenant unions.[109] Yamasaki Toyosada was one of the five. After identifying himself as a 'mere youth of 29,' inferior in education, experience, and knowledge to the 30 or so members of the committee, he spoke for roughly an hour, describing the problems that tenant farmers in Izumo had faced in the past, the goals and methods of the union movement he led, and his views on the need for the legislation under consideration.[110]

Concerning a law to redefine tenancy relations Yamasaki expressed enthusiasm. Existing law was geared to protecting landlords' rights to collect rents. What was required, he argued, was attention to productivity, that is, to encouraging tenants to raise output. Education in farming techniques was not enough. Tenants needed to have a stake in the land they cultivated, and the way to provide that was by giving them greater security of tenure.

Yamasaki then turned his attention to tenant unions, and urged the committee to leave them alone. Although proposed legislation would indeed grant de jure recognition to unions and to their right to engage in collective bargaining, it would at the same time subject them to government regulation – and that, in his view, would do far more harm than good. 'All other agricultural groups that exist today,' he observed, 'depend on official patronage . . . and leadership. They are weak, hothouse organizations.' In no other country at no time in history have such organizations ever achieved meaningful results. The only way to solve the problems villages face is to rely on 'natural,' not on 'manufactured,' organizations:

> Like a pine tree that has made a place for itself on a rocky crag, tenant unions have survived despite many obstacles. . . . It is because they have grown up in the wild that they are strong, and that wild strength [*yasei no chikara*] is the only means by which the countryside can be led to a bright future.[111]

Yamasaki's positive view of 'the wild strength' of tenant unions was not shared by the Japanese government. On the contrary, the very existence of 'wild,' unregulated organizations challenged bureaucratic conceptions of the state. At the same time, cooptation – bringing those organizations into the state's administrative structure and making them channels for the implementation of state policy – was not an acceptable response, for that would entail recognizing and legitimizing the interests, however broadly or altruistically defined, of a single social class.[112] Despite some sentiment within the Ministry of Agriculture in favor of a tenant union law, no such legislation was ever enacted. Instead the bureaucracy sought to eradicate tenant unions. To do so it employed two different approaches. The first was repression, which began with petty harassment in the early 1920s and culminated in the arrests of 'radical' unionists in 1928, 1929, and 1931. The second approach was reform, first of the machinery for dealing with landlord–tenant conflict, and ultimately, albeit only partially, of the tenancy system.

Official harassment of unions and unionists took many forms. Terada Noriaki recalled that the police would drop by his house unexpectedly, asking him interminable questions and making it hard for him to meet deadlines for the reports and articles he had to write.[113] Elsewhere, officials prevented local newspapers from reporting the details of tenancy disputes. Plainclothes policemen were sent into the countryside to learn about union plans and, if possible, to discover damaging personal information about union leaders. Auditors were dispatched to investigate the account books of unions for possible misuse of funds.[114]

Beginning in 1921 in Gifu, officials in a number of prefectures with active tenant movements issued revised police regulation (*keisatsuhan shobatsurei*) to define and establish penalties for a wide variety of illegal acts. Making collective action by tenants difficult, if not impossible, was clearly a major purpose of these regulations. The Shimane regulations, for example, included provisions that called for the imprisonment and/or fining of those who: participated in civil or criminal suits, non-litigation cases, or any other matters in which they had no direct, personal interest, or encouraged others to make complaints or file suits unless permitted by law; engaged in violent acts or incited others to such acts during the course of a dispute (*fungi*); engaged in mass demonstrations or attempted to negotiate en masse during the course of a dispute; employed gongs, drums, conch shells, or bugles to assemble or arouse others during the course of a dispute, or used fireworks, bonfires, pine torches, or banners for the same purpose; and incited or mobilized others not to pay taxes or public imposts.[115]

Rather than preventing collective action, however, these regulations appear on balance to have contributed to what can be termed the 'modernization' of the methods unions employed. Anxious to avoid fines and imprisonment, which imposed a heavy burden both on union treasuries and on themselves, union leaders were motivated to devise new procedures for conducting disputes and for creating and sustaining solidarity among union members. Those they devised were not only legal but more effective as well. To enable them to take part in suits and other matters in which they had no direct interest, union officials were formally elected as bargaining agents by the tenants concerned and granted power of attorney, duly executed and stamped, to act on the tenants' behalf. Armed with these documents, they did not have to persuade landlords to deal with them; landlords were constrained to do so by the law itself.[116] Instead of beating drums or lighting bonfires to assemble or arouse union members, they used posters, newsletters, and lecture meetings; when they needed to notify tenant unions in other communities that their help was needed – for example, to harvest crops before they could be sold at auction – they sent out telegrams.[117] Prevented from organizing boycotts not only of local taxes but also, in some prefectures, of local schools and such traditionally communal events as funerals,[118] they concentrated on direct forms of exerting pressure on landlords and on political action (such as getting tenants or their allies elected to hamlet and village assemblies) to bring about desired changes in local policy. Instead of violence, which was hard to control and often created resentments that were difficult to overcome, they emphasized disciplined and orderly behavior at union meetings and in disputes. Far from being a drawback, that proved an asset. On the one hand, it enhanced the respectability of union membership in the eyes of local tenant farmers and helped prevent resignations. On the other hand, it deprived landlords of an opportunity to evade the issues involved in disputes; having no grounds on which to summon local police, they had to respond to tenant demands.[119]

The final stage in the repressive approach to tenant unions began on March 15, 1928, when more than 3,000 suspected communists were arrested throughout Japan. Virtually all of the members of Nichinō's executive committee were included among those arrested, much to the relief of the current minister of agriculture, Yamamoto Tatsuo, who announced to his officials that the countryside finally was being freed from the grip of dangerous radicals.[120] Further arrests followed in April 1929 and March 1931, the latter including such local union activists as Kimura Kamezō and the leaders of the Zennō youth branch in Shimane.[121]

Not even Yamasaki escaped imprisonment. In February 1931 he was sentenced to eight months in jail for interfering with a government official in the performance of his duties (*kōmu shikkō bōgai*). His crime, committed in December 1926, had been to grab hold of a bailiff to prevent him from terminating an auction of standing crops that had been ordered by a local court to compensate the owners of the land in question for their tenants' refusal to pay rents. Yamasaki had mobilized nearby union members to attend the auction, and they so dominated the proceedings that the crops were being sold, to the tenants, for only a fraction of their market value. When the bailiff realized what was happening, he started to leave the scene. It was then that Yamasaki grabbed him, in effect to make him perform his duty, not to prevent him from doing so. Not even Yamasaki's legal skills, however, were adequate to mounting a successful defense in the repressive atmosphere that prevailed, although he was able to prolong the proceedings against him by means of appeals for over four years.[122]

The repressive approach to unions accorded fully with the view, discussed earlier, that unions were the product of alien forces that had penetrated rural society and contaminated tenant farmers with subversive ideas. In that sense, the arrests of union leaders represented an attempt to sanitize the countryside. Bureaucrats appear to have recognized, however, that removing leaders from the scene would only provide a palliative, not a cure. In addition to repression, they also employed reform.

In the early 1920s, at the same time that they were harassing existing tenant unions, bureaucrats had tried to enlist landlords in efforts to prevent new unions from being organized. Three measures had been recommended: that landlords voluntarily reduce rents in order to deprive tenants of an issue on which disputes, and hence unions, might be based; that they refer any disputes that did occur to local agricultural associations (*nōkai*) for resolution; and that they organize their tenants into conciliation associations (*kyōchō kumiai*) to promote mutual understanding and goodwill.[123] The responses these recommendations generated were far from gratifying. Few landlords lowered rents of their own volition. Rather than submitting disputes to *nōkai*, they continued trying to settle them independently or in concert with other landlords. Although some landlords organized conciliation associations, at no time before the mid-1930s did those associations rival tenant unions in either number or membership.[124] As officials in Shimane reported with a touch of exasperation, landlords remained indifferent to all warnings until after problems with their tenants had arisen, by which time it was usually too late to prevent the formation of tenant unions.[125]

The recommendations made to landlords by bureaucrats had been predicated on the assumption that landlords would rally to the cause of village and social harmony, that is, that landlords were reliable agents of state policy who would transcend private interests to work for the common good. Given evidence that landlords had a considerably less disinterested sense of vocation, bureaucrats began to realize that the countryside itself, not just external influences upon it, required their attention.

The first manifestation of this realization was the tenancy conciliation law of 1924. Instead of relying on landlords and local *nōkai*, the government established new machinery, under the direct control of the bureaucracy, to resolve tenancy disputes.[126] Next, in 1925, bureaucrats proposed, and the Diet enacted, regulations to promote the establishment of owner-cultivators; low-interest loans were made available to tenants to enable them to buy the land they cultivated, in what amounted to an attempt, however inadequately funded, to prevent tenants from joining unions or to encourage union members to resign.[127] The industrial association law (*sangyō kumiai hō*) of 1900, which despite its name had a greater impact on farming than on factories, was revised to make it easier for communities to establish consumer cooperatives for the purchase of basic necessities. Finally, in 1939, as the nation mobilized for war, bureaucrats were able to overcome the objections of landed interests in the Diet and secure passage of a law to establish fair rents (*tekisei kosakuryō*); a ceiling of one *koku* per *tan* in rent was imposed on top-grade land, with rents on lesser grades of land to be determined accordingly. Both landlords and tenants were to participate in determining rent levels.[128]

Implicit in these measures was the acknowledgement by bureaucrats that tenant unions, although unacceptable as organizations, had served legitimate needs among tenant farmers. To eradicate unions those needs had to be met in some other way. This was as close to equity as tenants were able to get until the postwar land reform.

Notes

1 Kenneth Pyle, 'The Technology of Japanese Nationalism,' *Journal of Asian Studies*, 33 (November 1973), 58–60, 65; Fukutake Tadashi, *Japanese Rural Society*, trans. Ronald Dore (Tokyo, 1967), pp. 169–70.
2 As I will discuss later, bureaucrats believed in early Taishō that landlords acted on behalf of rural society as a whole. Not until the 1920s did they begin to perceive that landlords, too, had class interests that landlord unions (*jinushi kumiai*) were designed to protect.
3 Data on unions and union membership appear in Nōchi seido shiryō hensan iinkai, *Nōchi seido shiryō shūsei* (Tokyo, 1969), 3: 514, 524 (hereafter cited as NSSS). Data on the number of tenant households appear in annual editions of *Teikoku tōkei nenkan*.
4 NSSS, p. 514.
5 Richard Smethurst, for example, observes that 'Farmers' unions at the peak of their organizational activity enrolled only a *minuscule* segment of the nation's tenants' (emphasis added): *A Social Basis for Prewar Japanese Militarism* (Berkeley and Los Angeles: University of California Press, 1974), p. 146. I do not agree that the segment was minuscule, but in the absence of agreed-upon standards for evaluating levels of popular unrest I can only assert my opinion. I think that a more fruitful approach to evaluating Japanese tenant unions is suggested by Henry A. Landsberger in his essay on 'The Role of Peasant Movements and Revolts in Development: An Analytical Framework,' *I.L.R. Reprint Series*, No. 236 (Ithaca, 1968), in which emphasis is placed on the characteristics, not the quantity of protest. I have found Landsberger's framework very helpful in my research.
6 '*Yonaoshi* in Aizu,' in *Conflict in Modern Japanese History: The Neglected Tradition*, ed. T. Najita and J.V. Koschmann (Princeton: Princeton University Press, 1982), pp. 164–76.
7 For a brief discussion of tenant protest before the 1920s see Ann Waswo, *Japanese Landlords: The Decline of a Rural Elite* (Berkeley and Los Angeles: University of California Press, 1977), pp. 21–3; Irwin Scheiner, 'The Mindful Peasant: Sketches for a Study of Rebellion,' *Journal of Asian Studies*, 32 (August 1973), pp. 579–91.
8 Usually bylaws made no mention of a time limit for the union's existence, although in some cases a period of ten or twenty years was specified. See Nōshōmushō nōmukyoku, 'Honpō ni okeru nōgyō dantai ni kansuru chōsa (1924),' reprinted in NSSS, p. 31. Of the 4,650 unions in existence in 1932, 2,601 (56 percent) had been established prior to 1927 and 620 (13 percent) has been established prior to 1922; NSSS, p. 516.
9 They also employed a variety of new means, which I will discuss at a later point. For a detailed explication of protest methods, both old and new, see Mori Kiichi, *Kosaku sōgi senjutsu* (Tokyo, 1928).
10 See Vlastos, '*Yonaoshi* in Aizu.'

11 The Ministry of Agriculture undertook its first general survey of tenant unions in cooperation with the Imperial Agricultural Association in 1916. In 1920 it began making its own surveys, although it relied on quantitative data on unions compiled by the Home Ministry until 1925. Until 1922 the Home Ministry was also the sole source of quantitative data on tenancy disputes. Thereafter the Ministry of Agriculture kept its own tabulations, consistently reporting substantially more disputes than did the Home Ministry, just as, after 1925, it consistently reported a slightly greater number of tenant unions. No satisfactory explanation for the discrepancies between the data reported by these two ministries has yet been uncovered. Conversation with Nishida Yoshiaki, Tokyo University. See also Nōmin undōshi kenkyūkai, *Nihon nōmin undōshi* (Tokyo, 1961), pp. 665, 672, 685, 883 (hereafter cited as NNUS).

12 Calculated from data in Nōrinshō nōmukyoku, 'Jinushi kosakunin kumiai ni kansuru chōsa (1926),' reprinted in NSSS, pp. 54, 59–63.

13 'Honpō ni okeru nōgyō dantai,' NSSS, pp. 30–1. In some cases membership was open to owner-cultivators as well, or to nonfarmers approved by the membership as a whole. Less frequently membership was restricted to individuals who tenanted at least a specified area of land (such as 2 *tan*) or to those of 'good character' (*hinkō hōsei naru mono*) only. 10 *tan* = 1 *chō* = 2.5 acres.

14 NSSS, p. 520. It is possible that bureaucrats used the term *ōaza* to describe hamlets (*buraku*) that were not officially part of the administrative structure of the countryside.

15 'Honpō ni okeru nōgyō dantai,' NSSS, pp. 31–2.

16 Ibid., p. 32.

17 Nōshōmushō nōmukyoku, 'Kosaku kumiai ni kansuru chōsa (1921),' reprinted in NSSS, p. 599; Takahashi Iichirō and Shirakawa Kiyoshi, eds., *Nōchi kaikaku to jinushi sei* (Tokyo, 1955), p. 101. For examples of union leaders, see Hayashi Yūichi, 'Shoki kosaku sōgi no tenkai to Taishōki nōson seiji jōkyō no ichi kōsatsu,' *Rekishigaku kenkyū*, No. 442 (March 1977), pp. 1–16; Suzuki Masayuki, 'Nichi-Ro sengo no nōson mondai no tenkai,' *Rekishigaku kenkyū* (1974 special issue), pp. 150–61.

18 'Kosaku sōgi ni kansuru chōsa (1921),' NSSS, p. 600. 100 *sen* = 1 yen.

19 'Honpō ni okeru nōgyō dantai,' NSSS, pp. 32–3.

20 Ibid., p. 26; Nōrinshō nōmukyoku, *Jinushi kosakunin kumiai kiyaku jirei* (Tokyo, 1926), p. 1. The latter report contains many examples of union bylaws. For a 'representative' sample, incorporating all of the most common features found in bylaws, see Nōshōmushō nōmukyoku, *Kosaku sōgi ni kansuru chōsa*, 1 (Tokyo, 1922), 211–17.

21 Unless otherwise noted, the source of the following description of union activities is 'Honpō ni okeru nōgyō dantai,' NSSS, pp. 33–5.

22 Tenants who violated these stipulations generally were subject to fines or ostracism.

23 For a discussion of rice inspection, see Waswo, *Japanese Landlords*, pp. 42–56. To compensate landlords for the loss or soilage of rent rice during transit and storage, tenants in many parts of the country had long been required to pay an extra measure of rice (known variously as *sashimai*, *komimai*, *kanmai*, etc.) per bale of rent. In late Meiji, many landlords began requiring

that tenants use double-layer bales for rent payments instead of the single-layer bales that had been employed in the past. Tenant objections to these requirements will be discussed at a later point.

24 See also Mori, *Kosaku sōgi senjutsu*, pp. 32–56; *Jinushi kosakunin kumiai kiyaku jirei*, pp. 2–4.

25 Unions also advocated educational reforms and the abolition of 'oppressive' taxes; *Jinushi kosakunin kumiai kiyaku jirei*, p. 4.

26 See, for example, 'Honpō ni okeru nōgyō dantai,' NSSS, pp. 21, 24. Bureaucrats later cited the victory of the British Labour party as a cause of increasing political activity by unions; 'Jinushi kosakunin kumiai ni kansure chōsa,' NSSS, p. 54.

27 Quoted in Kawamura Nozomu, 'Kosaku sōgiki ni okeru sonraku taisei,' *Sonraku shakai kenkyū nenpō*, No. 7 (Tokyo, 1960), p. 108.

28 Fukutake, *Japanese Rural Society*, pp. 86, 133, 214; George M. Foster, 'Interpersonal Relations in Peasant Society,' *Human Organization*, 19 (1960–61), 174–8.

29 Three excellent case studies by Nishida Yoshiaki, two concerning a district in Niigata Prefecture and one a village in Yamanashi Prefecture, examine this issue in detail: 'Shōnō keiei no hatten to kosaku sōgi,' *Tochi seido shigaku*, No. 38 (1968), pp. 24–41; 'Kosaku sōgi no tenkai,' in *Meiji Taishō kyōdoshi kenkyū hō*, ed. by Furushima Toshio *et al.* (Tokyo, 1970), pp. 346–69; and 'Kosaku sōgi no tenkai to jisakunō sōsetsu iji seisaku,' *Hitotsubashi ronsō*, 60 (1968), 524–46.

30 Nishida, 'Shōnō keiei,' p. 25.

31 Ushiyama Keiji, *Nōminsō bunkai no kōzō, senzenki: Niigata ken Kambara nōson no bunseki* (Tokyo, 1970), pp. 100–1. The author presents a detailed discussion of unions in 'headless' communities on pp. 97–103; the problems faced by unions in communities with landlords in residence are discussed on pp. 130–8. For a general discussion of absentee landlords and the effects of absenteeism on landlord–tenant relations, see Waswo, *Japanese Landlords*, pp. 81–93.

32 Bureaucrats observed in 1924 that the involvement of unions in cooperative activities was 'something to note,' but they made no further comment on the subject. 'Honpō ni okeru nōgyō dantai,' NSSS, p. 35. As I will discuss later, I think bureaucrats were slowly becoming aware that the breakdown of other institutions designed to meet farmers' needs had contributed to the growth of tenant unions.

33 Tenants in a given community did not have to experience every step of this process themselves, but could profit from the example of tenants in neighboring communities. For discussion of the ways in which tenants could and/or did discover the utility of unions on their own, see Ushiyama, *Nōminsō bunkai*, pp. 109–13; Takahashi and Shirakawa, *Nōchi kaikaku to jinushi sei*, pp. 86–9; Mori, *Kosaku sōgi senjutsu*, pp. 4–5, 54.

34 Examples appear in George O. Totten, 'Labor and Agrarian Disputes in Japan Following World War I,' *Economic Development and Cultural Change*, 9, part 2 (October 1960), 204; NNUS, pp. 890–902. See also the discussion that follows on the tenant movement in Iwami.

35 Ushiyama, *Nōminsō bunkai*, pp. 111–12, 120–23; Suzuki, *Nichi-Ro sengo no nōson mon*dai,' pp. 150–61. See also the discussion that follows on the union movement in Izumo.

36 That the case study I am about to present is typical in any statistical sense of developments in Japan as a whole is highly unlikely. I have selected it primarily because it is well-documented, enabling one to penetrate the anonymity that surrounds the subject of tenant protest and get some idea of the issues as tenants and their leaders perceived them. For a justification of the case study method, not as a basis for generalizing about the whole of a phenomenon but as a laboratory for examining social processes that affect all constituent parts to one degree or another, see Maurice R. Stein, *The Eclipse of Community: An Interpretation of American Studies* (Princeton: Princeton University Press, 1960), pp. 94–113.

37 Compiled from data in Shimane ken nōrinbu, nōchi kaikaku ka, *Shimane ken nōchi kaikaku shi* (Hirata, 1959), pp. 104, 106–8 (hereafter cited as SKNKS). Data on the number of tenant households are from *Shimane ken tōkeisho*, 1922 (Matsue, 1923), p. 7.

38 'Yamasaki Memo,' quoted in Yoshioka Yoshinori, 'Shimane ken nōmin undōshi,' NNUS, p. 818.

39 'Taishō Shōwa nōmin undō ni kansuru zadankai' (hereafter cited as 'Zadankai'), in SKNKS, pp. 316–17. Tenant union leaders in Nōgi and Yatsuka *gun* took part in two separate symposia in 1956, of which this is the transcript. Bylaws of two early tenant unions in Shimane, one established in 1898 and the other in 1902, appear in SKNKS, pp. 118–20, nn. 11, 12.

40 'Yamasaki Memo,' NNUS, p. 818.

41 Ibid., pp. 818–19.

42 Nōshōmushō nōmukyoku, *Kosaku sōgi ni kansuru chōsa*, 2 (Tokyo, 1922), 344; SKNKS, pp. 123–5, 130–3 n. 7.

43 *Kosaku sōgi ni kansuru chōsa*, 2, pp. 344, 339; 'Yamasaki Memo,' NNUS, pp. 818–19. Faced with the prospect of having to pay rents in rice of at least third-class quality (or pay a penalty in rice), tenants in a village in neighboring Tottori prefecture protested that 60 percent of the rice they grew was of fourth-class quality; SKNKS, pp. 123–4. For data of a similar sort from Gifu prefecture, see NNUS, p. 651.

44 *Kosaku sōgi ni kansuru chōsa*, 2, pp. 341, 342. Another objection was that the area of fields was now measured accurately, depriving tenants of the 'slack' they had enjoyed in the past; ibid., p. 349.

45 SKNKS, pp. 113, 121 n. 14.

46 *Kosaku sōgi ni kansuru chōsa*, 2, pp. 344, 347–53.

47 See the general discussion of these points in Landsberger, 'The Role of Peasant Movements and Revolts,' pp. 72–5.

48 Itō Kikunosuke, ed., *Shimane ken jinmei jiten* (Matsue, 1970), p. 267; 'Zadankai,' SKNKS, p. 325. Yamasaki died in 1964. Portions of what follows are based on autograph letters written in the late 1950s by Yamasaki to Yoshioka Yoshinori. To distinguish between the unpublished and published portions of the letters, which I will also be referring to below, I will cite the former as 'Yamasaki MS' and the latter as 'Yamasaki Memo,' NNUS. I owe thanks to Mr. Yoshioka for allowing me to photocopy the letters.

49 'Yamasaki MS'; 'Zadankai,' SKNKS, p. 325.
50 'Yamasaki MS'; 'Zadankai,' SKNKS, pp. 325–6.
51 Vetch, used as cattle fodder, a diuretic, and an antipyretic, was a major secondary crop in Izumo.
52 'Yamasaki MS'; 'Zadankai,' SKNKS, p. 326.
53 Ibid., p. 317; Yoshioka, NNUS, p. 816.
54 Ibid., p. 815; 'Zadankai,' SKNKS, p. 317.
55 Yoshioka, NNUS, p. 816.
56 'Yamasaki MS.'
57 'Yamasaki Memo,' NNUS, p. 816.
58 'Yamasaki MS.'
59 Yamasaki's testimony before the Kosaku Chōsakai, to be discussed later, as reported in *Kosakunin*, October 10, 1926, p. 3.
60 Yoshioka, NNUS, p. 817; SKNKS, pp. 153, 228.
61 'Yamasaki Memo,' NNUS, pp. 817–18.
62 Ibid., p. 817.
63 'Zadankai,' SKNKS, pp. 320, 325. Yamasaki described the establishment of the Nōgi federation as a 'revolt of youth against age.' 'Yamasaki MS.' Another characteristic leaders had in common, which can be inferred from these examples, was an above-average level of literacy.
64 SKNKS, p. 192 n. 2. The proclamation of the Tenant Federation of Yatsuka District, which does not refer explicitly to the emperor, appears ibid., pp. 200–3.
65 'Zadankai,' SKNKS, p. 324. For examples of subsequent scholarly opinion, see Hayashi, 'Shoki kosaku sōgi no tenkai,' especially p. 5; Yoshioka, NNUS, p. 821. Profiles of Yokota and Sugai appear ibid., pp. 1157–62.
66 'Zadankai,' SKNKS, p. 324. For the first issue Terada composed the slogan, 'Until the light shines brightly on the countryside.' Beneath it appeared a crude drawing of 'tenant farmers pushing the globe toward a bright future.' I think the symbolism here is significant: tenant farmers were to achieve their goal by their *own* actions.
67 'Yamasaki Memo,' NNUS, p. 819. Each issue sold for one *sen*; a year's subscription, including postage, cost 50 *sen*. Issues for February through December 1926 are on file at Hōsei daigaku Ōhara shakai mondai kenkyūjo, Tokyo.
68 *Kosakunin*, February 10, 1926, p. 6.
69 Polite verb forms were used in articles addressed to women; see, for example, *Kosakunin*, July 10, 1926, p. 3.
70 *Kosakunin*, February 10, 1926, p. 6. Among other contributions from readers was a rice-planting (*taue*) song composed by the women's association of a hamlet in Araijima village entitled 'Landlords' Punishment.' In rough translation: 'Landlords get rich and fat by squeezing tenants/Then Heaven punishes them with illness/They waste their money on fancy doctors/But that won't cure them/They should try being kind to their tenants instead.' *Kosakunin*, June 10, 1926, p. 1.
71 *Kosakunin*, June 10, 1926, p. 3.
72 '[It] can be done before breakfast'; *Kosakunin*, March 10, 1926, p. 4.
73 *Kosakunin*, May 10, 1926, p. 1.

74 *Kosakunin*, March 10, 1926, p. 1.
75 *Kosakunin*, June 10, 1926, p. 1. What I have rendered in translation as 'idle landlords' was expressed in the original as *norari kurari to asonde kurashite iru* landlords, not as *kiseiteki* (parasitic) landlords. The latter, more abstract term was popular among contemporary leftists but was avoided by Yamasaki.
76 *Kosakunin*, March 10, 1926, p. 3.
77 *Kosakunin*, March 10, 1926, p. 2.
78 *Kosakunin*, April 10, 1926, p. 3.
79 'Yamasaki Memo,' NNUS, p. 819.
80 'Kōsei naru kosakuryō,' published in 1924 in the journal *Kaizō*.
81 'Zadankai,' SKNKS, p. 325; 'Yamasaki Memo,' NNUS, p. 819; 10 *to* = 1 *koku* = 5.1 bushels (US dry measure).
82 'Yamasaki Memo,' NNUS, p. 819; see SKNKS, pp. 169–74 for examples of these accounts.
83 'Zadankai,' SKNKS, p. 335. Yamasaki regarded Nichinō's advocacy of 30 percent rent reductions on all tenanted land as 'unrealistically mechanical'; ibid., p. 323.
84 'Yamasaki Memo,' NNUS, pp. 831–2. For a description of a difficult case, see 'Zadankai,' SKNKS, pp. 336–7.
85 The federation retained a lawyer, but according to Yamasaki gave him more business than money; ibid., p. 327. Training courses and workshops are discussed ibid., p. 323; Yoshioka, NNUS, pp. 825, 826.
86 'Zadankai,' SKNKS, pp. 323, 329–30. Yamasaki observed that some landlords, receiving a court summons for the first time in their lives as a result of action taken by their tenants, felt that 'the world had been turned upside down.'
87 Ibid., p. 332. See also Mori, *Kosaku sōgi senjutsu*, pp. 77–104.
88 'Zadankai,' SKNKS, p. 327. No tenant looked forward to crop failure, but the utility of a minor decline in yields in pressing for concessions was widely recognized enough to be proverbial: *kosaku ni wa fusaku no hō ga toku datta* (in tenancy poor harvests pay off); quoted in Takahashi and Shirakawa, *Nōchi kaikaku to jinushi sei*, p. 97. I think this attitude helps to explain why poor harvests were reported as the major cause of disputes in the 1920s. When yields declined, tenants had grounds to seek improvement in the terms of tenancy. Opportunity, not desperation, motivated their actions.
89 'Zadankai,' SKNKS, pp. 323, 327. Yamasaki was not the only tenant leader to perceive advantages in the conciliation law. A union official in Niigata observed; 'Conciliation is like [the game of] pole-pushing. The side with patience and strength in reserve wins. It's the side that can make the last strong push after a lot of feints that gets the victory'; quoted in Mori, *Kosaku sōgi senjutsu*, p. 103.
90 SKNKS, p. 176 n. 11.
91 *Kosakunin*, June 10, 1926, p. 3.
92 *Kosakunin*, December 10, 1926, p. 1 of special section. Apparently many of the cooperatives that were established in 1926 went bankrupt within a few years; SKNKS, p. 222.
93 *Kosakunin*, July 10, 1926, p. 3 and June 10, 1926, p. 3. The June article emphasized the spontaneous (*jihatsuteki*) nature of the undertaking: 'It is not

like other efforts at cooperative farming that only exist on paper and whose leaders devote their time to getting money from the government.'

94 For an example of how tenants won such voting rights, see Kawamura, 'Kosaku sōgiki ni okeru sonraku taisei,' pp. 119–26.

95 Nōrinshō nōmukyoku, 'Taishō jūyon nendo chōsonkai giin kaisen ni okeru kosakunin gawa jōsei ni kansuru chōsa,' reprinted in NSSS, pp. 68, 70 and 72 (tables 1, 3, and 5). Tenants previously had occupied a total of 3,669 village assembly seats out of 42,738; ibid., pp. 71, 73 (tables 4, 6).

96 Ibid., pp. 68–73 (tables 1, 3, 4, 5, and 6). As in Shimane, 86 percent of the tenants elected to village assemblies in 1925 had 'no connection' with tenant unions; ibid., p. 70 (table 3). Why more tenant union members did not run for or succeed in obtaining village assembly seats throughout Japan is an interesting question that merits further study.

97 *Kosakunin*, February 10, 1926, pp. 1, 2. Recommendations for tax reform included the elimination of taxes on bicycles and carts, items that many tenants possessed, and the imposition of taxes on such 'luxuries' as gardens, villas, and concubines. Chief among the educational improvements called for was the creation of more lower-level agricultural continuation schools to benefit the children of tenant farmers.

98 SKNKS, p. 220.

99 *Kosakunin*, May 10, 1926, p. 3.

100 Ibid.

101 Yoshioka, NNUS, pp. 820, 830–1.

102 Ibid., pp. 827–9. Toyowara returned to Tokyo in June 1927. Ogawa moved to Osaka to work in Nichinō headquarters at the end of that year; ibid., p. 832.

103 Ibid., pp. 837–8.

104 Ibid. pp. 833–6, 839–42.

105 Ibid., pp. 842–3.

106 'Yamasaki Memo,' NNUS, p. 838.

107 Ibid., p. 832.

108 Yoshioka, NNUS, pp. 844–46.

109 Summaries of their remarks, and the remarks of other witnesses, most of them landlords, appear in 'Kosaku chōsakai tokubetsu iinkai gijiroku,' in NSSS, Supplement II, 157–257.

110 Since no complete transcript of his remarks exists, what follows is based on the summary, ibid., pp. 217–20, and on his report of his testimony as published in *Kosakunin*, October 10, 1926, p. 3.

111 'Kosaku chōsakai gijiroku,' p. 220; *Kosakunin*, October 10, 1926, p. 3.

112 Bernard Silberman, 'The Bureaucratic State in Japan: The Problem of Authority and Legitimacy,' pp. 242–6. In *Conflict in Modern Japanese History*, ed. T. Najita and J.V. Koschmann (Princeton: Princeton University Press, 1982).

113 'Zadankai,' SKNKS, p. 326.

114 The above examples are from Gifu prefecture, as reported in NNUS, pp. 669–70, 689, 690–1.

115 The complete text of these regulations, revised in November 1924, appears in SKNKS, pp. 177–8 n. 13.

116 Mori, *Kosaku sōgi senjutsu*, pp. 44–7.
117 For an example, see NNUS, p. 530.
118 Ibid., pp. 663, 667, 669–70.
119 Mori, *Kosaku sōgi senjutsu*, pp. 9, 13–18, 64.
120 Yamamoto's remarks are quoted in Hayashi, 'Shoki kosaku sōgi no tenkai,' p. 15.
121 Yoshioka, NNUS, p. 846.
122 Ibid., p. 830; 'Zadankai,' SKNKS, pp. 334, 336–8.
123 Hayashi, 'Shoki kosaku sōgi no tenkai,' pp. 3, 10. Yamasaki believed that conciliation associations posed a serious threat to the tenant movement and criticized them at every opportunity.
124 Data on the number and membership of conciliation associations appear in NSSS, pp. 540–1, 550–1. In 1929 there were 1,986 conciliation associations (less than half the number of tenant unions) with a total membership of 244,943 (77.6 percent of the membership of tenant unions). Not until 1936 were there more members of conciliation associations than there were members of tenant unions.
125 *Kosaku sōgi ni kansuru chōsa*, 2, p. 347.
126 Ogura Takekazu, *Tochi rippō no shiteki kōsatsu* (Tokyo, 1951), pp. 395–425.
127 For a discussion of the impact of these loans, see Nishida, 'Kosaku sōgi no tenkai,' pp. 537–40.
128 'Zadankai,' SKNKS, pp. 334, 335–6; Ogura, *Tochi rippō*, pp. 720–32.

6 Building the model village

Rural revitalization and the Great Depression

Kerry Smith

Introduction

It must be almost second nature by now to view rural Japan as perched on the brink of disaster. The list of economic crises, social ills and ecological calamities that have afflicted farming communities is a long one. From the start of the modern era, as this volume certainly helps illustrate, towns and villages throughout Japan were subject to a series of difficult transitions, from the sharp shocks of the Matsukata Deflation of the early 1880s to the subtler challenges of industrial capitalism and the rise of the nation's cities. The increased visibility of tenancy and tenant movements around the time of the First World War highlighted growing divisions of wealth and power within villages, and between commercially successful regions and those less able to break old habits. Joined to these economic problems was a series of programs and policies designed by the state to protect farmers and their communities. The introduction of industrial cooperatives and agricultural associations, local improvement in its various forms and tenancy conciliation laws all grew out of elite and bureaucratic concerns over the fate of the countryside. That even the postwar land reform and farm subsidies can be understood as part of the ongoing attempt to address gaps between agriculture and industry, and between changing agricultural technologies and static landholdings, speaks to the intransigence of the problems facing Japan's farmers.

This seemingly permanent crisis in farming masks the extent to which the 1930s and the war years reflect a new set of circumstances for rural Japanese. What this chapter and the two that follow will do is explore some of the ways the Great Depression and the Second World War transformed rural communities. Together they suggest that local and national responses to the era's crises marked important departures from past practices, and helped set the stage for the post-surrender reconstruction of the countryside and agriculture. One such departure, for example, was the new emphasis on emigration as both a solution to the 'farm village problem' and as an element of national policy. The connections between social stability, the idealized farm village, and Japan's imperial aspirations had never been so clearly drawn as they were in the aftermath of the 1931 Manchurian Incident. Japan's deepening involvement in China after 1937 led to even grander roles for colonist-farmers. The chapters by Wilson and Mori examine the implications and realities of emigration policies in the 1930s and 1940s, and suggest how significant these developments were to the nation's conception of the countryside, and rural citizens' sense of their place in the nation. The repercussions of these policies would extend well beyond the emigrant community itself.

Imagining what a fresh start in Manchuria or Korea might look like was one facet of a broader effort to improve rural life in the 1930s. The multiple crises at the start of the decade highlighted how much the countryside had already been changed by years of economic hard times and demographic shifts. Local leaders and state officials had to scramble to replace old models of social stability with new and more resilient ones. In mid-1932, these multiple models coalesced into a single framework for rural reform. From that summer until 1941, the Farm, Mountain and Fishing Village Economic Revitalization Campaign, or Nōsangyoson keizai kōsei undō, provided a national template for local efforts to respond to the Great Depression. Almost four-fifths of Japan's villages participated in the campaign at some point, and although the degree to which residents embraced its methods and rhetoric could vary from place to place and year to year, themes and experiences common to many communities are not hard to identify. This chapter explores the campaign's impact and its implications for our understanding of rural Japan (see Smith 2001 for an extended analysis of these issues). That exploration begins with an overview of the circumstances unique to the crises of the 1930s.

Hard times

Otoyo:	Has it really been five years?
Yōsuke:	And another five years to go. Just a little longer now . . .
Shūsaku:	(A little angrily) You say 'five years' like it was nothing. That was no ordinary five years!
Yōsuke:	Well, I guess it was the same all over. Still, you must be feeling a little better about your situation by now, right?
Otoyo:	(Nodding) Our debt has been reduced by half . . .

Shūsaku: And yet think of the difficulties our family had to go through to get to this point. (Looking down at his hands and feet.) I wonder if we'll be able to keep this up for another five years . . .

(Nukada and Takagi 1936: 67).

It might be hard to imagine busy men and women taking the time to stage this play for their fellow farmers, but at least some villagers did (see Figure 6.1) and it is easy to see why the editors of the magazine *Ie no hikari* urged them to do so. The drama is set in a generic rural village in the mid-1930s; the earliest dialogue, some of which is excerpted above, explains to readers that, at the time of the events depicted in this scene, the deeply impoverished family was only halfway through a ten-year plan to restore the family's finances, pay back its substantial debt, and diversify its crop holdings. Mother, father and their two sons describe the depths to which the family has sunk since the start of the depression, and reveal that their sole hope for revival lies in the continued pursuit of the aforementioned recovery plan. Both the struggle already endured and the hard work ahead are held up as difficult but necessary steps toward better times.

The tension in the play is not over whether to honor the family's obligations, but over how to do so, and under whose leadership. The father's conservative approach to coping with the depression's effects is challenged by his sons. The eldest calls for radical reforms of how they go about the business of farming; his younger brother privately contemplates abandoning the farm altogether. To further complicate matters, the daughter of one of the village's absentee landlords drops in from the city for a series of encounters with the brothers, during which she openly expresses her contempt for their way of life. Why work so hard for so little, she asks, when the city beckons? The plot of 'Sandanbatake no kyōdai' ('The Brothers of the Three-*tan* Field'), such as it is, explores how the family eventually triumphs over these multiple challenges.

Readers no doubt found it edifying on several levels, not least because the play seemed to address many of the issues then confronting rural readers of magazines like *Ie no hikari.* The severity of the depression's effects, the apparent demise of rural communities, and the benefits of diligence and thoughtful responses in the face of both these crises were themes local leaders and magazine editors alike faced again and again in the 1930s. The play offers a useful starting point for a discussion of some of the more significant changes under way in rural life in the 1930s. Let me begin with the mechanics of the economic crisis itself.

Figure 6.1 A performance of the Economic Revitalization drama 'Sandanbatake no kyōdai' by members of the industrial cooperative in Osogi village (Nishitama *gun*, Tokyo).

Source: The photos originally appeared in *Ie no hikari* 12.4 (April 1936), p. 10.

Explaining why prices for farm products fell as fast and as far as they did during the Great Depression is reasonably straightforward; understanding how farmers' lives changed as a result much less so. Agriculture's primary economic problems in the 1930s were the product of three related developments. Wall Street's 1929 collapse pulled the rug out from under US consumer spending, and thus on purchases of imported Japanese silk. As prices for raw and processed silk plummeted, payments to rural cocoon producers eventually did the same, sharply reducing a key source of income for many of the nation's farmers. The same mechanism led to wage cuts and mass lay-offs in the nation's textile factories, which in good times employed large numbers of young women from rural communities.

A second development originated at home, but overlapped disastrously with the economic downturn abroad. The Minseitō party's return to power in 1929 was due in part to the new cabinet's promises to put the country back on the gold standard. Such a step would place Japan on an equal footing with the other advanced economies. Japan had joined them in leaving the standard during the First World War, but a series of financial problems (including the Great Kantō Earthquake of 1923) had prevented an equally timely return. The new Hamaguchi cabinet held out participation in the gold standard as a sign of international prestige and economic strength, and while noting that going back on the standard would almost certainly send the economy into a mild recession as Japanese exports became significantly more expensive on world markets, finance minister Inoue Junnosuke and others assured the nation that any such phenomenon would be short-lived. Brushing aside initial concerns about what was happening in the United States and Europe that autumn, the government and businesses alike began trimming budgets and staff in late 1929 in preparation for a January 1930 return to the gold standard. The effects of those intentional efforts to slow the domestic economy were soon amplified by the unanticipated impact of the Great Depression and a slowing world economy. Instead of the mild downturn politicians had promised and business leaders had prepared for, the nation was instead visited by unprecedented difficulties in almost every sector. The ranks of the newly unemployed swelled to include not just textile workers, but skilled laborers from heavy industry and laid-off white collar 'sarari-men.' Factory closings and the surreptitious flight of insolvent business owners were soon common enough events as to go almost unremarked.

A third and final factor affecting the economic well-being of the farmers was their own productivity. For years many had tried to offset the real and anticipated drop in commodity prices by raising even more of whatever it was they grew. A gradual increase in yields during the 1920s culminated in a record rice harvest in 1930. (Silk cocoon production had been similarly ramped up in the late 1920s and early 1930s.) Once the government announced its estimate of the size of that autumn's crop, rice prices, already on a downward slide paralleling that of other basic commodities, dropped even more precipitously. By early in 1931 a unit of rice was selling for about half as much as it had the year before – the average price of farm products in general fell by about 45 percent between 1929 and 1931. The countryside's willingness to kept the nation supplied with rice and other commodities even at those desperately low prices worked to the advantage of factory workers and other wage laborers, and helped fuel the relatively rapid recovery of the industrial sector from the grip of the depression. Rural communities had a much longer wait before they were able to realize the full benefits of their own hard work. Prices for rice and silk, and thus the income they generated for farmers, remained at pre-depression levels until long after the rest of the economy had turned around (Shimizu 1987: 156; Nakamura 1988: 307).

Lost income and low prices were of course serious matters for farmers, and the extent and persistence of these factors were part of what made this downturn different from others in recent memory. Yet they were just a part – the list of reasons the crises of the early Showa era mark a significant shift in the countryside's relationship with the rest of the nation is a long one. Demographic changes are certainly part of the picture, as the growth of the nation's urban centers in the 1920s and 1930s went unmatched by rural communities. Only about one Japanese in eight lived in a community of more than 100,000 in 1930; by 1935, one in four did (Tasaki 1989: 179). A similar shift was under way in the economy, as the industrial sector gradually surpassed farming as the primary producer of the nation's wealth. Such trends were evident well before the depression struck, but the sharp shocks to the agricultural sector and the scrutiny of village life that followed highlighted the gaps between town and country in no uncertain terms.

Rural citizens were also better informed of these changes, and of their own vulnerabilities. The effects of the economic downturn and new avenues of public discourse reached the countryside almost simultaneously. By the time 'Sandanbatake no kyōdai' appeared in 1936, magazines like *Ie no hikari*, *Kingu* and others were assiduously cultivating rural audiences. *Ie no hikari* was one of the most widely read publications in the countryside. In its best years the magazine reached close to one in every three rural households. Circulation topped 200,000 in 1932, and broke the one million mark only three years later (Itagaki 1992: 54–6; Iwasaki 1976: 240, 244; Adachi 1973: 106). Print journals, film (attendance at movie theatres nationally rose by almost 60 percent between

1926 and 1934) and radio (heard by a million listeners in 1930) were a part of popular culture and rural life as never before (*Dai Nihon tōkei nenkan* 1930–36). Even a quick glance at the format of media directed at the countryside suggests that it was meant to appeal to a broad audience of men and women, younger and more mature readers alike. Special sections for children, forums, and topical articles intended for wives and mothers were increasingly common features in these mass-market publications. Editors responded to what was a very real demand for material directed toward, and useful to, rural citizens, and sustained high levels of engagement with them throughout the 1930s. Consumers of the new media responded enthusiastically as well; letters to the editor, essays submitted by local authors, and a constant series of roundtable discussions were only some of the public forums available to rural readers to express their points of view.

The rural depression was thus very much a part of the emergent public spectacle of the 1930s, one which included the military's exploits on the mainland, an ongoing fascination with the possibilities of urban decadence, and political terrorism. The involvement of farmers and agrarianist groups in acts of terrorism in the early 1930s marks another break with past practices and patterns. Such political violence highlighted the sense of desperation many rural Japanese felt, and heightened both the public's and the state's awareness of the countryside's volatility (Vlastos 1998). Farmers' associations whose activities normally revolved around scheduling contests to determine the best locally-produced fertilizer were in 1931 and 1932 moving in new directions, developing their own responses to the depression and demanding that the state do more to help. These demands were often couched in language that spoke of the government's abandonment of the countryside, and of the harm that would befall the nation should such neglect persist. It mattered too that farmers were not the only ones making such claims. Young officers and other critics of the state's policies connected rural impoverishment at home with threats to Japan's international standing, and especially to its new and vital interest in Manchuria. The early 1930s' juxtaposition of economic, diplomatic, and political crises was unprecedented. That the countryside was deeply implicated in each of them speaks to the new circumstances confronting farm families and rural communities.

Saving the family farm

Serious efforts to respond to the rural crises did not take shape until almost three years after the depression began. The return to power of the fiscally promiscuous Seiyūkai in late 1931, the involvement of farmers in the violence surrounding Prime Minister Inukai's assassination on May 15, 1932, and the Diet session scheduled for June set the stage for some sort of action by the state. Further pressure was brought to bear by a motley assortment of activists, rural radicals, and stodgy spokesmen for established rural elites. Using a combination of old-fashioned petition campaigns and media-savvy lobbying efforts, these groups depicted the miserable state of the countryside in considerable color. A sympathetic public expressed dismay at reports of impoverished families and malnourished children – ignoring or simply ignorant of the fact that the depression had greatly exacerbated, but not created, such conditions – as similar concerns were eventually voiced in the Diet as well. Though June's legislative session produced little in the way of concrete policies, it did end with a solemn promise that another, extraordinary, session would be convened later that summer, one devoted to helping farm and fishing communities. Lobbyists, politicians, and bureaucrats immediately went to work defining the scope and focus of the promised rural relief.

By the time the 63rd Diet convened in August, the premises behind the state's efforts to rescue the countryside were clear. Relief would come in three parts. The legislature tacitly acknowledged the severity of the economic problems then facing farm, fishing, and other rural communities by offering first a substantial package of short-term direct aid, mostly in the form of public works projects. The proposed budget for these projects topped 800 million yen, far larger than any prior allocations to the countryside for a similar purpose. News of the Diet's largesse was balanced by the knowledge that the spending would neither continue for very long, nor reach every needy family. The Home Ministry and the Ministry of Agriculture and Forestry, through which most of the public works funding would flow, stressed that such levels of spending were temporary – three years was the longest anyone would commit to. Similarly, they argued that this form of 'emergency relief' was only supposed to supplement diminished rural income by providing ready cash in exchange for work on small-scale, labor-intensive, and local public works projects. Ditch-digging, road repair, and the like were imagined, not the construction of new infrastructure on the scale of the emerging New Deal in the United States. There were no handouts, and no guarantees that work on the projects would provide farmers and their families with enough money to get by. Still, it was hard to argue with the observation that 800 million yen was a significant improvement over the paltry sums available up to that point, and the works projects were a tried-and-true response most localities could adapt to with ease (Miwa 1979; Yasutomi 1994).

Rural relief's second tier focused on debt. Before the depression, anecdotal evidence and the few limited surveys that were conducted suggested that many farmers had accumulated large debt burdens over the course of the 1920s, as they borrowed to pay for farming inputs, household expenses, and medical emergencies. The realities of credit often meant that these funds were obtained at very high rates of interest from private lenders, the sort of low-interest loans offered by banks and some government institutions being unavailable to the typical farmer. Borrowing in one form or another was very much a part of community life, and was both quite common and necessary for the day-to-day functioning of the family farm. The depression introduced a new set of circumstances, however, in that what might have been a manageable debt burden while commodity prices were at 'normal' levels quickly became something else entirely after 1929. Because the cost of most inputs for farming (fertilizer, seeds, and so on) also declined, on paper it can be made to appear as if income and spending achieved a rough equilibrium soon after the depression began. The addition of debt to the equation suggests just how uncommon such an outcome would have been for a typical farmer. Unable to keep up payments on the loans they already had, and often without access to any alternative sources of funding, farmers across Japan ran the risk of losing their property and other collateral to their creditors. Some farmers kept up a constant cycle of borrowing from one source to pay back another, while others tried to curtail spending on all but the barest essentials just to keep making payments on what they owed.

Such practices could not go on forever, however, and by 1932 increasingly frantic calls for help from farmers' associations and rural activists pushed the government to take a closer look at the problem. A well-organized and highly publicized petition campaign for a moratorium on farm debt, run by an ad hoc collection of agrarianists (most of whom had not been directly implicated in 1932's violence), was clearly a major impetus behind the state's willingness to act. The petition campaigns had a broad appeal, and sparked a flood of similarly intentioned delegations of farmers and local leaders into Tokyo that summer. They brought with them both detailed descriptions of local hardship and their proposals for dealing with the crises in the countryside; some form of policy dealing with debt was inevitably near the top of their lists.

One of the first developments to flow out of the campaigns for relief was an effort to quantify the depression's impact on all aspects of farming, but especially rural debt. Ministry of Agriculture and Forestry surveys, together with those generated by prefectural officials, revealed that farmers were carrying a staggering debt burden. The fictional family depicted in 'Sandanbatake no kyōdai,' for example, had worked for five years to cut their 5,000-yen debt in half. Such a heavy burden for a single household would have been unusual but not unheard of. Rural debt nationally in 1932 was estimated at roughly twice the value of all farm production that year. Individual families in many instances were thought to owe between two and three times their annual incomes. While local variations produced even greater gaps between what farmers earned and what they owed, it was clear that the phenomenon was a national one (Teruoka 1984: 79–80). Loans cut two ways; at interest rates that could approach 20 percent, borrowers could easily find themselves turning over most of their already depressed income to creditors, while lenders, many of them local farmers and small businessmen, faced financial ruin if their loans proved unrecoverable. The combination of rock-bottom prices, crushing debt, and a widespread sense of long-term vulnerability were new economic realities for the countryside. 'Sandanbatake no kyōdai' and works like it described circumstances that were all too familiar to rural readers.

The government's response to these circumstances was informed both by a recognition that rural debt was a real issue for many families, and an understanding by bureaucrats and politicians that neither a debt moratorium nor any significant debt forgiveness was likely to win legislative approval. In their place the Ministry of Agriculture and Forestry assembled a collection of legal reforms and institutional incentives designed to channel additional low-interest credit into the countryside. Many existing village- and hamlet-level farmers' organizations were given new opportunities to apply for low-interest loans, and thus bail out at least some of their members. In addition, the Diet authorized the creation of new local 'debt arrangement unions,' which would be formed for the express purpose of helping borrowers negotiate new terms of repayment with their creditors (Kase 1979). Note that the process of debt arrangement assumed at all times that existing loans would be repaid in time, and in full. The unions and the new funding that accompanied their creation at best bought time and lower interest rates for farmers, not a complete amnesty from debt.

Public works projects and debt adjustment were rural relief's two big-budget items in 1932. Together they represented a sharp break with past practice in terms of the scope of state spending on the countryside. The Ministry of Agriculture and Forestry's budget almost doubled between 1931 and 1932, and by 1934 was enjoying an allocation almost three times the size of its mid-1920s' funding. Much of that growth reflected new spending on public works and other efforts to channel money towards farming communities (Smith 2001: 139–45). It was the third and final element of the state and local response to the depression, however, that became the primary vehicle for a broader reconsideration of rural reform and recovery. The Farm, Mountain and Fishing Village Economic Revitalization Campaign, or Nōsangyoson keizai kōsei undō, took shape alongside public works and debt arrangement policies in the summer of 1932. The Ministry of Agriculture and Forestry, under whose control the campaign fell, needed little input from the legislature to make the campaign functional. Its budget requirements were minimal, for reasons described below, and the Ministry had the additional advantage of being able to adopt what was essentially a prefectural program of rural 'self-revitalization' to its own needs. The Hyōgo Prefecture Agricultural Association, assisted by the Imperial Agriculture Association, lobbied hard to have its approach to recovery from the depression taken up and given national application that summer.

That approach brought together what had been separate but not uncommon elements of existing rural reform programs into a single package. Building on practices that had been around since the Tokugawa era, for example, Hyōgo farmers had been encouraged to conduct thorough and uncompromising surveys of the state of their family and farm finances, beginning with each and every household and ending with a report that encompassed the entire community. With that data in hand, the next step was to construct an equally detailed recovery plan, one that outlined each family's efforts to boost income, cut back on expenditure, and diversify its production of crops, crafts, and fertilizer. Linked to these planning exercises was the creation of new village or improved village-level institutions – committees to oversee the development and implementation of local recovery plans, financially empowered cooperative unions and the like, all focused on the shared task of revitalizing the village economically, socially, and culturally.

Ministry of Agriculture and Forestry bureaucrats embraced what Hyōgo's activists had designed. It is not hard to see why. The Ministry's officials were well aware that similar campaigns had been publicized by the national agricultural association, and that many local branches of the same association had been receptive to them. That the campaign originated from outside the Ministry's offices was thus an asset on several levels; ministry bureaucrats would not have to design a campaign from scratch, they were guaranteed the support of the Agricultural Association, and, perhaps most importantly, an Economic Revitalization Campaign could be put in place at very low cost to the Ministry. The state's financial commitment to the campaign was limited at first to providing only very small amounts of seed money to a few towns and villages, distributing the paperwork necessary for planning, and publicizing the campaign's goals. Since the campaign by design placed the burden of surveying, planning and implementation on the communities themselves, the central government had only to oversee their efforts, not take an active or direct role in each and every locale. Unlike the public works programs and debt arrangement programs, which did represent a significant transfer of resources to the countryside, the Economic Revitalization Campaign implied no such commitment.

The first descriptions of the campaign and invitations to participate in it were sent out to village officials in September 1932. Designation of applicant villages as Economic Revitalization Campaign communities began soon afterwards, and continued until the campaign's final months in 1941. As noted above, by that time almost four-fifths of the nation's rural communities had been designated as campaign participants. In an era marked by short-lived reforms and a bewildering array of campaigns, Economic Revitalization stands out. Its particular focus on the countryside marks it as different, as does its longevity. The next section explores some of the changes the campaign brought to the countryside through depression, recovery, and mobilization.

Recovery

By design the Economic Revitalization Campaign was very much a local event, one that directed towns and villages to look inward, and to shun comparisons across even proximate borders. The interactions between the campaign and rural communities can thus be hard to pin down. The involvement of several thousand villages, distributed across the national landscape, further complicates careful analysis of the experiences common to residents of those communities. Not even the Ministry of Agriculture and Forestry, a consummate acquirer of statistics and reports, attempted much in the way of a generalized, careful assessment of what the campaign had accomplished, and why.

At the same time, however, the uniformity of the campaign's basic structures and premises makes some general observations possible. This section uses a single community, the village of Sekishiba, as a template for an exploration of developments unfolding throughout rural Japan. This is not to suggest that what happened in Sekishiba happened the same way everywhere else, or that Sekishiba's experiences reflect the full range of possible developments within the campaign. My purpose here is limited to identifying a few of the features evident in Sekishiba's encounter with the depression and with the Economic Revitalization Campaign, and to drawing from these examples some informed conclusions about similar transformations under way on a larger scale.

Sekishiba became a village in 1889. It stopped being one in 1954, when the town next door absorbed it and six other nearby villages, creating the city of Kitakata. These communities are located at the northern end of the Aizu basin, in northeastern Japan's Fukushima Prefecture. In the 1930s the closest urban center was Wakamatsu city, at the other end of the basin and less than an hour away by rail. It was through Wakamatsu that visitors and goods passed on their way to and from Tokyo and Japan's other urban and industrialized areas. While not isolated by any means, Sekishiba and its neighboring communities were defined by the mountain ranges that surrounded the Aizu basin, and by the importance of farming to their survival. Before the postwar amalgamation did away with its separate, independent character, Sekishiba was in many respects a fairly typical farming community. During the depression it was home to close to 400 families, most of whom raised rice, some silk cocoons, and other farm products to support themselves. The distribution of land holdings was not remarkable for a village of its size; landowners slightly outnumbered the landless, and those with medium-sized holdings were far more common than either the land-poor or the few residents with very extensive local holdings. At the village's northern end residents grew mulberry bushes and other upland crops in the dry fields there – most of the farmland in the village, however, was given over to rice paddies, criss-crossed with a complex network of irrigation ditches and footpaths, linking each of Sekishiba's fourteen hamlets to the rest of the community.

It will come as no surprise that Sekishiba's farmers were hit hard by the depression. They suffered the collapse of rice and silk prices along with the rest of the nation, and responded initially in much the same way as everyone else, namely by growing more of their staple crops. The 1933 rice crop was the village's largest to date, for example, and yields in other crops were similarly higher on average during the 1930s than they had been before the depression (Kitakata-shi shi hensan iinkai 1993: 796–9). Persistently depressed prices for these same crops, however, meant that farm families could not reap any windfalls as a result of their new-found productivity. Household income remained below pre-depression levels until 1935 or 1936, and was further burdened (and here too Sekishiba's farmers stayed true to national patterns) by substantial debt. One mid-decade estimate placed the average household debt at more than 1,800 yen, far higher than it had been earlier in the 1930s, and a multiple several times over of the average annual income from farming for those families ('Nōsakubutsu sakujō chōsa ni kansuru ken' 1934; 'Keizai kōsei keikaku kihon chōsa' 1934).

Plans to involve the village in the Revitalization Campaign were discussed in 1933, but unprecedented crop failures in 1934 temporarily delayed any serious efforts at reform and recovery. The campaign's first concrete effects were not visible in the village until 1935. By that point the industrial sector and to some extent the national economy more broadly had returned, more or less, to pre-depression levels. That the village leaders stuck with their earlier plans, and in fact eventually expanded them in scale, helps illustrate the extent to which the countryside's problems extended beyond issues of crop prices alone. As village leaders in Sekishiba made clear in their written and public commentary, they understood economic revitalization as a tool with which to address a whole range of deeply rooted problems in rural life. In this they shared sentiments expressed within the Ministry of Agriculture and Forestry, and by rural spokesmen in communities throughout Japan.

Sekishiba's normality is one of the qualities that makes it a useful template for a discussion of rural life in the 1930s. That the village was an early and well-documented participant in the Economic Revitalization Campaign is another. The mayor and other local notables kept the village engaged in the campaign throughout the 1930s, winning for it access to much sought after funding from the government, and some measure of notoriety in the area. Looking back on the considerable transformations in local farming practices, social life and institutional activity that marked the decade, the village's leaders were quick to attribute Sekishiba's changes for the better to the campaign's effects. While the extent to which the campaign was responsible for broader changes then under way in rural communities is certainly open to debate, there is little question that the practices of revitalization bear close scrutiny for what they can reveal about the nature of that transformation.

Planning for recovery

Revitalization insinuated itself into the lives of average farmers in a variety of ways. From the start, residents of communities participating in the campaign were committed to documenting, and thus quantifying, the important and not-so-important details of their lives. Forms distributed to every home in the village called on residents to report on income, family size, the productivity of their farms, and how much they spent on everything from salt to funerals. It was these documents, collected by the local leaders of the campaign, which established the baseline against which all future developments, familial and communal alike, were judged. In Sekishiba as in most villages, the campaign was the first time that such a detailed and comprehensive assessment of the state of the community had been attempted. Though most towns and villages compiled aggregate statistics on annual production and other economic indicators, it was not at all common for them to query average citizens, and certainly not in such detail. For most farmers, the campaign thus marked a new level of official interest in their personal circumstances. That the 'research' phase of the campaign included all households and not just the well-off landed farmers, up to that point the traditional targets of most rural reform efforts, is significant as well. The campaign's processes made it clear that everyone's participation was important, even as they implied that revitalization's benefits could accrue throughout the village.

The initial research and documentation phase of the campaign thus established at least three things. First, the surveys and reports regularized and defined the crises then confronting the community, suggesting in the range and number of questions asked that it was possible to quantify, to fully come to terms with, the depression's impact. Second, insisting that each household address essentially identical sets of questions and categories made it clear that the rural crisis affected everyone in more or less the same ways, and that the differences from one family to the next were likely to be matters of degree and not substance. While not exactly a leveling out of class and other differences, which were real and significant factors in rural life, the survey process markedly downplayed their importance. A similar stance is evident as well in the careful mapping out of each family's (and each community's) long-term goals for improving their economic, social and cultural circumstances, changes that were to be made real through reforms in family finances, farming technologies, and social practices. Together these constitute a third component of the campaign's early effects on the lives of average farmers.

These were no simple plans. Each mirrored the format of the highly detailed initial survey in insisting that households spell out exactly how they would get a handle on their debt, cut costs and boost income, and diversify their crops, to mention just some of the categories encompassed in a typical household's plan, every year for five years. Although the planning documents did not spell out a preferred result for farm families, or for their communities for that matter, the implications of the planning process were clear enough. As local plans in Sekishiba attest, farmers sought to grow more and more varied crops, to spend less on fertilizer, entertainment, and in other categories where cost-savings could be realized, and in general to pursue a more highly managed and rational existence.

Those parts of Sekishiba's revitalization plan that focused specifically on farming include the following highlights. Local farmers proposed producing almost 20 percent more rice and barley at the end of the first five-year planning period. Over the same time span, the village's planners relate, the local vegetable crop would more than double in yield, handicraft production would generate almost four times as much cash, and the community would move in a major way into animal husbandry. While the same farmers suggested that they would likely see reductions in some crops (in silk cocoons, for example), for the most part the trend was toward a noticeable increase in the production of key staples (like rice), the introduction of several new products, and quite sharp increases in what had until that point been almost secondary crops. In short, Sekishiba's farmers imagined a future in which their productive capabilities were altered significantly from pre-depression norms (Smith 2001: 260–2).

Farmers in other communities thought along similar lines, or at least those in communities participating in the Revitalization Campaign did so. In 1938 Ministry of Agriculture and Forestry officials compiled the data from all the revitalization plans then available, and generated an estimate of how the campaign might transform the nation's rural economy. As Table 6.1 suggests, the several thousand communities then active in the campaign had mapped out an ambitious vision of a much more productive, diverse and robust farming economy. Not only were staple crops like rice and wheat in line for a sharp increase in production, but so too were a wide array of other, sometimes even obscure, farm goods. Persimmons were listed alongside peas and pumpkins as crops worthy of special attention, and were thus among those that farmers proposed to harvest in far greater volume than ever before. As in Sekishiba, planners laid out a blueprint for change that sustained their ability to meet the nation's needs for rice and other staples, while at the same time moving

Table 6.1 Summary of economic revitalization planning (selected crops), 1932–36

Crop	*Proposed changes in*			*Number of village plans including this crop*
	hectares under cultivation (%)	*crop production (%)*	*yield per hectare (%)*	
Paddy rice	2	20	18	4,453
Wheat	34	72	28	4,137
Barley	14	38	21	2,779
Mulberry	–26	18	59	2,434
Soy beans	20	42	19	1,945
Potatoes	62	90	17	1,859
Persimmon	79	112	6	1,692

Source: Nōrinshō keizaikōseibu, 1985.

Note

Figures reflect five-year goals in plans submitted to the Ministry of Agriculture between 1932 and 1936.

aggressively into new markets with vegetables, fruits and a diverse array of cash crops.

How farmers would manage such a revolution in productivity within five years is a question planners confronted at all levels. Although the Revitalization Campaign generally did not lay out specific solutions to the problems then confronting the countryside, it did offer a series of basic premises about how they might be addressed. As suggested above, one consistent theme was an emphasis on a more rational application of existing resources. Planners did look forward to opening up some new land for farming, and this helps account for some of the increases in harvest size expected over the first five years. (The ability to develop new land must have varied considerably from region to region and village to village; Sekishiba's plans included almost no expansion in the total area under cultivation.) Far more important to the campaign than new farm land, however, were new farming techniques and technologies. Some sense of this is evident in the fact that planners called for significant increases not just in the total volume of the harvest from year to year, but for sharp boosts in yields per hectare. Referring again to Table 6.1, it is evident that farmers claimed in their planning documents that they would be able to coax more of any given crop from their land than they had in the past. Some of the improvements were more modest than others, but it would be hard to argue that an 18 percent change in yield per hectare for paddy rice production was insignificant. In Sekishiba, where as noted above farmers were less likely to open up new fields for rice cultivation, the community was supposed to realize its 20 percent growth in the size of the rice harvest almost entirely through improvements in yield per hectare. Planners there estimated that yields over the first five years would improve on average from 2.7 to 3.3 *koku* of rice per tenth of a hectare (Fukushima-ken keizaibu 1935: 123–6; Smith 2001: 260).

The specific techniques and technologies that would fuel such improvements would of course vary from crop to crop and region to region, but here Sekishiba's circumstances can provide some clues as to how many communities expected to proceed. In Sekishiba, planners explained that the higher yields would stem from a series of innovations and new practices. Included on that list was the introduction of new strains of rice and other crops, replacing existing less productive varieties. Double cropping and the more aggressive use of existing fields (planting fruit trees alongside rice paddies in land that would otherwise go unused, for example) would make a difference, as would a more scientific application of better, store-bought fertilizers. These steps would not be easy, and local leaders had few illusions about the likelihood of individual farmers pursuing such innovations on their own. The success of this component of revitalization was closely tied to changes in the organization and leadership of the village.

Organizing for recovery

The planning process in any campaign community included a large component devoted to the reform of existing village institutions. One of the reasons that farmers and Ministry of Agriculture bureaucrats alike were often optimistic about the campaign's potential was that it did link local improvement with better local leadership and technical instruction. Two groups in particular were thought to be essential to any community's economic recovery; the local branch of the Imperial Agricultural Association was one of them. This national body, long active in Tokyo on behalf of landlords and farmers in general, usually in that order, had local branches in most farming communities as well. Although the local associations were prohibited from addressing the financial needs of farmers, they were important channels for technical instruction and the sharing of best practices. When villages could afford them, the associations often hired full-time agricultural engineers to advise local farmers, and oversee test projects and the introduction of new technologies. Sekishiba's revitalization plan, as was common in many communities, took as one of its principles that the local agricultural association would be reinvigorated, and encouraged to maintain just such a full-time engineer to keep farmers abreast of the latest developments. This is in fact what happened in Sekishiba; the association's engineer was a regular and apparently persuasive participant in village meetings and other forums designed to get local farmers to make the right choices about crops, tools, and techniques.

A second and no less important local institution was the industrial cooperative, or *sangyō kumiai*. A part of rural life since the government had fostered their development near the turn of the century, the cooperative served farmers as creditor, marketing advisor, and discount broker, to name but a few of its roles. The cooperative provided loans in its capacity as a local credit union, for example, thus servicing the needs of local farmers even as it leveraged its national buying power to get lower prices for its members on essential supplies for the farm, fertilizer and seed among them. As a marketer, the cooperative assisted local farmers in transporting and selling their goods at prices better than other middlemen could provide. Though ubiquitous in the countryside, the cooperatives were, by the 1930s, suffering from poor funding and a diminished membership base. The cost of dues kept many farmers out, and the spiraling descent of commodity prices in the 1930s was the kiss of death for many struggling local cooperatives. Sekishiba's was more or less defunct by the mid-1930s; only a strenuous effort on the part of local leaders got it back on its feet and active in the community once again. They were helped in this by a series of initiatives spearheaded by Revitalization Campaign advocates within the Ministry of Agriculture and Forestry. Those initiatives greatly lowered the barriers to entry into local cooperatives, thereby assuring that all farmers had access to the resources associated with the cooperative. At the same time the state acted to shore up its financial support for the cooperatives, thus helping preserve their ability to provide credit and other services to local farmers.

Sekishiba's experiences offer some sense of how the industrial cooperatives and Revitalization Campaign were intertwined. By the end of the decade, Sekishiba's cooperative had begun playing the role that planners had expected of it. Not only did the cooperative handle more and more of the community's purchases of basic farm supplies (Sekishiba's handled four times as much fertilizer in 1937 than it had in 1933) and provide the credit necessary to improve farming practices, but it also took on the responsibility for selling an ever larger share of Sekishiba's rice and other crops to buyers outside the village – 60 percent of the village's rice sales in 1937 were handled by the cooperative (Smith 2001: 265, 277). Of equal importance was the fact that the cooperative membership extended by the end of the 1930s into almost every farm household in the village. Whereas membership prior to the campaign had declined sharply from already low pre-depression levels, revitalization brought with it efforts to bring old members back in, and to enroll farmers who had previously felt themselves too marginal or impoverished to participate. The campaign emphasized the benefits of full participation, and local leaders went to considerable efforts to see to it that just about everyone had access to the cooperative's resources. One can see in this further signs as well of the campaign's inclusionist tendencies. That is, by bringing together landed, middling and tenant farmers within the same hamlet and village-level structures, the campaign implicated everyone equally as victims of the depression, and as participants in recovery. The technical instruction and even more so the tangible resources associated with easier credit and cheaper fertilizer were, under the campaign's aegis, accessible to all comers and no longer the privileged domain of the village elites.

This sort of coordination manifested itself in other ways as well. An Economic Revitalization committee, created at the outset of the village's participation in the campaign, brought together leaders from many of the institutions central to village life. Its members included the mayor and most of his staff, teachers from the local elementary school and its principal, members of the village council, and the heads of each of the village's numerous business and farming unions and organizations. The committee's role was multifold; it provided much-needed coordination within Sekishiba's complicated network of overlapping institutions and groups, and facilitated the spread of information about the campaign to the members of those bodies. That no such structure had been put in place before the campaign is itself telling, and if nothing else the committee served as a visible reminder of how revitalization was transforming the institutional life of the community.

That same process was evident in other settings as well. Soon after the campaign started in Sekishiba, organizers began holding monthly meetings within each hamlet. These *buraku jōkai* brought together representatives of all the hamlet's households for lectures and discussion. The specific topics varied from session to session, but all related in some fashion to revitalization. The economic and social crises facing the village were recurring themes. Sekishiba's local agricultural technician was likely to speak on proper farming technique, while the mayor, a regular speaker at many sessions, could be counted on for a blend of moral exhortation and village boosterism. The assemblies were designed to foster cooperation in spirit and practice within each hamlet, but they also made it that much easier for village leaders – and the state – to reach into each of the village's homes on a regular basis with the latest slogans, reports, and suggestions for personal and communal improvement. In Sekishiba at least, local leaders never faltered in their support for the meetings, which were consistently well-attended over the course of the campaign.

Organizational reforms had at least one other effect on village life in the 1930s. Structures like the Economic Revitalization committee and the other re-invigorated civic groups created new opportunities for leadership at the local level. These opportunities had both quantitative and qualitative components, in that bodies such as the revitalization committees sharply expanded the number of people who could be officially involved in overseeing the local reform and recovery process. At the same time, the Ministry of Agriculture and Forestry used its influence over campaign communities to broaden definitions of who was qualified to fill those leadership positions. While in some ways reminiscent of the earlier Ministry attempts to reshape local leadership described previously in this volume by Tsutsui, the Revitalization Campaign reflected a significantly different perspective on who might guide local farmers, and why. Revitalization Campaign guidelines encouraged local committees to include younger and more technically skilled individuals within their ranks. Though seldom made explicit, the implication of such instructions was that the traditional sources of leadership were not up to the task at hand, 'traditional' in these instances referring to landlords and other local elites, long the power brokers in many rural communities.

In order to foster the development of a new generation of technically savvy and reform-minded leaders, the Ministry worked through the campaign to identify and help train groups of 'local mainstays.' Local committees were encouraged to send promising young men to Ministry-endorsed seminars and schools for instruction in advanced farming techniques, revitalization planning, and modern farm management. Although the total number of those able to attend these sessions was never large, the Ministry was clearly in search of cost-effective ways to influence local leaders. The cumulative effect of identifying even a few mainstays was thought to be significant. Those able to attend one of the regional training centers, or even a much shorter seminar, were expected to share what they had learned with the rest of the village. Since those chosen for additional training were presumably already in some way part of the local revitalization or leadership apparatus, it is easy to see how their new-found expertise would make itself felt in the day-to-day functioning of the village (Smith 2001: 302). In Sekishiba, which sent a number of young men out of the village for training, hamlet meetings were a useful venue for these expositions. And though it has been hard to pin down the particular impact of programs targeting local mainstays, it is clear that village leadership nationally in the late 1930s and early 1940s was undergoing some significant changes. Village council members, union leaders, and occupants of other positions of (admittedly limited) power were younger and better educated than their predecessors had been; it was not unheard-of for some of them to be tenant farmers, itself a remarkable transformation from circumstances of only a decade or so earlier. It is reasonable to conclude that some of the impetus for these changes came from the campaign, and, if nothing else, reflects the new realities of the post-depression countryside.

Mobilization, war, and recovery

Astute observers of the countryside will note that such efforts at institutional reform and communal harmony were nothing new. Policy makers from the Tokugawa era on through the Local Improvement campaign had pursued similar goals, and sometimes with similar methods. One quality which sets the pursuit of revitalization in the 1930s apart, however, is that the campaign's tenure overlapped with a significant and real transformation in farming practices and outcomes. This transformation is visible across several fronts at once. Crop diversification is one of them, increased productivity another. In the depression's aftermath the nation's farmers moved quickly to introduce new varieties of produce, or expand production of existing cash crops (Teruoka 1981: 172–4). Some sense of what this meant at the local level is evident in Sekishiba's experience, where the results of revitalization planning were impressive. The number of plum trees, for example, grew from 400 to 1,400 over the first five years of the Revitalization Campaign; the persimmon crop doubled, even as the village tallied the addition of some 3,000 rabbits and chickens to earlier livestock counts. These developments took place at the same time that local farmers were able to realize equally impressive improvements in the yields of local staples. Rice yields per hectare, after growing only 4 percent between 1926 and 1932, rose 8 percent between 1935 and 1936 alone, and by 1940 were 15 percent higher than in the middle of the decade ('Keizai kōsei keikaku jikkō hōkoku' 1936–41).

Such gains are significant, but it is worth pointing out that local farmers seldom did as well as they had said they would in their revitalization plans. In 1934 village residents assigned production goals to close to 50 different crops, livestock, and farm products. As of 1939, farmers had met those goals for only a dozen items. That the campaign was deemed a success and not a failure despite such shortcomings reflects something else about the recovery process. What was perhaps most important was that these changes in productive strategies had a measurable impact on the financial well-being of local farmers. By the end of the 1930s (and the end of five years of revitalization planning) an average Sekishiba household was producing goods that were worth almost three times as much as the value of production in 1931. Even adjusted for inflation those are significant gains. As a result of these changes savings rates were up, and the once crushing levels of debt were reportedly under control by the end of the first campaign planning cycle. Given where the village was in 1932 and the bleak assessments of the countryside's future that were commonplace then, these were welcome developments.

Sekishiba's success did not go unnoticed. In 1937 the village was chosen as one of only a handful of villages in the Aizu region able to participate in a new component of the Economic Revitalization Campaign, one that made available substantial new funding to help the community implement its revitalization plans. A year later another honor was bestowed on Sekishiba, as the national government identified it as one of only two Fukushima communities to receive an award marking the fiftieth anniversary of the nation's system of local government. The village's achievements in the Revitalization Campaign were featured prominently in the documents explaining Sekishiba's qualifications to receive the award. Local leaders also pointed to the hamlet assemblies as indicators of their commitment to reform, and as a sign of how far reform had progressed. From the time the first meetings were held in the early autumn of 1934, attendance was consistently high and the sessions themselves productive. For many participants, such changes were proof of the campaign's efficacy, and of its promise for a better future.

Assessing the economic recovery of villages like Sekishiba is complicated, to say the least, by the fact that it coincides with the nation's mobilization for war. That the countryside benefited from the massive military build-up of the 1930s goes without saying; rural Japanese were among those taking on new jobs in the industrial sector, even as a prosperity-driven boom in consumer spending helped farmers sell their goods at a premium for the first time in many years. Though village leaders and rural activists were loath to give much credit to the broader workings of the market when asked to account for the apparent recovery of the countryside, and focused instead on the importance of local reforms and initiatives, it was clear that farms and villages were being pulled along as the economy geared up for war.

Revitalization and mobilization overlapped in other ways as well. As the war in China dragged on, the Ministry of Agriculture and Forestry began to modify the Revitalization Campaign in support of the war effort. What that meant in practical terms was a noticeable shift away from revitalization as a set of methods for recovery and reform and toward the use of the same methods in the direct service of mobilization. The early emphasis on crop diversification and recovery plans unique to each household, for example, gave way to more focused efforts to boost production of certain key crops for the entire community. Fertilizer rationing and the distribution of other key inputs for farming were among the many new responsibilities of the local revitalization committees. ('Keizai kōsei iinkai jōseikin kōfu shinseisho' 1939).

Hamlet assemblies provided ready and consistent access to each household – the reinvigorated industrial cooperatives and agricultural associations played similar roles. In short, the very methods, new institutions and rhetoric that had begun to reshape the community in the aftermath of the depression were readily adopted to the needs of mobilization, and probably made it easier for the state to harness local resources and the commitment of rural citizens than would have been possible otherwise. The language of revitalization was one of communal solidarity, cooperation, and the application of scientific methods to vexing but surmountable problems. Once co-opted by the government for the purposes of mobilization, all these qualities and more made it possible to redefine the goals of revitalization on a national scale, and thus to connect continued economic stability with the very structures of the wartime state.

Conclusion: Missing pieces

Shūichi: I don't take pleasure in eating good food, or wearing nice clothes, or just walking around having fun. Happiness is in my heart. Raising up this hoe and bringing it down with all my might, at that moment my pleasure knows no bounds!

Ayako: (Laughing derisively) What a joke! That's something that's written in every single one of those books for farmers. They're just flowery words designed to put a damper on young people's spirits. It's just morphine.

Shūichi: (Strongly) You're wrong! You . . . , no, not just you, but city people in general, you all think of farmers as completely ignorant, as something out of the past, but that only shows how little you understand. We farmers are constantly studying and researching. And not just about our work, either. We're aware of what is going on ideologically, and in the world at large. We're not going to be tricked/provoked by you. We're here because we want to be, not because we don't have any skills.

Ayako: Which is precisely why I say you should come to Tokyo! You being here is a waste of talent.

Shūichi: That may be. But if I leave, Japan will collapse.

Ayako: Well, listen to you talk.

(Nukada and Takagi 1936: 76)

Sekishiba's postwar history is unremarkable. In 1954, the village and its neighboring communities were absorbed by the town next door – together they became the city of Kitakata. The newly formed city remains a hybrid of light industry and farming. Local farmers continue to supply rice and other crops both to local consumers and to buyers in distant markets. A similar pattern of amalgamation and of a blurring between town and country took place throughout the nation.

If Sekishiba/Kitakata's postwar experiences stand out in any way, it is in the particular strategies the community pursued to maintain economic and cultural vibrancy at the end of the century. The city has transformed itself, quite deliberately, into a tourist and travel destination for Japan's urban leisure class. Its marketing strategies rest on the twin foundations of Kitakata ramen, a local version of the common noodle-soup dish, and on *kura*, tile and mortar storehouses rare elsewhere in Japan but ubiquitous in Kitakata (Kitakata-shi shi hensan iinkai 1998: 830–1, 838). These attractions had long been part of local lore; beginning in the 1970s both were introduced to a national audience. Television programs devoted to travel and campaigns encouraging Japanese to experience 'exotic Japan' played key roles in commodifying the city's past, a process that was strongly encouraged by local leaders. The result has been a steady stream of television crews and tourist buses into the city, and an equally robust export of Kitakata ramen to grocery store shelves nationwide.

While the particulars of Kitakata's strategy to overcome economic obsolescence are unique, the developments that necessitated a turn to tourism are not. As John Knight suggests later in this volume, a number of rural communities have developed their own strategies of reinvention and reinvigoration to address similar problems. Which is another way of suggesting, it seems to me, that, as successful as the Economic Revitalization Campaign appears to have been at shaping the course of recovery and defining rural Japan's response to the crises of the early 1930s, it could not begin to resolve all of the countryside's problems.

This was certainly the case where tenancy was concerned. Tenancy and its implications for productivity and social stability were simply not issues that the campaign ever addressed in any significant way. Quite the contrary – eligibility for designation as a campaign village, and even more so for access to key campaign funding, was contingent on the absence of landlord–tenant struggles within the community. The state thus helped insure not only that participating villages would not be sidetracked by local conflicts, but also that recovery itself would rest on residents' willingness to keep discord from bubbling over. At no time did the Ministry, or the campaign, suggest that responding to the crises of the depression era would have to include addressing questions of land ownership, access to land, rents, and so on. As other chapters in this volume make clear, the Ministry of Agriculture and Forestry eventually turned to other policies to help address tenancy's costs. These policies were never intended to cut wide swaths in the countryside, nor did they address more than a handful of those potentially in search of some resolution to their problems with land, rent, and security. As broadly as the Revitalization Campaign sought to define its mandate to reform rural life, its silence on something as central as tenancy meant that it would require an occupation and a land reform to finally create a workable set of solutions to those particular problems.

The campaign also provided a forum for, but could not resolve, other concerns about rural life. The dialogue from the closing act of 'Sandanbatake no kyōdai' ('The Brothers of the Three-*tan* Field') excerpted at the beginning of this section hints at a discourse that emerged out of the crises and local responses to them. If revitalization laid out a range of possible responses to the depression, it also seems to have made more visible a public dialogue about the purposes of recovery. That is, was the value of recovery simply that it allowed rural citizens to escape destitution and poverty? Or could it be something more ambitious, perhaps even that a revitalized community meant that farmers could live more like their urban counterparts, and enjoy the same forms of amusement and personal improvement?

In Sekishiba, these questions were raised in multiple forums throughout the 1930s. Local leaders made strong and consistent connections between economic revitalization and the 'reform of daily life,' or *seikatsu kaizen*. Hamlet assemblies returned again and again to questions of the village's future, and how residents hoped to live in the years ahead (Kitakata-shi shi hensan iinkai 1991: 653–4). By this local leaders seem to have referred to both a transformation of physical culture (through better cooking techniques and architectural changes, for example) and to less tangible matters of citizenship and personal empowerment. At one point the Economic Revitalization committee even produced a 'Sekishiba Village Agreement on Economic Retrenchment and Moral Reform,' a lengthy list of suggestions for changes in daily habits, social practices, and attitudes. The agreement urged residents to be more punctual, to refrain from excess spending, and to think carefully about questions of health and diet ('Keizai kōsei keikaku jisshi ni kansuru ken' 1935; Smith 2001: 319). Education loomed large as well – local planners outlined the steps that families themselves could take to make sure that their children were learning not only useful subjects but also productive ways of imagining their place in the nation. The 'reform of daily life' thus linked improvements in the economic well-being of the community with a positive and productive attitude toward rural life and rural culture. Prosperity and recovery were thus tied not simply to an alleviation of abject poverty, but to the construction of a vibrant 'good life,' rich on its own terms, and definitely not a mirror image of urban modernity.

The same topics were being taken up outside of Sekishiba as well. The exchange between Shūichi and Ayako, the landlord's daughter, dramatizes some of the tension between efforts to define the countryside either as a backwater or as a separate and powerful counterweight to city life. *Ie no hikari* offered frequent and perhaps more realistic examples of local attempts to address these same concerns throughout the 1930s. In a forum discussion on 'The rebuilding of rural life' published in October 1934, leaders from business, the military, education and representatives of local governments held forth on the proper course of reform in nutrition ('Don't stick with the practices of the past – find nutritious ways to cook!' or 'Don't get seduced by urban cooking – develop rural tastes!'), toilet design, and clothing styles ('Nōson seikatsu no tatenaoshi' 1934:

113) In short, these critics sought to construct patterns of daily life that were at once enjoyable and modern, while not replicating whatever passed for normal in the cities. Accounts from two local activists in Tottori Prefecture were even more down-to-earth in their battle against the lure of the city. They had waged a two-year struggle to convince the village's young men to cut their hair very short (a style soon known locally as 'the *kōsei* cut') as a sign of their commitment to revitalization and the community. It was also a tangible sign of their having given up clandestine visits to the nearby town and its cafés. The young women in those cafés, it was reported, were partial only to men with long hair ('Kōsei keikaku wa dore dake jitsugen shita ka' 1935: 69).

As suggested earlier, wartime mobilization complicated but also intensified these dialogues. Before the realities of diminishing resources and manpower put an end to speculation about a brighter future for rural citizens in the near term, magazines like *Ie no hikari* and other forums for public discussion sustained debates about modernity, rational social practices, and the purposes of prosperity for many years (Itagaki 1992: 278–9). In Taiwan, colonial administrators started a *buraku shinkō* (hamlet development) campaign in the mid-1930s, which closely paralleled the goals and methods of revitalization in the metropole (Fix 1993). The campaign, which eventually involved several thousand Taiwanese rural communities and is credited with helping to bring about significant improvements in agricultural productivity, was never entirely distinct from ongoing efforts to replace Taiwanese culture with Japanese practices. One of the ironies here is that bureaucrats and local activists within Japan were at the same time doing their best to convince farmers that the future required abandoning Japan's traditions and long-standing practices in favor of the new and rational.

It will come as no surprise then that rural communities and the state revisited many of these same issues in the aftermath of the war- and occupation-era reforms. The Ministry of Agriculture's New Village Campaign of the mid-1950s is arguably little more than a re-labeling of Revitalization Campaign practices and purposes, less successfully implemented. The new campaign's program of planning, crop diversification, and the like was designed to help farmers maintain the gains they had made relative to factory workers and city dwellers over the course of the war and in the aftermath of the postwar land reform. The boom years of the Korean War had again favored the modern industrial sector over agriculture, and soon found farmers lagging behind the rest of the nation's improving standards of living and income levels. Revitalization in its new guise was unable to correct those disparities, something participants in the New Village Campaign were quick to discover.

The 1961 passage of the Basic Agricultural Law reflected the state's abandonment of self-help as the first line of defense for rural communities. In its place the state committed itself to a sweeping set of new benefits for farmers, including guarantees of a rough parity in income between farmers and factory workers. No such redistribution of the nation's wealth had been thought possible or even desirable before. The state's willingness to take such a step reflects both the importance of agriculture and rural communities to the nation's sense of itself, and a recognition that nothing short of parity would provide the sort of stability the state needed to sustain rapid economic growth.

Interestingly, even as Japan was moving away from a reliance on revitalization-like programs for the countryside, South Korea was embracing them. Park Chung Hee's government, after almost a decade of planning, in 1970 set in motion the Saemaul Undong (New Community Movement). In language reminiscent of earlier efforts in Japan, the movement's rhetoric 'centered on the idea that individual effort and sacrifice could solve the economic problems of the rural sector,' even as its practical components focused on the development of local infrastructure, cosmetic improvements to housing, and the introduction of scientific farming techniques (Brandt and Lee 1981; Abelmann 1996: 209). Largely abandoned by the mid-1980s, the Saemaul movement nevertheless defined more than a decade of rural reform efforts in South Korea at a particularly contentious period in that nation's history. While far from identical in conception or implementation, the similarities with what had been attempted in rural Japan in the 1930s are unmistakable and intriguing. If nothing else, these convergences suggest that local and national elites in both countries shared similar understandings of what qualities a modern countryside ought to possess. It would, in their vision, leave existing class structures more or less untouched, maintain political and social order, and preserve those qualities of harmony, cooperation, and diligence long associated with rural life.

These model villages were always much easier to imagine than to build. In the decades after the land reform and the 1961 Basic Agricultural Law, farmers did indeed share in the nation's prosperity, thus appearing to resolve at least some of dilemmas that revitalization's advocates had struggled to confront. As later chapters in this volume will suggest, however, and Sekishiba/Kitakata's forays into the exotic rural attest, the countryside continues to contest its place in modern Japan, and its future course.

References

Abelmann, N. 1996. *Echoes of the Past, Epics of Dissent, A South Korean Social Movement*. Berkeley: University of California Press.

Adachi Ikitsune. 1973. 'Jiriki kōsei undōka no "Ie no hikari",' *(Kikan) Gendai shi* 2 (May): 105–14.

Brandt, V.S.R. and M.-g. Lee. 1981. 'Community Development in the Republic of Korea.' In *Community Development: Comparative Case Studies in India, the Republic of Korea, Mexico and Tanzania,* ed. Ronald Philip Dore, Zoe Mars and Vincent S.R. Brandt. London: Croom Helm.

Dai Nihon tōkei nenkan. 1930–36.

Fix, D.L. 1993. *Taiwanese Nationalism and its Late Colonial Context*. Berkeley: University of California Press.

Fukushima-ken keizaibu. 1935. *Shōwa 9 nendo nōsangyoson keizai kōsei keikaku gaiyō: keikaku juritsu*. Fukushima-shi: Fukushima-ken keizaibu.

Itagaki Kuniko. 1992. *Shōwa senzen, senchūki no nōson seikatsu*. Tokyo: Sanrei shobō.

Iwasaki Akira. 1976. 'Atarashii media no tenkai.' *Shisō* 624 (June): 240–55.

Kase Kazutoshi. 1979. 'Nōson fusai seiri seisaku no ritsuan katei – Manshū jihenki nōgyō seisaku taikei no ichireimen.' *Tōkyō suisan daigaku ronshū* (March) 14: 11–38.

'Keizai kōsei iinkai jōseikin kōfu shinseisho.' 1939. Kitakata shiritsu toshokan shi-shi hensan shitsu: Sekishiba mura yakuba. Keizai kōsei kankei shiryō, March 17.

'Keizai kōsei keikaku jikkō hōkoku.' 1936–41. Kitakata shiritsu toshokan shi-shi hensan shitsu: Sekishiba mura yakuba.

'Keizai kōsei keikaku jisshi ni kansuru ken.' 1935. Kitakata shiritsu toshokan shi-shi hensan shitsu: Sekishiba mura yakuba. Keizai kōsei kankei shiryō, September 9.

'Keizai kōsei keikaku kihon chōsa.' 1934. Kitakata shiritsu toshokan shi-shi hensan shitsu: Sekishiba mura yakuba.

Kitakata-shi shi hensan iinkai (ed.). 1991. *Kitakata-shi shi*. Kitakata City, Kita Nihon insatsu.

—— (ed.). 1993. *Kitakata-shi shi*. Kitakata City: Kita Nihon insatsu.

—— (ed.). 1998. *Kitakata-shi shi*. Kitakata City: Kita Nihon insatsu.

'Kōsei keikaku wa dore dake jitsugen shita ka.' 1935. *Ie no hikari*: 60–9.

Miwa Ryōichi. 1979. 'Takahashi zaiseiki no keizai seisaku.' In *Senji Nihon keizai 2*, ed. Tōkyō daigaku shakai kagaku kenkyūjo. Tokyo: Tōkyō daigaku shuppankai.

Nakamura Masanori. 1988. *Shōwa no kyōkō*. Tokyo: Shōgakukan.

Nōrinshō keizaikōseibu. 1985. 'Nōsangyoson no keizaikōsei keikaku chū ni araretaru nōsanbutsu no seisan keikakuhyō.' In *Nōsangyoson keizai kōsei undōshi shiryō shūsei,* part 1, vol. 7, ed. Takeda Tsutomu and Kusumoto Masahiro. Tokyo: Kashiwa shobō.

'Nōsakubutsu sakujō chōsa ni kansuru ken.' 1934. Kitakata shiritsu toshokan shi-shi hensan shitsu: Sekishiba mura yakuba. Kangyō kankei shorui, September 28.

'Nōson seikatsu no tatenaoshi.' 1934. *Ie no hikari*: 112–22.

Nukada Roppuku and Takagi Kiyogaku. 1936. 'Sandanbatake no kyōdai, Keizai kōsei geki.' *Ie no hikari*: 66–80.
Shimizu Yōji. 1987. 'Nōgyō to jinushi sei.' In *Sekai daikyōkō ki 2*, ed. Ōishi Kaichirō. Tokyo: Tōkyō daigaku shuppankai.
Smith, K. 2001. *A Time of Crisis: Japan, the Great Depression, and Rural Revitalization*. Cambridge, Mass.: Harvard University Asia Center; Distributed by Harvard University Press.
Tasaki Nobuyoshi. 1989. 'Toshi bunka to kokumin ishiki.' In *Kōza Nihon rekishi 10*, ed. Rekishigaku kenkyūkai. Tokyo: Tōkyō daigaku shuppankai.
Teruoka Shūzō. 1981. *Nihon nōgyō-shi*. Tokyo: Yūhikaku.
—— 1984. *Nihon nōgyō mondai no tenkai*. Tokyo: Tōkyō daigaku shuppankai.
Vlastos, S. 1998. 'Agrarianism Without Tradition: The Radical Critique of Prewar Japanese Modernity.' In *Mirror of Modernity: Invented Traditions of Modern Japan*, ed. Stephen Vlastos. Berkeley: University of California Press.
Yasutomi Kunio. 1994. *Shōwa kyōkōki kyūnō seisaku shiron*. Tokyo: Hassakusha.

7 Securing prosperity and serving the nation

Japanese farmers and Manchuria, 1931–33

*Sandra Wilson**

In October 1932, 423 army reservists and their families left Japan to settle in Manchuria. Supposedly, they were to be the first of a great wave of farmers who would emigrate to northeast China, newly brought under Japanese control following the Manchurian Incident of September 1931, in order to secure Japan's rights in the area, solve the problem of overpopulation in the homeland, grow food to send back to their undernourished compatriots suffering during the acute economic depression, and ensure regional peace as well. In fact, Japanese emigration to Manchuria never achieved any of these lofty aims. The farmers who did go encountered numerous obstacles, from attacks by 'bandits' to labor shortages to outbreaks of dysentery, and many settlements failed. At every point recruits proved elusive, and emigration targets were not met. In the first five years, fewer than 3,000 households moved from Japan to Manchuria. Though the project received significant government support in 1936, it was swiftly undermined by the outbreak of full-scale war with China the following year, with its attendant labor shortages in rural Japan.

This chapter considers the movement to send rural settlers to Manchuria in the first years after the Manchurian Incident, with particular reference to the kind of arguments used in attempts to persuade farmers to emigrate. In this period the concrete achievements of those who sought to promote emigration were negligible; yet in rural Japan the idea of emigration to Manchuria had considerable rhetorical power. An investigation of the appeal to farmers to leave their homeland for Manchuria shows two critical features. First, emigration was clearly presented as a personal solution to the economic difficulties of Japanese farmers during the crisis of the early 1930s, even though the real motive of advocates

* This chapter builds on arguments first presented in my article 'The "New Paradise": Japanese Emigration to Manchuria in the 1930s and 1940s', *International History Review*, 17(2), 249–86.

of emigration was undoubtedly military and strategic. Thus the Japanese army boldly exploited the very real difficulties of the countryside in the pursuit of its own aims. Second, the call for emigrants was openly linked with an abstract nationalist rhetoric that encouraged settlers to see themselves as vital contributors to the preservation of the homeland and the expansion of Japanese influence abroad. In this sense, the appeal for settlers for Manchuria drew upon decades of effort by both official and civilian ideologues to persuade ordinary Japanese people to think in terms of the nation, and to identify their own interests as coterminous with the national benefit – while also revealing a certain confidence that such appeals would by now prove effective. More immediately, calls for emigrants reinforced particular rhetorical constructions of the nation that had been elaborated in detail during the crisis provoked by Japan's invasion of Manchuria in 1931–32, constructions of Japan as small and crowded but nevertheless vigorous and economically and culturally advanced (Wilson 2002: 225–6). The campaign to send emigrants to Manchuria now suggested a concrete way for ordinary Japanese to participate in furthering the national mission, and in so doing, to demonstrate the superior cultural attributes of the Japanese people.

In the early 1930s, then, Manchuria offered the vision of an alternative future for Japanese farmers – a future in which life would be both prosperous in personal terms and significant in national terms, in stark contrast to reality in the villages at the time. Though comparatively few took concrete steps to embrace the proffered new life, ideas about Manchuria and Japanese opportunities there lingered long in public rhetoric and in popular culture, no matter how divorced from reality they turned out to be.

The Great Depression

In rural Japan, the early 1930s were marked above all by the experience of the Great Depression. The income and welfare of farmers had already fallen in the 1920s, due to an absolute decline in prices for agricultural goods caused by competition from rice imports from Korea and Taiwan; the government's effort throughout the decade to deflate the economy sufficiently to allow a return to the gold standard, abandoned in 1917, at prewar parity; and a fall in world prices for agricultural goods (Patrick 1971: 218–19; see also Smith's chapter in this volume). Against such a backdrop, the worldwide decline in export prices for agricultural goods from 1929 onward plunged rural Japan into crisis.

The drop in silk prices in particular was catastrophic, given that 40 percent of all farm households raised silk, with much higher dependence on silk in certain areas. In 1930, spring cocoon prices dropped to about half those of the previous year, and during 1931 the price for silk thread also fell by more than half compared to January 1930 (Nakamura 1988: 274–5, 306–7). In Nagano Prefecture, a major cocoon-producing region, 80 percent of farm households raised silkworms in 1930. However, a middle-level farm household producing 100 *kan*, or 375 kg, of cocoons per year would have earned only 200 yen in 1930, compared to 1,000 yen in 1925 (Kobayashi 1977: 20). Then, in October 1930, prices also plummeted for rice, the other staple of Japanese agricultural production. In 1925 rice had sold for 41 yen per bushel (*koku*). In August 1930 the price had fallen to 30 yen and 50 sen per bushel, in September to 28 yen and 70 sen, and in October to 19 yen (Nakamura 1988: 307; Mori 1999: 16). A bumper rice crop was partly responsible for the sudden, catastrophic drop during 1930.

In 1931, the average price for rice was 18 yen and 46 sen per bushel, but the cost of production was 20 to 23 yen per bushel (Hashimoto 1984: 193–4). The result, unavoidably, was an increase in farm household debt, which rose in 1932 to an average of 846 yen per household. At the time, the average annual income for tenant farmers, including earnings from both agricultural and non-agricultural sources, was 552 yen; so average debt was more than 1.5 times higher than the average annual income for tenant farmers (Nakamura 1989: 42–3). In 1930, 59 percent of owner-farmers and 76 percent of tenants were in debt. Opportunities to increase the household income through wage labor decreased as the textile mills which had employed so many young rural women closed or suspended operations in the depression, and as wages for agricultural labor fell. According to figures produced by the Imperial Agricultural Association (Teikoku nōkai), the cost of agricultural production fell by 24.1 percent between 1930 and 1931, with 35.2 percent of this decrease attributable to wage reduction (Hashimoto 1984: 194). In the Tōhoku region, where economic suffering was acute, the selling of daughters into prostitution became a media issue from October 1931 onwards. Across the country, the plight of landless second and third sons of farming families, who were to become particular targets of the emigration campaign, was also severe.

The government's major strategy for tackling the depression is represented by the economic revitalization movement (*keizai kōsei undō*), which is discussed elsewhere in this volume by Kerry Smith (see also Smith 2001). In this context farmers were exhorted to be frugal, to rely on themselves and each other and, eventually, to restructure their villages economically. In the early 1930s, however, an alternative strategy was also espoused by some: struggling farmers, it was said, could save themselves by emigrating to Manchuria, now that the Kwantung Army had brought it under Japanese control. There they would have quantities of land they could not dream of in Japan, plus the opportunity to grow food to send back to the homeland and a chance to participate in the historic mission of the Japanese race to spread beyond Japan's borders.

Promoting emigration to Manchuria

The campaign to send farmers to Manchuria after September 1931 was in no way spontaneous; nor was it an extension of any significant previous experience of emigration to that region. Neither was it, from the point of view of its proponents, a genuine response to the domestic economic crisis, even though the appeal to potential emigrants was couched in those terms. Rather, it was the product of planning by the Kwantung Army in the service of its own military and political goals: to secure and extend Japanese gains in Manchuria and to defend the border between Manchuria and the Soviet Union. Thus the emigration movement was the orchestrated result of a particular military-political nexus produced by the events of 1931–32 in northeast China. In other words, the campaign to send emigrants to Manchuria developed not from any existing social basis but because of persistent efforts by key people within and outside the Kwantung Army, and because of the growing influence of military priorities in political affairs.

In itself, the idea of Japanese emigration was not new, though numbers of emigrants had always been tiny compared to those from other countries. Internally, emigration to Hokkaido in particular had begun during the Meiji period, and continued spasmodically in the 1920s and 1930s. From the early twentieth century, the main overseas destination for Japanese settlers was Brazil, which continued to provide serious competition for Manchuria as a target area after 1931. Emigration to Manchuria had also had its advocates from at least 1905. Prominent proponents of the military and strategic need for Japanese settlements there included Gotō Shinpei, first president of the South Manchurian Railway Company, Komura Jutarō, foreign minister from 1901 to 1905 and again from 1908 to 1911, and elder statesman Yamagata Aritomo. Very small numbers of emigrants had in fact attempted to settle in Manchuria in the 1910s and 1920s. Basically, however, their attempts had failed, for a variety of reasons including difficulties in securing land for the settlers (see Wilson 1995: 252–3). It was not until Japan's invasion of Manchuria had produced an entirely new framework that emigration began to be taken seriously. What changed in 1931–32 was, first, that the Kwantung Army now had a significant incentive to promote emigration, in order to secure its new territorial gains; second, that Chinese opposition to Japanese attempts to establish farms could be more readily overcome, by the use of Kwantung Army force; and third, that Manchuria itself had been elevated to a much higher position in public rhetoric about the Japanese nation. The only thing that remained was the need to attract Japanese farmers to emigrate.

Though there was no sound basis for the large-scale emigration of Japanese farmers to Manchuria in practical terms, the intellectual analysis which ostensibly provided the foundation of the overall emigration movement was more firmly established. Land was central to this analysis. Fundamentally, the scholarly argument was that rural poverty had been produced by over-population and a consequent shortage of land. Internal and overseas emigration was one of the solutions proposed, though the more perceptive analysts recognized that emigration was never likely to prove a realistic solution, and that industrialization was the only real option in the long term. Most significantly for our purposes here, the possibility of emigration to Manchuria had been discussed within this academic and bureaucratic debate during the 1920s, only to be dismissed by most. Various reasons were offered to justify this position, but one of the most persuasive was that Japanese farm laborers would not be able to compete economically with Chinese and Koreans already in Manchuria because of the very low standard of living of those Chinese and Koreans. Before September 1931, the scholarly and bureaucratic consensus was that, if emigration were to be taken seriously at all, then emigrants should go to Brazil, where at least there was a relatively substantial Japanese experience of settlement upon which to draw (Wilson 1995: 253–6). Thus, the academic and bureaucratic discourse before 1931–32, and afterwards too to some extent, actually emphasized Manchuria's unsuitability for Japanese settlement. Nor was there much popular consciousness of Manchuria in any context.

Nevertheless, a vigorous call went out for emigrants after the Kwantung Army's invasion of Manchuria, with the first official group departing in October 1932, as we have seen. The years 1932–36 are known as the period of 'trial emigration' or 'armed emigration' to Manchuria. During these years five groups of emigrants were sent, comprising a total number of less than 3,000 households. Their quasi-military function was quite evident: they were sent to settle areas in northern Manchuria, close to the border with the Soviet Union and prone to anti-Japanese guerrilla activity by a variety of forces; they were armed with weapons, including machine-guns; and the first group, at least, contained some serving soldiers, while men with military experience continued to be favored recruits to later groups. In 1936, the government announced a 'twenty-year plan,' during which one million households, or five million people, would be sent to Manchuria. Though initial reactions in some areas were promising, the labor shortage produced by the war with China which began in July 1937 soon put paid to the possibility of getting anywhere near the emigration targets. Government and army did not lessen their attempts to send emigrants, but their efforts met with continual and worsening obstacles. In the first five years of the 20-year plan, the number of new Japanese households settled in Manchuria fell more than 22,000 short of the target. Still, that nevertheless meant that 77,600 Japanese households did go in that period, making a total of roughly 270,000 individuals (Nakamura and Jinno 1995: 63; Kobayashi 1977: 110).

The campaign to settle Japanese farmers in Manchuria between 1932 and 1945 has thus been seen by some historians as a sign of the successful mobilization of the people in the service of imperialist goals, with thousands of Japanese rushing to join their nation's colonialist project in northeast China (for example, Young 1998). Others, focusing on the undeniable fact that numbers of emigrants never reached the desired levels, have branded the emigration project a failure. Wherever the overall emphasis in historical interpretation is placed, however, the early period of emigration after the Kwantung Army's takeover of Manchuria needs to be seen in its immediate context, distinct from later years when formal structures were put in place to facilitate recruitment of settlers. In the period immediately after the Manchurian Incident, the emigration movement had neither the government sponsorship it achieved after 1936, nor the complex bureaucratic apparatus to encourage recruitment. Its success therefore depended directly on the ability of the advocates of emigration to persuade suitable individuals to go. While the later period has been analyzed by a number of scholars in terms of the capacity of the emigration apparatus to further the integration of state and imperial society (see especially Young 1998), in the early 1930s, by contrast, the idea of emigration to Manchuria was presented primarily as one expression of the desire to solve the problem of poverty in the villages. At the same time, there was also a clear nationalist appeal to poor villagers to participate in a very direct and personal way in securing Japan's new territorial gains in northeast China.

Between 1931 and 1933, however, emigration to Manchuria, as a supposed solution to the rural depression, had to compete not only with settlement in Brazil, but with other, rival solutions which insisted on the possibility of renewal from within the village and the nation. Though there was a degree of overlap between advocacy of emigration and support of the government's economic revitalization movement, with some arguing that the former was part of the latter, advocacy of emigration in this period essentially constituted a declaration that life in the villages at home held no hope. Sometimes, arguments in favor of emigration included an explicit or implicit rejection of the government's other strategies. For one writer, for instance, the economic revitalization movement amounted to theoretical nonsense with no practical applicability, at least in the present. Japanese villages were not going to recover from the depression through the ideology of self-reliance. Further, official speakers supposedly spreading the message about revitalization mainly went to the big towns and stayed only briefly. They were not often heard by those who were most in need of instruction, according to this view, and in any case their message was too abstract for farmers to understand. 'In the end all they do is temporize a bit and relieve the feelings of the people a bit. It would have to be regarded as very doubtful that they achieve any lasting success' (Nagata 1933: 51–2, 154).

Emigration to Manchuria, on the other hand, was represented as an extremely practical solution to the difficulties faced by farmers, which stemmed above all, it was said, not from lack of rationality and planning, deficiencies that were addressed in the economic revitalization movement, but from lack of land. This was a problem which could be solved instantly in Manchuria, or so the proponents of emigration claimed.

Manchuria in the Japanese imagination: empty land

After September 1931, Japanese settlement of Manchuria was promoted at the highest levels because the Kwantung Army saw it as a way to secure areas of strategic importance and to ward off both Chinese guerrillas and any military forces which might stray across the Soviet border and threaten Japanese gains. Though senior army officers were not always completely confident of the level of rural support for the military in general (Smith 2001: 168; Wilson 2002: 130–2), in the context of Manchurian settlement the Kwantung Army was quite prepared to use country people for its own purposes. As the 1930s progressed, emigration to Manchuria was also promoted by prefectural and village officials in certain areas, as a way of reducing surplus population in the villages, probably also because of a general desire to cooperate with government policy, and possibly as an anti-revolutionary measure to defuse class tensions in the village by exporting some of the poorest members (see, for example, Takahashi 1997; Kimijima 1978; Kobayashi 1977).

The appeal to potential emigrants in the earlier period was based largely on the prospect of owning land. In Japan, land was scarce in relation to population, class relations in the village were often strained, and the rural economy was depressed. Manchuria, on the other hand, was said to have land in unlimited quantities, and publicity about emigration was directed at the poorest farmers, including those who had no land at all. The attractiveness of emigration varied according to the circumstances of the village concerned, but often there was special emphasis on the advantages of emigration for second and third sons, whose avenues of employment had contracted throughout the 1920s, because of reduced opportunities for agricultural laborers and shrinking job markets in the towns and cities (see, for example, Sunaga 1966: 488; Mori 2001: 202–3). As one advertisement for emigration in Nagano Prefecture put it in 1936:

> Farm land is scarce [here]; each farm household has only about eight *tanbu* [1.96 acres]. When cocoon prices were high, one could have a considerable income with eight *tanbu*, but that is now a dream of the past. . . . Along with rehabilitation of farm households, the problem is to find the way ahead for second and third sons. There is no land to establish branch families, and faced with the present shortage of work, parents and children inevitably lose heart.
>
> (Quoted in Kobayashi 1977: 85–6)

For many officials, reconstruction of the village depended on dealing with these surplus second and third sons. It is likely, too, that these were the very people considered most likely to cause unrest if they remained in the village with no prospect of improving their lot. Village harmony, then, might be enhanced if they left.

Propaganda about emigration to Manchuria often promised 10 or 20 *chōbu* (24.5 or 49 acres) of land per household. The appeal of such a prospect can be gauged from the fact that in 1933, 68 percent of farm households in Japan (including Hokkaido) owned one *chōbu* (2.45 acres) or less. Excluding Hokkaido, only 12,500 farm households owned five *chōbu* or more (Nihon gakujutsu shinkōkai 1937: 99). In the promise of land and, implicitly, upward mobility, there are striking similarities with other cases: with the view of Australia propagated in Britain during the nineteenth century, and the view of the United States popular in Italy, for example. In each case the destination would be a land of opportunity for those who had no hope at home.

A crucial additional element in propaganda about opportunities in Manchuria amounts virtually to the concept of 'terra nullius.' The 'Manchurian paradise' was consistently represented as a land of 'empty plains,' with Japanese propaganda clearly implying that no one lived there, apart from a few brave Japanese pioneers left over from earlier emigration projects and some incorrigible Chinese 'bandits.' As one enthusiast declared in 1932: 'the vast virgin plains, unhampered by tradition, are ready to welcome armies of fresh immigrants' (Hijikata 1932). Settlers would simply take up previously uncultivated land, and of course, being Japanese, would quickly make it productive. Thus one writer urged his fellow villagers in Nagano Prefecture to 'build [another] Izumida village in the limitless expanse of the Manchurian plains' (Matsui 1932). There was no hint that, in fact, millions of Chinese and others inhabited the supposedly endless and empty Manchurian plains, and that what actually happened in many cases was that Japanese settlers forcibly drove Chinese farmers off their land, and settled on land already long cultivated.

Much evidence suggests that the apparent availability of large tracts of land, and the prospect of owning it, were indeed powerful attractions to potential Japanese emigrants. Popular songs about Manchuria in the 1930s romanticized the idea of an empty land, very often mentioning sunsets, for example – always sunsets across vast plains affording spectacular and uninterrupted views of the horizon. Snowy expanses of plain were also popular, as was anything that emphasized space and emptiness, even loneliness since that implied space and an absence of other people. Reports from early emigrants echoed the same themes, along with frequent references to the cold climate of Manchuria. One of the first 'armed emigrants' sent this account of the initial three months of his new life in northern Manchuria back to his Nagano village:

> The loud noise of my boots on the frozen road . . . the majestic sound of the fixing of my bayonet . . . the voice which challenges, 'Who goes there?' . . . the cold, howling wind cutting straight through me . . . standing guard alone in the moonlight. . . . The sound of the rifle firing . . . the cries of donkeys and stray dogs – in such lonely guard was I occupied.
>
> (Ishii 1933a)

As for land ownership, one emigrant, reminiscing decades later about his motive for going, said simply, 'I yearned for ten *chōbu* of land.' Another explained:

> I went because I wanted to become the owner of ten *chōbu* of land. As the child of a tenant farmer, I had an endless longing for the title of 'landowner.' Since my parents were dead, it was the thing to do for a second son.

More than one-third of the 57 respondents to this 1975 survey of former emigrants mentioned rural poverty or being a second or third (or in one case, eighth) son as a motive for going to Manchuria ('Tairiku ni yume haseta koro' 1975). There was a cheerful air in Japanese villages, claimed a magazine article in September 1932, because there was so much land available in Manchuria, and farmers were simply awaiting their chance to go ('Mada mehana no tsukanu Manshū imin' 1932: 188–9).

In fact, Japanese farmers in Manchuria did not obtain as much land as had been promised, whether in the period of 'trial emigration' or the later years of emigration. Survivors of one settlement recall that they held an average of about three *chōbu*, or 7.35 acres, much more than they had owned at home but a far cry from the promised 10 or 20 *chōbu* (Kobayashi 1977: 142). Nor, for that matter, did the departure of the emigrants significantly improve the economic situation in their villages in Japan: for one thing, although the emigrants' land was supposedly to be redistributed to others who remained, it made little difference as few of those departing had owned much land in the first place. Many, as rural tradesmen, day-laborers, small shopkeepers or tenant-farmers, or as the younger brothers or sons of small landholders, had owned no land at all (for example, Mori 2001: 214–15).

Taking part in the national vision

The evidence on emigration to Manchuria leads inescapably to the conclusion that self-interest was not the only magnet for emigrants. Presumably, if it had been, emigrants would have preferred to go to Brazil, a much more stable environment for Japanese settlers. Going to Manchuria, on the other hand, combined an expectation of personal gain with an expression of patriotism. It was a way of supporting state policy, of taking part in the great project of planting Japanese civilization abroad, of guiding more backward people toward modernity. The two types of motivation – personal and 'national' – were probably not clearly separated in the minds of many potential emigrants in any case. Since the late Meiji period, Japanese leaders, officials and civilian ideologues had devoted a great deal of effort to promoting the view that what was good for the nation was good for the individual household, and much rhetoric, as is well known, mentioned family and state in one breath, often maintaining that they were analogous to each other. Emigration to Manchuria, it was now claimed, would further the welfare of both.

The rhetoric in Japan about settlement in Manchuria was always idealistic, even romantic, and emigrants' stories indicate that these appeals did find their mark. The most commonly used rhetorical phrases included not only Manchuria as the 'paradise' or 'new paradise,' but also, especially, 'Manchuria, Japan's life-line,' a phrase in which there is an unmistakable emphasis on national needs and goals rather than personal economic opportunity. Manchuria was said to have limitless potential and resources of all kinds and Japanese farmers would be the ones to realize this potential for the sake of the nation. Emigrants could relieve population pressure in Japan, grow food in Manchuria to export back to those who remained behind, and play a part in protecting Japan's 'rights and interests' in Manchuria. As the audience was told at a memorial service at the end of 1931 for soldiers killed in Manchuria, 'The Manchurian-Mongolian paradise is a huge resource which will support the [Japanese] nation' (Kimura 1937a: 167).

To go to Manchuria, however, was to do more than serve the national interest in a narrow sense. Allegedly it also contributed to Japan's international role, playing its part in the construction of a vision of national identity that transcended geographical boundaries. As Peter Duus has pointed out, the Greater East Asian Co-Prosperity Sphere of the later 1930s was considered by Japanese ideologues to be of world-historical significance and to showcase Japan as a creator of history rather than a backward country (Duus 1996: xxiii). Rhetoric about settling Manchuria clearly shows that, for some, consciousness of such a mission predated the Co-Prosperity Sphere: it was in Manchuria that Japan would show its attributes as a world-class nation. The emigration campaign strongly reinforced the notion that Japan could (and should) exist outside the physical nation – that is, that being Japanese was essentially a spiritual, cultural and racial thing. As one village official proclaimed, the emigration movement itself was a spiritual movement, whose purpose was 'to bring out clearly the fact that we are Japanese' (Yunoki 1982: 66).

In this sense, emigration provided an emotional focus for a cluster of issues concerning Japan's place in the world. From at least the 1920s, emigration in general had functioned virtually as a symbol of the status of Japan as a nation. It was closely associated with views of Japan's advance into the ranks of the powerful nations, its strength and vitality, and its equality with Western countries. Great nations were believed to be nations which sent their people to settle in and develop other places; certainly, great nations needed more resources than were to be found within Japan's borders. The comparison, usually unstated, was of course with the British Empire, despite the rejection of European colonialism in official rhetoric from the later 1930s. The more blatant publicists made this explicit. For example, the Nagano Prefecture activist Nagata Shigeru (Shigeshi) (1881–1973), an indefatigable advocate of emigration and author of over a dozen books on Japanese overseas settlement, wanted Japan to take over where he felt that Great Britain had left off, as the leading nation of the world. The Japan-centered settlements Nagata envisaged in Manchuria and Brazil were really bases from which the Japanese race would eventually expand over the whole of Asia and South America (Nagata 1933: 212–26). Significantly, however, it was only in 1932 that Nagata began to consider Manchuria for Japanese settlement as well as South America, indicating that his fervor for northeast China was much more strongly related to the Kwantung Army's new control of the region than to any obvious potential for settlement that he himself might have detected. More modest advocates of emigration maintained – and Western experts often agreed with them – that the Japanese population needed more space, and as a civilized, vital and growing nation had as much right to it as Western nations had felt they had at an earlier time (Wilson 1995: 253–4). For some, too, emigration to Japan's overseas sphere of influence was a way of compensating for the slight from Western nations like Australia, the USA and Canada which had closed their doors to Japanese immigration.

In material directed at prospective emigrants, the military agenda was often freely admitted, and appeals were openly made to national pride. Japanese women, for instance, were called upon to take their place as emigrants so that Manchurian women could learn from the sterling example they would provide through their hard work ('Manshū shintenchi de wa nōson fujin o motomu' 1932: 22–3). The efforts of the emigrants more broadly, according to another, would determine whether or not Manchuria truly became Japan's 'lifeline,' since the farmer-settlers would be pioneers in the development of Manchukuo. For Nasu Hiroshi, Tokyo Imperial University professor of agriculture, Japan would not be able to maintain the rights and interests it legitimately possessed in the region unless a great many settlers went there; by doing so they would also solve Japan's problem of overpopulation ('Manmō kaitaku no nōgyō imin zadankai' 1932: 46–51). Foodstuffs could be grown by settlers in Manchuria for Japanese consumption instead of imported from foreign countries, enthused an army officer. Mongolian sheep would substitute for imports of wool from Australia, and Manchuria would also provide meat for Japan (Iwasaki 1932: 37). The capacity to grow foodstuffs was in fact of paramount importance, according to Nagata Shigeru. Conceivably, Japanese villages might one day collapse economically; in that case, however, they would be saved by the efforts of the farmer-settlers, who would have built up Manchuria's agricultural resources to the extent that they could support the entire population of Japan! (Nagata 1933: 110–11)

On a grander scale, it was commonly claimed that the Manchurian settlers would contribute to peace in the entire East Asian region, and by their presence bring order to an unstable part of the world. Some propagandists went much further. Nagata Shigeru wrote that founding a state in Manchuria, together with a new Japanese model for world civilization in South America, were the twin national missions of the Japanese. Both enterprises had to be based firmly on Japanese agricultural emigration, because there was no other way to implant a permanent Japanese racial influence. In fact, both the sound development of Manchuria and the maintenance of peaceful relations between Japan and Manchuria absolutely required that a minimum of five million, and preferably 15 million Japanese people should move to Manchuria, the great majority of them to engage in agriculture (Nagata 1933: 212–26). Similarly, another writer opined that emigration – though not necessarily to Manchuria – was necessary to develop and expand the 'superior Yamato race' ('Kaigai ijū gappō' 1934: 11).

A specific vision of racial harmony also informed the idealistic version of Japan's potential contribution to Manchuria. To an extent this contradicted the idea of empty plains awaiting immigrants, because it recognized the existence of a number of different ethnic groups already there. Official Manchukuo ideology did stress 'racial harmony,' however, and the Japanese role within this scheme was clear: it was to lead and guide the other races and to bring rationality and organization to Manchurian agricultural management. The publicist Nagata, who by 1934 was working for the Kwantung Army, offered a striking metaphor. Manchuria, he wrote, was like a concrete structure, with the Chinese the stones, the Koreans the sand, and the Russians and Mongolians the water. No matter how they were mixed, stones, sand and water would not make concrete. It could not be done without the Japanese race as the cement. It did not apparently occur to him that each of the other elements was equally indispensable (Nagata 1933: 214–15). A more cultured version of the same idea referred specifically to the relations between Japanese and Chinese settlers, alluding to their common Confucian heritage. One village head advised 42 emigrants about to leave Miyagi Prefecture for Manchuria in 1932 to teach and to 'improve' the people of Manchuria, becoming their elder brothers, teachers and friends. They should study the *Analects* of Confucius and guide the natives kindly on the basis of the ethics it contained (Kimura 1937b: 209–12).

Potential emigrants seemingly did respond to the appeal to participate in a great patriotic undertaking. Many of the 57 former emigrants in the 1975 survey mentioned above ('Tairiku ni yume haseta koro' 1975) said they had wanted to support state policy: they went to 'develop the new paradise,' to produce food for Japan, or simply because it was national policy. When the movement to send 'brides' for the settlers got under way in the later 1930s many of those young women, too, went for patriotic reasons according to their later reminiscences (Jinno 1992). Again, reports from emigrants in the first groups emphasized the same themes. One wrote that he had gone to build a new Japan, and promote friendship between Japan and Manchuria ('Dokusha kurabu' 1933: 188). Another settler proudly assured his fellow villagers at home that 'even in the remote areas . . . with their boundless space and dense fields of sorghum waving in the breeze, the Japanese flag flies high in the sky every day' (Ishii 1933a). Several months later he reported that his group had at last reached the area allocated to it for farming, listing the number and type of animals and plows the settlers possessed and the crops that would be grown. All the people who formerly lived within the cultivated area, he noted laconically, had moved. For this young Japanese settler, however, watching their dispossession was a lesson in power politics rather than an occasion to reflect on the hypocrisy of those who told people at home that Manchuria was an empty land: 'Every day they are loading up with their household goods and leaving. It makes me acutely aware of how pitiful it is to have a weak country' (Ishii 1933b).

Criticism of the emigration campaign

Despite the efforts of enthusiasts inside and outside of the Kwantung Army, the promotion of emigration from rural areas to Manchuria in the early 1930s attracted a certain level of criticism as well as a large amount of indifference. The negative view held by scholarly and bureaucratic experts continued to be expressed, though no doubt more cautiously after the Manchurian Incident than during the 1920s. The economist Ueda Teijirō, for example, who believed that Manchuria's resources were not in fact extensive, told Kwantung Army officers in January 1932 that there was little prospect there for Japanese settlers, and that, instead, Japan should welcome Chinese settlers to the region (Ueda 1963: 168). Similarly, for the influential liberal economist and journalist Ishibashi Tanzan, the idea that Japanese in any numbers could live in Manchuria was an 'absurd notion' which, if pursued, would produce a large number of victims on the one hand, and very few benefits on the other. Ishibashi took issue with all the standard arguments about advantages Japan could gain from the exploitation of Manchuria, adding that any economic prosperity which might eventually result from the development of the region rightfully belonged to its existing inhabitants, not to an outside power (Ishibashi 1996).

In the villages too, some were clearly critical. In Izumida village in Chiisagata-gun, Nagano Prefecture, one writer sought to debunk the propaganda about opportunities in Manchuria. An earlier article in the young men's association newspaper produced in the village had shown considerable enthusiasm about the cheap labor available in Manchuria, citing the low wages of adult males as a positive factor from Japan's point of view. The second writer responded: 'I cannot condemn the writer, with his vision of being a splendid rural landowner through the use of cheap labor; but I would like him to be aware that we too are "adult males."' Manchuria, he continued,

> is certainly not the paradise dreamt of here. The only role allotted to us over there is to spend our blood and sweat in toil. Dreams of success without that hardship should be left to people like party politicians and the *zaibatsu*.
>
> ('Utsuriyuku jidai no sō' 1932)

In January 1933, young men in Aoki village, also in Chiisagata-gun in Nagano Prefecture, denounced attempts by the authorities to raise money to send emigrants to a new settlement in Manchukuo. Their objections were both practical and ideological. On the one hand, they pointed out that villagers could not afford to raise the 201 yen required as the contribution from Aoki. On the other, they believed that the campaign to 'protect Japan's rights and interests' in Manchuria was no more than a disguised attack on Soviet and Chinese communism and should therefore not be supported in any case (quoted in Ide 1991: 43–5). In more personal terms, one village school principal, as Mori Takemaro shows, rejected all the rhetoric about noble service by Japanese settlers in Manchuria. To him, the emigrants had simply been 'discarded' by their homeland. The principal himself was adamantly opposed to 'abandoning young people to Manchuria,' and refused to have anything to do with the campaign (Mori 2001: 211–12).

By the end of 1932, in fact, key institutions in the countryside had lost interest in the movement to send farmers to Manchuria, in view of the serious obstacles encountered by those who did go, and perhaps because of the early signs that the Japanese economy was beginning to recover from the depression. There was a general admission that 'emigration to Manchuria in 1932 ended in failure' ('Manshū, Burajiru tokōsha no tame ni mono o tazuneru kai' 1933), and warnings were issued to prospective emigrants against excessive eagerness. It might take a long time, advocates of emigration now acknowledged, for Manchuria to achieve its destiny as a 'paradise' for Japan. The agricultural cooperative (*sangyō kumiai*) movement and the Imperial Agricultural Association lost interest in the campaign, maintaining a quite critical stance toward it until emigration to Manchuria became government policy in 1936. Few officials in the Ministry of Agriculture and Forestry or the Home Ministry had ever shown interest in the project, and in fact there was little support from any part of the government at this stage (Takahashi 1997: 115–16; Wilson 1998: 128–30). Government support for emigration to Brazil, on the other hand, continued. The national budget for 1933–34 included 5,744,749 yen for the protection and encouragement of emigrants and for colonization enterprises, most of it earmarked for Brazil. By contrast, a separate item of just 382,075 yen was allocated for emigration to Manchuria (Grew 1933). Most significantly of all, there was little interest on the part of the rural population itself. For the great majority of Japanese, life at home was preferable, no matter how precarious. As one diplomat observed, 'in spite of all inducements, the average Japanese farmer would rather cinch in his belt and stay on his own acre of rice paddy than adventure to the ends of the earth after greater riches' (McClintock 1933: 27). Those who did choose to emigrate continued to prefer Brazil, with its relatively established Japanese population, rather than Manchuria.

Conclusion

Propaganda about emigration to Manchuria was directed at both farmers and decision-makers, in order to encourage the first group to emigrate and the second to provide support for the project. The call for emigrants was directed firmly at poor farmers. Ironically, however, by the time the campaign got seriously under way, it was no longer necessary to consider such drastic solutions to poverty. Conditions in the countryside had improved somewhat, with rises in prices for agricultural goods. By 1936, the price of both silk cocoons and rice was more than one-and-a-half times higher than in 1931 (Banno 1997: 219). Then, the outbreak of full-scale war with China in July 1937 produced a labor shortage which made nonsense of the argument that Japan required emigration as a solution for overpopulation, as young people from the villages were drawn into the military or to the munitions factories in the cities. By 1941–42, land was standing uncultivated in some areas because of the labor shortage, and landlords, fearing further labor shortages and a fall in both land values and rents, were opposing emigration (Sunaga 1966: 488; Mori 2001: 211). In the ultimate irony, Chinese and Korean laborers brought forcibly to Japan began to be put to work, sometimes in the very places from which farmers were being persuaded to go to Manchuria in order to alleviate the 'population problem' (Kobayashi 1977: 109). The Kwantung Army's desire to promote settlement in Manchuria hardly lessened, however, and emigration remained an important government policy, with publicity appealing to both patriotism and economic self-interest continuing in the villages throughout the war. As late as 1941, the following appeared in a journal aimed at prospective emigrants:

> If you become a Manchurian pioneer, you can be an owner-farmer with ten *chōbu*, and you will see permanent prosperity for your descendants. Manchuria itself is the basis of the East Asian Co-Prosperity Sphere. Manchuria, where 100,000 [Japanese] lives have been lost, must be protected with our hoes . . . . There is no way to revive the villages other than developing Manchuria.
>
> (Kobayashi Hitoshi 1941, quoted in Kimijima 1978: 302)

The myth of Manchuria as the place that would cure all the personal and national ills suffered in Japan thus proved to be an enduring one, even in circumstances which provided remarkably little justification for such claims.

References

Banno Junji. 1997. *Nihon seijishi: Meiji, Taishō, senzen Shōwa*. Revised edn. Tokyo: Hōsō daigaku kyōiku shinkōkai.

'Dokusha kurabu'. 1933. *Ie no hikari* (February): 188.

Duus, Peter. 1996. 'Introduction/Japan's Wartime Empire: Problems and Issues'. In *The Japanese Wartime Empire, 1931–1945*, ed. Peter Duus, Ramon H. Myers and Mark R. Peattie. Princeton: Princeton University Press.

Grew, Joseph. 1933. Ambassador Joseph Grew to Secretary of State, monthly reports for January–April 1933 (Nos. 76–79), United States National Archives, Washington DC, Records of the Department of State, Record Group 84 (Post Records, Tokyo, 1933).

Hashimoto Jurō. 1984. *Dai kyōkōki no Nihon shihonshugi*. Tokyo: Tōkyō daigaku shuppankai.

Hijikata Seiji. 1932. 'New Manchurian State Makes Good Beginning'. *Trans-Pacific* (April 7): 17. (Originally published in *Chūō kōron*.)

Ide Magoroku. 1991. *Owarinaki tabi*. Tokyo: Iwanami shoten.

Ishibashi Tanzan. 1996. 'Shina ni taisuru tadashiki ninshiki to seisaku'. *Tōyō keizai shinpō* (February 6, 1932). In *Dai Nippon shugi to no tōsō (Ishibashi Tanzan chōsakushū 3: seiji gaikō ron)*, ed. Kamo Takehiko. Tokyo: Tōyō keizai shinpōsha.

Ishii Uichi. 1933a. *Izumida jihō* (February): 1.

—— 1933b. 'Iyoiyo katsudō o kaishi shita'. *Izumida jihō* (May): 1.

Iwasaki Tamio. 1932. 'Shihonka ya seitōsharyū no Manshū ni suruna no koe'. *Ie no hikari* (June): 37.

Jinno Morimasa. 1992. *'Manshū' ni okurareta onnatachi: tairiku no hanayome*. Tokyo: Nashi no kisha.

'Kaigai ijū gappō'. 1934. *Ie no hikari* (February): 11–17.
Kimijima Kazuhiko. 1978. 'Fashizumuka nōson ni okeru Manshū imin: Hanishina-gun bungō imin no jisshi katei'. In *Nihon fashizumu no keisei to nōson*, ed. Ōe Shinobu. Tokyo: Azekura shobō.
Kimura Tadashi. 1937a. 'Dai nikai ireisai ni ikeru saimon' (December 18, 1931). In *Kimura Tadashi sensei kōenshū 'Sonchō jūnen'*, ed. and publ. Kimura Tadashi sensei kōenshū *Sonchō jūnen* kankōkai. Sendai.
—— 1937b. 'Manshū shimin shokun o okuru' (October 2, 1932). In *Kimura Tadashi sensei kōenshū 'Sonchō jūnen'*, ed. and publ. Kimura Tadashi sensei kōenshū *Sonchō jūnen* kankōkai. Sendai.
Kobayashi Kōji. 1977. *Manshū imin no mura.* Tokyo: Chikuma shobō.
'Mada mehana no tsukanu Manshū imin: saikin senkushita imin no hanashi'. 1932. *Ie no hikari* (September): 188–9.
'Manmō kaitaku no nōgyō imin zadankai'. 1932. *Ie no hikari* (May): 46–51.
'Manshū, Burajiru tokōsha no tame ni mono o tazuneru kai'. 1933. *Ie no hikari* (March): 110–19.
'Manshū shintenchi de wa nōson fujin o motomu'. 1932. *Nōson fujin* 1(3) (May): 22–3.
Matsui Masao. 1932. 'Akeyuku Manmō'. *Izumida jihō* (March): 1.
McClintock, Robert Mills (US Vice-Consul, Kobe). 1933. 'Japanese Emigration to Brazil'. November 1, 1933. United States National Archives, Washington DC, Record Group 59, M/F: LM 058, Roll 25, 894.56/69: 1–28.
Mori Takemaro. 1999. *Senji Nihon nōson shakai no kenkyū.* Tokyo: Tōkyō daigaku shuppankai.
—— 2001. 'Manshū imin: teikoku no susono'. In *Rekishi ga ugoku toki: ningen to sono jidai*, ed. Rekishi kagaku kyōgikai. Tokyo: Aoki shoten, pp. 197–224.
Nagata Shigeru. 1933. *Nōson jinkō mondai to ishokumin.* Tokyo: Nippon hyōronsha.
Nakamura Masanori. 1988. *Shōwa no kyōkō.* Tokyo: Shogakkan.
—— 1989. *Shōwa kyōkō* (Iwanami bukkuretto, shiriizu Shōwashi, No. 1). Tokyo: Iwanami shoten.
—— and Jinno Morimasa. 1995. 'Ashitaka-mura Manshū nōgyō imin'. *Numazu-shishikenkyū* (4): 61–89.
Nihon gakujutsu shinkōkai. 1937. *Manshū imin mondai to jisseki chōsa.* Tokyo: Nihon gakujutsu shinkōkai.
Patrick, Hugh T. 1971. 'The Economic Muddle of the 1920s'. In *Dilemmas of Growth in Prewar Japan,* ed. James William Morley. Princeton: Princeton University Press.
Smith, Kerry. 2001. *A Time of Crisis: Japan, the Great Depression, and Rural Revitalization.* Cambridge, Mass.: Harvard University Asia Center.
Sunaga Shigemitsu (ed.). 1966. *Kindai Nihon no jinushi to nōmin: suitō tansaku nōgyō no keizaigakuteki kenkyū – Nangō-mura.* Tokyo: Ochanomizu shobō.
'Tairiku ni yume haseta koro: kyū Manmō kaitaku seishōnen giyūgun Tōnei daiichi chūtaiin ni kiku'. 1975. In *Ichiokunin no Shōwashi*, Vol. 1: *Manshū jihen zengo – koritsu e no michi.* Tokyo: Mainichi shinbunsha, 1975, pp. 175–8.
Takahashi Yasutaka. 1997. *Shōwa senzenki no nōson to Manshū imin.* Tokyo: Yoshikawa kōbunkan.

Ueda Teijirō. 1963. *Ueda Teijirō nikki*, Vol. 3. Tokyo: Ueda Teijirō nikki kankōkai.
'Utsuriyuku jidai no sō: takanaru fassho kōshinkyoku'. 1932. *Izumida jihō* (September): 4.
Wilson, Sandra. 1995. 'The "New Paradise": Japanese Emigration to Manchuria in the 1930s and 1940s'. *International History Review* 17(2): 249–86.
—— 1998. 'Bureaucrats and Villagers in Japan: *Shimin* and the Crisis of the Early 1930s'. *Social Science Japan Journal* 1(1): 121–40.
—— 2002. *The Manchurian Crisis and Japanese Society, 1931–33*. London: Routledge.
Young, Louise. 1998. *Japan's Total Empire: Manchuria and the Culture of Wartime Imperialism*. Berkeley: University of California Press.
Yunoki Shun'ichi. 1982. 'Manshū imin undō no tenkai to ronri: Miyagi-ken Nangō-mura imin undō no bunseki'. *Shakai keizaishigaku* 48(3): 52–71.

8 Colonies and countryside in wartime Japan

Mori Takemaro

Introduction

This chapter explores the relationship between rural villages in Japan and Japan's colonies during the wartime period, with particular reference to the emigration of Japanese farmers to Manchuria (Manchukuo). For a thorough understanding of this relationship it would be necessary to consider capital and commodities as well as labor, but here I confine my attention only to labor, in the form of the movement of people. My aim is to identify some of the key characteristics of Japanese emigration during this period and, by means of a comparison with emigration to Korea at roughly the same time, to reveal some of the distinctive features of the Manchurian case. I will focus mainly on Yamato Village in Yamagata Prefecture. The prefecture itself ranked second in the nation as a source of emigrants to Manchuria, and the village ranked with Ōhinata Village in Nagano Prefecture and Nangō Village in Miyagi Prefecture as one of the top three villages nationwide in terms of the total number of emigrants produced.

The Rural Economic Revitalization Campaign

The rural crisis engendered by the Showa Depression in the early1930s proved a historical turning point for Japan, paving the way for war and fascism. The collapse of farming operations brought about by a sharp increase in the debts owed by farm households threatened to destabilize rural society, and the agonizing impoverishment of the countryside figured as a rationale in attempted *coups d'état* by young officers in the Imperial Japanese Navy and Imperial Japanese Army from the May 15th Incident of 1932 to the February 26th Incident of 1936. To cope with the rural crisis, the government encouraged farmers to commit themselves to what was called the 'Rural Economic Revitalization Campaign,' the basic principle of which was economic recovery by means of the self-help efforts of farmers themselves. As later attempts by the government to promote emigration to Manchuria, in particular the plan announced in 1936 to send one million Japanese farm households there over a 20-year period, were carried out as part of this campaign, it would be useful to begin by summarizing its main features (Mori 1999; see also the chapter by Smith in this volume.)

The Rural Revitalization Campaign was launched in 1932 as a means of dealing with the effects of the depression. As part of the campaign, the government designated 76 percent of all towns and villages in the country as revitalization localities, and farmers were urged to reconstruct their villages on the basis of self-help. From late 1938 onward, the campaign shifted from promoting recovery from the depression to increasing food production, functioning thereafter as part of wartime controls over agriculture.

The first goal of the campaign was the clearing of farm household debt, and one important measure in this direction was encouraging farmers to keep detailed accounts of their income and expenditure. By doing so, farmers were expected to learn the theory and practice of 'rational management' and take steps to improve their operations. One consequence would be greater diversification, with the introduction of such new commercial crops as fruits, vegetables and livestock in those parts of the country that had specialized in sericulture in the past. At the same time, the commercial activities of farmers that had developed fairly autonomously in the 1920s would be increasingly influenced by the state. As a result, 'the agriculture of rice and silk' that had prevailed in the countryside to that point gradually became less uniformly structured, and the basis for development of a wide range of new commercial crops in the postwar era was created.

The second goal of the campaign was the 'planned and systematic renewal' of the countryside, with a key institutional role assigned to the industrial cooperatives (*sangyō kumiai*) that were to be revivified in those villages where they already existed and established where none had yet been formed. This paved the way for the postwar development of the agricultural cooperative unions (*nōgyō kyōdō kumiai*, or *nōkyō*). At the same time, the government also put great emphasis on linking the hamlets within each village to the village's industrial cooperative, and the farm practice associations (*nōji jikkō kumiai*) that were formed in hamlets at this time functioned as the lowest unit of state control measures during wartime.

The third goal of the Rural Revitalization Campaign was to nurture 'village mainstays' (*nōson chūken jinbutsu*) as the agents of its policies in the countryside. Most of those recruited for this role were middling farmers, that is, owner-cultivators with fairly typical holdings for the area or farmers from the upper ranks of local owner-tenants. Some had been active in hamlet youth groups in the 1920s and were still quite young. Others were older, veterans of the tenancy disputes of the previous decade or of other local efforts to improve farming and raise living standards. They were sent for training at Kato Kanji's well-known private academy, the Japan National Higher Level School (Nihon kokumin kōtō gakkō) in Tomobe, not far from the city of Mito in Ibaraki Prefecture, and, later on, to the farmers' training centers (*nōmin dōjō*) which the Ministry of Agriculture and Forestry had established throughout the country, where a concerted effort was made to indoctrinate them with emperor-centered nationalism and agrarianism (*nōhonshugi*), the central ideologies of state-sponsored rural revitalization. This had the effect of distancing middling farmers from various campaigns influenced by socialist thought and such specific concerns of the tenant movement in which some of them had been involved as rent reductions and security of cultivating rights, instead mobilizing them in service to what was portrayed as the national interest.

Those who would coordinate the activities of village mainstays at the local level were designated 'village leaders' (*nōson chūshin jinbutsu*), but they did not come from the largest local landowning families that had monopolized village leadership positions hitherto. On the contrary, they represented the new leadership stratum that had developed within many villages by the late 1920s, a sort of 'local intelligentsia' consisting primarily of the sons of small and medium-sized cultivating landlords who possessed higher than average educational qualifications. Many were graduates of agricultural schools or had completed training courses in farming, working thereafter as technicians in local agricultural associations or as organizers of industrial cooperatives. Once the depression had ended, they rose to such posts as village mayors, deputy mayors and officials of local agricultural associations. They therefore played key roles both in efforts at rural revitalization during the harsh years of the depression, defending the interests of middling farmers in ways that the former leadership elite of large, non-cultivating landlords would not necessarily have found congenial, and in the implementation at the local level of subsequent control measures during wartime.

In contrast to rural revitalization, which sought domestic solutions to the crisis of the countryside in the depression years, policies promoting emigration to Manchuria sought to defuse the crisis by exporting one perceived cause of it: the surplus population of Japanese villages. In the next section I will trace the evolution of these emigration policies from their inception in the early 1930s to the announcement in 1936 of the government's plan to send one million emigrant households to Manchuria.

Official promotion of emigration to Manchuria

Policies promoting emigration to Manchuria began in the aftermath of the Manchurian Incident of September 1931 and the subsequent founding of the Japanese puppet state of Manchukuo in March 1932, these policies reflecting the military and political needs of running Manchuria as a de facto Japanese colony. Of course, the rural poverty caused by the depression also played a part, so it can be said that in emigration to Manchuria a linkage of war and the plight of the Japanese countryside occurred (Asada 1976: 104–7).

Before further discussion of the case of Manchuria, it will be helpful to outline the general contours of twentieth-century emigration from Japan. As shown in Figure 8.1, the number of Japanese immigrants resident in such Japanese colonies as Korea, Karafuto (southern Sakhalin), Taiwan and southern Manchuria (a Japanese leasehold since 1905) began to increase in the years following the Russo-Japanese War. During the 1920s, the increase in Korea was particularly striking, rising from about 300,000 in the late 1910s to almost 600,000 in 1930. During the 1930s, however, the most striking increase took place in Manchuria, with the total number of Japanese immigrants resident there surpassing the number in Korea in about 1935. In addition, we can also see that the number of Japanese immigrants resident in China proper escalated from a fairly low level from the mid-1930s on, especially after the outbreak of hostilities between China and Japan in 1937. That is to say, it is clear that from about 1930 onward the balance shifted from emigration to Korea, Karafuto and Taiwan to emigration to Manchuria and China proper, with the number of Japanese resident in Manchuria rising from 200,000 in 1930 to 1,000,000 in 1940. Turning now to destinations beyond Japan's colonial empire, it is apparent that the number of Japanese immigrants resident in North America increased until the mid-1920s, but stabilized after passage of the Immigration Act of 1924 in the United States, one of the chief aims of which was to end immigration from Japan. From about that time, an increasing number of Japanese began to emigrate to Central and South America. During the initial four decades of the century, then, there were two main categories of emigration from Japan: that destined for Japan's formal and informal empire and that destined for the Americas. The former consisted of 'colonists' backed by national policy, and the latter consisted of 'economic migrants' who sought to improve their lives and who received relatively little in the way of official encouragement

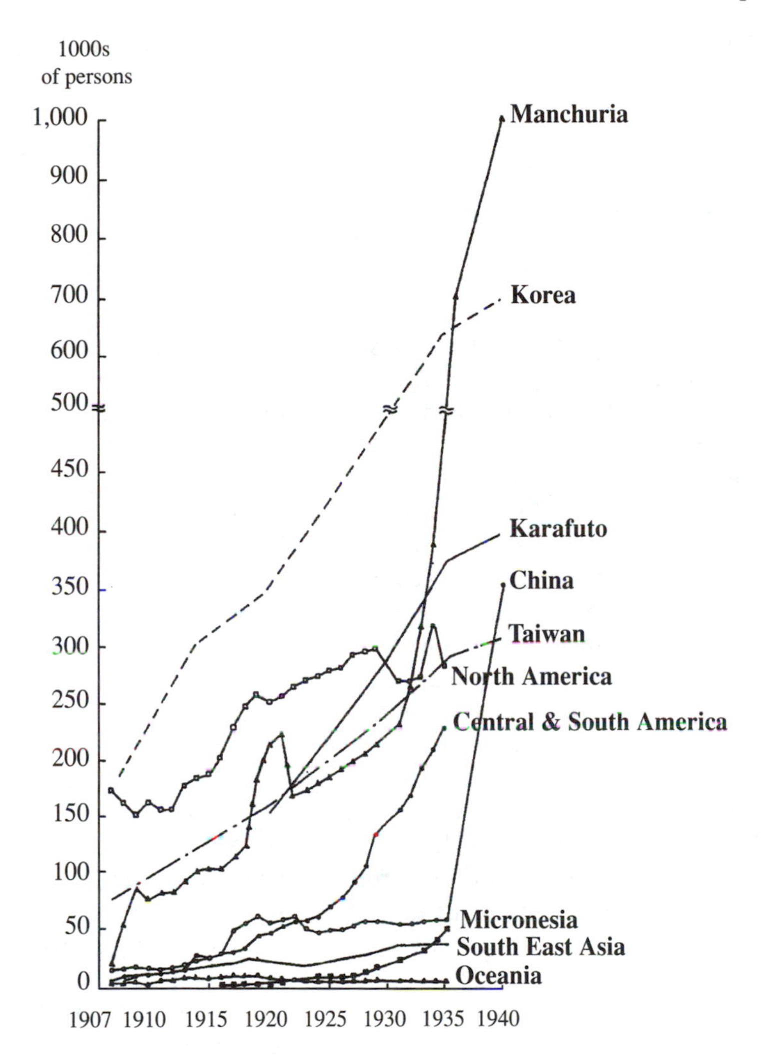

Figure 8.1 Japanese emigrants by destination.

Source: Takahashi Yasutaka, *Shōwa sensenki no nōson to Manshū imin* (Tokyo: Yoshikawa kōbunkan, 1997), p. 13.

(Takahashi 1997: 4). That Manchuria was the focus of emigration during the 1930s is also clear.

Now, let us move on to a brief overview of emigration to Manchuria. In July 1932, a little more than a month after the May 15th Incident, Captain Tōmiya Kaneo, a subordinate to Ishiwara Kanji on the staff of the Kwantung Army, and the agrarianist Katō Kanji met in Japan and decided that a program of emigration to Manchuria was desirable. Katō (1888–1967) was to play a key role in bringing that program about. After graduating from the Faculty of Agriculture at Tokyo Imperial University he had worked part-time for the Home Ministry and the Imperial Agricultural Association before becoming a teacher in 1913 at the Anjō School of Farming and Forestry, which was directed then by the well-known agrarianist Yamazaki Nobukichi. While there, Katō became a devotee of the 'Ancient Shinto' teachings of Kakei Katsuhiko, which stressed commitment to the emperor and to farming as the essence of the Japanese spirit, and to put these teachings into practice Katō established his own school in Kamiyama, Yamagata Prefecture in 1915. By 1925, he had embarked on the Ogino reclamation project in nearby Shinjō, with support from the War Ministry, as a means of providing plots of land to the non-inheriting second and third sons of farm families in the prefecture. The community of new settlers that resulted from this project would later be used as a model for the subsequent Japanese settlement of Manchuria. Katō had thought the Manchurian Incident provided an excellent opportunity to provide much greater opportunities for Japanese farmers, and with the help of Ishiguro Tadaatsu, then Vice-Minister of Agriculture, he had been able to present his case for a concerted policy of emigration to Manchuria to the Ministry of Colonial Affairs in January 1932. He would organize an Imperial Farmers' Corps of emigrants in as many villages as possible, those corps to be led by local village leaders (*chūshin jinbutsu*) and mainstay farmers (*chūken jinbutsu*).

The May 15th Incident, in which some civilian agrarianists had also taken part, triggered a flood of petitions from groups representing farmers to politicians and bureaucrats demanding attention to rural relief, and among the demands put forward by the Local Autonomy Farmers' Conference (Jichi nōmin kyōgikai) was 50 million yen in state aid for emigration to Manchuria. A much more modest appropriation of 200,000 yen 'to conduct feasibility studies on the farming and other economic opportunities available to those who went to Manchuria' was approved by the Diet in 1932, sitting in an emergency session known as 'the Rural Rescue Diet.' Emigration to Manchuria as a national policy began thereafter.

Among the very first to emigrate, beginning in October 1932, were 70 trainees from Katō Kanji's Japan National Higher Level School in Ibaraki, all of them carrying guns. In May 1936, in the aftermath of the February 26th Incident, the Kwantung Army and the Ministry of Colonial Affairs formulated a proposal 'for the dispatch of one million farm households to Manchuria,' which was approved by the Hirota Cabinet as a 20-year plan in August 1936. In November, the Hirota Cabinet also approved a plan to send 'volunteer youth corps' to Manchuria (Manmō kaitaku seishōnen giyūdan). Both plans were to be implemented from 1937. In this way, emigration policy evolved in two phases, the first after the May 15th Incident and the second after the February 26th Incident.

On March 11, 1936, just after the February 26th Incident, Katō Kanji met with Tanaka Nagashige, head of the Economic Revitalization Section within the Ministry of Agriculture and Forestry. It is worth quoting at some length from the record of their conversation:

> *Katō*: On the question of land, there's plenty available [in Manchuria] now at one or two yen per *tan*. Worrying about what we'd do if the price rises, the way some people do, makes no sense at all. In my opinion, we should just get on with it as quickly as possible. The Chinese and the Koreans don't bother trying to find out who owns the land they want. They just move in and take it over. If we waste time trying to track down owners and agree prices, we'll get left behind. The first group of armed emigrants didn't buy land before they left Japan, they bought it after they arrived. In Manchuria, no one knows who owns which parcels of land. If we Japanese don't get cracking, the Koreans and the Chinese will grab all the land there is.
>
> *Tanaka*: (Laughing) It sounds like theft to me.
>
> *Katō*: The conditions over there are not like those here at home. If you call what I'm talking about 'theft,' then you'd have to be against war, too, because war also involves theft as well as killing.
>
> *Tanaka*: (Laughing) You know, you sound like the head of a band of thieves to me.
>
> (Ide 1986: 85–6)

As the above quotation from the record makes clear, the two men did not agree about emigration to Manchuria. Whereas Katō insisted that the Japanese should acquire land there as quickly as possible and get on with Japanese settlement, Tanaka was highly skeptical. His stance was typical of the prevailing stance among most high-ranking Ministry of Agriculture and Forestry officials, where the entire venture was seen not only as likely to involve 'theft on a grand scale' but also as of dubious benefit to the Japanese settlers themselves on account of the difficulties they would face in operating their farms if and when they got them. In fact, it can be said that it was the military (especially the Kwantung Army) and the Ministry of Colonial Affairs that played the most active role in promoting the emigration project, and that the Ministry of Agriculture and Forestry was more or less carried along in their wake. That said, there were high-ranking officials in the latter ministry such as Ishiguro Tadaatsu and Kodaira Gonichi who did actively support Katō's project in the expectation that the dispatch of settlers abroad would contribute to relief of agrarian distress at home by freeing up land that could be redistributed among the remaining farmers, enabling them to expand their scale of operations.

Yet the essence of the emigration policy announced in 1936 lay not in the rescue of impoverished farmers, but in military necessity, as the following list of purposes makes clear (Yamada 1978). First of all, the bolstering of national defense. For the military, emigration to Manchuria was seen as 'the most important policy at present for defense of the nation and the realization of national objectives.' More specifically, it was needed: (1) to defend the South Manchurian Railway and areas experiencing raids by anti-Japanese forces; (2) to defend Japan against the Soviet Union, by the settlement of immigrants in northern Manchuria, especially near the border; (3) to insure that the 'Yamato race' would form the core race among the 'five races in harmonious coexistence' in the region; and (4) to provide for the defense of Manchuria's heavy industries. At the time, given these functions, Japanese emigrants to Manchuria were described as 'human pillboxes' (*ningen-tōchika*). Second, as a step toward the achievement of autarky. Japanese settlers were needed in Manchuria to provide Japan with feed for livestock and with improved stock breeds, and eventually with such staple foodstuffs as rice, wheat, and maize. More immediately, they were needed to guarantee self-sufficiency in food supplies for the rest of the Japanese population in Manchuria and for the Kwantung Army.

Third (and last of all), as a means of solving the problem of over-population in Japanese villages, which was widely regarded as a major cause of rural poverty, by sending the most marginal farmers – especially those with holdings of five *tan* or less – abroad as settlers. The Ministry of Agriculture and Forestry agreed to support emigration largely for this reason and set about encouraging villages to divide residents into two groups, one of which would emigrate and establish a 'branch village' in Manchuria and the other of which would take over the vacated holdings, thus expanding the scale of their operations and prospering at last.

A fairly simple calculation underlay the target figure of one million emigrant households: at an average of five family members per household, that was the number needed to insure that 10 percent of the population in Manchuria, which was projected to reach 50 million at the end of 20 years, would be Japanese. To achieve that target it would be necessary to get somewhat over half of the 1.86 million households farming less than five *tan* as of the mid-1930s to emigrate over the next two decades. As there were about 5.5 million farm households in Japan at the time, the plan required getting roughly 20 percent of them to emigrate.

In the eight years between 1937 and Japan's defeat in 1945, however, the total number of emigrants to Manchuria amounted to only 320,000, and at that rate, the goal of five million in 20 years' time would never have been achieved. In that respect, the policy of Manchurian emigration was an obvious failure.

Most Japanese emigrants ended up either in northern Manchuria, near the Amur River which marked the border with the Soviet Union, or in Dairen, Changchun and Harbin, near the South Manchurian Railway line. That they were concentrated there, rather than in the rural hinterland of southern Manchuria where it was possible to grow rice, shows that the Ministry of Agriculture and Forestry's concern with the economic opportunities available to migrating farmers was subordinated to the strategic concerns of the army. Granted, there were great stretches of unexploited land in the plains of northern Manchuria, but as in Manchuria as a whole virtually all of the land that was suitable for agriculture had already been occupied by Chinese, Manchurian or Korean farmers. The Public Corporation for the Development of Manchuria (Manshū kaitaku kōsha) was able to get those farmers to sell their holdings at very low prices and pass them on to Japanese settlers only because the Kwantung Army stood behind it, willing to apply force as and when necessary. In other words, the policy of emigration to Manchuria was indeed founded on pillage, or 'theft on a grand scale.'

Emigration to Manchuria and rural Japan

To begin with, let us look at the distribution of emigrants by prefecture. As shown in Table 8.1, Nagano Prefecture produced the largest number of emigrants. Yamagata Prefecture came a distant second, and Kumamoto Prefecture ranked third. Next came Fukushima, Niigata and Miyagi Prefectures. Overall, emigrants came primarily from the sericultural regions of central Japan, as exemplified by Nagano, and from the Tohoku region. To a degree, this reflected the fact that farmers in those regions had been hardest hit by the depression.

Although there were relatively few emigrants from southwestern Japan, two prefectures in that part of Japan did rank highly: Kumamoto as third and Hiroshima, eighth. This was probably because these two prefectures had sent a lot of people to North and South America and, when the

Table 8.1 Prefectural origins of emigrants to Manchuria

Rank	*Prefecture*	*Number of emigrants*	*Rank*	*Prefecture*	*Number of emigrants*
1	Nagano	37,859	13	Gumma	8,775
2	Yamagata	17,177	14	Aomori	8,365
3	Kumamoto	12,680	15	Kagawa	7,885
4	Fukushima	12,673	16	Ishikawa	7,271
5	Niigata	12,641	17	Yamaguchi	6,508
6	Miyagi	12,419	18	Iwate	6,436
7	Gifu	12,090	19	Okayama	5,786
8	Hiroshima	11,172	20	Kagoshima	5,700
9	Tokyo	11,111	21	Nara	5,243
10	Kōchi	10,082	22	Toyama	5,200
11	Akita	9,452	23	Fukui	5,136
12	Shizuoka	9,206	24	Yamanashi	5,105

Source: Manshū kaitakushi kankōkai, *Manshū kaitakushi*, 1966.

Note
Prefectures ranking lower than 24 have been omitted.

emigration to North America came to a halt in the 1920s, they started to send emigrants to Manchuria as an alternative. Okinawa had similarly sent many emigrants to North America but ranked forty-first when it came to Manchuria, possibly because the cold climate there did not appeal to local farmers.

Ibaraki Prefecture, where Katō Kanji now lived and a center of radical agrarianism during the depression era, came only thirty-third. Most of those who did emigrate came from the northern portion of the prefecture, where dry-field farming prevailed and where agrarianism was particularly popular. But there was little interest either in agrarianism or in emigration in the southern, rice-producing portion of the prefecture. That there were unusually extensive tracts of forest on fairly level land stretching from the western part of the prefecture to the southern, providing opportunities to bring new land under cultivation at home, no doubt helps to explain the lack of interest in Manchuria.

To some degree, then, the geographical distribution of emigrants reflected local economic conditions, but there were other important factors as well, ranging from personal ties and a local tradition of emigration to the presence of local leaders promoting emigration. The latter was of particular importance. It was usually the case that those who mobilized the poor farmers and landless agricultural workers in their villages into emigrant groups were the very mainstay farmers and, in some cases, the village leaders who had previously led local rural revitalization efforts.

Indeed, it was central to the whole emigration project that local mainstays persuade others in their communities to emigrate.

In Yamagata Prefecture the following six categories of people were listed as eligible to apply for emigration: (1) those who could command the respect of others and function in the future as the leaders of emigrant communities; (2) those with useful non-agricultural skills; (3) those with no land at all or insufficient land holdings; (4) those with a firm commitment to simplicity and honesty; (5) those who had engaged in agriculture for many years; and (6) those who were diligent and frugal (Mori 1999: 162).

The first category very clearly meant village mainstays. The 'useful skills' in the second category included plasterer, carpenter, blacksmith and car driver, combined with some farming experience. All the other categories applied primarily to poor farmers of one sort or another, from landless agricultural workers to tenant farmers with tiny holdings.

No educational qualifications were imposed. Although applicants up to 30 years of age who had passed the physical examination for conscription were preferred, anyone up to the age of 40 who was capable of physical labor was eligible. Even if married, applicants had to be willing to emigrate on their own and leave their families behind for at least one year; not need to send money back to their families; and be able to provide 30 yen toward the cost of getting to their destination and 20 to 30 yen for their expenses for a year. Most applicants were the fairly young second and third sons of farm families, who had no obligation to send money home.

Each successful applicant in 1937 was given a grant of 1,000 yen and ten *chō* of land in Manchuria, consisting of one *chō* of paddy land, three *chō* of dry fields and the rest in a portion of communal pasture land. No payments for the land were required for five years, and then the cultivator would have ten years to pay the amount due (*Tokyo asahi shinbun*, May 29, 1937).

Table 8.2 shows the socio-economic status of 20 residents who emigrated to Manchuria from Yamato Village in the Shōnai district of Yamagata Prefecture in 1941. The largest group, 13 of the 20, were agricultural workers either on a daily or annual basis. Four of the 13 also engaged in farming, probably as tenants. There was one carpenter, one factory worker and one rope maker, men who possessed some of the sought-after useful skills. All but one of the emigrants were married, not a few of them having large families with six to nine members. Their average age was 37.

Among those who emigrated from Yamato Village were three men who were members of the Imperial Farmers' Corps, two of them farmers

Table 8.2 Emigrants from Yamato Village, 1941

	Occupation	*Family size*	*Area land cultivated (tan)*	*Household tax paid (yen)*	*Age*	*Imperial Farmers' Corps*	*Industrial association (sangyō kumiai)*	
							Savings (yen)	*Loans (yen)*
1	Agricultural day laborer, farmer	3	2.4	0.24	53	–	30.00	20.00
2	Farmer, rice miller	5	5.0	0.34	36	–	–	–
3	Agricultural worker (annual)	7	–	1.65	25	–	–	–
4	Farmer	6	8.5	0.17	36	member	48.21	190.00
5	Agricultural day laborer	8	–	1.65	31	member	30.00	–
6	Agricultural day laborer	7	–	0.18	41	–	–	–
7	Farmer	8	21.6	0.35	36	member	150.00	1,431.00
8	Agricultural day laborer	7	–	–	39	–	60.00	165.00
9	Agricultural day laborer	4	–	15.13(*sic*)	42	–	–	–
10	Agricultural day laborer	6	–	0.24	25	–	–	–
11	Agricultural day laborer, farmer	6	1.8	0.24	42	–	90.00	332.00
12	Farmer, agricultural day laborer	9	7.0	0.55	38	–	60.00	150.00
13	Agricultural day laborer, farmer	6	2.6	0.24	45	–	60.00	170.00
14	Agricultural day laborer	5	–	–	36	–	60.00	–
15	Farmer	3	8.4	3.58	33	–	90.00	350.00
16	Agricultural worker (annual)	5	–	0.24	31	–	60.00	230.00
17	Carpenter	6	–	0.11	36	–	–	–
18	Agricultural day laborer	6	–	–	55	–	–	–
19	Factory worker	1	–	3.58	24	–	–	–
20	Rope maker	6	–	0.24	36	–	–	–
	Total	114	57.3	28.73			738.27	3,038.00
	Average (of entries)	5.7	7.2	1.69	37		67.12	337.56

Source: Sekisetsu chihō nōson keizai chōsajo, *Manshū nōgyō imin boson keizai jittai chōsa*, 1941.

with land holdings (at over two *chō* and 8.5 *tan*, respectively) that were considerably larger than the holdings of others in the group. These were clearly village mainstays, who fulfilled the criteria of 'commanding the respect of others and functioning in the future as leaders of the emigrant village.' Thus, this group of emigrants was stratified into a few mainstay leaders on the one hand, and a larger number of poor farmers and agricultural workers on the other. The latter, and the three men with useful non-agricultural skills, were probably the second and third sons of local farm households, who saw emigration to Manchuria as their only chance to establish themselves as landowning farmers.

Let us now turn our attention to one of the local mainstay farmers who played a crucial role in leading a group of emigrants from Yamato in 1943, Togashi Naotarō. Togashi was born in 1902. After graduating from upper elementary school and completing a middle-school correspondence course, he had spent some time in Tokyo. The eldest son in his family, he then returned home to succeed his father as family head. After becoming active in the administration of the local youth association (*seinendan*), at the age of 25 he had attended some of Katō Kanji's lectures in Kamiyama and was persuaded that the opening up of new farm land at home and abroad was a means of solving the problems facing the non-inheriting sons of farm families.

His own family had been owner-cultivators of two *chō* of land, but his father had been forced to mortgage the entire holding when a coal mining venture in Karafuto he had borrowed money to invest in had failed during the depression. Faced with a great burden of debt, Togashi eagerly committed himself to rural revitalization and played an active role in organizing an industrial cooperative in his village. Then, by dint of improvements to his farm management and hard work, he was finally able to repay his creditors and regain title to the family landholding. In addition, he rented 2.5 *chō*, thus becoming an owner-tenant cultivating 4.5 *chō* in all.

Sometime in the 1930s he had organized the Yamato Village Imperial Farmers' Corps and become a champion of emigration to Manchuria as a means of solving the problem of rural over-population and the bleak prospects of non-inheriting sons. In 1943 he won over potential emigrants with the promise that each of them would become the owner-cultivator of ten *chō* of land, obtained the necessary land from the Koreans who were cultivating it with the help of the Manchurian Development Corporation, and set off for Manchuria. In 1945, after the Soviet Union had entered the war and Japan had surrendered, local Manchurians attacked the settlement Togashi had established, killing 40 villagers. He tried to lead the remaining emigrants back to Japan, but they were captured by Red Army troops and imprisoned in Siberia for one year and a half (interview with Togashi Naotarō, 1991).

Back in the late 1930s Togashi wrote the following about the 'branch village movement' he led:

> (a) The branch village movement is of fundamental importance to rural regeneration, but village elders raise all sorts of objections to it. That's because they are trapped in conventional ways of thinking and contented with the status quo. They have no interest in building a new Japan. I feel that friction between people like them who think only of themselves and people with new ways of thinking is inevitable. After years of toil, I finally got our household finances straightened out, and then I got involved in this movement. Since then I've had no time at all for farming. . . . But then, no one determined to build an ideal society can expect an easy time of it.
>
> (b) 'Emigration' is not the movement of impoverished people to another place. Rather, it should be seen as a quest for independence, undertaken by comrades who understand the true importance of agriculture and who have awakened to the Japanese spirit. That's how I regard emigration by farmers. Those who dismiss agriculture, now that it has been devastated by the money economy, and who think that the only work worth having is that of an employee on monthly salary are mistaken, very mistaken indeed.
>
> (c) Japanese history is actually the history of emigration. Both the Eastern Expedition by Emperor Jimmu and the conquest of the Kumaso tribe in Kyushu by Prince Yamato-takeru were products of a genuine, unceasing effort. It is the same today with the many soldiers who leave their villages to cheering throngs and waving flags to attend to the sacred task of driving the Russians out of Asia. . . . The Hōtoku movement founded by the revered Ninomiya [Sontoku] and the colonization movement championed by Katō-sensei, leader of the Imperial Farmers' Corps, share the same essence. . . . Villages today are filled to overflowing with people, but finally there is a solution at hand to the wretchedness of residents' lives and livelihoods. . . . Aren't we brave men who don't worry about whether we live or die? Wouldn't we like to lay the foundations for later settlements all the way to the Urals?
>
> (Togashi 1938: 32–3)

It was in the above terms that one mainstay farmer, Togashi Naotarō, made the case for emigration to Manchuria. In (a) he emphasized that the branch village campaign had been opposed by 'village elders,' chiefly landlords we can assume, and represented a struggle to break free from the status quo and create an ideal society. Here we observe that so strong was his ideological commitment that he was even prepared to put his position as a middling farmer in jeopardy by neglecting his own fields. In (b) he professed his commitment to the central beliefs of agrarianism by means of a critique of the money economy and of urban salaried employees, confirming the importance of agriculture as a way of life and the importance of Japanese spirit. In (c) he made a case for emigration, in the process legitimizing his own actions. By citing examples of military expeditions since ancient (even mythological) times, he sought to present contemporary expansion onto the continent as an equally sacred project, in that the creation of a branch village would rescue all of those who had been impoverished emotionally and economically by the depression. Moreover, the expansion of the Yamato people he envisaged would eventually extend beyond Manchuria to reach as far as the Urals. The three elements of emperor-centered history, rescue of the countryside and emigration were thus combined in his thinking.

Although inspired by Katō Kanji, Togashi's ideas about emigration were also shaped by the dire straits of the countryside in the aftermath of the depression. Readers today will no doubt be struck by his ethnocentrism and enthusiastic support for the invasion of foreign lands, but it should also be noted that in the rural Japan of the time his ideas were considered revolutionary in that they, like the even grander schemes for a 'Showa Restoration' propounded by young military officers in the 1930s, sought to destroy the status quo. He regarded the acquisition of foreign territory not as an end in itself, but as a means of relieving rural poverty at home.

As the example of Togashi demonstrates, the promotion of emigration to Manchuria depended very greatly on the leadership of mainstay farmers and the recruitment efforts of the local Imperial Farmers' Corps to persuade second and third sons to sign up for emigration. It appears that, in the Tohoku region, emigration was further encouraged by some lineage groups (*dōzoku*, known locally as *maki*) and hamlets pressing for volunteers to emigrate for the greater good of all concerned (Yunoki 1977: 60).

The next matter to consider is the response of local landlords to Togashi's campaign. In Yamato Village, a few large landlords had long dominated village affairs, and they proved themselves decidedly cool to both rural revitalization and emigration to Manchuria. In fact, their stance toward the latter was hostile, leading Togashi to conclude that the only way forward against the opposition of 'village elders' who defended the status quo was to seek the radical reform of village politics. Large landlords in the village objected to emigration primarily because fewer tenant

Table 8.3 Views on the necessity of emigration to Manchuria, Ibaraki Prefecture, as surveyed in September 1936 (%)

	Not necessary	*Very necessary*	*Necessary*	*Fairly necessary*	*Somewhat necessary*	*Necessary in the future*	*Necessary in view of national policy*	*Logically necessary*
Village mayors	40	11	12	7	14	7	3	6
Agricultural association heads	59	7	29	7	15	7		4
Industrial association heads	35	16	19	9	2		7	2
Elementary school principals	31	20	11	3	12	11	3	1
Agricultural technicians	51	19	16	3	16			
Youth school teachers	23	28	21	5	14	7	5	1
Reservists' association heads	41	20	14	1	4	7	3	2
Youth group leaders	30	15	17	5	7	9	6	
Girls' youth group leaders	35	6	7	7	11			
Overall response rate	37	16	19	5	10	7	3	3

Source: Nōson kōsei kyōkai, *Tochi jinkō chōsei taisaku ni kansuru Ibaraki 4 gun nōson chōsa*, 1937.

farmers would reduce demand for their land, leading first to a decline in the rents they could charge and eventually to a decline in the value of their holdings. Some smaller cultivating landlords also objected to emigration on the grounds that it would reduce the plentiful supply of local labor, forcing them to pay higher wages to those they employed to work their fields.

The stance of the established local elite in Yamato does not appear to have been at all atypical. Consider the results shown in Table 8.3 of a survey conducted in villages in four districts of Ibaraki Prefecture in September 1936, in which residents who held various administrative posts within their communities were asked their views on emigration to Manchuria. Even though this survey took place at a time when emigration was official national policy and explicit opposition to that policy was difficult, more than 37 percent of those polled said they saw 'no need' for such emigration. Moreover, the largest groups among those so responding were heads of local branches of the Imperial Agricultural Association (59 percent), agricultural technicians (51 percent), heads of local branches of the Military Reservists' Association (41 percent) and village mayors (40 percent). As most leadership posts in branches of the Imperial Agricultural Association were occupied by landlords at this time and as most village mayors were landlords, it is apparent that landlords tended not to favor emigration.

Those expressing views in favor of emigration may be divided into two groups, 40 percent expressing what can be described as positive endorsement (either 'very necessary,' 'necessary' or 'fairly necessary') and 23 percent who might best be described as marginally or passively in favor (10 percent 'somewhat necessary'; 7 percent 'necessary in the future'; 3 percent 'necessary in view of national policy'; and 3 percent 'logically necessary.') The highest percentages recorded among those who regarded emigration as 'very necessary' were teachers in youth schools (at 28 percent), principals of primary schools (at 20 percent) and leaders of local military reservists branches (also at 20 percent). That suggests that it was primarily the educators within villages who promoted emigration, along with at least some with close ties to the military.

Among the reasons cited in the same report concerning why farmers in general were opposed to emigration were uncertainty about the conditions on offer, fear of Manchuria itself, the availability of land for reclamation within Japan, the peace and stability of their own villages, love for the homeland, parental objections, and opportunities to find work in Japanese cities (Nōson kōsei kyōkai 1937).

To sum up, it is clear that mainstay farmers with strong ideological convictions played a crucial role in mobilizing a fairly modest number of farmers to emigrate to Manchuria. It was very definitely not a program led by landlords as a means of defusing tension between themselves and their tenants, as some have argued (for example, Asada 1976), nor was it a venture to which poor farmers flocked in droves, eager to get their hands on ten *chō* of land, as others have argued (Takahashi 1997). On the contrary, poor farmers needed considerable persuasion to overcome their reluctance to sign on as emigrants.

Moreover, from the start of the Sino–Japanese War in 1937 and the boom in war-related industries that it triggered, there were plenty of opportunities for non-agricultural employment again, and poor farmers had the more attractive option of migrating to Japanese cities. That Nagano Prefecture continued to provide emigrants in significant numbers thereafter was in part because of the strength of agrarian thought within the prefecture and the activism of local mainstay farmers, and in part because of the continued economic distress caused by the collapse of sericulture in mountainous districts where arable land, and hence alternatives to sericulture, was scarce. Even then, it took the efforts of mainstay farmers and the urgings of such village leaders as elementary school teachers, youth school teachers and heads of military reservist branches to channel

Plate 8.1 Settlers from Yamagata Prefecture in Manchuria, 1943. Courtesy of Togashi Eiji.

the desire of poor farmers for more land into a decision to emigrate to Manchuria.

Roughly comparable circumstances prevailed in Yamagata Prefecture. On the one hand, many of the mainstay farmers in that prefecture, whether owner-cultivators or owner-tenants, saw the emigration of their poorer neighbors as a source of additional land for themselves, an important consideration in a region where the harsh winter climate permitted only one crop of rice per year, and actively supported the 'branch village' movement to achieve that outcome. On the other hand, there were far fewer factories of any sort in the prefecture or anywhere along the Japan Sea side of the country, whether war-related or not, than was the case on the other side of the country, facing the Pacific, and so there were relatively few opportunities for poor farmers and non-inheriting sons to find non-agricultural employment. As a result, the over-population of villages remained a problem, and campaigners such as Togashi Naotarō remained able to gain recruits for emigration.

Emigration to Korea

To shed further light on the relationship between rural society and emigration to Manchuria, I would like to make some comparisons with emigration to Korea. As noted previously, Korea had been the most popular destination for Japanese emigrants in the early decades of the century, especially after its 'absorption' into the Japanese empire in 1910. From then and throughout the 1920s, the Oriental Development Company (Tōyō takushoku kaisha) played an active role in promoting emigration (Matsunaga 2000: 31–57). For the purpose of comparison with Manchuria, however, I will confine my attention to emigration to Korea during the 1930s.

As an example, I will consider the efforts of Matsuoka Toshizo, a Diet Member from Yamagata Prefecture, to establish forestry operations in Korea. Matsuoka, who belonged to the Seiyūkai Party, represented the Murayama district and had played at active role in promoting rural relief projects there and in the Mogami district in the early years of the depression. From 1934 on, he began supporting the forging of closer transportation links between Japan and Korea – the so-called project to turn the Sea of Japan into a Japanese lake – and advocating the promotion of forestry in northern Korea, which would provide employment opportunities for emigrants from Yamagata and elsewhere in the Tohoku.

The project to turn the Sea of Japan into a Japanese lake involved developing new ports at Rajin and Unggi and the creation of a free-trade zone at the mouth of the Tumen River near the border between Korea and Manchuria as a means of promoting the development of northern Korea (Yoshii 2000: 260–79). It was part of the plan for the industrialization of Korea announced by the Japanese governor-general of the colony, Ugaki Kazushige, in the early 1930s (Hori 1995: 191–265), which brought about a marked change in Japanese emigration thereafter. Instead of farmers, emigrants who would contribute to Korea's industrialization were now sought.

Matsuoka's forestry project in northern Korea was a response to this new departure, aiming at the exploitation of 11,000 *chō* of state-owned forests along the upper reaches of the Tumen River to provide timber for the construction of factories and other industrial facilities elsewhere in the colony. He explained his objectives in an advertisement that appeared on January 6, 1937 in the Yamagata edition of the *Tokyo asahi shinbun*, with the headline 'All travel expenses paid. Call for volunteers to survey conditions in northern Korea.' The text read:

> Every sensible person knows that new enterprises should be developed more rapidly in northern Korea than in northern Manchuria. Northern Korea is situated at the very door of the whole northern Manchuria region, which stretches from Changchun to the Amur River at the border. Northern Korea, therefore, is a strategic point of ultimate importance. People from the Tohoku should most seriously concern themselves with northern Korea. It is more than obvious that, in every possible respect, northern Korea as a strategic point is more important than any other place. With Port Rajin and Port Chongin, is not northern Korea the most promising place for ambitious youths?
>
> Residents of Yamagata Prefecture tend to be traditional. . . . They find it difficult even in these troubled times to adjust to the new circumstances that prevail. High birth rates have forced farm families to divide up their holdings into smaller and smaller parcels, and as a result many farmers are now destitute. Like it or not, it is absolutely certain that the day will come when everyone, not just tenant farmers but landlords and wealthy owner-cultivators too, will face ruin.
>
> In contrast to the bleak situation here, northern Korea is like a blank sheet of paper. With a blank sheet, one can allow oneself to enjoy drawing whatever one wants. And one will be properly rewarded for one's efforts. Are you contented with the status quo, or do you want the chance of a better life by moving to the new frontier?
>
> I have devised this inspection tour as a test of the determination of the residents of Yamagata Prefecture. I am confident that right-

> minded people will come forward, and that is why I have placed this advertisement.

The advertisement alluded to the problems of overpopulation and poverty that had afflicted the Tohoku region. It then contrasted that problem-ridden region with a supposedly problem-free northern Korea, which was projected as an attractive 'new frontier' where young people would be able to realize their legitimate aspirations. We can see here an attempt to link the creation of the puppet state of Manchukuo with the industrialization of Korea, and to encourage Japanese emigration to northern Korea.

It was Kazama Kōemon, a large landlord owning 500 *chō* in the Shonai region of Yamagata, who provided finance for Matsuoka's project in northern Korea (Shibuya, Mori, Hasebe 2000: 300–14), and the combined outcome of his funding and Matsuoka's organizational efforts was the establishment of the Matsuoka Forestry Works (Matsuoka ringyō jimusho) on 11,000 *chō* of state-owned forest land along the upper reaches of the Tumen River. The inspection/emigration promotion tour advertised above took place in April 1937, visiting the Matsuoka works and some other sites in northern Korea. The 40 tour members recruited from Yamagata consisted of 30 farmers, seven shopkeepers, two teachers and one carpenter, all young men in their twenties who had met the selection criteria set out in the advertisement: 'It is essential that applicants come from families of moderate means or less, be literate, be sound in mind and body and robust in spirit. A reference [of good character] from the village mayor or police officer would be very useful' as would be 'enthusiastic commitment to the transformation of the people of northern Korea into loyal subjects of the Emperor.'

The tour group landed in Port Chongin on April 5, 1937 and, after inspecting Port Rajin, Port Unggi and the large coal-mine district of Aoji, it arrived at the headquarters of the Matsuoka Forestry Works on the 8th. To commemorate their visit to Korea and the 'union of the peoples of Japan and Korea,' tour members then joined with the 300 Korean workers at the works for two weeks of tree planting. Finally, the group crossed the Tumen River and visited a number of sites in Manchuria, including a sheep breeding farm operated by the Oriental Development Company, before returning to Japan in early May.

Only 15 of the original 40 tour members returned to Japan, however; 25 of them stayed on in northern Korea (or in two cases, Manchuria) as emigrants. As shown in Table 8.4, seven of them took jobs with the Matsuoka Forestry Works, but the majority found employment elsewhere, with those entering non-agricultural work of one sort or another far

Table 8.4 Employment found by the 25 tour members who became emigrants

Position/occupation	*Number*
Matsuoka Forestry Works	7
Farming	3
Business	4
Shop worker	3
South Manchurian Railway employee	2
Mitsubishi Corporation employee	2
Office worker in a fishermen's association	2
Office worker in a mining company	1
Chōsen Nichi Nichi newspaper	1
Total	25

Source: 'Hokusen mitodokedan zaisensha genzaibo,' in *Chōsen jigyō shokan tsuzuri* (June 1936–December 1938). Kazama-ke monjo.

outnumbering those taking up farming. They may have come from families of 'moderate means or less' and no doubt they were the second or third sons in those families, but as the requirement of literacy and character references from authority figures suggests, they were probably from somewhat more affluent backgrounds than emigrants to Manchuria. Even though many of them came from farm families, moreover, most opted for non-agricultural employment. Given the relative stability of Korea under Japanese rule and the on-going program of industrial development in the north, there appears to have been ample such employment available.

A further contrast with Manchuria concerns the role of landlords. As the sponsorship of Matsuoka's venture by Kazama illustrates, wealthy landlords in wartime Japan were gradually shifting away from investment in arable land to investments in forests at home and abroad, and they were keen to take advantage of the economic opportunities that forestry development in Korea offered. Rather than opposing emigration, as was the case with Manchuria, they actively supported it.

To sum up, by the mid-1930s emigration to Korea had evolved from the state-sponsored programs of the early decades of Japanese colonial rule there to something akin to the voluntary 'economic migration' of Japanese to North America that had taken place until the 1920s and the 'economic migration' that continued to Central and South America thereafter. Of course, in the Korean case that fairly voluntary migration took place within the context of firm colonial rule by the Japanese military, but the military itself was not directly involved (Lee 1999: 156–82).

Emigration to Manchuria was markedly different. It was focused on agriculture, poor farmers were its major target, and at every step it was controlled by the Japanese military. It was also conceived on a truly grand scale, as a 'national project' requiring the movement of one million farm households, almost one-fifth of all the farm households in Japan, from their home islands to that part of northeast Asia. As we have seen, recruitment proved difficult and by the time of Japan's surrender on August 15, 1945 only a total of 320,000 individuals had emigrated. Those who remained in Manchuria at that time would pay a heavy price indeed for having seized the chance of owning 10 *chō* of land. The troops of the Kwantung Army rapidly retreated when the Soviet Red Army crossed the Manchurian border on August 9, leaving the settlers behind and subject to reprisal attacks by the local population. Roughly one-third of them lost their lives. Many survivors, Togashi Naotarō among them, were captured and interned for a time in Siberia, and it would not be until after the restoration of normal diplomatic relations between Japan and the People's Republic of China in the early 1970s that the children of Japanese emigrants who had been separated from their parents in the confusion of retreat and revenge could be repatriated to Japan. In every respect that one can think of, Japan's wartime project to promote emigration to Manchuria was a total failure.

References

Asada Kyōji. 1976. 'Manshū nōgyō imin seisaku no ritsuan katei.' In *Nihon teikokushugika no Manshū imin*, ed. Manshū iminshi kenkyūkai. Tokyo: Ryūkeishosha.

Hori Kazuo. 1995. *Chōsen kōgyōka no shiteki bunseki*. Tokyo: Yūhikaku.

Ide Magoroku, 1986. *Owarinaki tabi*. Tokyo: Iwanami shoten.

Lee Junko. 1999. 'Shokuminchi kōgyōka ron to Ugaki Issei sōtō no seisaku.' In *Ugaki Issei to sono jidai*, ed. Hori Makoto. Tokyo: Shinhyōron.

Matsunaga Tatsushi. 2000. 'Tōyō takushoku kaisha no imin jigyō.' In *Kokusaku-gaisha Tōtaku no kenkyū*, ed. Kawai Kazuo *et al.* Tokyo: Fuji shuppan.

Mori Takemaro. 1999. *Senji Nihon nōson shakai no kenkyū*. Tokyo: Tōkyō daigaku shuppankai.

Nōson kōsei kyōkai. 1937. *Tochi jinkō chōsei taisaku ni kansuru Ibaraki 4 gun chōsa*. Tokyo: Nōson kōsei kyōkai.

Shibuya Ryūichi, Mori Takemaro and Hasebe Hiroshi. 2000. *Shihonshugi no hatten to chihō zaibatsu*. Tokyo: Gendai shiryō shuppan.

Takahashi Yasutaka. 1997. *Shōwa sensenki no nōson to Manshū imin*. Tokyo: Yoshikawa kōbunkan.

Togashi Naotarō. 1938. 'Bunson undō no senjin o abite,' *Hirake Manmō*, 2(11).

Yamada Shōji. 1978. *Kindai minshū no kiroku 6 – Manshū imin*. Tokyo: Shin-jinbutsu ōraisha.

Yoshii Ken'ichi. 2000. *Kan-Nihonkai chiiki shakai: Manmō, Kantō, Ura Nihon*. Tokyo: Aoki shoten.
Yunoki Shun'ichi. 1977. 'Manshū nōgyō imin seisaku to Shōnai gata imin,' *Shakai keizai shigaku*, Nos. 42–5.

9 Part-time farming and the structure of agriculture in postwar Japan

Raymond A. Jussaume Jr

Introduction

In a recent article, Penelope Francks (2000) analyzed postwar agricultural policy in Japan, Korea and Taiwan in order to determine whether an East Asian model of agricultural development can be said to exist and to have played a broadly similar role in industrial development in those countries. By means of a comparative analysis of the structures of agriculture and exploration of how each national government has interacted with its own agricultural sector, Francks concluded that there are three basic similarities in the evolution of postwar agriculture across these countries. These are: (1) the fundamental role of rice cultivation in the structure of agricultural production and food consumption; (2) an active 'developmental state' which intervened in the farm sector, with the assistance of agricultural cooperative organizations, to support farm incomes and protect family farm households; and (3) the spread of pluriactivity, or part-time farming, to a majority of farm households.

Francks' analysis helps us recognize that Japan is not a singular case of agricultural change. Although Japanese agricultural development may appear to have very little in common with that of the United States or Europe, it would be a mistake to conclude that the Japanese case is unique and does not share similarities with other East Asian societies, or even some Occidental ones. A long history of riziculture, mountainous landscapes, a tradition of strong central governments, and a Confucian heritage are a few of the conditions that are shared by Japan, Korea and Taiwan and that have affected parallel changes in agriculture. In addition, Japan's agricultural system, like those in other so-called 'developed' societies, has been under pressure to become more economically efficient within the context of globalization. Japan shares with Europe the facts of a peasant agrarian history, a prevalence of small-scale agricultural operations, and strong state involvement in agriculture. Thus, while there are aspects of Japanese agricultural and rural life that are unique, the conditions there are not exceptional.

Francks' work highlights the role of national state actors in agricultural development. Of particular emphasis is how, in each East Asian case, the 'state' was a merging of public and private sector actors. The key private institution that has worked with the government bureaucracy in all three settings to initiate and implement farm income support policies has been the producer cooperative. Although there have been differences in the policies enacted and how the relationships between the government and the cooperatives have worked, Francks argues that this strong public–private sector coordination is reflective of a state-centered form of development that has been successful in many parts of Asia.

Finally, Francks underscores how the spread of part-time farming has become a central element in the evolution of postwar agriculture in that part of the world:

> Thus the pluriactive farm household represents a key link in the model [of agriculture's role in industrialization in East Asia], acting as the vehicle through which rural incomes could be sustained while labour and other resources were transferred to the industrial sector, and as the basic unit in a policy network which both exploited and supported this form of agricultural organization.
>
> (Francks 2000: 49)

This model crystallized during the first two decades of postwar Japanese history, which was a period of rapid and remarkable transformations. While the majority of Japanese rural households in the late 1940s were farm households that earned most or all of their income from agricultural activities, by the latter half of the 1960s most rural households were obtaining more than half of their income off-farm. As Francks notes, this rapid growth of part-time farming came about in part because of changes in the agricultural sector as well as the larger economy. Pluriactivity was the strategy through which farm households could adapt to industrialization while simultaneously maintaining their links to agriculture and community. Thus, an analysis of part-time farming is useful for understanding the socio-economic forces affecting postwar rural Japan, and for understanding how farm households accommodated themselves to these changes.

The goal of this chapter is to provide such an analysis. I use Francks' recognition of the significance of the spread of part-time farming in East Asia as a point of departure for describing the evolution of the Japanese structure of agriculture in the decades after the Second World War. It is my assertion that this growth in part-time farming, particularly of the type in which over half of household income is from non-agricultural sources, occurred because it was the most feasible option for Japanese farm households to use to adapt to rapid social, political and economic change. The political-economic context of that period included the occupation of Japan by the United States military, food shortages, rapid domestic economic growth, accelerated agricultural mechanization, changing food and agricultural policies, and the growing integration of Japan into a global political–economy. However, I also contend that the spread of a part-time farming strategy cannot be fully appreciated without recognizing some of the continuities that existed between pre- and postwar rural Japan. The importance of rice in Japanese culture, farming as a business (rather than a peasant activity), the active role of the Japanese government in rural and agricultural policy, and familiarity with part-time farming were well established elements of the socio-economic environment in prewar rural Japan. Postwar reconstruction took place upon this foundation. Thus, I argue that the changes that took place in postwar rural Japan reflected historical continuities as well as adaptation to new postwar realities.

Historical continuities

While many changes took place in Japan during and immediately following the Second World War, it is incorrect to assume that the war created a total rupture with the social, political and economic realities of the prewar era. In many ways Japanese agricultural and rural development exhibited a consistent trajectory throughout the twentieth century. Although pluriactivity became so widespread in the decades following the war that observers began to think of it as a defining feature of postwar Japanese agriculture, part-time farming was by no means unknown in prewar Japan. Indeed, it existed in nineteenth-century Japan (Kada 1982: 368), as it did in nineteenth-century England (Hill 1984). And, as Ōkado demonstrates earlier in this volume, women played a key role in prewar Japanese agriculture as well, as women have done throughout history in agricultural systems around the world. The idea that farm household members would work at various agricultural and non-agricultural tasks as part of a shared income-generating strategy was an established way of life in rural Japan long before the Second World War.

Another significant constant of twentieth-century Japanese agriculture was the central role of rice. While there is a wide variety of agricultural commodities that can be grown in Japan, rice was, and continues to be, *the* dominant agricultural commodity. Rice production has a long history in Japan, as well as other East Asian cultures (King 1911: 6–8). During the Tokugawa era, the amount of land devoted to rice production grew from an estimated 1.5 million hectares in the seventeenth century to 2.97 million hectares by the eighteenth century (Amatatsu 1959: 6). This is roughly the same area that was devoted to rice cultivation in Japan during the 1980s (Ministry of Agriculture and Forestry 1999)! In addition, during the twentieth century, the area devoted to rice production generally has exceeded the area devoted to the production of all other agricultural commodities combined. Given that context, it is not surprising that rice production and rice policies continued to be pivotal to postwar agriculture.

Certainly, the production and consumption of rice evolved during the twentieth century. Tremendous technological innovations in rice production, both biological and mechanical, contributed to a steady increase in yields for most of the century (Ogura 1980: chapter 3). In addition, the culture of rice consumption also changed, particularly in the 1960s and 1970s, when the percentage of calories in the national diet derived from rice began to decline: in 1960, nearly half of all calories consumed in Japan were from rice, but by 1990 that ratio had declined to approximately 25 percent (Nōrin Tōkei Kyōkai 1998). However, despite these changes, rice cultivation continues to be a defining feature of rural Japan. Indeed, as foreign pressure to liberalize rice trade has increased, some Japanese have begun to argue that rice paddies are an indispensable element of Japanese ecology, in part because they help retain water in the countryside that would otherwise contribute to flooding during the rainy season (Tashiro 1992: 43). Rice also is said to be the most important agricultural commodity produced in Japan from economic, political, symbolic and religious perspectives (Francks 2000: 46).

The prominence of rice in the political economy of twentieth-century Japan is reflected in the centrality of rice in Japanese food policy. Ongoing political demands from consumers for access to affordable rice in the prewar era, including actions like the Rice Riots that began in Toyama Prefecture in 1918, compelled the government to be actively involved in securing rice supplies, including rice imported from the colonies, and stabilizing consumer rice prices. A key legislative act was the adoption of the Rice Law of 1921 (Matsumoto 1959: 15), which provided a foundation for rice policy into the postwar era. Spurred on by rice shortages in the early postwar years, which were partly made up by imports from the United States (Jussaume 1991a: 94), the Japanese government strengthened the system by which it purchased rice directly from farmers and then sold that rice to consumers at reduced prices. During the 1950s and 1960s, the announcement of the official producer and consumer prices for rice was eagerly awaited throughout Japan, such that 'The price of rice may be thought of as representing politics itself in Japan' (Hemmi 1982: 235).

It is widely believed that these subsidized producer prices for rice were crucial in the spread of part-time farming in the postwar years, as they enabled farmers with small landholdings to combine rice cultivation with the off-farm employment of some, even most, family members. Due to economies of scale associated with the adoption of improved production technologies, large-scale rice farming is more economically efficient in Japan than small-scale farming. Yamaji and Ito (1993: 357–8) have presented evidence that the per hectare cost of producing rice on a farm greater than five hectares is nearly 40 percent less than on a 0.3 hectare farm. However, because the price of rice has been kept at a high level (Egaitsu 1982: 149), even small-scale farmers have been able to generate a net positive income from producing rice. While returns per hectare or per hour of labor are lower for small-scale farms, any net positive income fits within a household strategy of maximizing income from diverse sources, retaining access to land, and providing work opportunities for household members who do not work off-farm, such as the elderly.

The consistent historical pattern in the twentieth century of active Japanese government involvement in ensuring rice availability and affordability is mirrored throughout the broader arena of agricultural policy. While Japanese agricultural policy underwent a variety of changes during that century, particularly with the passage of the Basic Agricultural Law in 1961, for most of the time Japanese governments placed a priority, at least officially, on rural revitalization and improving the farm economy. One example of this can be found in various government projects to support land reclamation. According to Sasaki (1959: 21), 116,000 hectares of land were reclaimed in Japan in the 1920s and 1930s as a result of subsidies provided by the Land Development Furtherance Law of 1919. This is a relatively small area in comparison to the total area of rice paddy land under cultivation in Japan (less than 4 percent). But considering ecological limitations, government attempts to expand the area under rice cultivation by whatever means possible is a reflection of the importance placed by the government in expanding rice production.

Although this law was abolished in 1940, it was replaced by the Land Improvement Law of 1949, which differed from its predecessor primarily in scope and context. The goals of the two laws were similar, and reflected continuing government efforts to maximize agricultural production as well as create economic opportunities for farm households. The consistency of agricultural policies, including rice policies, throughout the twentieth century demonstrates that the strong role of the state in Japanese agriculture and rural areas was neither caused, nor seriously diminished, by events related to the Second World War.

While one purpose of Japanese agricultural policies may have been to improve the lives of rural inhabitants, another very important objective was to promote the interests of the state. The latter included the expansion of agricultural output to provide food for the nation and generate capital for industrial development. This meant that it was important to stress the production of *agricultural commodities*, i.e. crops that would be sold. The push, particularly after the Russo-Japanese War of 1904–5, to have Japanese farmers grow commodities and think of agriculture as a 'business' is one of the main points in Tsutsui's chapter earlier in this volume. The notion that Japanese agriculture and rural life were subject to increasing commodification throughout the twentieth century was also a central theme of Fukutake's work (1972, 1980). This means that the pluriactive strategies of Japanese farm households, throughout the century, were part of a farming, rather than a peasant, strategy. In other words, the Second World War did *not* have the effect of transforming rural Japanese households from peasants to farmers. That change had taken place decades earlier.

One institution that played a crucial role throughout this period in implementing government policies designed to promote the modernization of agriculture was the producer cooperative. In her recent article, Francks (2000: 47) points out that a strong association of agricultural cooperatives working cooperatively with the national government has been a key to agricultural development in Japan, South Korea and Taiwan. In Japan, the history of the agricultural cooperative movement is approximately 100 years old. In the early years, Japanese agricultural cooperatives 'were imbued with something like the "Rochdale spirit"' (Dore 1959: 278), as appears to have been the case with early consumer cooperatives as well. During the prewar period, the Japanese government began to form stronger ties with agricultural cooperatives, in part to ensure government control over food supplies. Those ties were solidified after the war, with government payments to farmers for the rice they grew being made through the producer cooperatives, and with cooperatives functioning as a mechanism for providing credit to farmers (Kato 1969: 345). Nonetheless, it should be noted that the seeds of the model of cooperative–government cooperation in promoting state policies were planted in the prewar era.

While many significant changes did take place in rural Japan after the war, including the rapid expansion of part-time farming, a trajectory of modern agricultural development was already in place. Prewar Japanese agriculture was characterized by a high degree of commercialization, and

Table 9.1 Pluriactivity in prewar Japanese farm households

	Agricultural income (yen)	*Non-agricultural income (yen)*	*Total income (yen)*
1921 owners	1,138 (82.4%)	242 (17.6%)	1,381 (100%)
1921 tenants	597 (78.1%)	168 (21.9%)	765 (100%)
1934–36 owners	593 (73.8%)	211 (26.2%)	804 (100%)
1934–36 tenants	361 (68.0%)	170 (32.0%)	531 (100%)

Sources: Ogura Takekasu, *Can Japanese Agriculture Survive?* (Tokyo: Agricultural Policy Research Center, 1980); Hayashi Yūichi, 'Dokusen dantai e no ikō,' in Teruoka Shūzō, ed., *Nihon nōgyō 100 nen no ayumi* (Tokyo: Yūhikaku, 1996), pp. 97–142.

the active role of the Japanese state in promoting rural development was well established. Before and after the war, the Japanese state had a policy goal of maximizing agricultural commodity production to promote rural development and maintain food supplies. Finally, pluriactivity was a well-established way of life in prewar rural Japan for many farm households, as shown in Table 9.1. In other words, Japanese farm household members before the war were well acquainted with the role of the state, and the market, in structuring their daily lives. They also were familiar with using a pluriactive strategy, which included all members of the household working at a variety of income-generating activities, for navigating their lives in the social, economic and political world that surrounded them. This is the foundation upon which the postwar expansion of part-time farming was constructed.

Postwar changes in Japanese agriculture

Although part-time farming in the context of commercialized agriculture was well established in Japan before the Second World War, major transformations did take place after the war that contributed to its adoption by an increasing percentage of farm households. Some of these changes were related to the fact that Japan lost the war. While government bureaucracies remained largely intact, and the direction of government policies often remained consistent, there was also a great deal of political instability. The United States government, by virtue of its occupation of Japan, proposed numerous policy initiatives, some of which were embraced by local reformers. The thrust of these programs was to promote the economic and political reconstruction of Japan.

Perhaps the most important governmental act taken during the occupation affecting Japanese agriculture and rural life, and one that is sometimes under-emphasized by contemporary observers, was the Japanese land reform. This 'bourgeois' land reform (Tuma 1965: 140) reinforced the ideology of household land ownership and sought to end the extraction of wealth from tenant farmers via land rents. In essence, the land reform set restrictions on the amount of land that any farmer could own and that any resident landlord could rent out to tenants. All land in excess of these limits, as well as all tenanted land owned by absentee landlords, was sold to the government for a fixed price, and rents on remaining tenancy contracts were reduced and made payable in cash. All land purchased by the government was sold to the household that had tenanted that land at the price the government had paid for it, with the new owner allowed to pay for the purchase over a 30-year period at a 3.2 percent interest rate (Ogura 1980: 416).

At the time of its completion, the land reform was considered to be an overwhelming success. Whereas over half of all rice land and over a third of upland (or dry) fields were tenanted in 1941, by 1950 only a tenth of all land was still being tenanted (see Table 9.2). More significantly, the number of landless tenant households decreased by more than one million, or about 20 percent of all farm households in Japan. Significantly, the scale of farming operations and the number of farm households did not change drastically. What the land reform accomplished was to give ownership title to lands that were being farmed by tenant households. The land reform did not promote rationalization or redistribution of farm lands. Farm households remained on the land and in villages, which reinforced the ties they had with their communities.

The purpose of the land reform in Japan was the same as that of other land reforms that were supported by the United States government in South Korea and Taiwan (Deyo 1987: 1970), as well as other reforms sponsored by the United States government in occupied Japan. The goal was to promote economic *and* political stability by giving as many households as possible an ownership stake in the economic and political status quo. Some observers at the time believed that one consequence of the land reform was a broadening of support for conservatism in rural areas and an undermining of the attractiveness of 'leftist' political parties in postwar rural Japan (Beardsley *et al.* 1959: 419–21; Dore 1959: 407–12; Ogura 1980: 431). This finding has been challenged by Nishida, who argues that those rural regions of Japan that were progressive before the war remained progressive, at least until the early 1970s (Nishida 1994:

Table 9.2 Effects of the Japanese land reform (in *chō* of land and number of households)

	1941	*1947*	*1950*
Owner-cultivated rice paddies	1,489,000 (46.9%)	1,594,000 (55.9%)	2,592,000 (88.9%)
Tenant-cultivated rice paddies	1,686,000 (53.1%)	1,256,000 (44.1%)	319,000 (10.9%)
Owner-cultivated dry fields	1,689,000 (62.7%)	1,437,000 (66.5%)	2,084,000 (91.2%)
Tenant-cultivated dry fields	1,003,000 (37.2%)	725,000 (33.5%)	195,000 (8.5%)
Owner-cultivators	1,711,000 (31.2%)	2,154,000 (36.5%)	3,822,000 (61.8%)
Owner/tenants	2,239,000 (40.7%)	2,180,000 (36.9%)	2,002,000 (32.5%)
Tenants	1,524,000 (27.7%)	1,574,000 (26.6%)	312,000 (5.0%)

Source: Ronald P. Dore, *Land Reform in Japan* (London: Oxford University Press, 1959), pp. 175–6 (tables 8 and 9).

Note
1 *chō* = 2.45 acres = .992 hectares

37–8), by which time part-time farming had spread and the role of farming in rural life had become less prominent. The transformation of rural areas into a solid constituency for conservative parties may have been overestimated. However, the strengthening of the agricultural cooperative system, government policies for supporting the price producers received for rice, and the land reform all helped create a foundation for steady farm household income growth that began in the middle 1950s.

Another important change that contributed to the modernization of Japanese agriculture, as well as the spread of part-time farming, was its mechanization. As noted previously, Japanese agriculture had begun the process of commercialization decades earlier. Mechanization was part of this process, as Francks' study of the innovation of electrical irrigation pumps on the Saga Plain illustrated (Francks 1983). Nonetheless, as Hayami and Ruttan (1971) pointed out in their comparative analysis of agricultural development in the United States and Japan, prewar Japanese agriculture was characterized primarily by growth due to the introduction of yield-enhancing biotechnologies and the intensive use of labor. For example, rice yields were improved through the development of new varieties, as well as increased use of fertilizers and more intensive farming practices. In the United States, on the other hand, prewar agricultural growth was based in large part on the spread of labor-displacing technologies, such as the mechanical harvester.

The emphasis on improving yields through greater applications of labor and biotechnologies was broadened in postwar Japan, in part with assistance from United States-directed development programs. Added to this prewar development trajectory was the strategy of mechanizing Japanese agriculture. This change is highlighted in Table 9.3. There was a rapid expansion in the 1950s and 1960s in the number of electrical and kerosene motors used on Japanese farms, as well as the introduction of tractors and mechanical cultivators. This dissemination of labor-displacing technologies was particularly rapid in the 1950s. For example, the number of Japanese farm households that had tractors grew nearly four times from 1956 to 1959 (Okada and Kamiya 1960: 8). This rapid dispersal was made possible in part by rapidly increasing farm household incomes, both from farming and non-farming sources.

Unlike improved seed varieties, which lead to economic growth through expansion of yields, most agricultural machinery, like tractors and cultivators, contribute to growth by improving labor efficiency. While agricultural yields did continue to climb after the war, in part due to the expanded use of chemical fertilizers, pesticides and herbicides, this simply continued a trend that took place throughout the twentieth century (Table 9.3). The dissemination of machine technologies did not significantly alter the overall growth rate in rice yields. What changed in the postwar era was the additional emphasis on maximizing returns to agricultural labor through mechanization. One consequence of making labor more efficient is that it becomes redundant.

Table 9.3 The mechanization and productivity of Japanese agriculture, pre- and postwar

	1935	*1955*	*1965*
Electric motors	47,100	956,100	1,381,000
Kerosene motors	96,400	1,134,000	(superceded)
Tractors	–	1,000	63,000
Mechanical cultivators	–	89,000	2,490,000

	1885–99	*1915–19*	*1935–39*	*1955–59*	*1965–69*
Rice yields (kg/10 ares)	214	286	314	376	425
Index	100	133.8	146.8	175.7	198.6

Sources: Ogura Takekasu, *Can Japanese Agriculture Survive?* (Tokyo: Agricultural Policy Research Center, 1980); Ebata Akira, *Postwar Japanese Agriculture* (Tokyo: Shobi Printing Co.)

Plate 9.1 Bringing in the rice crop with a combine harvester, Gumma, 1978. Reproduced from *Shashin ga kataru Shōwa nōgyōshi*, (Tokyo: Fumin kyōkai, 1987), p. 172.

In the Japanese case, the increasing redundancy of rural labor came at a fortuitous historical moment. Due to a variety of domestic and global factors, the Japanese economy began a sustained period of economic growth in the mid-1950s that lasted until the early 1970s. This growth, which was based in large part on the expansion of heavy industry, provided numerous employment opportunities for rural labor (Ohkawa 1965: 480). The freeing up of agricultural labor through mechanization provided opportunities for farm household members, particularly males, to work off-farm. Simultaneously, increasing off-farm incomes provided farm households with the funds to mechanize farm operations. The rapid mechanization of agricultural tasks in Japan in the 1950s and 1960s was accompanied by a shift of farm household labor, particularly males, off-farm and an increase in farm household incomes.

The combination of (1) a solidifying of household ties to local place via expanded private ownership of land; (2) an increase in mechanization of agricultural tasks; and (3) rapid economic growth in the national

Plate 9.2 Pesticide spraying in a tea field, Kagoshima, 1987. Reproduced from *Shashin ga kataru Shōwa nōgyōshi*, (Tokyo: Fumin kyōkai, 1987), p. 179.

political economy were factors that accompanied the spread of part-time farming throughout Japan. This was particularly true in rural districts that were geographically proximate to cities and industrial districts (Jussaume 1991b: 95–7). My empirical research in Okayama Prefecture demonstrated that there was a geographical element to the spread of part-time farming in that it expanded out from urban areas towards more remote rural regions.

Not only did part-time farming become an increasingly popular strategy, but the nature of part-time farming also evolved. Table 9.4 shows that in 1955 the majority of Japanese farm households were obtaining the bulk of their income from the sale of agricultural commodities. This is similar to the way in which pluriactivity worked for many farm households before the war. In other words, farming was the primary labor activity and non-agricultural income sources were used to supplement the household's agricultural income. In more remote regions of Japan, particularly in the 1950s, one common method of pluriactivity of this type was called *dekasegi*. This was a practice wherein a household member, often a male, would temporarily migrate to an urban district to find seasonal work. Generally, households practicing *dekasegi* earned less off-farm than on-farm income.

However, during the late 1950s and early 1960s, an increasing number of farm household members began to secure full-time off-farm employ-

Table 9.4 Pluriactivity in Japanese farm households, 1906–95

Year	*Total farm households*	*Of which 'commercial' farm households*	*Full-time (%)*	*Part-time (%)*		
				Pre-1944	*Type I**	*Type II**
1906	5,378,337		71.0	29.0		
1915	5,451,189		68.8	31.2		
1925	5,463,001		69.8	30.2		
1935	5,518,275		74.1	25.9		
1944	5,536,508		37.3		38.3	24.4
1955	6,043,000		34.9		37.6	27.5
1965	5,664,800		21.5		36.7	41.8
1975	5,905,100		12.4		25.4	62.1
1985	4,228,738	3,314,931**	15.0		22.9	62.1
[non-commercial + class II			*11.8*		*17.9*	*70.3]*
1995	3,443,550	2,651,403**	16.1		18.8	65.1
[non-commercial + class II			*12.4*		*14.5*	*73.1]*

Sources: Agricultural Policy Research Center, *Statistical Yearbook*, various years (Tokyo: Ministry of Agriculture, Forestry and Fisheries); Hayashi Yūichi, 'Dokusen dankai e no ikō', in Teruoka Shūzō, ed., *Nihon nōgyō 100 nen no ayumi* (Tokyo: Yūhikaku, 1996); Kayō Nobufumi *et al.*, *Kaitei Nihon nōgyō no kiso tōkei* (Tokyo: Nōrin tōkei kyōkai, 1977).

Notes

* from 1944 part-time farm households were divided into type I (primarily agricultural) and type II (primarily non-agricultural) households.

** Currently 'commercial farm households' (*hanbai nōka*) are defined as those that farm at least 30 ares of land or sell at least 500,000 yen in farm produce annually. 'Non-commercial farm households' generally have very small holdings and grow crops only for their own consumption.

ment. This trend was made possible by a number of factors, including improved transportation, expanding job opportunities, labor redundancy in agriculture, and expanded formal educational opportunities for young people. By the 1970s, agriculture had become a supplementary economic activity for most Japanese agricultural households. By the mid-1970s, two-thirds of Japanese farm households earned more than half of their income from non-agricultural sources.

This does *not* mean that farm work ceased to be an important activity for many rural inhabitants. Constant references to part-time farming in Japan as *san-chan nōgyō* (agriculture practiced by mom, grandma and grandpa) implicitly recognizes that agriculture was, and continues to be, an important activity for many farm household members. Indeed, I would argue that the social and psychological significance of part-time farming has come to outweigh its economic importance. One of the more vivid memories I have of my year living in rural Japan in the early 1990s is

Plate 9.3 Feeding the chickens, Saitama, 1953. Reproduced from *Shashin ga kataru Shōwa nōgyōshi*, (Tokyo: Fumin kyōkai, 1987), p. 220.

of the large number of elderly residents making their way out to their households' fields early every morning. Many of the hamlet's residents, who had off-farm jobs and did little farm work, often remarked that the main reason their household kept possession of their agricultural lands was for the benefit of *ojiichan* (grandpa) or *obaachan* (grandma). This reflected the value given by most hamlet residents to providing elders with an opportunity to work and make a contribution to the household by providing food and pocket money.

This is not to suggest that we should dismiss the economic importance of farming to Japanese agricultural households or to the nation as a whole. However, for many rural Japanese households, farming has become a side economic activity, rather than a household's prime source of income. The persistence of pluriactivity, and the comparatively slow decline in overall farm numbers, particularly in the 1960s and 70s, occurred because a part-time farming strategy served a variety of household economic, social and even political needs. As Ruth Gasson has noted, part-time farming is 'an accommodation to gradually changing circumstances' (Gasson 1986: 364). Indeed, it is an ideal adaptive strategy, for it allows certain members of the household, often the young, the flexibility to participate in new economic opportunities, while maintaining the household's link to land and community. This is particularly of value to household members whose off-farm employment opportunities are limited.

Thus, as the Japanese economy changed in the postwar era, the form and role of part-time farming adapted along with it. This interpretation about part-time farming in the modern age is hardly unique. Cavazzani (1979: 25) developed a similar argument concerning European part-time farming 20 years ago. The persistence of part-time farming does *not* mean that farm households have not altered their approaches towards pluriactivity or that these strategies play a stagnant role in society. Indeed, two major strengths of pluriactivity that help explain its persistence are adaptability and variability. Given this, it would be reasonable to predict that, as Japanese society continues to change, Japanese agriculture as a whole, and part-time farming within it, will adapt and reflect the increasing diversity of Japanese society.

Recent trends in Japanese agriculture

In the previous two sections, I pointed out that, while pluriactivity was commonplace in twentieth-century Japanese agriculture, as it has been around the world, its scope and form evolved after the Second World War. This happened in tandem with changes in the Japanese political economy, and the dominant mode of agricultural production. I would now like to examine how the structure of Japanese agriculture continues to evolve, even while part-time farming remains the most prevalent strategy used by farm households (Yoshino 1997).

One trend that is continuing in Japanese rural areas is the spread of 'business thinking' in agricultural households and rural communities (Sakai 1993). As I noted previously, the notion that farming should be thought of as a business has existed in Japan throughout the twentieth century (Fukutake 1972). However, the belief that agriculture is just another form of business or industry is growing stronger in rural areas as a result of constant government prodding and changes in the national and international political economy (McMichael 1993). These pressures are ideologically expressed in the paradigm of neo-classical economics, and have resulted in constant calls for the rationalization of Japanese agriculture (Hayami 1988: 119; Roningen and Dixit 1991: 98–9). Japanese farmers are under constant pressure to industrialize their operations to an ever greater extent so as to compete against foreign agricultural producers in their home markets. Consequently, many farmers have come to accept the idea that they must constantly modernize in order to survive economically.

Responses to this constant pressure to rationalize are leading to the development of an increasing variety of new organizational forms in Japanese agriculture. Sakai (1993: 153–4) provides examples of joint corporate/farm household farming, such as a fertilizer firm farming land via contracts with farm households. Certain mechanized tasks are delegated to the firm, others to the farm household. Agricultural cooperatives, under pressure as their numbers and influence continue to wane, are also active in the creation of incorporated group farming enterprises.

Another organizational form that is beginning to take a foothold in Japan is corporate farming. I have written elsewhere about hydroponic cherry tomato production (Jussaume 1998: 34–5). In that case, a major Japanese electronics firm established a subsidiary to develop and manage a farm corporation, legally co-owned with some local farm households. The households' role was to provide the land for a five-hectare greenhouse cherry tomato operation. Yearly production was estimated at 500 to 550 tons, took place over a nine-month period from fall through spring, and much of the labor was provided by 'part-time workers' (i.e. full-time workers who are employed seasonally with minimal benefits). What is particularly interesting is that some of these part-time workers live in farm households, which are undoubtedly listed as part-time farm households even though some of their off-farm income comes from employment in the agribusiness sector.

Most Japanese farm households are not becoming part of corporate organizational structures. Many small farmers, like their contemporaries in Europe and the United States, are attempting to survive by producing high quality products that they market directly to consumers. One farm household I have studied, which produces beef and organic eggs for direct sale to local consumers, invites their customers to the farm to pick up their produce, as well as to participate in the occasional chicken barbecue. This direct marketing approach, sometimes of organically produced commodities, is increasingly being practiced in the United States, Europe and elsewhere. The success of this strategy is based in part upon building trust between consumers and producers.

Thus, despite the comparatively small scale of operations, many households, including part-timers, continue to farm in Japan, although the total number of farming households is in decline (Table 9.4). It is reasonable to expect that many part-time farm households will abandon farming in the near future, particularly as the elderly inhabitants of these households pass away. Yet Kada, a recognized expert on part-time farming in Japan, asserts that there will be a steady stream of retired Japanese who will U-turn to rural areas as part of a strategy to maintain a desirable lifestyle in their old age (Kada 1980). An interesting research project would be to investigate just how prevalent this form of part-time farming will become in Japan, and what the motivations and rewards will be for those who pursue it.

Kada's argument supports the interpretation that part-time farming in Japan continues to evolve and reflects many of the changes taking place in Japanese society as a whole. Examples of retirees who have not farmed in decades returning to their natal hamlets to take up farming once again does not merely offer a possibility that part-time farming may persist in some form. It also suggests that, in contrast with the push to make Japanese farms more business-like and economically rational, some people may persist or return to farming for reasons that include, but move beyond, economics. Unlike part-time farming in the early postwar era, where a pluriactive strategy often was a vehicle for younger farm members to find work in expanding industries, for some households at present part-time farming may be turning into a strategy for melding retirement and farming income, while simultaneously preserving a desirable, rural lifestyle.

I also have begun to wonder if, at least in some cases, part-time farming in Japan may be evolving from *san-chan* to *ni-chan* nōgyō (i.e. farming by grandma and grandpa only). Not only are there the above-mentioned cases where retired couples are returning to farm, but also young farm household wives, like their husbands, are increasingly working outside the hamlet in non-farm occupations and refraining from performing agricultural tasks. This is directly comparable to the situation in parts of Europe, where an increasing number of farm women are taking off-farm jobs, a trend that is leading to changes in gender roles and women's identities (Jewell 1999: 107–8; Oldrup 1999: 354). This trend is made increasingly possible in Japan by the further mechanization of farm tasks, which as Kumagai (1994) has noted, has had a differential impact on the time-allocation patterns of farm household residents by generation and gender. Younger household members, particularly wives, are no longer interested in helping on the farm, and their labor may no longer be needed, as older household members are able to perform farm tasks with the aid of machinery.

Finding young people, especially sons by birth or adoption, to work in agriculture (Sakai 1992: 56–7; Yoshino and Moberg 1989), continues to be a major challenge in Japanese rural areas, particularly in mountainous areas where off-farm employment opportunities, land resources and direct marketing opportunities are limited. This has led to a rapid aging of the rural population, particularly in communities located deep in the mountains (Takahashi 1988: 99–100), which face very different problems from peri-urban rural areas (Ouchi 1995). This suggests, too, the possibility that Japanese rural areas, and the types of agriculture practiced, could become even more diverse in the future. For example, while it is conceivable that rural areas near urban centers could witness an expansion of capital-intensive production of fresh produce for urban markets, farm households in mountainous areas may experiment with agro-tourism strategies, as is being done in parts of Europe. In addition, while few in number, there are now examples, almost unheard of a few generations ago, of younger Japanese of urban origin taking on farming, although the cost of land and difficulty in gaining acceptance from established local farm families makes this option difficult. In these cases, it may not be possible for new entrants to survive solely on farm income, and thus at least some part-time farming may result from households that resort to a pluriactive strategy to establish and support a farm-based, rural lifestyle.

Conclusion

In these pages, I have tried to use part-time farming as a vehicle for outlining some of the changes that have taken place in rural Japan during the postwar era. This is not to suggest that an examination of the transformation in the structure of agriculture can yield a complete picture of rural life. Rural does not equal agricultural. Indeed, the growth of part-time farming of the type where more than half of all household income is earned off-farm reveals that postwar life in rural Japan has become increasingly *less* dependent on agriculture. Certainly, many residents of contemporary Japanese 'farm households' no longer think of themselves as agriculturists, as people who are dependent on agriculture for their way of life.

The review of the growth of part-time farming also reveals that pluriactivity is a strategy that has been used by Japanese farm households to cope with the steadily increasing pressures of market and state. Many of the factors that have been cited as contributing to the growth of part-time farming – such as rice price support policies, mechanization and the commodification of agriculture – can be interpreted as economic and political influences that largely originated outside of rural communities. They denote a longstanding interest on the part of policy makers and business leaders to 'modernize' Japanese agriculture and have it contribute to the country's development. Part-time farming has been a popular way for farm households to respond to the opportunities and challenges presented by those conditions created by external agents.

The spread and evolution of part-time farming in postwar Japan, therefore, is a reflection of the de-agriculturalization of Japanese rural areas as well as the adaptation of farm household residents to the increased penetration of market and state in their lives. While agriculture continues to be an important activity for many Japanese rural households, neither hamlets nor rural households can be thought of as being primarily 'agrarian,' i.e. living a traditional lifestyle built around the seasonal cycles associated with the growth of domesticated plants and animals. This circumstance is neither surprising nor unique to Japan. The same condition has been observed in rural districts in Europe, the United States and elsewhere. In many parts of the world, particularly the so-called 'developed' countries, agriculture no longer is the primary influence in defining rurality, which has become a much more complex phenomenon than it was in the past.

Finally, I would argue that the declining influence of agriculture in rural Japan, and the accompanying spread of part-time farming, should be seen as the culmination of state policies and market trends that began in Japan at the turn of the last century. In other words, the declining significance of agriculture as an industry is a consequence of its having *become* an industry. One interesting element of the Japanese case is that farm household residents there are like farm residents in other parts of the world in that they preserve for themselves a role in agriculture, often for reasons that are interpreted by outsiders as 'irrational.' Certainly, from the perspective of maximizing returns to investments in labor and capital, small-scale, part-time farms are highly inefficient and thus illogical. Part-time farm household residents are aware of the inefficiencies in their farming operations, but do not abandon farming. I would argue that this is because households combine economic and non-economic goals into their decision making. For example, part-time farming strategies are utilized by some Japanese farm households to augment elderly members' self-worth by providing them with an opportunity to contribute to their household's well being. Thus, as in Europe, the persistence of part-time farming is indicative of a desire by many rural households to balance household members' needs and maintain a valued way of life. For these households, farming is not simply a matter of maximizing returns on land, labor and capital resources. A dilemma facing policy makers is whether it is in the interest of government to assist these households in the name of community development or maintaining the ability to produce food domestically.

References

Amatatsu Katsumi. 1959. *Growing Rice in Japan*. Agricultural Development Series. Tokyo: Agricultural, Forestry and Fisheries Productivity Conference.

Beardsley, Richard K., John W. Hall and Robert E. Ward. 1959. *Village Japan*. Chicago: University of Chicago Press.

Cavazzani, Ada. 1979. 'Part-time Farming in Advanced Industrial Societies: Role and Characteristics in the United States.' Cornell Rural Sociology Bulletin Series No. 106. Ithaca, NY: Cornell University Press.

Deyo, Frederick C. (ed.). 1987. *The Political Economy of the New East Asian Industrialism*. Ithaca, NY: Cornell University Press.

Dore, Ronald P. 1959. *Land Reform in Japan*. London: Oxford University Press.

Egaitsu Fumio. 1982. 'Japanese Agricultural Policy.' In *U.S.–Japanese Agricultural Trade Relations,* ed. E.N. Castle, K. Hemmi and S.A. Skillings. Washington, DC: Resources for the Future.

Francks, Penelope. 1983. *Technology and Agricultural Development in Pre-war Japan*. New Haven and London: Yale University Press.

—— 2000. 'Japan and an East Asian Model of Agriculture's Role in Industrialization.' *Japan Forum* 12(1): 43–52.

Fukutake Tadashi. 1972. *Japanese Rural Society*. Trans. Ronald P. Dore. Ithaca, NY: Cornell University Press.

—— 1980. *Rural Society in Japan*. Tokyo: University of Tokyo Press.

Gasson, Ruth. 1986. 'Part-time Farming: Strategy for Survival.' *Sociologia Ruralis*. 24(3–4): 364–76.

Hayami Yujiro. 1988. *Japanese Agriculture Under Siege: The Political Economy of Agricultural Policies*. New York: St Martin's Press.

—— and Vernon Ruttan. 1971. *Agricultural Development: An International Perspective*. Baltimore, MD: Johns Hopkins Press.

Hemmi Kenzo. 1982. 'Agriculture and Politics in Japan.' In *U.S.–Japanese Agricultural Trade*, ed. Emery N. Castle and Kenzo Hemmi. Washington, DC: Resources for the Future.

Hill, Berkeley. 1984. 'Part-time Farming in the United Kingdom: Plan of Work and Methodology.' Paper presented at the Conference on Mixed Income Farming, Bressanone, Italy.

Jewell, Anne Maxmes. 1999. 'Changing Patterns of Family Farming and Pluriactivity.' *Sociologia Ruralis* 39(1): 100–16.

Jussaume, Raymond A. Jr. 1991a. 'United States–Japan Food and Agricultural Commodity Trade in Theoretical Perspective: Fordism vs Niche Marketing.' *Japan Forum* 3(1): 91–206.

—— 1991b. *Japanese Part-time Farming: Evolution and Impacts*. Ames, Iowa: Iowa State University Press.

—— 1998. 'Globalization, Agriculture, and Rural Social Change in Japan.' *Environment and Planning A*. 30: 401–13.

Kada Ryohei. 1980. *Part-time Family Farming*. Tokyo: Center for Academic Publications Japan.

—— 1982. 'Trends and Characteristics of Part-time Farming in Post-war Japan.' *Geojournal*, 6(4): 367–72.

Kajita Masaru. 1959. *Land Reform in Japan*. Agricultural Development Series. Tokyo: Agricultural, Forestry and Fisheries Productivity Conference.

Kato Yuzuru. 1969. 'Development of Long-term Agricultural Credit.' In *Agriculture and Economic Growth: Japan's Experience*, ed. K. Ohkawa, B.F. Johnston and H. Kaneda. Tokyo: University of Tokyo Press.

King, F.H. 1911. *Farmers of Forty Centuries*. Emmaus, PA: Rodale Press, Inc.

Kumagai Sonoko M. 1994. 'Farm Mechanization and Women's Life Pattern.' *International Journal of Japanese Sociology* (3): 99–119.

Matsumoto Takeo. 1959. *Staple Food Control in Japan*. Tokyo: Chūō kōron jigyō shuppan.

McMichael, Philip. 1993. 'Japanese Agricultural Restructuring in Global and Regional Context.' SSRC Conference on Agriculture and Farming in Japan. Honolulu: East–West Center.

Ministry of Agriculture and Forestry. 1999. *Nōrin suisan tōkei* (pocket edition). Tokyo: Agriculture and Forestry Statistics Association.

Nishida Yoshiaki. 1994. 'The Rise and Decline of the Farmers' Movement and Transformation of the Rural Community in Postwar Japan.' University of Tokyo, Institute of Social Sciences, Occasional Paper 19.

Nōrin tōkei kyōkai. 1998. *Nōgyō hakusho*. Tokyo: Agricultural and Forestry Statistics Association.

Ogura Takekazu. 1980. *Can Japanese Agriculture Survive*? Tokyo: Agricultural Policy Research Center.

Ohkawa Kazushi. 1965. 'Agriculture and the Turning Points in Economic Growth.' *The Developing Economies* 3(4): 471–86.

Okada Ken and Kamiya Yoshiharu. 1960. *Nihon nōgyō kikaika no bunseki*. Tokyo: Sōbunsha.

Oldrup, Helene. 1999. 'Women Working off the Farm.' *Sociologia Ruralis* 39(3): 342–58.

Ouchi Masatoshi. 1995. 'Nōka kazoku no henbō to sengo nōsei.' *Sonraku shakai kenkyū* 1(2): 8–18.

Roningen, Vernon O. and Praveen M. Dixit. 1991. 'Reforming Agricultural Policies: The Case of Japan.' *Journal of Asian Economics* 2(1): 87–111.

Sakai Tomio. 1992. Nōgyō no gendai to kadai. *Hokuriku no sangyō to keizai* (March): 55–74.

—— 1993. 'Growth of Various Pioneer Farmers and Regional Agriculture.' *Ringyō mondai kenkyū* (113): 10–18.

Sasaki Shiro. 1959. *Land Development and Improvement Projects in Japan*. Tokyo: Agricultural, Forestry and Fisheries Productivity Conference.

Takahashi Akiyoshi. 1988. 'Japanese Agricultural Problem and Farming Family in Transition.' *Bulletin of the Faculty of General Education*. Tokyo: Tokyo University of Agriculture and Technology.

Tashiro Yoichi. 1992. 'An Environmental Mandate for Rice Self-sufficiency.' *Japan Quarterly* 39(1): 34–44.

Tuma, Elias H. 1965. *Twenty-six Centuries of Agrarian Reform*. Berkeley, Los Angeles: University of California Press.

Yamaji Susumu and Shoichi Ito. 1993. 'The Political Economy of Rice in Japan.' In *Japanese and American Agriculture*, ed. L. Tweeten, C.L. Dishon, W.S. Chern, N. Imamura and M. Morishima. Boulder, Colorado: Westview Press.

Yoshino Hideki. 1997. 'Nōgyō no jūyō na ninaite to shite no kengyō jūgyōin.' *Sonraku shakai kenkyū* 3(2): 8–21.

Yoshino Shigemi and Mark A. Moberg. 1989. 'Fostering of Rural Youth in Japan.' In *Young Successor Farmers in Asia and the Pacific*, ed. A.P. Organization. Seoul: APO.

10 Local conceptions of land and land use and the reform of Japanese agriculture

Iwamoto Noriaki

Introduction

Most studies of land issues in twentieth-century Japan have taken a legal or institutional approach to the subject. In contrast, this chapter focuses on the customs and norms regarding land ownership among farmers and rural communities, both before and after the postwar land reform. In my view, such a focus provides an essential basis for developing policies to deal with the crisis facing Japanese agriculture today. That crisis has both exogenous and endogenous origins: on the one hand, the liberalization of trade in agricultural commodities, including rice, and on the other, the rapid aging of the agricultural labor force. While the former has narrowed the options available to those Japanese farmers who wish to remain in business, the latter is steadily rendering the exploitation of such agricultural resources as land impossible in many parts of the country. Efforts to promote the structural reform of agriculture – in particular, land-extensive farming and more efficient management of local agricultural resources – have yielded few positive results to date. Those who speak of the threatened collapse of agriculture in Japan have considerable basis for their concern.

To be sure, a historical analysis such as this one will not automatically yield a prescription for solving the problems facing agriculture at present. But just as distinctive customs and norms related to the ownership and use of land have developed over time in other countries, so too have they developed in Japan and, as elsewhere, they remain salient (although by no means unchanged) today. They have affected the implementation of policy in the past, and any policy initiative that fails to take them into consideration will be unlikely to succeed. What follows, then, constitutes an inquiry into an essential prerequisite for achieving the elusive goal of structural reform: an understanding of the distinctive customs and norms concerning land that developed over time among rural *ie* and *mura* in the Japanese countryside.

As is well known to students of Japanese history, the *ie* (or house, in the sense of a lineage group) became the prevailing form of family structure in rural Japan in the Tokugawa period, accompanying the shift from serfdom to small-scale farming. The *ie* owned the family's property, occupation, surname and other heritable assets. These were controlled by the head of the family, almost always male, with the expectation that they would be passed on to the next generation. The *mura* (the natural village, or hamlet) was a clearly demarcated rural community made up of the *ie* within its borders, which performed such essential tasks for local farming as management of irrigation facilities and common lands. The *mura* also possessed self-governing functions and made its own rules, which local residents were expected to obey.

There were four noteworthy features of the *ie*'s attitudes toward land at this time: (1) that land was its most important possession, not only essential to the family's occupation but also a barometer of its standing within the community; (2) that land was the collective possession of the *ie*, merely entrusted to the current generation by the previous for transmission to the next; (3) that all decisions about the use of land were made by the head of the *ie* at any given time; and (4) that all of the *ie*'s land and other property would be passed on from one house head to another (almost always the current head's eldest son). Younger sons and all daughters were excluded from inheritance.

The *mura* also possessed its own customs in relation to land, which from the Tokugawa era onwards were as follows: (1) the periodic redistribution of land among local farmers, as a means of insuring that the burden of generating the tax payments, for which the community as a whole was then responsible, was equitably distributed among local *ie* (this custom was practiced only in those parts of the country where crop failures were common on account of harsh weather, etc.); (2) the return of pawned land to its original holder even when the date for redeeming the pawn had passed, if and when the borrower was able to repay the loan; and (3) the prohibition of transfers of holding or cultivating rights to land within the *mura* to persons living elsewhere or even pawning land to such persons, unless the permission of the *mura* had been obtained. The basic, and enduring, principle here was that 'the land in the *mura* should be used for the benefit of those who live in the *mura*.'

To be sure, these customary practices and attitudes began to change in the late nineteenth century, with the promulgation of the Meiji Civil Code and the development of capitalism. The concept of absolute, exclusive private ownership rights gradually spread within Japanese society.

But so far as farmers were concerned, that concept was added to prevailing attitudes toward land. Their fields were both private property and, at the same time, subject to *ie* and *mura* control.

The postwar land reform and local conceptions of land and land use

As an attempt to realize change in the ownership and use of farm land, the postwar land reform obviously had an impact on the customs and attitudes toward land that had developed over time in rural Japan. On the one hand, the land reform constituted a break with those customs and attitudes, but on the other hand – and very importantly in accounting for its success – the land reform also built upon them. In short, there were both ruptures and resonances. Chief among the latter were (1) the sharp distinction the land reform drew between resident and absentee landlords; (2) the emphasis on farm households, not individual farmers; (3) the priority given to promoting owner-cultivation; and (4) use of hamlet-based expertise. I will discuss each of these in turn before turning to the ruptures.

First, thinking of land ownership and use in terms of hamlet boundaries was deeply rooted in Japan's rural society, and such notions as 'the hamlet's land is for use within the community' and 'outsiders should not gain control of the hamlet's land' were widely diffused among local residents. In making a sharp distinction between resident and non-resident landlords at the time of the land reform and treating the latter more harshly, agricultural policymakers were in harmony with the thinking of most farmers. Indeed, even before the land reform itself, in the context of state management of rice supplies that had begun in 1940, policymakers had drawn a sharp distinction between resident and absentee landlords, allowing the former as well as producers to retain some rice for their own use, but denying that benefit to absentee landlords. Behind this differential treatment lay the assessment that, whereas resident landlords were pillars of their communities and often important agents of agricultural improvement, absentee landlords were concerned only with the collection of rents and, as such, an undesirable source of tension and conflict in the countryside.

The land reform was predicated on a similar distinction, with resident landlords permitted to retain some of their previously tenanted land, up to specified acreage limits for owner-cultivation in their locality, and absentee landlords not permitted to retain any previously tenanted land whatsoever. In defining resident and absentee landlords, however, the architects of the land reform chose to employ the legally recognized administrative boundaries of cities, towns and villages used in local government, whereas to most farmers it was the boundaries of the natural village – that is, the hamlet or *ōaza* (section) – that determined whether a landlord was resident or absentee. There had been debate about how to define absentee landlords in the Diet, but it is worth noting that 'not even government spokesmen questioned the principle that absentee landlords should hand over all of their tenanted land' (Ōwada 1981: 73).

Second, in carrying out the land reform, the unit employed in determining mandatory land transfers and the maximum acreage resident landlords or existing owner-cultivators could retain was the household, not the individual. Designed primarily as a means of preventing landlords from avoiding the forced sale of their holdings by redistributing ownership title among family members, this policy at the same time resonated with the traditional view among farmers that land was a family, not an individual, possession.

Third, the priority given to owner-cultivation, too, resonated with traditional village norms. Since early modern times, the ideal rural community had been viewed as one in which cultivators and the land they cultivated were united. In this sense, tenancy was undesirable, because it impinged on that unity, and if the political or social tensions brought about by tenancy exceeded a certain point, efforts to restore the desired unity would commence. The custom of the return of alienated land mentioned earlier was one manifestation of this view. Many of the tenancy disputes of the early twentieth century were also an expression of it, in the sense that they represented attempts to restore communal solidarity (Saitō 1974: 235–7), as were official efforts to promote owner-cultivation as the most desirable form of farm management thereafter (Tanaka 1987: 529–41; Iwamoto 1987: 509–24).

Fourth, the hamlet assistants appointed by land commissions insured that communal interests would figure prominently in the implementation of the land reform. There were some 260,000 such assistants nationwide, or on average 25 assistants per municipality, and it is fair to say that no hamlet was without at least one. It was their task to carry out the basic surveys that were needed in planning local land purchases and sales (Nōchi kaikaku kiroku iinkai 1951: 156–7). That meant first recording the details of every single parcel of land in the hamlet – its location, type, area, owner, cultivator, the amount of any rent charged and the existence of any mortgage or other lien on the property – then specifying the parcels that were to be transferred under the terms of the land reform, and finally drafting a plan for those transfers. In short, the work of the hamlet assistants was a vast and complicated undertaking (Nishida 1998a: 187). As Nishida notes, these hamlet assistants were to be chosen from among those 'with good knowledge of local farming conditions' and 'an understanding of the land reform program' (Nishida 1998a: 186). However, I disagree with his assessment that the activities of these assistants amounted to 'direct democracy within the community' and signified the 'participation of [ordinary] farmers' in the reform (Nishida 1998b: 92–3). There was, after all, a marked tendency to choose such influential residents as heads of hamlet agricultural practice associations and heads of hamlet assemblies as hamlet assistants (Nōchi kaikaku kiroku iinkai 1951: 157). They were indeed 'insiders' whose mobilization contributed to the success of the land reform, but rather than 'direct democracy' or 'the participation of farmers,' what they represented were the interests of the community and its long-established values.

Nowhere was the continuity between the land reform and communal norms more apparent than in the outcome of efforts by resident landlords to regain cultivation of their tenanted land. Some 88,000 *chō*, or 4 percent of all tenanted land, were given back to landlords after the war. Most such returns of land took place in 1945 and early 1946, but some returns were agreed informally even after the land reform had begun and all land transfers supposedly made subject to close scrutiny. Rather than a simple expression of the coercive power of landlords (although that was a factor in some instances), what was operative here was communal problem-solving of a traditional sort. Most of the land so returned had first been let to tenants when the owners had been conscripted into military service during the war or had left to settle in one of Japan's Asian colonies (Dore 1959: 164). As members of the community who had contributed to local society as resident landlords in the past, their right to survival now had to be respected. Without doubt, concessions such as these helped to defuse landlord opposition to the land reform (Dore 1959: 173; Ōwada 1981: 269).

In the ways outlined above, there were resonances between the aims and methods of the land reform and the long-established norms of rural *ie* and *mura*, and these resonances certainly contributed to the land reform's overall success. But there were ruptures as well, which conflicted with very powerful rural norms, and it is to those I now turn.

The clearest manifestation of rupture in the implementation of the land reform at the local level was the land commission secretariat. Municipal land commissions had three secretaries in their service, on average, and those secretaries were expected 'to be progressive in their thinking, able to understand complicated legislation and committed to scientific approaches based on accurate statistical data' (Nōrinshō nōchika 1949: 715). In normal times it would have been impossible to employ large numbers of people with these abilities in rural areas, but on account of widespread unemployment following Japan's surrender and the demobilization of its military forces there actually were many individuals with appropriately high educational qualifications living in the countryside. 'They became secretaries and kindled the enthusiasm for the land reform that was essential to Japan's rebirth' (Ōwada 1981: 207).

According to Ministry of Agriculture and Forestry (MAF) figures, there were 11,035 land commissions in existence in August 1948, serviced by 32,462 secretaries (23,735 men and 8,727 women). The average age of these secretaries was 30 (34 for men, 21 for women), and fully 96 percent of them had completed education beyond the compulsory level: upper elementary school graduates, 36 percent; middle school graduates, 56 percent; university or college/professional school graduates, 4 percent. Some 20 percent of all secretaries consisted of evacuees from urban areas, demobilized military personnel and repatriates from Japan's former colonies (Ōwada 1981: 208). These secretaries 'replaced conservative landlords as local leaders and, as pioneers of rural democratization, devoted themselves to realizing land reform. . . . That they worked directly with culturally deprived, politically inexperienced farmers to implement the tasks of land commissions is the main reason why the land reform was able to achieve greater than anticipated success in the short span of only two years' (Nōrinshō nōchika 1949: 721). As the above description makes clear, the land commission secretaries functioned as outsiders, bringing new and far less parochial ideas and norms to the communities in which they worked (for an example, see Dore 1959: 155–6). Without their contributions, the land reform would not have been at all as thorough and comprehensive as it was.

A second rupture relates to one of the underlying principles of the land reform, the idea that the ownership and use of farm land entailed obligations to society as a whole. The record of litigation challenging the constitutionality of the land reform – some 119 such cases had been lodged in district courts by 1950 – shows that this idea went well beyond prevailing conceptions. At issue in these cases was article 29 of the [postwar] constitution:

> The right to own or to hold property is inviolable. Property rights shall be defined by law, in conformity with the public welfare. Private property may be taken for public use upon just compensation therefore.

Plaintiffs asserted (1) that selling the land they had been forced to surrender to tenants in order to create owner-cultivators violated clause 3 of article 29 in that the land thus transferred was not destined for 'public use'; and (2) that the purchase price paid to them did not amount to 'just compensation.'

The Supreme Court handed down a final decision in one of these cases on December 23, 1953. This particular case concerned the matter of just compensation, not the constitutionality of the land reform per se, but no decision about compensation could be made without reference to the public character of the land reform. As the following citations from the decision make clear, that public character was recognized.

In relation to article 29, for example:

> Property rights are determined by law to insure public welfare. Thus, when necessary to maintain or promote public welfare, restrictions may be placed on the right to use, dispose of or otherwise benefit from property, and similarly, specific restrictions may be placed on the value of property, rather than consigning its price solely to market forces'.
>
> (Quoted in Nōchi kaikaku shiryō hensan iinkai 1978: 693)

Moreover, the decision cited the controls imposed on the ownership rights of farm land during the war:

> Even before passage of the land reform legislation, restrictions on the free disposition of farm land were in place, as were restrictions on using cultivable land for non-agricultural purposes. Where rents were payable in cash, they were set at a uniform level, and even the price of farm land was regulated. In these ways, strict controls were placed on the ownership rights of landlords, and eventually the price of land was so controlled by law that there was virtually no scope for market values to exist. . . . Such changes to the character of ownership rights as applied to farm land were legal measures to realize the continuing national policy of establishing owner-cultivators. In other words, these changes must be seen as having been carried out by law in a manner in conformity with the public welfare as set out in clause 2 of article 29 of the Constitution (quoted in Nōchi kaikaku shiryō hensan iinkai 1978: 696–7).

Nowhere in this decision was it explicitly stated that the land reform was in all respects consonant with the public welfare, but a high court decision of November 25, 1953, which the Supreme Court used as a precedent, had so determined:

> As is clear from the statement of purpose in article 1 of the Owner-Farmer Establishment Special Measures Law, the land reform which that law set in motion aimed at realizing such essential benefits to

> the public welfare as security for cultivators of the land, the rapid and widespread establishment of owner-cultivators who could enjoy the just fruits of their labor and, by the more effective use of land for agricultural purposes, the promotion of greater agricultural production and of democratic trends in rural communities.
>
> (Quoted in Hosogai 1978: 328)

Thus, the redistribution of private property with just compensation to its original owners was in the public interest because it promoted the eminently public goals of rural democratization and greater agricultural output. The land reform was constitutional.

In so deciding, the Supreme Court also found in favor of the principle of land ownership rights on which the land reform was premised: that such rights had a public character (Noda 1998: 192). As noted earlier, there was also a 'public' dimension in the traditional conception of land ownership and use in the countryside: farm land was not owned by individuals, but by the *ie*, and was subject to control by the *mura*. To a degree, then, in denying that farm land was simply private property, the land reform resonated with this traditional view, but its definition of 'public' went well beyond that prevailing in the countryside. In the traditional view, the public interest was confined to each particular rural community and involved only its collective residents. In contrast, the land reform introduced a far more sweeping definition of the public character of land ownership, which applied to the nation as a whole.

Agricultural legislation in the aftermath of the land reform

How did the conception of land ownership introduced by the land reform fare in subsequent years? Not at all well, in my opinion. Beginning almost immediately after the completion of the reform in 1948, mechanisms for the public control of land ownership were steadily weakened, a process which culminated in the enactment of the Agricultural Land Law in 1952. The full implications of this would become apparent during the years of Japan's so-called 'economic miracle,' *c.* 1955–72, and during the 'bubble economy' of the late 1980s and early 1990s. I will return to these implications later, but first it will be useful to examine the retreat from public control of land ownership in greater detail.

First, there was the ending of preemptive purchase of land affected by the land reform. The stipulation that the state had the right of preemptive purchase of any land that had been sold to cultivators at the time of the land reform was one of the clearest manifestations of the reform's public character, and one to which Occupation officials in the Natural Resources Section (NRS) attached great importance. A memorandum of June 28, 1946 which H.G. Schenck, the NRS chief, showed to Agriculture Minister Wada insisted that a ban on the alienation of any land purchased from the state during the land reform, whether money changed hands or not, should remain in force for a period of 30 years; in those cases where the state acknowledged that continuing owner-cultivation was no longer possible, the state itself should purchase the land in question. MAF responded with a policy of compulsory state purchase of such land in perpetuity. However, the revision of the Land Registration Law in July of 1950 eliminated the recording of rental values, which had served as the basis for determining the price of land to be purchased during the land reform, thus undermining price controls on farm land and rendering the operation of the existing preemptive purchase system impossible. Seeing no chance of re-establishing that system, MAF instead opted for an ordinance requiring that, if land purchased from the state at the time of the land reform was sold during the ten years following its purchase, a portion of the difference between the original purchase price and subsequent sale price must be repaid to the state. This approach was retained in the Agricultural Land Law, but by the late 1950s the original ten-year period had expired, and any state claims on such land transactions ceased to exist (Ōwada 1985: 113). Precisely why the right of preemptive purchase was allowed to lapse remains unclear to this day, but an explanation later offered by an official active in agricultural policymaking at the time may be relevant: ‘Because the operation without time limit of controls of this sort [on only one category of land, that transferred to owner-cultivators during the land reform] would have destabilized the agricultural land market as a whole’ (Satake 1998: 15).

Second came the abolition of price controls on farm land. Although the Japanese government was inclined to maintain controls on agricultural land prices after the land reform, Occupation headquarters [SCAP] was not, and the NRS insisted to MAF that they be eliminated. The reason given was that, with continued regulation of the maximum size of holdings and of tenant rents, price controls were unnecessary, but the general uneasiness within SCAP about direct interference in private property rights was also at work here.

The issue first surfaced in 1950, when the land registration law was revised as part of the general revision of the local tax system in accordance with the Shoup Recommendations. As mentioned in passing above, the recording of rental values that had been central to the price control policy was eliminated in the revised law. The government responded immediately by issuing an ordinance stipulating that any land still changing hands under the terms of the land reform could only be sold to cultivators at its former controlled price and that the price paid for any land now acquired by the state to maintain the acreage limits decreed by the land reform would be equivalent to ten times the average rental value of the land in question. MAF officials thought at the time that this ordinance could be used to control land prices. (Nōrinshō nōchikyoku nōseika 1950: 1027).

The issue of price controls resurfaced during Diet interpellation of the Agricultural Land Law. In response to a question from the floor, a government spokesman stated that as clause 3 of article 3 of the proposed law required official permission for any change in the title to arable or pasture land, it would be possible for the state to attach conditions that restrained undue price increases. However, shortly after the law had been passed, the vice-minister of agriculture advised regional agricultural officials that the clause in question could not in fact be used to attach conditions that affected price in the absence of any overall policy of price control (Nōchi kaikaku shiryō hensan iinkai 1980: 1160). Precisely what had brought about this change in interpretation remains unclear, but once again the assessment of Satake Goroku provides some insight: 'At a time when land prices were escalating everywhere in the country, it was likely that the feasibility of realizing price controls of any meaningful sort would be called into question' (1998: 15).

The third factor was the demise of the idea of public management of farm land. As the land reform was nearing completion in mid-1948, MAF began considering post-reform agricultural policy. An internal paper dated August 2, 1948 by Ōwada Keiki put forward particularly wide-ranging proposals to 'assure effective farm operations that built on the achievements of the land reform.' These included 'efforts to increase output by overcoming the problems caused by overly small-scale farming' and, most significantly, reliance on municipal land commissions as an instrument of state oversight of farm land to insure its efficient use. Specifically, land commissions would be empowered to regulate all changes to ownership rights, leases of land and changes in cultivating rights within their jurisdictions (Nōchi kaikaku shiryō hensan iinkai 1975: 738–43).

Based on the same principle of the public character of farm land that had infused the land reform, Ōwada's proposals aimed at solving the pressing problem of food supply facing Japan in the late 1940s by promoting the structural reform of agriculture. Continued control of all rights pertaining to land would now be used to encourage farming on a larger, more efficient scale than that achieved by the land reform itself, whether by getting groups of very small landowners to join together in cooperative farming or by allowing the most committed and capable farmers to gain cultivating rights of one sort or another to additional land.

This proposal, representing the thinking within MAF at the time, met with resistance from two quarters. On the one hand, members of the conservative parties in the Diet were uneasy about any further regulation of property rights, and provisions relating to the management of farm land by land commissions or agricultural cooperatives were struck from the proposed legislation (Nōchi kaikaku shiryō hensan iinkai 1975: 780–1). On the other hand, and much more decisively, SCAP was opposed. The thrust of Occupation policy had begun to shift in 1948, and a reconsideration of previous policy toward capital and labor was taking place. This manifested itself in two ways so far as the land reform was concerned. First, there was a narrowing in SCAP's definition of the scope of reform from the total reorganization of agriculture to the redistribution of ownership rights to land under cultivation at the time. Second, while committed to efforts to maintain what the (now more narrowly defined) land reform had achieved – thus differing from the conservative parties in the Diet – SCAP was opposed to the introduction of any measures not already included in the land reform legislation. Continued state interference in ownership rights and now in farm management, as Ōwada's proposals intended, was therefore found to be objectionable (Iwamoto 1979: 217–22).

Despite this setback, efforts by agricultural officials to realize the public management of farm land at the community level continued thereafter, notably in discussions leading to passage of the Basic Agricultural Law of 1961. For example, at a meeting of the Sub-Committee on Structural Problems in December 1959, Ogura Takekazu put forward a draft policy to the effect that 'all transactions in farm land should be supervised by a government agency in order to stabilize land prices at a reasonable level and contribute to structural policies.' In the discussion that followed, committee member Ōuchi Tsutomu supported the idea but took it a step further: 'There should also be local bodies, whether at the village or hamlet level, to develop plans for the use of farm land and facilitate at least a degree of cooperative management among local farmers' (Kajii 1999: 110).

The sub-committee's final report took up this point, stating that 'some form of public management of farm land *at the municipal level* is essential to deal with tenanted land and land transfers, although its precise form and methods will require further scrutiny' (emphasis added). The report also observed that 'the cooperative management of farm land to plan and execute improvements in agricultural technology and the structure of farm management at the municipal level might also be included in this public management system' (Sekiya 1994: 10).

The same point of view was manifested in proposals for the establishment of land management associations in the mid-1960s. Not only would these associations serve to promote the expansion of farm operations by their regulation of all land transfers and leases, but it was also expected they would play a role in bringing about the rationalization of land prices (Nōrinsuisanshō hyakunenshi hensan iinkai 1981; Ōwada 1965). However, the draft legislation put before the Diet in 1965 and again in 1966 met with resistance from both the ruling Liberal Democratic Party and the Japan Socialist Party, and failed to become law (Tōbata 1965: 132). Numerous reasons have been cited for the bill's failure – that as it offered no inducements to get marginal landowners to abandon farming, it was unlikely to promote structural reform; that intervention of the sort proposed could only work to the disadvantage of small-scale farmers; and that the proposed associations would be unable to cope with the volume of work caused by rising land prices (Nōrinsuisanshō hyakunen hensan iinkai 1981: 324). But escalating land prices almost certainly were the key factor, as they rendered the sort of controls on land transfers envisaged by the legislation virtually impossible (Kurauchi 1998: 79). As we shall see in the next section, those same price increases led the governing conservative party to concentrate in the future on agricultural policies that appealed to farmers as the owners of ever more valuable real estate.

The 'economic miracle,' land price escalation and attitudes toward land

It was the dramatic increase in all land prices during the postwar era that exerted the most profound impact on farmers' attitudes toward their land. Land prices began increasing in the early 1950s, just when Japan's economic recovery from the war was nearing completion, and they continued to increase thereafter at a rate far outstripping increases in both GNP and wholesale prices. There were three periods of particularly rapid increase: from the late 1950s to early 1960s; during the early 1970s; and from the late 1980s to the early 1990s. Although various land policies were attempted in these periods, they only treated the symptoms of the underlying problem, and the economy was ever more influenced by land values.

The increases in the value of farm and forest land were also dramatic, nowhere more so than in the case of farm land near expanding cities and in areas considered prime targets for development as golf courses, ski resorts and other leisure facilities. That these price increases heightened awareness of agricultural land as an asset is widely recognized, and it is

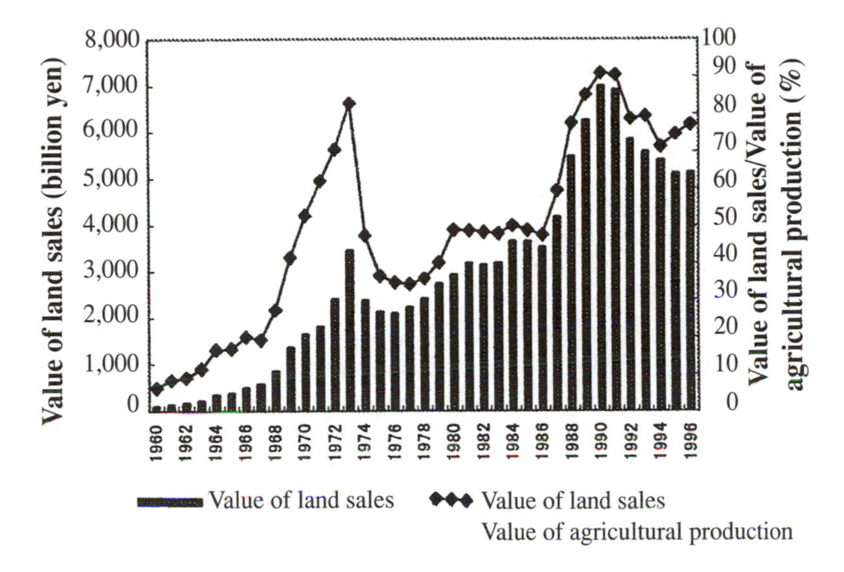

Figure 10.1 Value of agricultural land sales and the ratio of that value to the total value of agricultural production, 1960–96.

Source: Based on data in *Nōgyō shokuryō kanren sangyō no keizai keisan*.

worth noting that price increases also had a direct impact on cash flows in the farm household economy. As shown in Figure 10.1, the total value of agricultural land sales began to increase after 1960, rising above three trillion yen in 1969 and exceeding six trillion yen (an amount equivalent to more than 80 percent of the value of agricultural production) during the turbulent early 1970s. The value of land sales declined thereafter, but rose sharply again during the bubble economy of the late 1980s and early 1990s, reaching 90 percent of the value of agricultural production before leveling off to roughly 80 percent in subsequent years. It seems clear not only that farmers were increasingly aware of their land as an asset, but also that a significant number of them were cashing in on its enhanced value.

As discussed previously, public control of farm land prices was abandoned in the process of formulating the Agricultural Land Law. Nor was there any serious consideration of price policies in discussions leading to passage of the Basic Agricultural Law, even though the purchase or leasing of additional land was essential to the creation of self-sustaining farm households at which that law aimed. This remains one of the great puzzles of postwar agricultural policymaking, but some idea of why virtually no attention was paid to land prices can be inferred from the recollections of key participants. For example, according to Tōbata

Seiichi, who chaired the Commission on the Basic Problems of Agriculture, 'There was no discussion of land prices during the year the commission met. . . . Indeed, it was as if MAF was delighted with price increases, as evidence of the flourishing state of agriculture. Ogura tried to bring the matter up, but others in the ministry told him not to and he appeared to have given up' (Nōrinsuisanshō hyakunenshi hensan iinkai, 1981: 796–7). Ōwada Keiki observed: 'There were various opinions [about land prices] in the ministry, but no one argued that the ministry itself should take steps to bring prices down. The increases weren't welcomed, at least not openly, but they weren't really condemned either. They were just accepted as more or less inevitable, and as a result it is clear that intervention of any sort was delayed' (Nōrinsuisanshō hyakunenshi hensan iinkai 1981: 807). According to Kajii Isoshi, several items related to land prices had been included in the discussion papers prepared by the MAF secretariat, but none of them was discussed in any detail in the sessions of the Commission on the Basic Problems of Agriculture. Ogura, the head of the secretariat, then stressed the problem of land prices in his explanation of the report on the Agricultural Basic Law and urged MAF to take urgent action (Kajii 1993: 203). Perhaps the most one can say is that, while at least some officials were aware of the land price issue, they were even more keenly aware of the political and administrative difficulties of resurrecting any sort of price controls.

With no mention made of land prices in the Agricultural Basic Law and the idea of local land management associations stymied, all chance of the direct control of land prices was lost. The one remaining possibility was to use the provisions relating to changes in land use in the Agricultural Land Law to keep the price paid when a change of use was permitted from affecting land prices in general. This proved well-nigh impossible in practice, however – and indeed the Agricultural Land Law itself proved to be a weak instrument for promoting rational land use and the preservation of high-quality farm land in the absence of any effective system of control over land-use planning nationwide. In such circumstances, agricultural policymaking in Japan steadily veered toward policies predicated on continued price increases and the appeal of those increases to Japanese farmers. The easing of criteria for approving changes in land use is a typical example, with the easing facilitated by the fact that the criteria were not specified by law or ordinance, but by vice-ministerial directive. At the same time, the ruling Liberal Democratic Party found diverse ways of garnering votes in rural districts, including support for zoning changes, highway construction and the location of public facilities and factories on the 'new' parcels of non-agricultural land that could be set aside for such purposes when field boundaries were straightened in land adjustment projects. Portrayed as contributing to rural development, such measures also increased the value of the parcels of land affected, and the revenue from their sale to the state or to private interests went directly to at least some local farmers. Catering to the property owning instincts of farmers, especially those in urban areas, proved a very effective vote-winning strategy indeed.

Looking ahead to the structural reform of agriculture

Without doubt, the attitudes of farm families and rural communities toward land changed markedly during the period of rapid economic growth, in no small measure because of the thrust of agricultural policies in those years, which increasingly appealed to farmers as the owners of land. The public character of agricultural policy, particularly of policy toward agricultural land, which had infused the land reform got lost in the shuffle as the main architects of that policy – MAF officials, Diet Members (especially those belonging to agriculture-related *zoku*, or 'policy tribes') and agricultural cooperatives – each sought their own greatest advantage. That is one of the major reasons why the Japanese public lost confidence in the nation's agricultural policy, and unless its public character is re-established – in an atmosphere of greater transparency than has been the case during the past 40 years or so – that confidence will not be regained.

In that connection, it would be relevant to return to the main theme of this chapter, the attitudes of the *ie* and *mura* toward land that first came into being in the early modern era. Granted, changes in those attitudes have occurred as market forces have penetrated the countryside. Indeed, the patriarchal *ie* itself was legally abolished when a new civil code was implemented in 1948. But the attitudes still exist, albeit in attenuated form, and still influence the behavior of rural households and rural communities. The desire to pass on the family assets to the next generation is, after all, one of the main factors that sustains those farmers in less-favored areas in their farming operations, and recent attempts at organizing group farming operations can be traced in many respects to early *mura* norms and practices in regard to the community's land.

Table 10.1 presents those findings (excluding Hokkaido) relevant to communal norms in surveys carried out for the Agricultural Censuses of 1970 to 1990, and from it the following conclusions can be drawn:

1 Communities have become increasingly mixed in population, with the non-agricultural population reaching 84 percent in 1990. Farmers are now a minority within 'farming' communities. Yet it is important

Table 10.1 Results of surveys of farm communities, 1970–90 (excluding Hokkaido)

	1970	*1980*	*1990*
Number of farm communities	135,206	135,200	133,147
Average no. households per community	83	142	174
farm households (%)	45.8	23.8	16.0
non-farm households (%)	54.2	76.2	84.0
Communities by proportion of farm households (%)			
50% or more	78.0	64.3	51.8
80% or more	50.0	34.2	18.4
Territorial boundaries of the community (%)			
its arable land clearly demarcated	82.6	–	–
its forests and open fields clearly demarcated	57.9	–	–
overall boundaries of the community clear	79.4	–	–
Date of community's establishment (%)			
before the Meiji era	95.0	–	–
after the Meiji era	3.2	–	–
post-Second World War	1.8	–	–
Farm communities owning forests and fields (%)	46.5	43.3	–
exclusive ownership	25.8	–	–
shared with other community or communities	12.8	–	–
both of the above	7.9	–	–
Farm communities owning arable land (%)	6.8	5.0	–
Farm communities owning reservoirs or ponds (%)	18.2	12.4	–
Local road maintenance and repair (%)			
carried out as group work	73.6	–	–
all households take part	53.1	–	–
Farm path maintenance and repair (%)			
carried out as group work	74.0	70.8	66.2
all households take part	52.0	–	–
Irrigation and drainage facilities (%)			
maintenance work carried out as group work	63.8	64.5	76.1
all households take part	43.6	–	–
Number of community meetings per year (%)	–	–	–
1–2	–	17.8	23.3
3–4	–	22.0	22.9
5–6	–	22.7	20.3
7–9	–	7.4	6.1
10–12	–	19.2	18.6
13 or more	–	10.9	8.9
Communities where farmers participate in agricultural production organizations (group cultivation, joint use of equipment, livestock organizations, etc.) (%)	–	24.2	40.3
Communities involved in group crop diversification (%)	–	–	17.7

Source: Based on data in *Nōgyō shūraku chōsa hōkokusho* for the relevant years.

to note that even in 1990 farm households constituted over half of all households in 52 percent of all rural communities.

2 The great majority of agricultural communities possess clearly defined borders, and hence a sense of territorial specificity.
3 The overwhelming majority of rural communities were established before the Meiji era.
4 Over 40 percent of rural communities own such property as forests and fields.
5 Even in the mixed rural communities of today, the maintenance of field paths and irrigation facilities is usually carried out by local residents, often including non-farming residents.
6 Regular community meetings are held (although their frequency varies markedly from roughly one per year to one or more per month).
7 The proportion of communities whose residents participate in agricultural production organizations of one sort or another has risen, with most of those organizations being based in the community itself.

It is therefore clear that there has been continuity as well as change, and a variety of important communal activities (such as management of field paths and irrigation facilities) are still carried out.

Now let us turn to a survey into the attitudes of the members of farm households. Tables 10.2 and 10.3 show the results of a survey carried out by the Nippon Agricultural Research Institute in 1991 among 91 households in the Toyohara district of Yamagata Prefecture, the Iwamuro district of Nara Prefecture and the Yashirohara district of Yamaguchi Prefecture, in which all household members in residence who were over the age of 20 were asked to complete a questionnaire. A total of 247 questionnaires were returned, with those in their twenties or thirties constituting 20 percent of the total, those in their forties or fifties constituting 40 percent and those over 60 also constituting 40 percent. The questionnaire contained 20 questions in all, with questions 1 through 13 dealing with *ie* consciousness and questions 14 through 20 dealing primarily with *mura* consciousness.

Concerning the former (Table 10.2), affirmative answers (agree; somewhat agree) to all questions outnumbered the negative (disagree; somewhat disagree). Affirmative answers were particularly pronounced in relation to the importance of family ancestors (questions 1 and 2) and the importance of everyone working together to make farming a success (question 10). There was also a fairly high proportion of affirmative answers to questions related to the importance of retaining ownership of the family's land so that it could be passed on to (ideally, one member of) the next generation, that is, assuring the future of the *ie* (questions 3, 12 and 13)

Table 10.2 The *ie* consciousness of farmers (% responding to each question)

	Question	*Agree*	*Somewhat agree*	*Cannot decide*	*Somewhat disagree*	*Disagree*
1	It is essential to maintain ancestral graves and ceremonies for the ancestors.	87.9	8.1	3.2	0.0	0.8
2	I believe our ancestors watch over our family's future.	68.4	15.0	13.8	0.4	2.4
3	I hope our family always remains in farming (even if only part time).	44.1	16.2	32.0	4.0	3.6
4	It is all right to adopt a son-in-law to secure a successor.	41.3	11.7	34.0	4.9	8.1
5	It is the responsibility of the successor to care for his parents.	52.6	16.2	22.3	1.6	7.3
6	It is best for the successor to live with his parents, even if he is married.	42.2	16.0	36.3	3.4	2.1
7	Until the successor comes of age, the head of the family should remain fully responsible for management both of farming operations and all other household matters.	63.2	14.6	16.2	4.0	2.0
8	When a parent and a child disagree, the child should defer to the parent.	22.7	14.2	47.4	6.5	9.3
9	A daughter-in-law should defer to the views of her mother-in-law.	27.1	19.0	42.5	2.4	8.9
10	In farming it is important that everyone in the family pitches in and cooperates unselfishly to get the work done.	72.1	16.2	8.5	1.6	1.6
11	Even those in the family who have other jobs should help with the farm work as much as possible.	55.9	21.1	17.8	2.4	2.8
12	The land inherited from the ancestors is held in trust, to be looked after carefully and passed on to the next generation.	54.7	17.4	21.4	4.0	2.4
13	Only one person should inherit the house and land, so that the family can continue with farming.	59.1	13.0	20.6	2.8	4.5
	Average of responses	54.0	15.3	23.2	2.8	4.7

Source: Akashima Masao, 'Kazoku to nōgyō ni kansuru ankeeto,' Nippon nōgyō kenkyūjo, *Nōgyō mondai*, no. 5 (1992), pp. 65–6.

and doing everything possible to assist in the family's farming operations (question 11). On the other hand, there were relatively few affirmative answers to questions 8 and 9, both of which concerned intergenerational relations within the family. That parent–child relations (question 8) generated more negative responses than did relations between daughters-in-law and mothers-in-law (question 9) may well reflect sample bias.

Although not to the same degree as in *ie* consciousness, affirmative answers to questions concerning *mura* consciousness (Table 10.3) outnumbered negative responses. This was particularly the case in relation to the role of the community (question 14). In addition, there were many affirmative responses to questions about the value of local festivals and beliefs (question 16) and community service (question 17). On the other hand, there were relatively few affirmative responses to question 15 concerning the binding power of decisions made by the community and to question 18 concerning the participation of the community in decisions about local land use or sale. Indeed, there were relatively few negative responses to those questions either, with most people opting for a neutral answer to both. It would appear that the older idea that 'land in the community should be cultivated by members of the community' was still operative (questions 18 and 19), but some resistance to intervention by the community in the exercise of private property rights (that is, transactions in land or changes in land use) had now surfaced.

As the author of this questionnaire himself acknowledges (Akashima 1992: 72–3), some caution is necessary in interpreting the results of opinion surveys, especially when the survey deals with attitudes toward the *ie* and the *mura*. One is likely to get 'conventional' or 'expected' (*tatemae tekina*) responses rather than candid opinions (*honne*), and as a result one might be tempted to conclude that orientations toward the *ie* and the *mura* remain stronger than in fact they are. That only adult family members still in residence were surveyed and those who had left home were excluded is a further problem. It is therefore likely that this survey over-reports affirmative attitudes.

That said, it is truly surprising that despite all the massive changes in the actual circumstances of both *ie* and *mura* over the past 20 to 30 years there does not appear to have been an equivalent degree of change at the normative level. Today's rural families and rural communities have not succumbed totally to the logic of market economics, and regional and intergenerational differences notwithstanding, long-established customs and attitudes related to land survive. Rather than being an obstacle to 'progress,' as most political theorists believed during the heyday of modernism, this legacy of the past could well prove the basis for important new departures in Japanese agriculture.

Table 10.3 The *mura* consciousness of farmers (% responding to each question)

	Question	*Agree*	*Somewhat agree*	*Cannot decide*	*Somewhat disagree*	*Disagree*
14	The role of the *mura* (hamlet community) in farming villages will remain important in the future.	57.5	20.6	18.2	1.6	2.0
15	Residents should abide by *mura* decisions, even if they find them to their disadvantage.	29.6	22.7	36.8	4.5	6.5
16	Customary rites and celebrations in honor of the guardian deities of the *mura* should always be observed.	52.2	24.3	16.6	3.6	3.2
17	No matter how busy they are, everyone should make time to perform the communal tasks the *mura* has agreed.	53.8	24.3	17.8	0.8	3.2
18	If at all possible, title to arable land within the *mura* should not be transferred to anyone outside the *mura*.	41.3	19.8	32.4	2.8	3.6
19	Efforts should be made to insure that all land within the *mura* is cultivated by residents of the *mura*.	42.5	20.6	29.5	3.2	4.0
20	The consent of the *mura* should be obtained for the sale or change in use of any arable land within its boundaries.	20.6	15.8	39.7	6.9	17.0
	Average of responses	42.5	21.2	27.1	3.3	5.7

Source: Same as for Table 10.2.

Just as those postmodern political theorists in North America who argue for a new communitarianism to combat the problems of apathy and anomie in their societies (for example, Avineri and de-Shalit 1992; Mulhall and Swift 1996) are not engaging in mere nostalgia for the past, so too I am not indulging here in nostalgia for some 'golden' rural past in Japan. On the contrary, the communitarianism of rural families and hamlets was parochial in the extreme, and the 'public' interest served was confined to those living within the hamlet's borders. That sort of inward-looking narrowness must be transformed into the more open communitarianism of civil society. The campaigns for organic farming and the direct delivery of fresh, wholesome produce to urban consumers that have expanded rapidly in recent years, as well as diverse other forms of closer contact between city and countryside, have great promise as a means of achieving just that. Infused as such campaigns are with voluntarism, pluralism and the partnership of ordinary citizens in a common enterprise, they constitute not only a quest for a counterweight to the powers of the modern state and market economy, but also a means to broaden the definition of 'public interest' to include all participants, in this particular case both farmers and urban residents, and to ease the conflicts of interest and resultant social frictions that might well occur between them from time to time.

And there will be a need for agricultural policies that coincide with and support the growing 'communitarianism of civil society' of this sort. More specifically: (1) Once the proper sphere of the central government has been clearly delineated (to include such matters as trade in agricultural commodities, the preservation and use of farm land, regulation of supply and demand in agricultural commodities, price policies, etc.), a considerable degree of authority should be delegated to the regional and/or local level to determine how best to meet agreed policy objectives; (2) Regional and local policy should be based to the greatest possible extent on the best practices that have been developed by farmers and urban consumers in those areas, as a vital means of empowering residents and giving them a greater stake in policy outcomes; and (3) Behind-the-scenes 'interest-trading' should be eliminated and transparency restored to decision making at all levels so as to reaffirm the public character of agriculture, which would result not only in encouraging farmers to consider the public good in their actions, but also in restoring the confidence of the broader Japanese public in their country's agriculture and agricultural policy (Iwamoto 1999).

References

Akashima Masao. 1992. 'Kazoku to nōgyō ni kansuru ankeeto,' Nippon nōgyō kenkyūjo *Nōgyō mondai*, No. 5.

Avineri, Shlomo and Avner de-Shalit. 1992. *Communitarianism and Individualism*. London: Oxford University Press.

Dore, Ronald P. 1959. *Land Reform in Japan*. London: Oxford University Press.

Hosogai Daijirō. 1978. 'Kaisetsu.' In *Nōchi kaikaku shiryō shūsei*, vol. 8, ed. Nōchi kaikaku shiryō hensan iinkai. Tokyo: Nōsei chōsakai.

Iwamoto Noriaki. 1979. 'Nōchi kaikaku.' In *Taikei Nihon gendai shi 5: senryō to sengo kaikaku*, ed. Kanda Fumito. Tokyo: Nihon hyōronsha.

—— 1987. 'Sengo nōsei to jisakunōshugi – nōgyō kihon hō o meguru rongi o chūshin ni. In *Family Farms no hikakushiteki kenkyū*, ed. Shiina Shigeaki. Tokyo: Ochanomizu shobō.

—— 1999. 'Sengo nōsei no wakugumi to "shin kihon hō".' *Nōgyō keizai kenkyū*, 71(3).

Kajii Isoshi. 1993. 'Shūraku nōjō sei no gen dankaiteki igi.' In *Ie to mura no nōseigaku*, ed. Nihon nōgyō kenkyūjo. Toyko: Nōsangyoson bunka kyōkai.

—— 1999. *Nōgyō kōzō no henka to nōchi seido*. Tokyo: Zenkoku nōgyō kaigisho.

Kurauchi Sōichi. 1998. 'Nōgyō kōzō seisaku to tochi mondai.' *Nōgyō keizai kenkyū* 70(2).

Mulhall, Stephen and Adam Swift. 1996. *Liberals and Communitarians*. 2nd edn. Oxford: Blackwell Publishers.

Nishida Yoshiaki. 1998a. 'Nōchi kaikaku to nōson minshushugi.' In *Demokurashii no hōkai to saisei*, ed. Minami Ryōshin, Nakamura Masanori and Nishizawa Tamotsu. Tokyo: Nihon keizai hyōronsha.

—— 1998b. 'Sengo kaikaku to nōson minshushugi.' In *20 seiki shisutemu*, vol. 5, ed. Tōkyō daigaku shakai kagaku kenkyūjo. Tokyo: Tōkyō daigaku shuppankai.

Nōchi kaikaku kiroku iinkai. 1951. *Nōchi kaikaku tenmatsu gaiyō*. Tokyo: Nōsei chōsakai.

Nōchi kaikaku shiryō hensan iinkai. 1975. *Nōchi kaikaku shiryō shūsei*, vol. 3. Tokyo: Nōsei chōsakai.

—— 1978. *Nōchi kaikaku shiryō shūsei*, vol. 8. Tokyo: Nōsei chōsakai.

—— 1980. *Nōchi kaikaku shiryō shūsei*, vol. 12. Tokyo: Nōsei chōsakai.

Noda Kimio. 1998. 'Sengo tochi kaikaku to gendai – nōchi kaikaku no rekishiteki igi.' *Nenpō Nihon gendaishi*, No. 4.

Nōrinshō nōchika. 1949. 'Shichōson nōchi iinkai no shoki ni kansuru chōsa.' In *Nōchi kaikaku shiryō shusei*, vol. 6 (1977), ed. Nōchi kaikaku shiryō hensan iinkai. Tokyo: Nōsei chōsakai.

Nōrinsuisanshō hyakunenshi hensan iinkai. 1981. *Nōrinsuisanshō hyakunenshi*, ka.

Ōwada Keiki. 1965. 'Nōchi kanri jigyōdan no kōsō o megutte.' *Nōgyōhō kenkyū*, No. 3.

—— 1981. *Hishi Nihon no nōchi kaikaku*. Tokyo: Nihon keizai shinbunsha.

—— 1985. 'Nōchi kaikaku – shōgen to kaiko, hansei.' *Nōgyō to keizai*, special edition.

Saitō Hitoshi. 1974. Tochi seisaku ron no mondai ten – kosaku sōgi o chūshin to shite.' *Ajia shokoku ni okeru tochi seisaku*. Tokyo: Ajia keizai kenkyūjo.
Satake Goroku. 1998. *Taikenteki kanryō ron*. Tokyo: Yūhikaku.
Sekiya Shunsaku. 1994. 'Nōyōchi kanri shisutemu ni tsuite.' *Heisei 5-nendo nōyōchi yūkō riyō hōsakutō ni kansuru chōsa kenkyū jigyō hōkokusho*. Tokyo: Nōsei chōsakai.
Tanaka Manabu. 1987. 'Nihon ni okeru jisakunōshugi no keifu.' In *Tōnan Ajia no nōgyō gijutsu henkaku to nōson shakai*, ed. Takiqawa Tsutomu. Tokyo: Ajia keizai kenkyūjo.
Tōbata Shirō. 1965. 'Kihon hō nōsei o megutte.' *Chōsa jihō*, no. 4.

11 Agricultural public works and the changing mentality of Japanese farmers in the postwar era

Kase Kazutoshi

Introduction

Publicly financed civil engineering projects occupy a larger share of GDP in Japan than in other developed countries, leading some critics to describe Japan as a 'state dominated by construction companies' (*doken kokka*). That the share of public works projects related to agriculture has remained high while the share of agriculture in the national economy has declined precipitously has been a particular target of criticism in recent decades. Until the 1970s, however, the importance of such public works projects was widely acknowledged, not only by farmers, but also by the general public.

In paddy field agriculture, unlike in other types of agriculture, both the stabilization of output and increases in output are highly dependent on improvements to irrigation and drainage, land readjustment, and other civil engineering projects. The rapid increases in the productivity of paddy fields and in the productivity of agricultural labor in the postwar era would have been impossible without agricultural public works. During the 1950s and 1960s, Japanese farmers were enthusiastic about engineering projects and paid what was often a substantial portion of the costs themselves, although rising rice prices and inflation eased the burden of repayment. In these years farmers were keen to achieve higher incomes and relief from arduous labor, and they saw agricultural engineering projects as a vital means toward these goals.

Since the 1970s, however, farmers' attitudes toward engineering projects have become more diverse, as rice prices have stagnated due to falling demand and the need to switch to other crops has become apparent. This in turn has complicated relations among farmers within the same rural community. Those who cultivate relatively large holdings and have children willing to succeed them have aimed at expanding their scale of cultivation, made possible by the increasing efficiency of agricultural labor, and have remained enthusiastic about engineering projects, but those who cultivate small holdings and have no successors have tended to be reluctant to put up the money required. In addition, those who are thinking of selling their farmland for housing or other non-agricultural purposes at some point in the future tend to base their decision to accept a proposed project or not on whether it will facilitate or hinder later sales, and whether or not it will increase the value of the land.

Because agricultural public works projects apply to all the agricultural land within a specific area, it is essential that all the farmers concerned agree to the proposed project, or that those who are against it can be constrained into participation. Legally, there are mechanisms for compelling participation in cases where opponents are few in number, but it has always been clear that resort to compulsory measures would have a damaging effect on relations among the farmers within a given community. Hence, achieving unanimous support within the community was viewed as essential, and it was expected that farmers who were enthusiastic about a proposed project would join with local officials and officials of the land improvement district to persuade those among their neighbors who were opposed or reluctant to consent to it.

Since the 1990s, the prices Japanese farmers have received for the rice they produce have fallen sharply, as the rice imports agreed at the GATT Uruguay Round began and as the price support system in effect hitherto could no longer provide them with the equivalent of urban wages for the hours they worked. In terms of their profits from farming alone, farmers were no longer able to shoulder their share of the cost of engineering works. State appropriations for rural public works projects increased at this time, partly as a means of countering the disruptive effects of the Uruguay Round in rural Japan and partly as a general response to the deep recession afflicting the Japanese economy as a whole. Faced with the necessity of spending the funding that had been allocated to their region, local authorities became increasingly concerned about achieving the necessary consensus among farmers on which public works projects depended.

In this chapter I will take a closer look at agricultural public works, with particular attention to the impact of changes in farmers' attitudes toward farm management and agricultural investment throughout the postwar era on the kind of projects proposed and implemented.

About agricultural public works in general

Two sorts of agricultural public works can be identified: (1) those designed to create new agricultural land by means of drainage and reclamation;

and (2) those designed to improve existing agricultural land. Projects of the former sort were actively pursued immediately after Japan's defeat in 1945, a time of the severe food shortages, but it is projects of the latter sort that predominated thereafter. Moreover, the primary focus has been on paddy fields, where rice is grown, and projects aimed at improving dry fields (*hatake*) and pasture land have been of secondary importance.

Paddy field improvements can be divided into the following categories: (1) irrigation and drainage works to improve the water supply throughout a given area; (2) projects to improve the fields in a given area, such as land readjustment, bringing in topsoil, the construction of culverts for drainage, and so on; and (3) projects to improve farm roads.

Irrigation and drainage works are the key projects that improve the fundamental conditions for growing rice in the area. In order to secure water for paddy field agriculture, rainwater alone is not enough. Water has to be taken from rivers and reservoirs to fill the paddies before the rice seedlings are transplanted, and the proper depth of water must be maintained for most of the time that the rice is growing. Accordingly, each paddy field has to be connected to a channel that draws water from a river or other source, and the soil within it has to be level. It is also essential to be able to drain water from the paddy fields after heavy rainfall, when the roots of the plants need exposure to air and at harvest time.

In the days when only very simple civil engineering projects were possible, rice could only be cultivated on land immediately adjacent to rivers. Not only was the labor involved in growing rice more arduous and crop yields far lower than at present, but also the area of land that could be utilized as paddy was limited by available technology. Moreover, there was considerable variation in yields among local paddy fields, because those in low-lying positions received too much water and those at higher elevations received too little. Irrigation and drainage works overcome this kind of situation, providing all land within a given area with uniformly favorable water supply conditions. Embankments are built to prevent flooding, pumps are installed to draw water from the river to any paddy field in the area, and channels connecting each field are dug to drain water back into the river as and when necessary.

The second type of public works for paddy fields are those that improve the conditions of individual fields. For example, when the mechanization of farming really got under way in about the 1960s, the floor of each paddy field had to be strengthened before any machinery could be used – if a piece of machinery is put into a muddy paddy field with a weak floor it will sink due to its weight alone. Moreover, in order to make the operation of the machinery more efficient, it was essential to make the shape of each field into as large a rectangle as possible. To that end, large

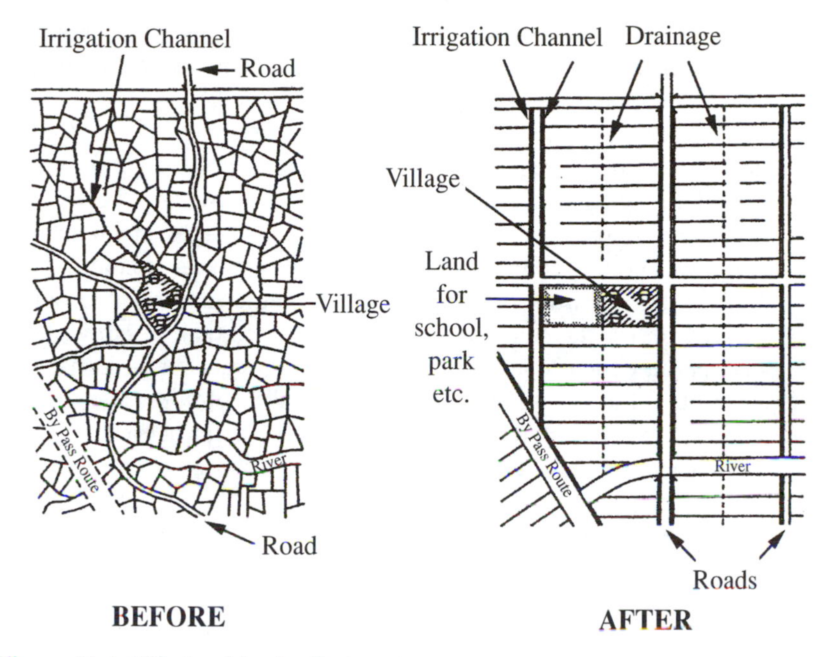

Figure 11.1 Effects of land adjustment.

Source: redrawn from Fukushima ken nōgyōshi hensan iinkai, ed., *Fukushima ken nōgyōshi*, vol. 3 (1985), p. 1,273.

numbers of farmers took part in land readjustment projects, which involved exchanging the various small paddy fields they owned with others to create one contiguous holding and then straightening the boundaries.

The third type of agricultural public works are the farm road improvement works that have widened, straightened and paved the narrow and winding farm roads so as to make the passage of farm machinery (from the second half of the 1950s) and cars (from the second half of the 1960s) possible. As a result of this, the transportation time for moving farming equipment and bringing in the harvest has been greatly shortened, and labor much reduced. Figure 11.1 illustrates the effects of the second and third type of agricultural public works.

Agricultural public works up to the early 1950s

The scale of agricultural public works that had been carried out during the decades prior to the Second World War had been limited, in part because of technological constraints and in part because of conflicts of interest among the parties concerned, which impeded both the planning and execution of improvement projects. Those conflicts of interest had been of the following two sorts: between colonial and domestic agriculture and between landlords and tenant farmers in Japan.

The Japanese government had encouraged improvements to rice cultivation in Taiwan and Korea, not only as a means of promoting economic development in those two colonies, but also as a means of providing the cheap food imports that would keep industrial wages in Japan low, thus strengthening the competitive position of Japanese manufactured goods in international trade. Given that much greater increases in output could be secured for the same outlay in the colonies than at home, there was a marked tendency to concentrate the limited state funding that was made available on agricultural public works in the colonies, and insufficient funding was provided domestically. Japanese farmers thus found they had to shoulder more than half the cost of any projects undertaken, and with the slump in rice prices in the 1920s and 1930s they saw little chance of realizing any profit even if the money required could be scraped together. As a result, the pace of agricultural public works projects was slowed.

The second factor slowing land improvement projects was conflict of interest between landlords and tenant farmers. More than half of all rice paddy was cultivated by tenants in the prewar period – in 1930 only 46.3 percent of paddy fields were cultivated by owner-farmers – and the increasing number of disputes over rent levels between tenants and their landlords proved an obstacle to agricultural public works. It was the owners of land, not the cultivators, who agreed to improvement projects and assumed responsibility for their share of the costs. What landlords sought from such projects was a net increase in the rents they received, either by stabilizing yields so they need not grant rent reductions when crops were poor or by increasing yields so they could demand higher rents. If that proved impossible they saw little point in bearing the costs involved. As tenant farmers became organized after the First World War and as tenancy disputes increased in number, raising the rent after the completion of improvement works became difficult to achieve. As a result, from the 1920s on hardly any progress in agricultural public works was possible at all in western Japan where the tenant movement was strongest, and they came to be carried out primarily in the Tohoku region where disputes organized by tenant unions remained relatively uncommon.

During the Second World War the import of rice from the colonies became difficult, and in response to growing food shortages within Japan attention focused on agricultural public works that would bring about higher rice yields at home. Tenant rents were controlled, on the basis that, if the actual cultivators of rice were not given a measure of protection, they would have no incentive to increase yields, and consequently the stalemate in agricultural land improvement due to the conflict between landlords and tenant farmers eased. In 1941 the Agricultural Land Development Act came into force and government subsidies were greatly increased. Because of severe shortages of raw materials and labor, however, the majority of projects were stymied early on and would only be completed after the war.

When Japan surrendered in August 1945, rice from the former colonies could no longer be imported at all, and that reality combined with shortages of fertilizer and farm implements made the food crisis even more severe than during the war itself. There was widespread malnutrition among urban residents until the autumn of 1948, and as the government was unable to fulfill its responsibilities for the rationing of food, people who were unable to purchase food at black market prices were on the verge of starvation. Accordingly, increasing the area of agricultural land and raising the productivity of existing land became urgent priorities. In addition, a fair proportion of people who had lost their jobs due to the dissolution of war-related industries at the end of the war returned to farming, while those second and third sons of farming families who could not get jobs in other industries sought out new agricultural land.

In these extreme conditions, policies towards agricultural land improvement works were strengthened, and two particular sets of circumstances had a favorable effect on the development of projects immediately thereafter. First, the conditions that had limited agricultural land improvement works before the war were eliminated, owing to the loss of the colonies and the virtual extinction of the landlord class as a result of the postwar land reform, and, second, in view of the food crisis, a considerable proportion of spending on public works was concentrated on agriculture.

As a result, many of the works that had been planned during the war but that could not be carried out because of shortages of raw materials and labor were executed in a short space of time. 'Urgent land reclamation works' to create new arable land were given priority, as it was felt they would have a greater immediate impact than improvements to existing land and would make the best use of such raw materials as were available. Most projects were relatively small in scale.

In addition, the Land Improvement Act in 1949 became the basic law for postwar agricultural land improvement works. Under its provisions, the separate irrigation associations and land improvement associations that had existed in the past were unified into one body to oversee improvements at the local level. The law also effected a change in the locus of decision making about agricultural land improvement works from the prewar 'landowner principle' to the 'cultivator principle,' so that in instances of proposed improvements that involved any fields remaining in tenancy only the tenant farmers as the actual cultivators were empowered to decide whether or not to participate.

To sum up, relatively little in the way of improvements was actually achieved during the early post-surrender years, but some very crucial groundwork was laid for the development of agricultural land improvements in the future.

The 1950s and 1960s

The food shortages and economic chaos that beset Japan after 1945 finally came to an end in the early 1950s, and from 1955 to the early 1970s the Japanese economy grew rapidly, with GDP increasing at an annual rate of about 10 percent and non-agricultural job opportunities expanding dramatically. The younger members of farm households, whether those who had returned to the countryside at the end of the war or those who had just completed the now mandatory nine years of compulsory education, increasingly found employment in industry and commerce, and the surplus population within farming villages soon began to disappear.

While the wages paid to non-agricultural workers increased, farm incomes remained relatively stable. To resolve what came to be seen as a serious problem, the Agricultural Basic Law was enacted in 1961, and a new policy for determining how much farmers would be paid by the state for the rice they produced was implemented. Not only would their actual costs of production each year be taken into consideration, but so too would prevailing wages for industrial workers, and farmers would receive a roughly equivalent 'wage' for the hours they had worked. The state would then sell the rice to the public at a lower price, absorbing the cost of doing so. Table 11.1 shows the changes in state rice prices over time, revealing stable price levels during the latter 1950s and rapid increases between 1960 and 1968.

At roughly the same time, the prices of easy-to-use agricultural machinery produced by the expanding machinery industry fell to levels that ordinary farmers could afford, and their greater use of machinery, combined with their greater use of chemical fertilizers, pesticides and improved rice strains, led to higher yields for less labor. As Table 11.1 also shows, the average yield of rice on 0.1 hectare of paddy rose dramatically from about 300 kg in the early 1950s to some 450 kg in the late 1960s. Table 11.2 indicates that the labor required per 0.1 hectare to grow rice declined from 199 hours in 1950 to 116 hours in 1970, a decrease of some 42 percent, for a farmer with a holding of from one to 1.5 hectares. Clearly, a considerable degree of change for the better – albeit

Table 11.1 State purchase price for rice, 1950–99

Year	*Price/60 kg yen*	*Rice yield/ tan (kg)*	*Year*	*Price/60 kg yen*	*Rice yield/ tan (kg)*
1950	2419	324	1975	15440	481
1951	2820	306	1976	16432	427
1952	3000	334	1977	17086	478
1953	3384	278	1978	17176	499
1954	3704	305	1979	17176	482
1955	3902	393	1980	17536	412
1956	3788	345	1981	17603	453
1957	3898	362	1982	17797	458
1958	3880	377	1983	18112	459
1959	3886	388	1984	18505	517
1960	3902	398	1985	18505	501
1961	4129	384	1986	18505	508
1962	4562	404	1987	17404	498
1963	5030	397	1988	16615	474
1964	5772	396	1989	16615	496
1965	6228	390	1990	16372	509
1966	6936	400	1991	16266	473
1967	7592	453	1992	16266	504
1968	8088	449	1993	16266	367
1969	8090	435	1994	16266	544
1970	8152	442	1995	16266	509
1971	8482	411	1996	16266	525
1972	8880	456	1997	16092	515
1973	10218	470	1998	15741	499
1974	13491	456	1999	15500	515

Sources: Kayō Nobufumi, *Nihon nōgyō kiso tōkei*; Shokuryō-chō, *Shokuryō kanri tōkei nenpō*.

Note
The purchase prices listed are for third-class, unhulled rice.

within the confines of small-scale family farming – was occurring in the lives and livelihoods of farmers.

In 1952 the Ministry of Agriculture and Forestry announced a 'Five-year Plan to Increase Food Production,' which aimed at the achievement of self-sufficiency in food by 1960. This plan was later revised, but until the mid-1960s efforts to increase the production of rice and other agricultural products received official encouragement.

There was a gradual reduction in the land reclamation projects that had been emphasized immediately after the war, in part because suitable land was now harder to find, and attention focused in the 1950s on the improvement of existing fields. After 1963, the main emphasis shifted from irrigation and drainage works to the readjustment of individual paddy

Table 11.2 Hours of labor per 0.1 hectare to grow rice, by scale of cultivation

	Scale of cultivation (ha)							
Year	*Average*	*<0.5*	*0.5–1.0*	*1.0–1.5*	*1.5–2.0*	*2.0–3.0*	*3.0–5.0*	*5.0+*
1950		250.0	185.6	199.0	187.9	178.8	165.1	
1956	183.2	209.6	193.8	180.8	166.9	162.9	141.4	
1960	172.7	193.6	182.8	172.7	165.3	155.2	144.1	
1965	141.2	156.2	148.5	138.5	138.4	130.9	117.0	
1970	117.8	141.6	129.5	115.8	111.9	102.6	88.8	
1975	81.5	107.8	94.6	82.7	70.0	65.9	55.4	
1980	64.4	81.7	70.5	62.0	54.1	52.8	49.3	31.8
1985	55.1	72.7	63.3	52.9	47.5	44.9	44.4	32.1
1990	43.8	57.7	51.0	43.8	40.4	37.3	35.4	26.7
1995	39.1	57.6	46.7	40.5	35.2	33.1	30.1	23.5
1998	36.1	53.0	42.9	36.7	32.8	30.8	28.0	21.3

Sources: Kayō Nobufumi, *Nihon nōgyō kiso tōkei* (revised ed.), pp. 488–9; Nōrinshō tōkei jōhōbu, *Kome oyobi mugirui no seisanhi*, relevant years.

fields. At the same time the main effect of projects changed from increased productivity per unit area to savings in labor.

In the early 1950s the standard size of paddy field created by readjustment was the one-*tan* plot (1,000 sq.m., in a rectangle 25 m by 40 m), but gradually the standard area was increased to two *tan* (2,000 sq.m., in other words 25 m by 80 m), and after 1963 a three-*tan* plot (3,000 sq.m., 30 m by 100 m) was recommended. Central government subsidies were provided to promote such works, amounting to 45 to 50 percent of the total cost after 1965. In addition, it was standard practice for prefectures to provide 30 percent, leaving farmers responsible for no more than 20 to 25 percent (or even less if the municipalities in which they lived were willing and able to contribute toward the cost). Not only did such readjustment projects begin changing the rural landscape by providing expanses of uniformly rectangular paddy fields, but also – and of more immediate importance – they made possible the use of machinery: the cultivators and small tractors that spread rapidly from the late 1950s to the early 1960s, and the harvesters (at first binders, then combine harvesters) that became available in the late 1960s.

It was of vital importance to the success of the policies implemented at this time that all farmers supported land improvement. That in itself made it relatively easy to overcome any reluctance some of them might feel at parting with bits of what had previously been 'their land' and to negotiate the land transfers to create unified parcels of suitable size. Village officials and officials of the local land improvement district sought the required consent of all farmers in the proposed project area, and if any problems arose over land transfers it was usually possible to resolve them fairly swiftly by calling for compromise, so that 'a project that everyone wants can be realized as soon as possible.' At a time when the benefits of land readjustment were easily appreciated by one and all, such arguments usually proved persuasive.

Moreover, at a time when further inflation and further increases in rice prices were to be expected, the real burden on farmers of their share of land improvement costs lightened every year, and farmers tended to think that the sooner the works were carried out the greater their profits would be. Consequently, in cases where government subsidies were not granted to projects, it was not unusual for the works to be carried out immediately with no subsidy (in other words, with the farmers themselves bearing the full cost). Rather than postpone the works in order to apply for subsidy again the following year, farmers believed they could quickly repay any loans taken out to pay the costs involved.

Of course, the enthusiasm among farmers for agricultural public works was greatest in those parts of the country where the greatest effects could be expected. That many projects were carried out in the Tohoku and Hokuriku regions and relatively few were carried out in western Japan was because yields per *tan* had long been low in the former regions on account of the harsh winter weather and the poverty of local farmers, and improvement projects promised to increase yields significantly. This was indeed to be the case. By the late 1950s rice yields per *tan* in the prefectures of the Tohoku and Hokuriku regions had increased to well above the national average, and as a result of further increases in the 1960s these prefectures became the chief rice-producing districts of the country. Farmers there, and in the northern Kanto region, 'were busy converting every possible plot of flat land into rice paddy' in what were known as 'self-funded paddy conversions' (*jiko kaiden*) (Baba 1975: 259). In parallel with those 'self-funded paddy conversions' and other land reclamation projects, projects to improve existing agricultural land were also carried out.

The fifth column of Table 11.3 shows the percentage of paddy fields on which land readjustment works had been completed by 1963. The national average stood at 27 percent, but the two regions of Hokuriku and Tohoku had considerably higher rates of 47 percent and 44 percent respectively. It can also be seen that the Kinki and Chugoku regions in western Japan were well below the national average, while Hokkaido had the lowest percentage of all.

As we shall see in the next section, the prospect of converting agricultural land to such other uses as housing sites would impede agricultural

Table 11.3 Percentage of adjusted rice paddy fields by agricultural region, 1963 and 1993 (1,000 ha, %)

	August 1963					*March 1993*		
	Total area of paddy	*Adjusted fields*				*Total area of paddy*	*Adjusted to 0.3 ha or larger*	
		Area	*Area adjusted to 0.2 ha or more*	*Adjusted (%)*	*Adjusted to 0.2 ha or more*		*Area*	*Adjusted (%)*
	(a)	*(b)*	*(c)*	*(b/a)*	*(c/a)*	*(d)*	*(e)*	*(e/d)*
Japan	3428	912	83	27	2	2782	1424	51
Hokkaido	237	15	2	6	1	241	215	89
Tohoku	647	283	13	44	2	664	329	50
Kanto	626	189	12	30	2	505	258	51
Hokuriku	403	190	22	47	5	313	161	51
Tokai	239	62	9	26	4	156	83	53
Kinki	318	39	2	12	1	206	94	45
Chugoku, Shikoku	496	46	12	9	2	333	107	32
Kyushu	462	87	11	19	2	363	176	49

Sources: *Poketto nōrinsuisan tōkei* (1977); Nōrinshō nōchi kyoku, *Tochi kairyō sōgō keikaku chōsa hōkoku* (1967), p. 67.

public works from the 1970s on, but during the 1960s that was not the case. On the contrary, the very creation of large, level, uniformly rectangular plots was viewed as a plus by those farmers who were contemplating sales of their property for non-agricultural use as well as by those who intended to continue farming, and until 1969 virtually no legal restrictions existed on such sales. Indeed, farmers who owned land near rapidly expanding cities could expect to recoup far more than they had been required to invest in land readjustment from the higher prices such readjusted land would fetch from developers.

The 1970s and 1980s: an era of change in agricultural public works

The favorable conditions for rice farming in the 1960s were at the same time preparing the ground for the subsequent deadlock in Japanese agriculture. The first problem to surface was an excess in the supply of rice over demand. Spurred on by annual increases in the price they received for rice, farmers made continued efforts to increase yields per *tan*, but at the very same time the dietary preferences of urban consumers had been shifting away from rice to bread as part of the westernization of lifestyles during the years of rapid economic growth. Annual rice consumption per capita reached a peak of 118 kg in 1962 and then swiftly fell to 93 kg in 1971, a decrease of over 21 percent in just nine years. By the late 1960s the Food Control Account was in serious deficit, because projected revenue from sales of rice to consumers (at lower prices than producers received) was significantly less than anticipated. From 1968 efforts began to curtail increases in the producers' rice price, and in 1970 the first rice production controls (*gentan*, or set-aside policies) went into operation.

A second problem was that as Japan entered the ranks of the economically advanced nations it encountered demands for the abolition of trade restrictions from its first-world trading partners, including demands for the ending of restrictions on the import of certain agricultural commodities. While, on the one hand, new policies to discourage rice production envisaged that farmers would be induced to switch to growing vegetables, fruit and livestock, on the other hand, with increasing imports of foreign agricultural commodities that had been produced far more cheaply than was the case in Japan, domestic prices for those commodities fell, and so many of the crops seen as alternatives to rice became unprofitable to grow.

The third problem stemmed from changes within rice farming itself. When mechanization even of rice planting became feasible in 1975 or thereabouts, almost the entire process of growing rice became freed from time-consuming hand labor. Consequently, even someone with a full-time job in the non-agricultural sector now found it possible to grow rice, and the number of type 2 part-time farmers (those earning more from non-agricultural employment than from agriculture) increased dramatically. As car ownership had become more widespread in rural Japan than in cities by the early 1970s, farm household members were able to contemplate even longer daily journeys to their non-agricultural jobs, and at the same time an increasing number of factories were relocating to the countryside in response to efforts to reduce pollution in cities, creating a substantial increase in non-agricultural employment opportunities relatively close to hand. The interest of type 2 part-time farmers in farming was relatively weak; they were considerably less keen than full-time farmers to pay their share of local agricultural public works projects, and they tended to be more interested than their full-time farming neighbors in the possibility of selling their land holdings. After 1969, when a law came into effect imposing severe restrictions on the subsequent change in use of any land in designated agricultural promotion districts that had received a state subsidy for public works, they were likely to oppose proposals for such projects on the grounds that future sales of land would be impeded.

With rice now in over-supply, the nature of agricultural public works projects underwent marked changes. First, the number of projects to create new paddy fields was reduced, and the improvement of existing arable land took center stage. In that regard, emphasis was now placed on the conversion of paddy fields into dry fields (for example, improving the drainage of paddy fields so they could be used as dry fields too) and on projects to improve dry fields themselves.

Second, agricultural public works were rescheduled as part of attempts to reduce rice production. Previously it had been standard practice to begin works in the autumn after harvesting was over and to finish the works by rice-planting time the following year so as not to interfere in any way with the rice crop. Now works during the summer months were encouraged, first by means of set-aside subsidies (*kyūkō shōrei hojokin*) from 1970 and then by year-round works subsidies (*shūnen sekō hojokin*) from 1974. Within a very short space of time, many projects were being carried out on the latter basis.

Third, there was an increase in 're-improvement' projects on paddy fields that had been improved previously. With the introduction of large rice-planting machines and the increased size of other machines used in rice production, farmers found it desirable to increase the size of the 0.1 or 0.2 hectare plots that had been created during the 1960s. Moreover, in cases where part-time farmers had entrusted the cultivation of the paddy fields they owned to other full-time farmers, or to a producers' organization, it was essential that the farmers looking after the fields were able to make efficient use of mechanical equipment. Hence, in order to even out the differences in elevation between adjacent small-scale paddy fields and combine them into one large paddy field, further readjustment was necessary.

Fourth, projects to provide farmers with independent access to water were undertaken for the first time. Previously, it had been necessary for all the farmers in a given area to coordinate the flooding of the paddy fields they cultivated, but with the increase in part-time farming this sort of coordination became difficult and independent access to water became necessary. Works to supply water to individual fields were carried out, and piped water came into general use with separate taps being installed in each field.

Fifth, the scope of agricultural public works projects was expanded from the early 1970s to include purposes other than increasing agricultural output. Road construction and the laying of sewers in villages can be cited as examples of projects that benefited all rural residents, not just farmers alone. Although such projects were carried out by the Ministry of Construction in urban areas, they were carried out by the Ministry of Agriculture and Forestry in the Japanese countryside, so as to maintain that ministry's share of public works appropriations at a time when farmers were increasingly divided over the value of purely agricultural public works.

As shown in Table 11.4, the charges farmers had to pay for land improvement works and irrigation rose from the equivalent of about 2 percent of their gross income from rice cultivation in the mid-1960s to 8 percent in the late 1980s, and from about 3 percent of their cash income from rice to about 9 percent during the same period. In terms of net income, generally estimated at about half of gross income, the burden of charges rose from 4 percent to 16 percent.

The above are average figures. As shown in Table 11.5 the actual burden varied inversely with size of holding. That is, the smaller the holding, the higher the percentage of land improvement charges to gross income. This would lead us to expect that enthusiasm for land improvements would vary according to size of holding. On the one hand, small-scale farmers – among whom the vast majority farmed only part-time – would be reluctant to pay for works, and on the other hand, large-scale farmers would be enthusiastic about them, especially if the works enabled them to use machinery more effectively. In this way, differences in the scale of operation among farmers in any locality and their differing approaches to rice farming would produce differing stances

Table 11.4 Agricultural income and the cost of land improvement works to farmers, 1965–98 (national averages, 1,000 yen)

	Gross agricultural income			*Cost of works*	*c/a (%)*	*c/b (%)*
	Total	*From rice only*				
		Total (a)	*Cash (b)*	*(c)*		
1965	639	274	188	5.6	2.04	2.98
1966	726	308	217	6.2	2.01	2.86
1967	870	380	283	7.8	2.05	2.76
1968	926	406	302	8.8	2.17	2.91
1969	969	402	306	10.2	2.54	3.33
1970	985	374	280	10.9	2.91	3.89
1971	961	335	245	12.1	3.61	4.94
1972	1128	388	297	13.6	3.51	4.58
1973	1411	463	357	15.2	3.28	4.26
1974	1777	652	511	17.7	2.71	3.46
1975	2081	784	634	21.1	2.69	3.33
1976	2214	772	624	23.9	3.10	3.83
1977	2332	891	737	26.9	3.02	3.65
1978	2399	857	742	28.9	3.37	3.89
1979	2447	820	685	32.7	3.99	4.77
1980	2421	706	576	33.4	4.73	5.80
1981	2552	771	632	37.9	4.92	6.00
1982	2576	788	654	42.0	5.33	6.42
1983	2691	803	669	43.5	5.42	6.50
1984	2857	957	813	47.9	5.01	5.89
1985	2897	942	808	50.5	5.36	6.25
1986	2817	964	832	58.4	6.06	7.02
1987	2658	846	732	58.2	6.88	7.95
1988	2678	791	688	63.0	7.96	9.16
1989	2872	846	739	67.2	7.94	9.09
1990	3002	848	748	67.2	7.92	8.98
1991	3012	798	701	68.4	8.57	9.76
1992	3796	1137	1023	88.2	7.76	8.62
1993	3671	965	868	89.6	9.28	10.32
1994	4025	1355	1234	96.5	7.12	7.82
1995	3791	1136	1029	90.9	8.00	8.83
1996	3801	1113	1014	87.1	7.83	8.59
1997	3642	987	892	84.9	8.60	9.52
1998	3705	986	899	84.8	8.60	9.43

Source: Nōrinshō tōkei jōhōbu, *Nōka keizai chōsa* (relevant years).

Notes

1 'Cost of works' includes cost of land improvement and irrigation maintenance expenses.

2 From 1992 on, the data are for 'commercial farmers' (*hanbai nōka*) only, currently defined as those who farm at least 30 ares of land or sell at least 500,000 yen in farm produce annually.

Table 11.5 Cost of land improvement works and irrigation maintenance expenses to farmers by their scale of cultivation (excluding Hokkaido) (1,000 yen)

		Gross agricultural income		*Cost of works*	*b/a*
		*Total**	*Rice only** *(a)*	*(b)*	*(%)*
All farmers	1965	830	340	7.0	2.06
		676	242	7.0	2.89
	1975	1971	747	19.1	2.56
		1729	595	19.1	3.21
	1985	2694	905	47.6	5.26
		2465	769	47.6	6.19
0.1–0.5ha	1965	643	68	1.1	1.62
		550	24	1.1	4.58
	1975	569	240	5.4	2.25
		419	128	5.4	4.22
	1985	684	267	14.7	5.51
		528	162	14.7	9.07
0.5–1ha	1965	553	207	3.5	1.69
		423	120	3.5	2.92
	1975	1730	564	12.4	2.20
		1503	410	12.4	3.02
	1985	1839	648	34.3	5.29
		1640	516	34.3	6.65
1–1.5ha	1965	893	343	7.4	2.16
		729	241	7.4	3.07
	1975	2922	941	25.0	2.66
		2615	758	25.0	3.30
	1985	3293	1052	56.4	5.36
		3048	900	56.4	6.27
1.5–2ha	1965	1141	510	10.4	2.04
		952	394	10.4	2.64
	1975	3698	1451	42.5	2.93
		3347	1254	42.5	3.39
	1985	4869	1529	76.9	5.03
		4578	1360	76.9	5.65
2ha+	1965	1495	854	20.6	2.41
		1270	716	20.6	2.88
	1975	5414	2491	67.3	2.70
		4955	2273	67.3	2.96
	1985	8138	2709	141.8	5.23
		7697	2525	141.8	5.62

Source: Nōrinshō tōkei jōhōbu, *Nōka keizai chōsa (relevant years).*

Note

* The top figure for each year is total gross income; the bottom figure is cash income only.

toward any agricultural public works proposed. Instead of easily achieved consensus as in the 1960s, there would be conflict.

An example from the village of Shiranegō in Niigata Prefecture illustrates the divisions that did in fact materialize. When a proposal was put forward to 're-improve' local rice paddies by enlarging them from 0.1 hectare to 0.3 hectare each, the responses of farmers were as follows: large-scale farmers enthusiastically supported the proposal, medium-sized farmers agreed with reservations, and small-scale farmers not only expressed opposition but also formed a group to campaign against the proposal. According to the authors of a study of this case:

> Those cultivating small holdings were entirely satisfied with the existing 0.1 hectare plots and as they saw no personal benefit in further enlargement, they saw no point in further investment. Given that they viewed [the proposal] as a waste of their money, it was only natural that they opposed it. Those who agreed with reservations did not like the prospect that their existing machinery would become redundant. This middling group farmed too little land to rely on farming alone, nor could they afford new investment to continue as part-time farmers. So they sought as many concessions as possible from the land improvement district to reduce the financial burden on them that [the proposed] paddy enlargement project would impose.
> (Arita and Kimura 1997: 50)

In another case, farmers with large-scale holdings proposed lining all earthen watercourses in the locality with concrete, but other farmers in the community objected to the plan. At issue here was the fact that the minority of large-scale farmers had to attend to the maintenance of the existing watercourses on their own – weeding the earthen channels, dredging work, and so on – because the majority of farmers had jobs in the non-agricultural sector and could not get time off to help. Concreting the channels would have eliminated what the large-scale farmers saw as unfair burden-sharing, but the small-scale farmers objected to the costs of the work and rejected the proposal.

In order to secure the necessary consent from the many part-time farmers for projects that would promote more efficient large-scale farming, bring about substantial increases in yields on poor-quality land and/or produce substantial labor savings, local authorities and officials of land improvement districts now resorted to one or more of the following strategies.

First, methods were devised which resulted in no financial burden at all being imposed on local farmers. For example, if as a result of land readjustment an additional parcel or two of land could be created for public use, the local authority could purchase that land and the proceeds from the sale could be used to cover all the costs that farmers would otherwise have been expected to pay. In districts close to expanding cities where land prices had escalated, the proceeds from such sales might even be sufficient to provide each local farm household with a share of the proceeds (Okabe 1997).

Second, it was possible to re-zone some of the land within the project area so that subsequent changes in use were possible. This proved a useful means of obtaining the consent of those farmers who saw no economic merit in the proposed project so far as their own farming operations were concerned, but who were interested in the eventual sale of at least part of their holdings for housing or other non-agricultural development.

Third, in cases where some farmers found it difficult to find the time to cultivate all of their holdings and were thinking of leasing or entrusting part of their land to others, the municipality could intervene and withhold the necessary approval for such arrangements until agreement on the consolidation and enlargement of paddies was secured.

Of course, older methods of persuasion would be used as well. Farmers were reminded that they could take out long-term loans to cover their share of the expenses, and so the annual payments due would not be large. Indeed, they would hardly notice the payments if they arranged to make them by means of automatic transfers from their savings accounts with the agricultural cooperative, and before they knew it the loan would be repaid. Another argument was that, if the proposed works were not carried out, it would prove difficult to survive as a rice-producing district, and local land values would decline. Appeals to the traditional spirit of mutual assistance within the community were also made, stressing the duty of other residents to come to the aid of those among them who suffered from poor conditions and were anxious to see improvements carried out.

As for the actual process of securing agreement, it was usual for state and prefectural staff involved in agricultural public works as well as officials of the local land improvement district to participate and for repeated meetings with all the farmers in the community to be held. Once the agreement of the majority of the farmers seemed assured, then efforts were concentrated on persuading any hard-line opponents. Although it was legally possible to carry out works on all fields, including those of opponents, on the basis of a two-thirds majority in favor, and to levy charges on the dissenting farmers, in practice efforts continued to gain well-nigh universal consent so as to avoid permanent damage to social relationships within the community. Opponents would be reminded of the provisions of the law and urged to reconsider on the grounds that 'since the project is going to be carried out anyway, surely it will be better to carry it out amicably.'

Usually, projects were authorized once the agreement of at least 95 percent of local farmers had been secured. That could take considerable time, and as a general rule at least several years would pass from the initial drafting of plans to the start of actual work. Cases requiring up to 20 years or more before work commenced were not that unusual. An example which took well over a decade, and which finally went ahead despite significant local opposition, is described below.

A public works project that had just been agreed in Nangō-chō, located in a major rice-producing area of Miyagi Prefecture, was suspended when the *gentan* policy to reduce rice production went into effect in 1970. At that time, the municipality had distributed the following letter to farmers:

> The market for rice will continue to become ever more competitive, and in order to survive as a rice-producing district, the improvement of our fields is undoubtedly essential. Although there is agreement on the general aim of these works, the burden on farmers will be large and long-lasting, and many farmers have been uneasy about the future direction of national agricultural policy. It was therefore decided that it would be best to reconsider the project once that direction has been determined. . . . It is clear that opinions within the municipality are divided. [Although] we have found many supporters of the project among farmers in younger age groups and among those who farm inferior land, there was [also] a lot of opposition to taking on the considerable costs of the project at a time of uncertainty about Japanese agricultural policy.
>
> (Nangō-chō 1985: 1031)

Some years later the proposed works were again put forward for implementation, in part because of renewed campaigning by those local farmers who had always supported the project and in part because of the desire among local officials to promote Nangō as a leading center of rice production. Despite the determined lobbying of farmers who objected to the project, some of whom organized an 'Alliance to Prevent the Proposed Field Improvements,' the project was finally approved as a prefectural undertaking in 1982 and work commenced in 1983. Objecting to the high costs involved, as had opponents of the project since 1970, some 46 out of 379 local farmers (12 percent of the total) resisted all attempts at persuasion and remained in opposition even as work began.

The 1990s: agricultural public works at a time of crisis in Japanese agriculture

Under the agreements reached late in 1993 during the Uruguay Round of GATT negotiations, the Japanese government was to end price supports for domestically produced rice and enforce a 'minimum access' system for rice imports as of 1995. Rice prices fell dramatically, threatening the viability of Japanese rice farming. Among those hardest hit were the very farmers whom the Ministry of Agriculture had been trying for years to promote: those with large holdings, who could make the best use of machinery to produce rice more cheaply. Still relatively few in number, those farmers had been gradually expanding their scale of operations, primarily by taking on the cultivation of paddy fields owned by their elderly neighbors. The steady aging of the many small-scale farmers in Japan, most of whom lacked children willing or able to continue farming the family's land, was contributing to the achievement of efficient agriculture. With the collapse of rice prices, however, the potential profitability even of large-scale farming operations was thrown into doubt.

Not surprisingly, the deterioration in agricultural profits made small-scale farmers even less interested in agricultural public works than previously. Large-scale farmers, who were far more likely than the majority to be full-time farmers without additional sources of income, now faced a severe dilemma. Not a few abandoned their expanded operations at this time, and lost interest in agricultural public works as a result. Some others sought to weather the storm by expanding their operations even further. In particular, those who had borrowed heavily to finance expansion by means of land purchases, or perhaps more commonly, by purchases of machinery to farm leased land, found it necessary to continue expanding, if for no other reason than to generate the revenue from increased crop sales at lower prices that would enable them to service their loans. But with rice prices down and prohibitions on growing rice under the set-aside program now extending to 30–40 percent of all paddy fields, not even they could see any point in land improvements.

Spending on public works of all sorts was expanded in Japan during the 1990s as a means of counteracting the ongoing recession and, as a result of competition among ministries for budgetary allocations, the share of public works spending carried out by the Ministry of Agriculture increased significantly. As shown in Table 11.6, that ministry had received an annual allocation of about 0.9 trillion yen between 1980 and 1991, but its allocation rose to 1.76 trillion yen in 1994 and remained at the level of about 1.5 trillion yen thereafter. Given that farmers both small and large were now considerably less interested in agricultural public

Table 11.6 State spending on agricultural public works, 1967–98 (billion yen)

	Total	*Land improvements*	*Farmland development*	*Land reclamation*
1967	121	86	21	13
1968	139	99	25	15
1969	162	116	29	13
1970	190	140	36	11
				Development projects in designated regions
1971	247	192	41	8
1972	316	251	50	8
1973	326	258	52	7
1974	356	281	52	11
1975	426	339	58	16
1976	468	371	64	20
1977	637	513	83	27
1978	775	625	105	31
1979	856	692	115	36
1980	913	746	116	34
1981	916	749	114	36
1982	904	739	111	37
1983	899	734	112	35
1984	893	729	111	34
1985	879	718	110	31
1986	889	738	112	31
1987	958	802	119	28
1988	854	703	116	31
1989	867	717	110	30
1990	867	720	108	30
		Farmland improvements	Village improvements	Farmland conservation
1991	909	611	197	90
1992	1239	705	410	112
1993	1657	839	673	146
1994	1760	821	769	158
1995	1618	853	570	173
1996	1597	817	606	162
1997	1533	774	585	161
1998	1459	738	545	163

Source: Ōkurashō shukei kyoku, *Kessan setsumei*, annual editions.

Note

Figures for total spending include administrative costs.

works, much less in assuming any financial burden for their cost, new means had to be devised to secure the consent of local farmers to projects so that spending to the level of appropriation could be achieved.

One such means was further reduction in the financial burden farmers would be expected to assume. This was achieved in some cases by extending the period of the loans farmers took out to cover their share of the costs so that their annual payments (although not their total indebtedness) would be less. In other cases, the charges would be halved from 20 to 10 percent if certain officially approved targets for the creation of larger fields and the expansion of large-scale farming in the area were met.

Another means was to increase the number of projects that aimed at improving the daily life of rural residents. As is also shown in Table 11.6, Ministry of Agriculture spending on the now separately listed category of 'village improvements' (*nōson seibi*) increased rapidly from 1991, and in 1994 it constituted over 43 percent of the total spent on public works in the agricultural sphere. Because it was difficult to get farmers to agree to purely agricultural public works quickly enough, the Ministry applied more of its funding to laying sewers and constructing roads in the countryside.

Conclusion

Hardly any raw data related to agricultural public works have been made public, and most of the statistics that have appeared have been organized in a manner that prevents analysis of the precise nature and scale of projects in any given region at any given time. As a result, no comprehensive assessment of the changes that have taken place in agricultural public works during the postwar era is yet possible. However, by returning to Table 11.3, which compares 'completed improvements' to paddy fields in 1963 and 1993, it is possible to grasp some of the most significant changes that have occurred.

The first point to note is that there was a 19 percent decrease in the total area of paddy fields, from 3.43 million hectares in 1963 to 2.78 million hectares 30 years later. Only in Hokkaido and Tohoku did the area of paddy fields increase somewhat. In all other regions there were marked decreases, as paddy fields were converted to such other uses as housing sites. Second, we can see that considerable progress was made during this 30-year period in improvements to paddy fields. As of 1963, only 27 percent of fields had been improved in any way, and only 2 percent had been enlarged to the then standard 0.2 hectare size. By 1993, fully 51 percent of all fields had been enlarged to at least 0.3 hectare. The increase in

Hokkaido, to 89 percent, was truly spectacular, especially as Hokkaido had ranked lowest in the nation in improved land of any sort in 1963. Clearly, efforts to promote paddy field improvements there had been vigorously pursued, and considerable increases in labor productivity had been achieved. At the same time, however, the burden of loans that Hokkaido rice farmers had taken out to finance their share of improvement works had increased proportionately, and when rice prices plummeted in the early 1990s, those among them who farmed the largest and most efficient holdings in the region found themselves the most vulnerable to globalization. Burdened by debt and almost totally dependent on agricultural income for their livelihoods, many of them were forced into bankruptcy or into abandoning farming.

The fate of the supposedly fittest and most modern of Hokkaido farmers set off alarm bells in rural communities throughout Japan, further intensifying the uneasiness that had been brewing among farmers for years. For the past half century or so, agricultural public works had effected sweeping changes in the countryside, providing the infrastructure and other improvements for rice cultivation that no individual farmer could carry out to any meaningful degree entirely on his own. No doubt additional public works projects would be necessary in the future, especially in creating even larger fields, and as in the past the costs would be substantial. But the era in which farmers would happily bear the financial burden which those projects imposed on them was now very definitely over.

References

Arita Hiroyuki and Kimura Kazuhiro. 1997. *Jizokuteki nōgyō no tame no suiden kukaku seiri*. Tokyo: Nōrin tōkei kyōkai.

Baba Akira. 1975. 'Sengo tochi kairyō jigyō no tenkai.' In *Sangyō kōzō henkakuka ni okeru inasaku no kōzō*, vol. 1, ed. Furushima Toshio. Tokyo: Tōkyō daigaku shuppankai.

Nangō-chō. 1985. *Nangō-chō shi*, vol 2. Miyagi ken, Nangō-chō.

Okabe Mamoru. 1997. 'Tochi kairyō jigyō to gōi keisei.' *Nōson kenkyū*, No. 85.

12 Organic farming settlers in Kumano

*John Knight**

Introduction

Since the 1970s a new migration trend has emerged in industrial societies. It is rural resettlement: the migration to the countryside of idealistic urbanites to enact a new way of life, usually centered on farming. With its emphasis on recovering a connection to land and nature, this migration expresses opposition to the dominant values of the larger urban-industrial society (for Britain, see Pepper 1991; for France, see McDonald 1989; for the United States, see Berry 1992).

In Japan, too, small numbers of urbanites have been migrating to the countryside to take up farming. In this chapter I describe an example of such rural resettlement in the municipality of Hongū in the mountainous Kumano district of the Kii Peninsula, Wakayama Prefecture, where I carried out ethnographic research in the 1980s and 1990s. I show how the newcomers, dedicated to organic farming, pursue an alternative lifestyle amid local neighbors. Their lifestyle is often a source of friction with those neighbors, but it also holds out the prospect of contributing to rural revitalization.

Depopulation

In postwar Japan there has been a large-scale redistribution of the population from the countryside to the cities. The effect of this outmigration has been to depopulate rural Japan, especially the remoter upland areas, resulting in demographically skewed rural populations consisting of a

* Portions of this chapter first appeared in 'The Soil as Teacher: Natural Farming in a Mountain Village,' in *Japanese Views of Nature: Cultural Perspectives*, ed. Pamela J. Asquith and Arne Kalland (London: Curzon Press, 1997), pp. 236–56.

high proportion of elderly people and very few young people. This trend is clear among the inland municipalities of the Kii Peninsula. Most local youths have left for the larger cities of the Kansai region and beyond. Between 1955 and 1995, these areas lost over half of their population.

In the postwar period, Hongū has been afflicted by large-scale outmigratory depopulation. In 1955 the population of Hongū-chō stood at 10,276 people, but by 1995 it had fallen to 4,310. Postwar depopulation in Japan can be broken down into a number of phases characterized by markedly different rates of decline. In the period 1965–70 alone, Hongū lost no less than one-fifth of its total population! Since this time the local population has continued to decline in number, but at much slower rates. Another feature of postwar depopulation is the discrepancy between the figures for individuals and for households. While the individual population of Hongū fell by over half, the number of households declined by around 20 percent, from 2,263 households in 1956 to 1,754 by 1995. This indicates that depopulation has been due, in general, to the outmigration of younger family members rather than of whole families. Consequently, there remains a large number of households, but they consist mostly of older people.

Depopulation is caused, in the first instance, by large-scale outmigration. Official records show that in the period 1965–95, 12,356 people outmigrated from Hongū. While this averages out at just over 400 outmigrants each year, the figure conceals enormous variations within the period. The peak of outmigration was reached in 1967 when more than one thousand people left, and the trough in 1991 when 177 people left. However, there is a second phase of rural depopulation in which population decline is principally accounted for by the low fertility rates arising from the removal of the reproductive age bands from the local population by outmigration. The birth rate in Hongū declined from 210 births in 1956 to 27 births in 1995. The mortality figure, by contrast, has remained relatively stable: 88 deaths in 1956, 61 deaths in 1995. Eventually, a threshold is passed whereby fertility rates fall below mortality rates; in Hongū this point came in 1970, the first year when local deaths exceeded local births: 69 to 65. This natural reduction of population is one of the features of rural areas in advanced states of depopulation (Mitsuhashi 1989: 23). Upland municipalities are faced with a crisis of social reproduction.

Another feature of depopulated Japan is that, in addition to its (diminished) residential population, it has attached to it a secondary population of migrant sons and daughters. Although Hongū has lost most of its natal population through outmigration, many of these migrants remain connected to their home town economically, ritually, communicatively, and through return visits. The main occasion for return-visiting is Bon, the great midsummer festival, during the three days of which the village populations swell to three times their normal size. Such migrant ties can make an important contribution to mountain village life – by helping local families to continue farming where otherwise they might abandon it; by reinforcing, through ritual, the sense of family unity, despite the reality of dispersion; and, insofar as they bind migrants to their natal localities, by expediting future return-migrations. However, the migrant connection can also contribute to the demoralization of the village. At the end of Bon the village returns to its earlier state of depopulated normality. Within a few short days, the excitement of the crowded village gives way to silence and stillness, a change which can produce a palpable sense of sadness and loneliness among villagers.

Another source of demoralization in depopulated areas is the environment. There is a proliferation of *akiya* or empty houses: my own survey (of four Hongū villages) showed that 31 of the 148 houses, or 21 percent, were unoccupied. There is also much abandoned farmland. In recent decades the area of farmland in Hongū has diminished by two-thirds, from 508 hectares in 1960 to 179 hectares in 1995. One consequence of this trend (accelerated by the government policy of rice field acreage reduction, known as *gentan*) has been a large reduction in the area of rice fields, many of which have been transformed into dry fields for the cultivation of vegetables and other crops, while the old dry fields at the forest edge have become scrubland or planted with conifer saplings to become, in effect, an extension of the forest. Consequently, throughout upland Japan the forest has expanded areally. In Hongū, forest has increased from 90.7 percent of the municipal area in 1970 to 92.7 percent in 1995. Although the increase in the forest area is proportionately small (in the case of Hongū only 2 percent), this extra forest has a considerable visual impact, making the village feel a dark, 'lonely' (*sabishii*) place.

Depopulated villages, with their proliferation of empty, run-down houses, closed-down schools, abandoned farmland, encroaching forest, grown-over footpaths, and unkempt graveyards, are typically viewed as depressing, 'spooky' (*bukimi*) places, places with no future, places forgotten by the rest of the nation – 'villages of death' (*shi no shūraku*), in the words of one observer (Aoyama 1994: 19–20). The decline of the timber forests, many of which were in effect commissioned by the nation in the aftermath of the war to regenerate the national timber resource, are a striking visual testament to the present-day national indifference to the domestic forestry industry and the forestry villages dependent on it in places like Hongū.

Rural resettlement in Japan

There have been a variety of governmental responses to depopulation, including infrastructural development, the attraction of industries from outside, the development of new industries and new products, and the promotion of tourism. But there has also been attention to population management. Since the 1970s, municipal and prefectural governments in Japan have actively encouraged return-migration. Prefectures have opened offices in Tokyo to publicize what is termed the U-turn option and to handle inquiries. Advertising campaigns have been carried out – through posters in the Tokyo subway, print advertisements, television commercials etc. – exhorting migrants from the regions to return to their *furusato*, or natal place. Rural municipalities have even offered monetary incentives to encourage return-migration.

Another response is to encourage direct migration to the village from the cities. Prefectures have established offices in metropolitan areas to field inquiries from would-be rural settlers of urban origin, especially those willing to take up farming. These settlers are referred to as 'I-turners' (migrating directly from cities to villages), as opposed to 'U-turners' and 'J-turners' (migrating from small towns to villages). The appeal to would-be new farmers is made through slogans such as 'With Your Hands, a New Agriculture' (*Anata no te de atarashii nōgyō o*) or 'Gather! For a Farming Adventure' (*Atsumare! Aguri adobencha e*) (Adachi 1994: 217–25). In particular terms, municipalities encourage incomers to take up farming by offering low rent or rent-free land, interest-free loans or subsidies for repair and maintenance work or for house construction, and other forms of back-up, support and assistance. For example, under the catchphrase 'We give land away' (*tochi o agemasu*), Honkyō-mura in Yamaguchi Prefecture offers land to those prepared to come and settle. Similarly, Tadami-chō in Fukushima Prefecture offers 'to give one *tsubo* [3.31 sq.m.] of land to you for free' (*tochi o hito tsubo tada de sashiagemasu*) (Kitsu 1994: 170). Usually, the land is not formally transferred immediately, but after a period of 10 or 20 years, but in the meantime only a nominal rent is charged. Aya-machi in Miyazaki Prefecture lends municipally owned farmland to new farmers until they are able to buy farmland of their own (Takeuchi 1993: 118).

Some prefectures have established offices in the major cities to field inquires on rural settlement. The Ministry of Agriculture has launched a scheme aimed at promoting farming-related rural settlement in remote areas – the 'I- and J-turn Farming Occupation Promotion Scheme' (Hidaka 1996: 2). Many prefectures have established assistance and training programs to attract 'new farmers' to their rural areas (see *Asahi Shinbun* 1993; Hidaka 1996: 188–97).

According to the figures published in the *Farming White Paper* (*Nōgyō hakusho*), in 1996 some 3,570 people made inquiries about rural resettlement (to the National New Farmers' Guide Center and Prefectural Advice Centers), and 384 people actually took up farming (NTK 1998: 174). In the period 1988–96, the same source records that 1,556 people took up farming (ibid.). However, much back-to-the-land rural settlement bypasses these channels, and the actual scale of rural resettlement would appear to be much higher. Thus since 1989 Nagano Prefecture alone has attracted 2,000 settlers from the large cities (Hidaka 1996: 173). Furthermore, the increasing trend is indicated by the fact that there were only 32 new farmers in 1988; 92 new farmers in 1990; 141 in 1992; 236 in 1994; and 384 in 1996 (NTK 1998: 174). In other words, twelve times more people took up back-to-the-land farming in 1996 than was the case in 1988 (ibid.).

Well-known examples of new rural settlements include Oak Village in Nagano Prefecture, which was established in 1974 by a group of idealistic university graduates (Iwamizu 1989: 19–64) and in the north of Wakayama Prefecture a new village was founded in the mid-1980s called Banjiro Mura ('Guava Village').

Often there is a clustering of new settlers in the same area, forming in effect a network or group. But there are also many examples of lone settlers – individual families which take up residence in a village amid local neighbors. Many of the settlers are young, unmarried or married and starting up a family, but there are also older people who have retired from their city jobs. One common characterization of new rural settlers is that they are 'double-cropping' (*nimōsaku*): in addition to the 'summer crop' that was their youth, they are undertaking a 'winter crop' for the second half of their lives.

The Kumano example

Since 1980 around 50 new families have come to settle in the Kumano area, where they rent empty houses and unused farmland in remote village settlements. Around 20 of these new families have settled in the upland municipality of Hongū-chō.

Hongū has undergone severe agricultural decline. As noted previously, the area of its farmland has diminished by two-thirds. Some of the former farmland has become housing land, but most of it has been planted over with conifer saplings to become timber forest. Despite the fact that more than half the 1960 ricefield acreage has been lost through conversion to other use, in 1995 over a quarter of the remaining Hongū riceland was unused. One of the causes of agricultural contraction in Hongū is outmigratory depopulation. The municipality has lost over half its population in the postwar decades. But there has also been a repudiation of farming among the remaining residential population. In 1955 two-thirds of the working population of Hongū worked in the primary sector (farming and forestry), but by 1990 this had fallen to 13 percent. In 1990 it was the tertiary sector (including tourism) which accounted for nearly two-thirds of the Hongū workforce. The combined trends of outmigration and deagrarianization create villages of empty houses and overgrown ricefields. It is in these vacated rural spaces that the newcomers have come to settle.

The Hongū newcomers originate, for the most part, from the major cities of Tokyo, Osaka and Kyoto, but some are of regional origin (e.g. Hiroshima, Shikoku and Aomori). They are typically young (in their twenties and thirties), university-educated, and their past occupations include company employee, designer, computer programer, gardener, livestock farmer, baker, Buddhist priest and artist. Most practice organic farming, and rent farmland on which they grow rice and a variety of vegetables and fruits, and keep farm animals. Many grow and eat 'natural food' (*shizenshoku*) – and are referred to by locals as 'the natural food people' (*shizenshoku no hito*) – and generally eat brown rice, in contrast to local people who share the usual Japanese preference of white rice. One or two new families follow a macrobiotic diet.

The settlers tend to be critical of modern urban life more generally. They have migrated to the Kumano region because it is different from Tokyo and Osaka. Many explicitly state that it is 'great nature' (*daishizen*) which has drawn them to Kumano. Some approach nature as an object of worship, and make the notion of 'gratitude' (*kansha*) central to their lives, particularly in relation to the food they grow and eat, and even characterize their new way of life as a religious austerity or *shugyō* (see Hidaka 1996: 157). A number of the Hongū settlers have visited India, and have been influenced by Indian mystical and religious traditions (including Bhagwanism).

The settlers are widely read in the area of alternative and ecological literature, and are familiar with the ideas of thinkers such as Steiner, Schumacher and Capra. Kumano is a mountainous region well-known in Japan for its shrines and as a site of medieval pilgrimage, but some of the newcomers represent the sacred character of Kumano in a global New Age idiom of energy lines, vibrations and meridians. Like Stonehenge and Mecca, Kumano is held to be one of the primary points in the earth's energy system. There is also a keen interest in indigenous cultures such as the Ainu, ancient Celts and North American Indians who stand as exemplars of a simple, natural lifestyle in stark contrast to modern materialism.

For many of the newcomers, the 'peasant,' like the indigenous hunter-gatherer, stands as a symbol of anti-materialism. The newcomers tend to refer to themselves as 'peasants' or *hyakushō*. In Japanese, the term *hyakushō* has certain negative connotations; as a noun it is readily paired with negative adjectives, such as *mugaku na hyakushō* or 'ignorant peasant'. Among Hongū people, the term *hyakushō* is sometimes invoked as a form of self-deprecation – for example, in explaining why young people leave the village (to escape 'peasant' life) or why farming sons cannot find brides (because young women refuse to marry into a 'peasant' family). Indeed, among larger farmers there is an effort to escape this 'peasant' imagery and to define farming as a modern occupation. Kelly describes how a particular part-time farmer 'styles his work identity and routine as a "scientific and rational occupation"' (Kelly 1986: 609), and goes on to stress the importance of new machines in creating a new, modern image of farm work in order to persuade younger farmers to stay on the farm.

But among the Kumano settlers, the term *hyakushō*, with its associations of a simple life of honest toil on the land, is invoked with a certain ironic pride. The 'peasant' lifestyle represents a kind of polar contrast to that of the salaried worker which many of them followed. In fact, a common media term applied to rural settlers is *datsusara* or 'salary-shedders,' a term encapsulating the point that the new settlers reject the very status and lifestyle – of the urban middle-class salaried worker – to which most young Japanese (including rural youth) aspire.

For some of the newcomers, the 'peasant' lifestyle is synonymous with autarky. They pursue a lifestyle of near 'self-sufficiency' (*jikyū jisoku*) in which household food is largely self-produced and participation in the money economy minimized. Some explicitly eschew the 'money economy' (*kahei keizai*), viewing money as the central symbol of the materialistic society they reject. They occasionally sell their produce for much-needed cash, but do so reluctantly. By contrast, their village neighbors have become absorbed by the cash economy through waged employment. Factory-employed farmers' wives are no longer able to contribute so much labor to growing vegetables and to making home-made foods such as *miso* (bean-paste), *tsukemono* (pickled vegetables), and *umeboshi* (pickled plums). As the newcomers were moving into the countryside to pursue the goal of autarky, rural families were increasingly 'buying their vegetables in stores instead of growing them and using processed foods instead of preparing them at home' (Nozoe 1981: 224).

In addition to this rejection of money, some new families have even refused to send their children to local schools. One Hongū family opposed school attendance because they believed that the schools simply served to regiment the children and to inculcate into them the materialistic values of the wider industrial capitalist society.

The settlers' farming differs from mainstream Japanese farming in a number of respects. There is a rejection of synthetic fertilizer – both because it is believed to be harmful to the human body, and because fertility is held to be something which should come from the soil itself. Pesticides are similarly rejected on safety grounds. The newcomers are therefore obliged to undertake the demanding task of weeding by hand. The newcomers' farming is largely unmechanized, in contrast to the mechanized farming of villagers. In some areas, there are even examples of rural settlers who have revived the old practice of plowing their fields with oxen (Saitō 1985: 38).

Some of the newcomers practice a more radical form of alternative farming, informed by the ideas of Fukuoka Masanobu. Fukuoka's 'natural farming' method involves the rejection of tillage and weeding. Tillage is eschewed in order to restore the integrity and fertility of the soil by increasing organic matter, and there is no weeding because weeds are seen as beneficial – naturally 'tilling' the soil through their roots and, on dying, providing nutrients to micro-organisms in the soil (Fukuoka 1983: 48–53). According to this method, the farmer does not really 'cultivate' (*tsukuru*) at all, but assists with the crop-growth which is generated from the powers of fertility intrinsic to the soil.

Some of the newcomers fertilize the soil with family waste. At a time when villagers increasingly opt for flush toilets instead of non-flush latrines (a symbol of the 'smelly' and 'dirty' character of the Japanese countryside), the newcomers positively opt for the latrine because it allows them to recycle night-soil as farm fertilizer in the traditional way. Another source of organic fertilizer for their fields comes from the domestic animals which many of the newcomers keep. Until the 1950s it was common for most farming households to have one or two cows and some chickens, but in the last few decades farm animals have largely disappeared from Japanese villages as machines replaced cows in farmwork and synthetic chemical fertilizers were used in place of animal wastes. But among the new farmers, animal droppings from chickens, cows and goats are used as farmland manure.

Another feature of 'natural farming' is the linkage of forest and farm. The use of the forest is seen as integral to earlier peasant farming. Mountain forests provided green fertilizer for fields, fodder for animals, as well as food, fuel and building wood. Fukuoka suggests that every new farmer should be able to draw on some nearby forest for organic fertilizer (1985: 137). Some of the new families in Hongū reject the use of modern forms of energy such as electricity and gas, preferring to use candles, oil lamps, and forest fuels such as firewood and charcoal. In this, they imitate the prewar pattern of energy usage in rural areas.

Many of the Kumano settlers opt to grow different rice varieties (such as *kogane masari*), which grow better under chemical-free conditions, and circulate seeds among each other. Earlier generations of Japanese farmers developed their own family or village rice seed, which was better suited to local conditions, but this has since been replaced by uniform, high-yielding rice varieties scientifically produced by government laboratories and distributed by the Agricultural Cooperative. The newcomers lament this loss of seed variety in rice farming.

In general, the newcomers grow the same range of crops as local families. But they also grow some crops which have been discontinued by villagers. The prime example is the newcomers' cultivation of a winter crop of wheat on their ricefields. Again, this 'double-cropping' practice, facilitated by the mild winters of western Japan, is associated with the peasant farming of the past.

Impact of settlers I: Frictions

Farming

Although the newcomers consider their farming to accord with the 'peasant' tradition of the Hongū area, in fact this form of farming is a source of friction with villagers.

The newcomers' farming can appear anti-social. Some of the new families use animal waste and/or human waste as fertilizer on their fields, but this can lead to local objections about the smell. Natural rice fields provide a sanctuary for insects, but these insects do not necessarily respect the boundaries with other ricefields. Adjacent farmers sometimes find their own fields adversely affected and their harvests reduced by the insects and other pests in the newcomers' pesticide-free rice fields. Some farmers have found themselves under pressure not to rent to such settlers in the future.

The newcomers' farming methods are viewed as inferior. One basis for this perception is the poor harvests of the newcomers – as much as 30 percent less than other farmers. But there are also doubts about the quality of the rice produced. These are expressed in stories circulating among villagers that, while wild animals such as wild boar damage the farms of villagers through crop-raiding, they tend to shun the farms of the newcomers!

Newcomers find that they have restricted access to certain basic farming inputs. Irrigation is one problem. The direct seeding methods employed by some of the newcomers entail a particular timetable for cultivation and specific irrigation requirements. Usually, village farmers coordinate seedling transplanting and collectively irrigate their fields. But this customary communal control of irrigation channels can lead to disputes with the newcomers whose own farming is hindered by a lack of control over irrigation (Fukuoka 1985: 179). Another problem arises with green fertilizer from the forest. In some cases, newcomers find that the forest is effectively out of bounds to them because of village requirements to join the local forest association (*kurinkai*) as a condition of forest access. For many of the cash-strapped newcomers the cost of doing so is prohibitive.

There is a local perception of the settlers as 'idlers' (*namakemono*). While some perform the demanding work of weeding the rice fields by hand, others eschew weeding altogether, which, as they do not use weed-killers, means that their fields become thick with weeds. This is something which offends the villagers' sense of what a field should look like and reinforces the local impression of the settlers' fecklessness and incompetence. Such misgivings are further fueled by tales of settlers who, rather than actually bend down to transplant seedlings in the traditional back-breaking way, opt to scatter the seeds (encased in small clay balls) by hand (see Nakamura 1991: 14).

Self-sufficiency

The settlers' pursuit of self-sufficiency, the reversion to a 'lamp life' (*ranpu no seikatsu*), recalls an earlier rural age, before the energy revolution of the 1950s. The newcomers are seen to embrace a lifestyle of virtual poverty that local people left behind decades ago. But this 'peasant' lifestyle is not one which evokes pride but is rather a source of embarrassment among locals. Pride attaches to the transcendence of that sort of situation. In particular, this leads to concern about the children of such families. One new family which became the object of gossip and criticism apparently sent its children to school with a *hinomaru bentō* (a simple rice meal with a single pickled plum), recalling the poverty of an earlier age.

The newcomers' pursuit of self-sufficiency, and rejection of waged work, can also arouse suspicion among local people. The settlers may aim for farming self-sufficiency, but everybody knows that, given the quantity and quality of the land they farm, they cannot do so completely.

Money is needed to pay their taxes and other local charges, to run their cars, to pay their telephone bills, to buy schoolbooks and uniforms for their children and to purchase goods from the mobile shop. There was speculation that one new family (which had satellite television) supported itself from the redundancy money of the husband's father in the city. Another rumor about this family was that the husband, who painted watercolors, was selling his paintings for enormous prices during his occasional visits to Tokyo, and that this explained how the family supported itself in the absence of any obvious source of income. There are also rumors that this or that new family, despite their apparent poverty, have extensive savings that they can draw on in times of need. Rural settlers in other areas have been the object of similar rumors among their neighbours (e.g. Nakamura 1991: 244).

Impermanence

The new farmers tend to be perceived as impermanent by their village neighbors. Typically, they rent rather than own the land they live and farm on. One reason for renting is the reluctance of rural families to sell off land. As Iwamoto makes clear in chapter 10, land inherited from earlier generations ('made with the tears and sweat of ancestors') is something that a family should endeavor to pass on to the next generation and never sell. But even when a villager does sell land, other villagers are customarily given first option to buy it. (In fact, in the 1980s and 1990s there has occurred a proliferation of rural land sales to outside buyers, but this has been in the context of large-scale tourist development and inflated land prices.)

A further reason for renting has to do with the settlers' rejection of land ownership and the restrictions on mobility and freedom that it entails. There has been a high turnover of newcomers on the Kii Peninsula and elsewhere in Japan. Some find their new way of life harder than anticipated, and give up after a few weeks or months. Others positively opt for successive migrations, moving on after a number of years to lead the same kind of farming lifestyle in other regions. One new family in Fukui Prefecture, for example, referred to themselves as 'guerrilla peasants' (*gerira nōmin*) who must move on in due course rather than stay in one place (Yamashita 1993: 113), while others refer to themselves as 'travelers' (*tabi no hito*) or 'ramblers' (*yūhojin*) (Takahashi 1984: 34). The same spirit of adventure that brought them in may well take them out again.

Impact of settlers II: Contributions

Repopulation

Despite these problems, the new settlers have usually been positively received by the depopulated villages they enter. They are viewed as beneficial in a number of ways. First of all, even though their numbers are small, they constitute an important demographic contribution to the depopulated villages of Hongū. They join in collective work tasks and duties of the village (such as path-clearing, fire-fighting drills, and funeral preparations). They contribute to collective farming tasks such as the maintenance of irrigation channels, the repair of protective fences (against forest wildlife), and cooperative rice transplanting and harvesting. As youthful newcomers to elderly villages, this physical contribution is often of inordinate importance and highly valued. Their children boost the numbers enrolled in the small village schools, and thereby help the locality to resist the pressure for school closure.

Morale

One of the effects of rural depopulation is the demoralization of the remaining population, as manifested most starkly in the high rates of suicide reported among the rural elderly. In addition to the increase in empty village houses, the abandonment and loss of farmland is a source of particular dismay and distress. The original reclamation of arable land is viewed in rural areas as a great ancestral achievement which is the object of gratitude and a source of pride among village descendents. 'For generations, farmers had considered it a virtue to reclaim land for paddies, a practice their forebears had begun centuries ago' (Ni'ide 1994: 18). Conversely, farmland that is overgrown or that has reverted to forest is one of the saddest of sights for elderly villagers, and arguably a contributory factor in rural demoralization.

But the new occupancy of long-vacated houses and the renewed cultivation of fallow rice fields help to offset this despair by suggesting that village decline may not, after all, be inexorable. The arrival of a new family in a dilapidated old village often generates great excitement among remaining inhabitants. For remote villages which had seemed destined to abandonment, the appearance of new settlers offers much-needed hope for the future.

The newcomers can also restore confidence in upland farming, something which has been seriously dented in recent decades. One major problem for Kumano farmers is wildlife crop-raiding which, while a perennial threat to farmland, has greatly worsened with depopulation. In some cases, elderly cultivators are forced to abandon outlying fields in the face of repeated depredations. New settlers too suffer such farm damage (despite the comments to the contrary of some of their neighbors), and this is one of the reasons why they too may give up farming and leave. But, in general, the presence of the newcomers, farming what is often the most vulnerable farmland located at the forest-edge, can also give the village new resolve to resist wildlife pests by erecting or repairing fences and investing in wildlife repellents and scare devices.

Public debate

The settlers can also radicalize the villages they enter. The Kumano settlers are often outspoken in their criticism of local industries such as forestry, construction and tourism, and have even become involved in protests against development initiatives such as road construction, dam construction or the establishment of nuclear power stations. This activism can lead to frictions with other villagers, especially where the perception is created that the newcomers are not committed to the cause of rural development. But there are clear examples where newcomers, by alerting the wider local population to the adverse environmental consequences of certain exogenous development plans such as golf course construction, have been the catalysts for a wider local protest (e.g. Moen 1997: 21–2). At a time when 'resort' development is transforming land use in rural Japan on an enormous scale, with metropolitan capital buying up large swathes of the Japanese countryside to build ski-grounds, golf courses and condominiums, and encountering little resistance from the dwindling numbers of rural dwellers, the new settlers constitute an important source of resistance.

The new settlers also oppose cultural standardization. They often bring with them a great enthusiasm for local customs and traditions and other aspects of village life and culture that are otherwise being discontinued and forgotten. They are keen attenders of village festivals, and some even undertake the documentation of village folklore. Settlers have played an important role in perpetuating or reviving such traditions, and in stimulating renewed local interest in them.

New ideas

Settlers are often champions of the 'natural' farming lifestyle. There is a certain amount of evangelizing among village neighbors. In Hongū a few local families have emulated their new neighbors and farm without chemicals, and many more have reduced their use of chemicals. Some of the Kumano settlers, in an effort to diffuse their ideas more widely, have established an induction course – nationally advertised in certain alternative magazines – for other would-be rural resettlers to come and learn how to lead a self-sufficient organic farming lifestyle. Settlers have also become involved in debates on local development, in some cases forcefully arguing that agrarian revival based on organic farming methods is the only solution to the widespread problem of rural depopulation (Yamashita 1993: 206–8).

Recent trends in the Japanese food sector have tended to facilitate a more positive local reception for the settlers' ideas about farming and food. Organic farming is of increasing commercial importance in Japan. There are widespread consumer concerns about the quality of purchased farm products and the perceived overuse of chemicals by output-maximizing Japanese farmers. One striking expression of such concerns is the rise in membership of consumer cooperatives in Japan. In 1996, the 688 primary Seikyō food cooperatives alone had a national household membership of 14 million (Moen 1997: 14). Many consumer cooperatives sub-contract rural producers to cultivate organic food for their largely urban membership (e.g. Inoue 1996: 62–8). Some rural municipalities offset the decline in mainstream farming by converting to market-directed organic farming (Takeuchi 1993: 117). The appearance of the new 'peasants' in rural Japan coincides with this new consumer trend.

Even though the Kumano newcomers are generally not involved in new rural enterprises, their organic farming ideas have had an impact on the development of local commercial products, some of which are marketed nationally as 'chemical-free' (*munōyaku*), 'additive-free' (*mutenka*) 'health foods' (*kenkō shokuhin*).

Publicity

Finally, the newcomers have attracted enormous mass media interest. The Hongū settlers were regularly visited by journalists and filmed by television camera crews. Rural resettlement is a phenomenon which captures the imagination of the wider Japanese society, especially where it involves young middle-class families willingly embracing the everyday hardships of the peasant past such as woodstove cooking and machineless farming. Some of the Kumano settlers have become minor media celebrities in their own right. This media attention is often encouraged by municipal authorities keen to maximize national publicity for the locality with an eye to tourist promotion and to the prospect of further insettlement.

Conclusion

Japanese farming in the modern era has undergone a number of transitions. One major transition was that from the prewar era of surplus extraction from farming to the postwar era of subsidization of farming. But at the end of the twentieth century another transition was evident: from the postwar 'rural bias' to the new phase of withdrawal of state commitment to farming as manifested in their trends of agricultural liberalization, deregulation and even prospective de-subsidization. The most emphatic demonstration of this shift – and of the prioritization of Japanese industry over agriculture – was in 1993 when the Japanese government agreed to a timetable for rice imports at the conclusion of the GATT talks. Although state support for the regions continues in Japan, support for farming lifestyles is effectively being withdrawn.

In the early 2000s the future of Japanese farming appears in great doubt. There is a dire shortage of younger farmers, and a shortage of brides for farmers. In recent times, the protesting farmer, descending on Tokyo to protest against farm imports or about the bride shortage, has become a familiar figure in the Japanese mass media. The Japanese farming sector appears incapable of reproducing itself into the twenty-first century. Some media commentary suggests that agriculture is set to succeed electrical appliances, industrial machinery, semi-conductors and automobiles, to become the latest Japanese industry to be translocated to other parts of Asia, with farmers in Thailand, Vietnam and China becoming the producers of the Japanese food supply, and even the growers of Japanese rice (by growing Japanese rice varieties [*japonica*]), in future (Kubō 1994: 8).

The plight of Japanese farming readily accords with modernist expectations of agrarian decline in advanced industrial society, whereby the peasant appears a doomed figure, unable to really exist in the present, much less the future, and therefore condemned to a fate of historical disappearance (Kearney 1996: chapter 3). This tendency has become pronounced in postwar Japan, with its much-vaunted 'economic miracle' and its assumption of 'economic superpower' status, where the peasant increasingly comes to occupy the past tense.

Yet twentieth-century Japan also provided a clear example of the way in which the disappearance of agrarian lifestyles may co-exist with the persistence of agrarianist motifs. One of the conspicuous features of Japanese modernity has been the ideological incorporation of peasant motifs and imagery as a central constituent of national identity in the industrial or post-industrial age. Along with the emperor and the family, the peasantry has served as an enduring symbol of cultural continuity and timeless national essence in the course of Japanese modernization. One of the themes of postwar social science in Japan has been the continuity of the agrarian past in the urban-industrial present in the form of latent principles of social organization. As Harootunian points out, postwar Japan represents a prime example of the way in which 'values of an agrarian order have been made to serve the requirements of a postindustrial society' (1989: 83). This transmutation of the peasantry into a latent motif of the industrial order legitimates Japanese modernization and, with it, de-agrarianization. Agrarianism in this abstracted form serves 'to sanction, not to resist, the modernizing changes Japan has realized' (Harootunian 1993: 216).

The new 'peasants' of Kumano have an ambivalent relationship to this process of modernist incorporation of the agrarian. On the one hand, they challenge the 'teleologic master narrative' (Kearney 1996: 73) of peasant disappearance in the course of modernization. Rejecting the urban salaried lifestyle in favor of the 'peasant' farmer, they invert – and potentially de-naturalize – the dominant trend of post-Meiji Japan. Moreover, by physically committing themselves directly to the land, they manifest the possibility of a literal agrarianism – as lifestyle – and thereby challenge the modern appropriation of the agrarian as a legitimating device for the urban-industrial order. As 'salary shedders,' they reject Japanese industrialism and, ipso facto, any latent agrarian legitimations of it. They embody the possibility of a direct continuation into the present of Japan's 'peasant' past.

Yet they cannot avoid becoming caught up in this national ideological process of agrarian symbol-mongering. Despite the autarkic goals animating much Japanese rural resettlement, in practice, as we have seen, there is a degree of conscription of the new settlers – their ideas and rhetoric, but also the settlers themselves – by their host localities to the cause of market-directed rural development. Rural municipalities have become aware of the instrumental potential of agrarian motifs in relation both to commercial product development ('hometown' food, organic 'health foods' etc.) and to tourism, as is indicated most strikingly by the emergence of what might be called agrarian tourism.

Fukuoka's back-to-the-land vision holds that the Japanese people en masse will reverse the urbanization process. According to this vision, a new age of farming lies ahead, whereby the Japanese people will return to the land. Many of the newcomers consider themselves at the vanguard of a new trend which will become more important in the decades ahead, as other urbanites realize the limitations of city life and opt to 'return' to the land. But, statistically, rural resettlement remains a minor phenomenon compared to ongoing agricultural contraction and rural depopulation.

Its principal significance is therefore probably not as rural repopulation, at least not on a scale commensurate with rural depopulation. Rather, it is as a concrete statement of the possibility of an agrarian future for rural Japan, one which represents a clear alternative to the current transformation of the Japanese countryside into a recreational space for urban-industrial society.

References

Adachi Ikutsune. 1994. *Hyakushō o yaritai*. Tokyo: Sanichi shobō.

Aoyama Hiroshi. 1994. 'Tenryō ringyōchi kara no hōkoku.' In *Sanson ga kowareru sono mae ni*, ed. Sanson keizai kenkyūjo. Tokyo: Nihon keizai hyōronsha, pp. 15–25.

Asahi Shinbun. 1993. 'Kasochi no datsusara shin nōmin.' March 19.

Berry, Brian J.L. 1992. *America's Utopian Communities: Communal Havens from Long-wave Crises*. Hanover and London: University of New England Press.

Fukuoka Masanobu. 1983. *Wara ippon no kakumei*. Tokyo: Shunjusha.

—— 1985. *The Natural Way of Farming: The Theory and Practice of Green Philosophy*. Trans. Frederic P. Metreaud. Tokyo: Japan Publications.

Harootunian, H.D. 1989. 'Visible discourses/invisible ideologies.' In *Postmodernism and Japan*, ed. Masao Miyoshi and H.D. Harootunian. Durham: Duke University Press, pp. 63–93.

—— 1993. In *Japan in the World*. Masao Miyoshi and H.D. Harootunian. Durham: Duke University Press, pp. 196–221.

Hidaka Kunio. 1996. *40-sai kara no inakagurashi*. Tokyo: Tōyō keizai shinpōsha.

Inoue Kazue. 1996. 'Guriin tsūrizumu to chiiki nōgyōzukuri.' In *Nihongata guriin tsūrizumu*, ed. Inoue Kazue, Nakamura Osamu and Yamazaki Mitsuhiro. Tokyo: Toshi bunkasha, pp. 59–71.

Iwamizu Yutaka. 1989. *Wakamono yo sanson e karere*. Tokyo: Seibunsha.

Kearney, Michael. 1996. *Reconceptualizing the Peasantry: Anthropology in Global Perspective*. Boulder: Westview.

Kelly, William W. 1986. 'Rationalization and nostalgia: cultural dynamics of new middle-class Japan.' *American Ethnologist* 13: 603–18.

Kitsu Kōichi. 1993. *Inaka urimasu*. Tokyo: Daiyamondosha.

—— 1994. 'Sanson no toshika ni tsuite.' In *Sanson ga kowareru sono mae ni*, ed. Sanson keizai kenkyūjo. Tokyo: Nihon keizai hyōronsha, pp. 170–80.

Kubō Hiroshi. 1994. 'Japan and rice: a new vision.' *Look Japan* 40(465): 4–8.

McDonald, Maryon. 1989. *'We are not French!' Language, Culture and Identity in Brittany*. London and New York: Routledge.

Mitsuhashi Nobuo. 1989. 'Kaso shichōson ni okeru jūmin ishiki ni tsuite.' *Nōson seikatsu sōgō kenkyū* 7: 23–44.

Moen, Darrell Gene. 1997. 'The Japanese organic farming movement: consumers and farmers united.' *Bulletin of Concerned Asian Scholars* 29(3): 14–22.

Nakamura Kenji. 1991. *Hyakushō shigan*. Tokyo: Shizenshoku tsūshinsha.

Ni'ide Makoto. 1994. 'Rice imports and implications.' *Japan Quarterly* 41(1): 16–24.

Nozoe Kenji. 1981. 'At dangerous crossroads – Japan's agriculture and food security.' *Japan Quarterly* 28(2): 217–26.

NTK (Nōringyō taiken kyōkai). 1998. *Nōgyō hakusho*. Tokyo: NYK.

Pepper, David. 1991. *Communes and Green Vision: Counterculture, Lifestyle and The New Age*. London: Green Print.

Saitō Emi. 1985. 'Mō hitotsu no mirai shakai.' *Gendai ringyō* No. 229. Tokyo: Zenkoku ringyō kairyō fukyū kyōkai, pp. 34–9.

Takahashi Yoshio. 1984. *Inakagurashi no tankyū*. Tokyo: Sōshisha.

Takeuchi Kazuhiko. 1993. 'Waga machi, mura o utsukushiku.' In *Mori-hito-machi tsukuri*, ed. Tanba no mori kyōkai (and Nakase Isao). Kyoto: Gakugei shuppansha, pp. 85–120.

Yamashita Sōichi. 1993. *Datsusara nōmin wa naze genki*. Tokyo: Ie no hikari kyōkai.

13 Whither rural Japan?

Nishida Yoshiaki and Ann Waswo

'Culturally deprived' and 'politically inexperienced.' That was how the authors of the Ministry of Agriculture report cited earlier by Iwamoto described Japanese farmers in 1949, and it is more than likely that their assessment was shared by most officials within that ministry, and within the Japanese bureaucracy as a whole. This would become one source of the negative evaluation of farmers in western scholarship thereafter. Another would be the wartime propaganda of the Japanese state, which had stressed the countryside as the locus of those cardinal virtues of loyalty and self-sacrifice that defined Japan's national essence, and young men of rural birth as the nation's best soldiers. Also contributing would be a few scholarly works by Japanese authors that had been translated into English and works by a handful of western authors (most of them using the secondary literature in Japanese as their sources), which emphasized the 'feudal' character of prewar village life (Smith 2001: 355) and the harsh exploitation – by landlords and/or by capitalism – of those who actually tilled the soil. Other voices spoke for rural Japan and its residents, and by and large what they said was accepted as accurate. A rather different assessment emerges when farmers are allowed to speak for themselves, and when the logic of their actions at any time is explored.

That there were serious problems in the Japanese countryside in the decades preceding Japan's defeat in the Second World War is beyond doubt, but what is striking is the extent to which farmers involved themselves individually and collectively in tackling those problems and in achieving largely positive results. Nishiyama Kōichi may have felt humiliated by his inability to pay the interest due on a loan from his main landlord during the early years of the Great Depression, and he – like most Japanese, both rural and urban – certainly supported the war effort, but neither his deference to those to whom he was beholden nor his commitment to the war effort prevented him from securing title to the land he cultivated in 1945 and working to make the land reform a success in his area. Indeed, one of the major themes to emerge from the first six chapters in this volume is the vital 'pre-history' of the postwar land reform. Rather than a sudden bolt from the blue, at a stroke destroying 'the economic bondage which has enslaved the Japanese farmer to centuries of feudal oppression' (General Douglas MacArthur, quoted in Dore 1959: 23), the land reform built upon longer-term trends in rural society, constituting more of a denouement than a radically new departure. Landlord power had been eroding in many parts of Japan since the early 1910s, a consequence both of the steady commercialization of farming and of the increasing opportunities available to the actual cultivators of the land, especially the younger and literate among them, to participate in local organizations and to work as the direct agents of agricultural improvement.

In the development theory that has prevailed since the 1970s (see, for example, Schultz 1988), a strong correlation has been noted between each year of basic schooling that farmers in low income countries have completed and the productivity increases they have achieved. A similar correlation can be detected in Japan in the early decades of the twentieth century, where the number of years of compulsory elementary education were increased from four to six after the Russo-Japanese war and where the output of the major crop, rice, was up by some 14 percent over its level in 1910–12 by the early 1920s (Table 2.1). Nor was that the only consequence of basic education in rural Japan. Keeping detailed diaries may have been an exceptional result, but studying farming techniques and keeping accounts of farming operations was not. As Smith has shown, those widely diffused abilities were of crucial importance in efforts to achieve rural revitalization during the depression years. Even earlier, basic literacy among local farmers had been utilized by the likes of Yamasaki Toyosada to create a viable tenant farmer movement in Izumo and to confront local landlords with scientific evidence they could not easily ignore. Yamazaki may have been unusual in his political (and legal) savvy, and the farmers of Osogi village may have been unusual in including the staging of a play in their revitalization efforts in 1936 (not exactly what one would expect from the 'culturally deprived'), but farmers everywhere in Japan, including a significant proportion of tenant farmers, were increasingly taking charge of their own lives. They were reading newspapers and magazines such as *Ie no hikari*, and discussing the issues of the day among themselves. Even if only a minority of tenant farmers were able to take advantage of the state program to establish owner-cultivators when it was revised in their favor in 1943, all of them benefited from the rent controls and the two-tier pricing structure for rice that the state had been constrained to implement to assure food supplies during wartime. And their benefit constituted loss – of both income and influence – for landlords. The latter had very little left to lose in 1945, although it is certainly true that their dispossession was more thorough and uncompromising than would have been the case had Japan not been subject to the directives of an occupying power.

A second theme is the nationalism of Japanese farmers in the prewar era. To date, only the most extreme, violent and overtly militaristic forms which that nationalism took have featured in the western literature on Japan: agrarianist ideologues like Katō Kanji and their committed followers, some of whom participated in the assassinations of members of the political and economic establishment in the interwar era, as well as army and navy officers, figure prominently, and there has been a tendency to assume that what they defined as the solution to the 'plight of the countryside' and the needs of Japan in the depression era were widely embraced by poor farmers. As both Wilson and Mori have shown, however, that was far from the case, and considerable prodding was required in the 1930s to produce a relatively modest number of emigrants to Manchuria. That said, it cannot be denied that most rural Japanese became increasingly aware of themselves as loyal subjects of the emperor in the early 1900s – like youngsters in the contemporary West, they had been taught patriotism as well as the 'three Rs' in school – and it is also likely that many rural boys became increasingly keen to 'accomplish brave deeds' as soldiers, as the village history quoted by Tsutsui suggests. Rural residents almost certainly participated more consistently than did their urban counterparts in the observances of Emperor Jimmu's accession, Army Day, Navy Day, and Japan's victories over China in 1895 and Russia in 1905, in no small measure because there were far fewer other events and entertainments available in the countryside to provide respite from work. As noted previously, they supported Japan's cause during the Second World War, contributing their labor to boost food supplies, the metal objects they possessed to produce bullets, and their sons. All this complicity in what proved to be a reckless spiral of aggression and conquest carried out in the emperor's name does not sit comfortably with the image of a basically gentle people 'misled by a handful of militarists' that was embraced by the Japanese public soon after Japan's surrender in 1945, and that tension attests to the still unresolved issues of broader war responsibility with which members of that public have only begun to grapple seriously since the death of the wartime Showa emperor in 1989. But there had been more to the loyalty of farmers to that emperor than just supporting Japan's ultimately disastrous and destructive actions abroad. Farmers had also used the rhetoric of loyalty to encourage agricultural improvements, as in Harazato village, and the rhetoric of 'boundless imperial grace' to legitimate protest against the inequities of the status quo, as in Izumo. These quests for better lives and livelihoods, and for justness and fairness in the treatment of all imperial subjects, especially the most disadvantaged among them, should also be taken into account in any final reckoning of the consequences of popular nationalism, in this instance popular nationalism in the countryside, on Japan's development.

A third theme emerges from the chapters dealing with postwar Japan: the effects of rapid economic growth during the 'miracle' years on farmers and farming. As Jussaume has demonstrated, there had been part-time farming in the prewar era, but back then the non-agricultural work which members of farm households did had generally served to supplement household income and to permit the maintenance or expansion of the household's farming operations. In the postwar era, part-time farming rapidly increased and off-farm work eventually came to provide the lion's share of income in the majority of farm households. Farming itself increasingly became a sideline for those households, a reversal of the relationship between farming and non-agricultural work before the war. Not only for them, but also for the minority of households who remained full-time farmers, the countryside became a more complicated place, and its formerly clear-cut function as the site for agricultural production became blurred by other considerations.

Moreover, as the papers by Iwamoto, Kase and Nishida make clear, the attitudes of farmers toward their land would change as the regional development spurred on by rapid economic growth caused land price inflation to one degree or another throughout the country. There had been great enthusiasm for farming in the 1950s and early 1960s, and for making the land more fruitful by all available means. State assistance for land adjustment and other improvements was available on a scale that the many farmers who had committed themselves to rural revitalization back in the depression era could scarcely have imagined. But over succeeding years, the fields that had formerly been seen as of crucial importance to agricultural production steadily came to be seen as an asset, whose value might well increase further if the right decisions about both farming and development prospects were made. That there were relatively few secure job opportunities for middle-aged farmers in a non-agricultural employment market that favored young school leavers and that little in the way of state social security provision was then available served to intensify the asset consciousness of the owners of farmland. As a result, the scope for farming and for giving priority to the needs of farming at the local level diminished further.

A fourth theme, focused on only by Ōkado but alluded to in passing by several of the other contributors to this volume, is the status of rural women. While they have played a vital role in family farming and in farm families throughout the twentieth century, their contributions have remained largely invisible to others, and in the recent international survey carried out by the Ie no hikari kyōkai, the self-evaluations provided by a sampling of them were strikingly low. The root of the problem would appear to be significant vestiges of patriarchy, despite the abolition of the patriarchal *ie* and the granting of equal rights to males and females in Japan's postwar constitution and civil code. Both in the inheritance of the family's land and in decision-making about the management of its farming operations, males continue to enjoy privileged status. Indeed, even on such matters as the management of the home and the upbringing of children rural women do not seem to feel they enjoy much influence. Inheritance of the farm by one successor may make sense, especially when small holdings of land are involved, but the exclusion of daughters from consideration for that inheritance does not. Nor have the messages delivered by inheritance practices and assumptions about who should make key decisions been lost on rural daughters. Increasingly throughout the postwar era, they have sought to escape from constant and unrewarded toil by leaving the countryside, or at the very least by marrying someone other than a farmer. The 'bride shortages' that have attracted attention recently in the West have already become 'bride famines' in some parts of rural Japan. Put another way, the 'pure and simple' farming life that appeals to those relatively few urban women who have participated with their families in rural resettlement, as described by Knight in this volume, very definitely does not appeal to many among those born and raised female in the Japanese countryside.

Which brings us to the present – and future – of rural Japan. According to one scenario, only the most marginal of farmers throughout the country and the most marginal of farming communities, whether in the mountainous hinterland or in isolated pockets within densely populated urban districts, will disappear from now on. Elsewhere, farming will thrive, on ever larger holdings (whether owned by their cultivators or jointly operated in some way, or owned and/or managed by corporations) and with ever greater economies of scale achieved. In a much more radical scenario, virtually all domestic farming will cease, except for a small number of specialist operations catering to especially lucrative niche markets, and Japan will rely on the international marketplace to supply the overwhelming bulk of its foods needs.

The latter reliance has already grown pronounced, it should be noted. According to a recent white paper (Nōrin tōkei kyōkai 2000), Japan had enjoyed a rather high 79 percent ratio of self-sufficiency in food (on a calorie basis) in 1960, but that ratio tumbled during the high-growth years that followed, and amounted to only 40 percent in 1999. This is markedly below the self-sufficiency ratio of 60 percent in Switzerland, said to be the lowest in Europe. Moreover, Japan's experience in this regard is almost exactly the opposite of Britain's, where the ratio was at the low level of 40 percent in 1970 but then rose to about 80 percent in 1999. Not surprisingly, food security re-surfaced as a major concern of the Japanese government in the late 1990s, and that concern contributed to passage of the New Basic Law on Food, Agriculture and Rural Areas in 1999, one aim of which was to boost Japan's self-sufficiency ratio. There is no intention to seek any dramatic increase in that ratio – as of March 2000, the goal of achieving just 45 percent self-sufficiency within ten years had been announced – but there are a host of questions being debated in policy-making circles and in the media relating to the implications of relying substantially on imported food, not only for Japanese consumers and the farmers elsewhere who supply that food, but also for the environment. Precisely how can reasonable standards for the safety of food be maintained in a globalized agricultural system, and the very supply of adequate food stocks be assured in the event of natural or man-made disasters elsewhere? Would the farmers of sub-Saharan African states and other less developed countries in Asia and Latin America, whom some economists see as the logical suppliers of food to the developed world (for example, Blank 1998), be forever consigned to 'low-wage dependent' agriculture, and their countries denied the development trajectories that the once predominantly agrarian countries of the nineteenth and early twentieth centuries have enjoyed? While food produced hundreds and even thousands of miles from Japan may well be less expensive than domestically produced food at present, even after transport costs have been factored in, what is all the fossil fuel needed to get that food to Japan by sea and by air doing to the ecosystems essential to life on earth? And, getting back to Japanese consumers, what bearing do all those additional 'food miles' have on the quality of food available to them?

The decline in Japan's food self-sufficiency ratio after 1960 reflected the very weakening of the bases for domestic agricultural production to which we have already referred. There had been slightly more than six million hectares of farmland in the country in 1960, but that area had fallen by 20 percent to only 4.8 million hectares in 2000. And in the latter year, farmers over the age of 65 accounted for fully 52.9 percent of all those engaged in agriculture. Within the next ten years, those farmers will have retired, and unless others fill their places, the area of land in cultivation may well decrease even further. As noted by Nishida at the end of Chapter 2, farming hamlets themselves were disappearing at the rate of 500 per year between 1990 and 2000, and that rate, too, is likely to quicken, if fields are left abandoned after the death of their owners and the population of the community falls below a critical point.

To be sure, there are some prospects for the materialization of replacements for the increasingly elderly Japanese farmers of the present. As mentioned by Knight, a fairly small number of young people have responded to advertising campaigns to take up 'a farming adventure' by I-turning from the city to the countryside, and as he also indicates, there are probably greater numbers of U- and J-turning rural resettlers as well, among them recent retirees from urban employment who have gone back to their native village or to some other village in the region of their birth to resume the farming they experienced as youths. The long recession in Japan since the early 1990s and the marked increase in unemployment in the secondary and tertiary sectors of the economy it has generated may well contribute to these trends. But it is highly unlikely that such settlement/resettlement alone will suffice to reinvigorate Japan's agricultural sector. To achieve that, considerably greater attention will have to be paid to creating the conditions locally, regionally and nationally in which farmers sense, as did their predecessors in the decades before the war and in the early postwar era, that opportunities exist for them to improve their farming operations. Moreover, as the chapters by Iwamoto and Ōkado indicate, considerable attention must also be paid to broadening the still narrow definition of 'public interest' that has survived in most rural communities to include the Japanese public as a whole, on the one hand, and to providing rural women with at least the same degree of equality in family life and the management of familial assets that urban women have gained, on the other.

Almost exactly thirty years ago, in the summer of 1973, the American biologist Paul Ehrlich described Japan as the 'canary' in the contemporary industrialized world's mineshaft, because it was then 'the most precariously overdeveloped nation' of all, whose collapse would serve as an early warning to other nations at work on the same natural resource-intensive and polluting coalface (*Mainichi Evening News* June 8, 1973). Japan managed that challenge, although not without difficulty or delay, by the imposition of a modicum of pollution controls and by a progressive shift to cleaner, knowledge-intensive industries. Now there is a new canary on duty, in the mineshaft of the industrial/post-industrial world's most precariously marginalized agricultural sector. Whether it can – or to what extent, it should – be revitalized is now at issue.

References

Blank, Steven C. 1998. *The End of Agriculture in the American Portfolio*. Westport, Conn.: Quorum Books.

Dore, Ronald P. 1959. *Land Reform In Japan*. London: Oxford University Press.

Nōrin tōkei kyōkai. 2000. *Zusetsu shokuryō nōgyō nōson hakusho*. Tokyo: Nōrin tōkei kyōkai.

Schultz, T. Paul. 1988. 'Education Investments and Returns.' In *Handbook of Development Economics*, vol. 1, ed. Hollis Chenery and T.N. Srinivasan. Amsterdam, London, New York and Tokyo: North-Holland.

Smith, Kerry. 2001. *A Time of Crisis: Japan, the Great Depression, and Rural Revitalization*. Cambridge, Mass. and London: Harvard University Asia Center.

Index